ON SCHACHT'S
ORIGINS OF MUHAMMADAN JURISPRUDENCE

ON SCHACHT'S ORIGINS OF MUHAMMADAN JURISPRUDENCE

M. Mustafa Al-Azami

Published by
THE OXFORD CENTRE FOR ISLAMIC STUDIES
and
THE ISLAMIC TEXTS SOCIETY

Copyright © 1996 M. M. Al-Azami

First published 1985
This edition first published 1996 by
Oxford Centre for Islamic Studies
George Street, Oxford OX1 2AR, UK
and
The Islamic Texts Society
Miller's House
Kings Mill Lane
Great Shelford
Cambridge CB22 5EN, U.K.

Reprint 2013

British Library Cataloguing-in-Publication Data.
A catalogue record for this book is
available from the British Library.

ISBN 978 0946621 46 0 paper

All rights reserved. No part of this publication may be produced,
installed in retrieval systems, or transmitted in any form
or by any means, electronic, mechanical, photocopying,
recording, or otherwise, without the prior written
permission of the publishers.

Cover design copyright © The Islamic Texts Society

The Islamic Texts Society is distributed in North America by:

Independent Publishers Group
814 North Franklin Street, Chicago, IL 60610, USA
www.ipgbook.com

ACKNOWLEDGMENT

The author would like to thank King Saud University, Riyadh for sponsoring the publication of this book. Thanks are also due to co-publisher John Wiley and their editorial staff.

King Saud University,   M.M.A.
Riyadh
1405/1985

Table of Contents

	Page
Key to Abbreviations	
Introduction	1

PART ONE: Law and Islam 5

Chapter 1: The Place of the Law in Islam 7
- The Role of the Prophet in Islamic Law 13
- Schacht on Law in Islam and the Prophet's Role 15

Chapter 2: Islamic Law in the First Century A.H. 19
- The Judicial Activities of the Prophet 20
- Legal Codes and Judgments 22
- First-Century Legal Literature 24

PART TWO: The *Sunna* of the Prophet and Islamic Law 27

Chapter 3: The *Sunna*: Its Meaning and Concept 29
- The Early Concept of the *Sunna* 29
  - The Word *Sunna*: Its Meaning and Usage 30
  - Other Meanings of the Word *Sunna* 31
- Schacht's Theory of the Early Concept of the *Sunna* 36
  - Ibn Muqaffa' 41
  - The Medinese School 43
  - The Syrian School 51
  - The Iraqian School 52

Chapter 4: The Living Tradition is More Authoritative than the *Sunna* of the Prophet 55
- The Medinese and the Living Tradition 56
- The Syrians and the Living Tradition 64
- The Iraqians and the Living Tradition 66

Chapter 5: The Authority of the *Sunna* of the Prophet in the Ancient Schools of Law 69
- The Attitudes of the Medinese, Syrian, and Iraqian Schools 69
- Abū Yūsuf and the *Sunna* of the Prophet 70
- Shaibānī and the *Sunna* of the Prophet 71
- The Attitudes of the Ancient Schools of Law According to Schacht 72
  - Schacht's Concept of the Antitraditionists 73
  - Weaknesses in Schacht's Thesis 76

	Schacht on the Medinese School	79
	Schacht on the Iraqian School	85
	Schacht on Auzāʿī's Attitude	90
	Further Questions on the Methods of the Antitraditionists	91
Chapter 6:	The *Sunna* of the Prophet in Transition....................	96
	Was the *Sunna* of the Prophet Imposed on the Old Idea of *Sunna*?	100
	Was the Living Tradition Projected Back into the Prophet?	105
	Opinions of Companions Allegedly Ascribed to the Prophet	105
Chapter 7:	On the Growth of Legal Tradition	109
	The Diffusion of *Aḥādīth*	109
	Method of Learning *Aḥādīth*	110
	Precautions Against Errors and Forgeries	111
	A Critique of Schacht's View Regarding *Aḥādīth*	115
	Inconsistencies Both in Theory and in Use of Source Material	117
	Unwarranted Assumptions and Unscientific Research Methods	118
	Mistakes of Fact	122
	Ignorance of Political and Geographical Realities	122
	Misunderstanding of the Quotation Methods of Early Scholars	122
	An Examination of Schacht's Examples	122
Chapter 8:	The *Isnād* System: Its Validity and Authenticity...	154
	Beginning and Development of the *Isnād* System	154
	Schacht and the *Isnād* System	165
	Origins of the System	166
	Arbitrary and Careless Creation of *Isnāds*	168
	General Uncertainty	177
	Gradual Improvement of *Isnāds*	182
	Creation of Additional Authorities	188
	Family *Isnād*	196
	The Common Link in a Chain	197
	Ḥadīth Barīra	200

Appendix 1:	The Use of *Isnād* in *Sīrah* and *Ḥadīth-Fiqh* Literature	206
	Ibn Isḥāq	206
	Abū Ḥanīfah	206
	Mālik	208
	Abū Yūsuf	209
	Shāfi'ī	211
Appendix 2:	Materials of Appendix 1 in Arabic	213
	ملحق	226

ابن اسحاق واستعماله للاسانيد
الإمام أبو حنيفة واستعماله للاسانيد
الإمام مالك واستعماله للاسانيد
الامام أبو يوسف واستعماله للاسانيد
الامام الشيباني واستعماله للاسانيد
الامام الشافعي واستعماله للاسانيد

Bibliography	227
Index	233

Abbreviations Used in the Footnotes

A.D.	Abū Dāwūd, *Sunan*
Annales	Ṭabarī, *Annales*
Auzāʿī	Abū Yūsuf, *Al-Radd ʿalā Siyar al-Auzāʿī*
A.Y.	Abū Yūsuf, *Āthār*. Numbers refer to Ḥadīth number.
Bu	Bukhārī, *Ṣaḥīḥ*
Ḥanbal	Aḥmad bin Ḥanbal, *Musnad*
Ḥujja	Al-Shaibānī, *Al-Ḥujja ʿalā ahl al-Madīna*
Ibn Abī Lailā	Abū Yūsuf, *Ikhtilāf Abī Ḥanīfa wa Ibn Abī Lailā*
Ibn Sʿad	A,-Ṭabaqāt al-Kabīr
Ikh	Shāfiʿī, *Ikhtilāf al-Ḥadīth*
Introduction	Schacht, *An Introduction to Islamic Law*
Kharāj	Abū Yūsuf, *Kitāb al-Kharāj*
Mu	Muslim, *Ṣaḥīḥ*
Mud	Saḥnūn, *Al-Mudawwana al-Kubrā*
Muṣannaf	ʿAbdur Razzāq al-Sanʿānī, *Muṣannaf*
Muw	Mālik b Anas, *Muwaṭṭaʾ*
Muw. Shaib.	Shaibānī, *Muwaṭṭaʾ*
Origins	Schacht, *Origins of Muhammadan Jurisprudence*
Risāla	Shafiʿī, *Risāla*
Studies	Al-Aʿzamī, *Studies in Early Ḥadīth Literature*
Tahd	Ibn Ḥajar *Tahdhīb al-Tahdhīb*
Taqrīb	Ibn Ḥajar *Taqrīb al-Tahdhīb*
Tir	Tirmizī, *Sunan*
Tr	Tr as used by Schacht in his book, *Origins of Muhammadan Jurisprudence* in chapterizing certain books.
Umm	Shāfiʿī, *Kitāb al-Umm*
Zurqānī	Commentary on Mālik's *Muwaṭṭaʾ*

INTRODUCTION

The Muslim view is that the origins of the Islamic legal code are rooted in the Qur'ān, the *sunna* of the Prophet, consensus, and analogy. This view, especially regarding the role of the *sunna*, was first challenged about a hundred years ago by such Western scholars as C. Snouck Hurgronje and Ignaz Goldziher. But it was only in this century, with the publication of *An Introduction to Islamic Law* (1964) and *Origins of Muhammadan Jurisprudence* (1950) by Joseph Schacht that the doubts about the validity of the classical account came to be articulated in a comprehensive theory which claimed to destroy it.

Schacht's *Origins of Muhammadan Jurisprudence* has won high acclaim among leading Orientalists. H. A. R. Gibb, for example, considers that "it will become the foundation for all future study of Islamic civilization and law, at least in the West"[1] and N. J. Coulson says that Schacht "has formulated a thesis of the origins of Sharī'a law which is irrefutable in its broad essentials."[2] It has also strongly influenced many other Orientalists, notably J. Robson, Fitzgerald, J. N. D. Anderson, and C. E. Bosworth, and has had a similar impact upon modern Muslim writers on Islamic law such as Fazlur Rahman, A. A. A. Fyzee, and others.[3]

Schacht's main thesis may be summarized thus:
1. Law as such fell outside the sphere of religion. The Prophet did not aim to create a new system of jurisprudence. His authority was not legal. As far as believers were concerned, he derived his authority from the truth of his religious message; skeptics supported him for political reasons.
2. The ancient schools of law, which are still the major recognized schools today, were born in the early decades of the second century A.H. By *sunna* they originally understood the "living tradition" *(al-'amr al-mujtama'alaih),* that is, the ideal practices of the community expressed in the accepted doctrine of the school of law. This early concept of *sunna*, which was not related to the sayings and

---

[1] H. A. R. Gibb, *Journal of Comparative Legislation and International Law*, 3rd series, vol. 34, parts 3-4 (1951), p. 114.
[2] N. J. Coulson, *A History of Islamic Law* (Edinburgh 1964), p. 4.
[3] Fazlur Rahman, *Islamic Methodology in History*, (Karachi, 1965), pp. 10-11. A. A. A. Fyzee, *Outlines of Muhammadan Law*, (Oxford 1964), pp. 26-28. Schacht's *Origins* has become the bible of Orientalists to such an extent that when the late Amīn Al-Maṣrī chose a critical study of the work as the subject of his Ph.D. thesis, his application was rejected by the University of London; he fared no better at Cambridge University. See Muṣṭafā Sibā'ī, *As-Sunna wa Makānatuhā* (Cairo, 1380/1961), p. 27.

deeds of the Prophet, formed the basis of the legal theory of these schools.[4]

3. These ancient schools of law gave birth to an opposition party, religiously inspired, that falsely produced detailed information about the Prophet in order to establish a source of authority for its views on jurisprudence.
4. The ancient schools of law tried to resist these factions, but when they saw that the alleged traditions from the Prophet were being imposed more and more on the early concept of *sunna*, they concluded that "the best they could do was to minimize their import by interpretation, and to embody their own attitude and doctrines in other alleged traditions from the Prophet"[5] – that is, they joined in the deception.
5. As a result, during the second and third centuries A.H. it became the habit of scholars to project their own statements into the mouth of the Prophet.
6. Hardly any legal tradition from the Prophet can, therefore, be considered authentic.[6]
7. The system of *isnād*[7] ("chain of transmitters"), used for the authentication of *ḥadīth* documents, has no historical value. It was invented by those scholars who were falsely attributing their own doctrines back to earlier authorities; as such, it is useful only as a means for dating forgeries.

Schacht argues that the picture painted by Muslim scholars of the origins of Islamic law, "concealed rather than revealed the truth; and I trust that the sketch by which I have tried to replace it comes nearer to reality." If that is indeed the case, not only the early legal history of Islam but its early literary history as a whole would be demolished, and the honesty and integrity of almost all Muslim scholars of the early centuries would be called into serious question. It is the aim of this book to examine such charges.

The question that immediately poses itself is the means Schacht used to produce findings so startlingly at variance with the Muslim view. Not only with the Muslim view but even against the historical facts known to every reader of Islamic history. As an example, I cite the case of Ibn Ḥanbal and his clash with the dogma and creeds of the Caliph and Muʻtazila sect. He asked the Caliph to bring forward a single *ḥadīth* of the Prophet that supported the official view. But the Caliph with all his power and an army of learned scholars was unable to produce one. The fact that it was impossible to fabricate a *ḥadīth* on the authority of the Prophet that could go unnoticed by the scholars speaks for itself.

---

[4] See *Origins* p. 80. According to Schacht, "Shāfiʻī was the first lawyer to define *sunna* as the model behaviour of the Prophet" (*ibid.* p. 2).

[5] *Introduction*, pp. 35–36.

[6] *Ibid.*, p. 34.

[7] For a detailed discussion of *isnād*, see below Chapter 6.

Schacht had two methods at his disposal: either to draw his conclusions from a study of the original sources of Islam, especially the Qur'ān, or to use the writings of early scholars as sources. He adopted the latter course. I have, therefore, carried out a rigorous study of these writings to determine what there might be in them that led Schacht to his conclusions.

It will be argued that, in broad terms, the writings of the early scholars support the classical picture; Schacht has apparently failed to consult some of the most relevant literature; he often misunderstands the texts he quotes; the examples he uses frequently contradict the point he is attempting to make; on occasion he quotes out of context; and, most important, he applies unscientific *methodology* for his research, thus drawing conclusions that are untenable when the evidence of the text as a whole is weighed. The arguments will be illustrated by using detailed, direct quotations from the early sources while scrutinizing the methodology applied by Schacht.

The book is divided into two parts. In the first part, which is divided into two chapters, I discuss Schacht's views on law and its place in Islam in the light of the specific injunctions laid down in the Qur'ān. It will be shown that, in theory at least, law did not fall outside the sphere of religion and that the Prophet created a distinct legal system which was in use in the first century A.H..

The second part is divided into six chapters. Chapter 3 deals with the early concept of the *sunna*. The next, Chapter 4, discusses Schacht's thesis that the ancient schools of law considered the generally agreed-on practice – the "living tradition" – more authoritative than traditions from the Prophet. Chapter 5 cites examples from the writings of the time to show that the ancient schools of law, far from being resistant to the *sunna* of the Prophet, in fact based their decisions on it on their best knowledge. Chapter 6 is a critical study of the examples Schacht adduces in his attempt to show how what he calls the fabricated *sunnas* of the Prophet imposed themselves on the original idea of *sunna*, and how the ancient schools of law, having been defeated by the traditionists, began to project their own doctrines into the mouth of the Prophet. Chapter 7 consists of a detailed discussion of the examples produced by Schacht in defense of his theory that the entire *ḥadīth* literature was an invention of the second and third centuries. In Chapter 8 there is a similar discussion of the examples Schacht uses to impugn the validity of the *isnād* system. It argues that he failed to understand the difference between the way *isnād* was quoted in the *sīra* and *Fiqh-ḥadīth* literature and its use in *ḥadīth* literature.

One of the factors that might have caused many mistakes by modern scholars is the lack of deep understanding of early scholars, their literary style, and their methods of quotation. This problem is discussed in my book, *Ḥadīth Methodology and Literature*, pp. 74–79, which shows what the early authors of *Ḥadīth* books recorded in their books on the authority of their teachers; apparently verbal narrations were drawn from the books of their teachers. These sources therefore may be legitimately used to trace the records of the narrations and doctrines of early authorities.

There are two appendices. One gives examples of *isnād* from *Sīra* and *Fiqh-Ḥadīth* literature (in English) that indicate the styles of early scholars of law and biographers of the Prophet using *Isnād*. The other consists of the same material as Appendix 1 in Arabic to facilitate comparison for research scholars.

There is a certain overlap in the examples used in the various chapters. In this I follow Schacht, who uses the same examples in many places, although because he frequently refers to page numbers rather than specifying the actual example under discussion, this may not always be readily noticeable to the reader.[8] Moreover, I consider it sufficiently important to treat each aspect of Schacht's theory comprehensively, even at the expense of some repetition. I hope the reader will bear with me if some of my arguments seem lengthy. Indeed, they would have been lengthier still if I had not confined myself to the most crucial points regarding *sunna* in Schacht's writing. A critique of all the areas in contention would fill many volumes.

---

[8] See, for example, *Khiyār al-Majlis,* pp. 64, 160, 167, 184, and 256.

Part One
Law and Islam

The primary purpose of any law is to make social life possible. In societies where laws are man-made, they reflect the values current in that society at any given time. The society starts out by deciding what it wants to make legal and illegal and formalizes its views in a legal code. Opinions about what consitutes a legal or illegal act change, sometimes diametrically, as values change. When this happens the law is changed accordingly.

The values of societies, although in many cases deriving their original authority from religious sources, are fixed by the societies themselves. There is often a dichotomy between what a society considers legal in a secular sense and what its religious teachings indicate. No such dichotomy exists in Islam.

The essential key to the understanding of the values of an Islamic society is *"Lā Ilāha Illallāh,"* "There is no god but Allah." In Islam, Almighty Allah is the Only Creator of the universe and everything in it, including man. He is the Sustainer, the Most Benevolent, the Most Merciful. It is He alone who fixes the values and possesses all legislative power. He alone has the authority to lay down what is lawful and unlawful. Thus, the law as revealed by Him in the Qur'ān and through the agency of the *sunna* of the Prophet is immutable and obligatory on all believers. Even the Prophet himself did not have the right to alter it of his own volition.

Schacht's central contention is that law as such fell outside the sphere of religion. He further maintains that Islamic law did not exist at all during the greater part of the first century A.H. If he were correct, the foundations of Islamic society would be cut away.

I will look in detail at these two contentions. Chapter 1 will deal with the place of law in Islam, quoting extensively from the Qur'ān to show that it was indeed part of the Prophet's function and duty to create a new system of law, that it was an accepted principle that the Prophet was *authorized* by Allah to legislate, and that his own behavior formed a model for Muslim society. Chapter 2 will show that these injunctions from the Qur'ān were reflected in practice, and that there were systematic Islamic legal activities throughout the first century A.H.

CHAPTER ONE

THE PLACE OF THE LAW IN ISLAM

In the sixth century of the Common Era, the Ka'ba in Mecca, the symbolic heart of monotheism,[1] was surrounded by and filled with no fewer than 360 idols.[2] The city itself was full of idol worshippers. Polytheism was rife throughout the Arabian peninsula; the small Jewish communities dotted here and there and the few tribes that had been converted to Christianity were the exception. As Muir writes: "The foundation of Arab faith was deep-rooted idolatry, which for centuries had stood proof, with no palpable symptoms of decay, against every attempt at evangelisation from Egypt and Syria."[3]

Commercial life was flourishing, especially in Mecca and Ṭā'if, while Medīna was a lively business and agricultural center. Usury was widespread. And with tribes as the social units, there was no organized government. There was, consequently, no agreed way of obtaining justice, let alone a system of legal practice. Disputes were settled either on a crude revenge basis or by calling in arbitrators acceptable to both sides. Although the Arabs had some excellent qualities, such as courage, hospitality, honesty, and love of freedom, they also had some evil and degrading vices.

It was into this environment that Allah sent Muḥammad with his Eternal Message. His influence was immediate: during the period of more than a decade that he preached in Mecca he was subjected, in a way that Christian preachers and other thinkers before him in the same area had not been, to continual ridicule and harassment. The ruling polytheists saw only too clearly the threat posed to their way of life by the core sentence of Muḥammad's message: "*Lā Ilāha Illallāh.*" "There is no god but Allah" was no dead metaphysical phrase but a living creed which demanded the total submission of man's will to the will of Allah and not to the will of other men. As Almighty Allah says:

قل إن صلاتي ونسكي ومحياي ومماتي لله رب العالمين [4]

---

[1] Qur'ān, 2:96.
[2] Muslim b. Ḥajjāj al-Qushairī, *Ṣaḥīḥ*, (Cairo 1374/1955) *Jihād* 87, cited hereafter as *Mu*.
[3] Sir William Muir, *The Life of Mahomet* (London 1894), pp. 82–83 (introduction).
[4] Qur'ān, 6:162.

Say: my prayer, my ritual sacrifice, my living, my dying all belong to Allah, the Lord of the Worlds.

If the principle of total submission of man's will to Allah is accepted, naturally and logically it leads to the belief that His Will ought to be the only law and that man must submit himself to these injunctions in their entirety. The Qur'ān says:

ألا له الخلق والأمر تبارك الله رب العالمين [5]

Verily, His is all creation and His is the command [law]. Blessed be Allah, the Lord of the Worlds.

And again:

ولا تقولوا لما تصف ألسنتكم الكذب هذا حلال وهذا حرام لتفتروا على الله الكذب إن الذين يفترون على الله الكذب لا يفلحون [6]

And do not say, as to what your tongues falsely describe, this is lawful, and this is forbidden, so that you forge a falsehood against Allah. Those who invent a lie against Allah will never prosper.

The Qur'ān makes it clear that, originally, legislative power belonged to Allah. He instructed His messenger thus:

ثم جعلناك على شريعة من الأمر فاتبعها ولا تتبع أهواء الذين لا يعلمون [7]

And now we have set thee [O Muḥammad] on a clear road [*Sharī'a*] of our Commandment; so follow it, and follow not the desires of those who know not.

Allah also bestowed certain powers on his Prophet in this regard:

ويحل لهم الطيبات ويحرم عليهم الخبائث ويضع عنهم أصرهم والأغلال التي كانت عليهم [8]

He will make lawful for them all good things and prohibit for them only the foul, and will relieve them of their burden and the fetters which were set upon them.

It is important to note, however, that only Allah Himself is the lawgiver. The Prophet's task was to explain this law by word and deed. His words were binding not because he was the lawgiver as such but because what he said about the law had originally been conveyed to him by Allah or had His approval. He is obeyed by Muslims because they are certain that his words and deeds express the will of Allah.

Further, Allah ordered the people to obey the Prophet without reservation and to take his life as a perfect model to be followed.[9] Thus, for the Muslim community, the orders of the Prophet were on an equal footing with the Orders of Almighty Allah. All his orders and personal

---

[5] Qur'ān, 7:54.
[6] Qur'ān, 16:116.
[7] Qur'ān, 45:18.
[8] Qur'ān, 7:157.
[9] Chapter 1 deals with this concept in the section concerning the Prophet as *Muṭā'*.

behavior, as well as deeds done by others that met with his tacit approval, were carefully noted by his Companions and put into practice.

In his lifetime, the Prophet saw almost the whole of the Arabian peninsula come under the guidance of Islam. Within a quarter of a century of his death, parts of what are now the USSR, Afghanistan, Iran, Iraq, Syria, part of Turkey, Egypt, Palestine, Lebanon, the Sudan, Yemen, Libya, and Tunisia were under Muslim control.

The task of spreading the message of Islam and developing the fledgling Muslim communities fell to the Companions of the Prophet. Those who were well versed in the Qur'ān and the *sunna* of the Prophet became teachers of Law. Great cities such as Mecca, Madīna, Baṣra, Kūfa, Damascus, and Fusṭāṭ (Cairo) became the centers of legal education. The central government gave constant guidance, although the methods it used varied. For example, we find hundreds of letters sent by the Caliph 'Umar to the Commanders and far fewer from other caliphs.[10] The learned Companions passed the word to the Successors, and when life settled down in the new territories, scholars began to travel to different parts of the Muslim world to acquire knowledge on a much larger scale.[11]

The authority of the law as revealed in the Qur'ān and the *sunna* of the Prophet was unquestioned by these scholars. The authority of the Qur'ān was part of Muslim belief, although obviously there were disagreements on interpretation and thus its application in certain cases. Similarly, although the rule that the *sunna* of the Prophet must be followed was a basic part of Islamic belief and, thus, unanimously accepted among Muslims, different methods of testing whether this or that practice was actually the *sunna* of the Prophet were in existence. Again, there were differences in interpretation of certain aspects of the *sunna* and, similarly in their application.

When a decision was being made about the correct interpretation of *sunna*, the opinions of the Companions were taken into consideration because of the fact that they participated with the Prophet in applying the Divine Orders and were intimately acquainted with the Qur'ān, its spirit, and its promulgation by the Prophet. They were also the first to be privy to the Prophetic orders. Yet although their explanations and their decisions carried much weight, later scholars had the right to differ from them in interpretation of both the Qur'ān and the statements of the Prophet; this was especially the case where the Companions themselves disagreed. By no means were all the issues requiring resolution explicitly dealt with either in the Qur'ān or the *sunna* of the Prophet; scholars had to use their discretion, *ijtihād*, which again sometimes resulted in disagreement. Moreover, in the second century A.H., when scholars began to travel extensively for the sake of knowledge, they found that certain aspects of the *sunna* of the Prophet had been unknown to certain scholars of the

---

[10] Chapter 2 discusses these letters.
[11] See Khaṭīb, *al-Riḥla*, edited by N. 'itr, 1395, pp. 107–183.

early period and thus their decisions were in conflict with those parts of the *sunna*.

Plainly, then, considerable disagreement inevitably existed among the early lawyers. But it is important to note that in many societies, legislators draw up constitutions embodying a framework of law. In Islam, the legislator is Allah and He fixed the legislative authority in Himself and His Prophet, or in other words, in the Qur'ān and the *sunna* of the Prophet.[12]

From the very meaning of the word *Islām*, that is "submission," or rather its Islamic meaning, which is "total submission to the will of Allah" — and the central legal concept that all legislative power rests with Allah,[13] four additional principles are either to be found in the Qur'ān or can be readily deduced from it:

1. The revealed principles of law cover all facets of human activity. As Islam demands total submission, it ought to provide laws and guidance to cover all facets of human activity. And, in fact, the Qur'ān, together with the *sunna* of the Prophet, covers all "legal aspects" of life, either in the form of general rules[14] or in great detail, as for example, in the laws of inheritance, marriage, and certain crimes.

2. The revealed law is binding on the whole community. Even the Prophet had to follow what was revealed to him. Allah says:

ثم جعلناك على شريعة من الأمر فاتبعها ولا تتبع أهواء الذين لا يعلمون [15]

And now We have set thee [O Muḥammad] on a clear road [*Sharīʿa*] of our Commandment; so follow it, and follow not the desires of those who know not.

It is thus clear that the whole community and the individuals in it are bound by the same laws. Allah says:

وهذا كتاب أنزلناه مبارك فاتبعوه واتقوا لعلكم ترحمون [16]

This is the Book We have sent down, blessed; so follow it, and be God-fearing, that perhaps you will find mercy.

The following verses from the Qur'ān may further serve to illustrate this principle. Almighty Allah says:

---

[12] Consensus and analogy were mentioned by the Qur'ān implicitly and by the Prophet explicity. Therefore it has always been the theory and belief of Muslim scholars that the whole of the legal system rests on two main sources: the Qur'ān and the *sunna* of the Prophet. Then there are sources or subsources, such as the consensus of Muslim scholars as a whole and the method of analogy, etc.

[13] See the discussion of "*La-Ilāha Illallāh*," earlier in this chapter.

[14] See A. S. Rusainī, Master's thesis, Sharīʿa College, Mecca, 1392, *Fiqh al-Fuqahā' as-Sabʿa*, chart of verses, p. 5.

[15] Qur'ān, 45:18.

[16] Qur'ān, 6:155.

واتبع ما يوحى إليك واصبر حتى يحكم الله وهو خير الحاكمين .[17]

And [O Muḥammad] follow that which is revealed to you, and forbear until Allah gives judgment. And He is the Best of Judges.

And again:

إنا أنزلنا إليك الكتاب بالحق لتحكم بين الناس بما أراك الله ولا تكن للخائنين خصيما .[18]

Lo! We reveal unto thee the Scripture with the truth, that thou mayest judge between mankind by that which Allah makes clear to thee, and be not a pleader on behalf of the treacherous.

The Qur'ān rebukes those whose conduct violates the above verse, and praises those whose conduct conforms to it. Allah says:

ويقولون آمنا بالله وبالرسول وأطعنا ثم يتولى فريق منهم من بعد ذلك وما أولئك بالمؤمنين . وإذا دعوا إلى الله ورسوله ليحكم بينهم إذا فريق منهم معرضون . وإن يكن لهم الحق يأتوا إليه مذعنين ، أفي قلوبهم مرض أم ارتابوا أم يخافون أن يحيف الله عليهم ورسوله بل أولئك هم الظالمون . إنما كان قول المؤمنين إذا دعوا إلى الله ورسوله ليحكم بينهم أن يقولوا سمعنا وأطعنا وأولئك هم المفلحون . ومن يطع الله ورسوله ويخش الله ويتقه فأولئك هم الفائزون .[19]

They say, "We believe in God and in the Apostle, and we obey," but even after that, some of them turn away: they are not truly believers.

When they are summoned to God and His Apostle in order that he may judge between them, behold, some of them decline [to come].

But if the right is on their side, they come to him in all submission. Is it that there is a disease in their hearts? Or are they in fear that God and His Apostle will deal unjustly with them? Nay, it is they themselves who do wrong. The response of the Believers, when summoned to God and His Apostle, in order that he may judge between them, is no other than this: They say, "We hear and we obey." It is such as these who will attain felicity. It is such as obey God and His Apostle, and fear God and do right, that will win [in the end].

And again:

ألم تر إلى الذين يزعمون أنهم آمنوا بما أنزل إليك وما أنزل من قبلك يريدون أن يتحاكموا إلى الطاغوت وقد أمروا أن يكفروا به ويريد الشيطان أن يضلهم ضلالا بعيدا .[20]

Have you not regarded how those who assert that they believe in what has been sent down to you, and what was sent down before you, desire to take their disputes to idols, although they have been commanded to disbelieve in them? But Satan desires to lead them astray into gross error.

It is not only those who profess Islam who are rebuked if their conduct falls short of what is demanded. The Jews, for example, were rebuked for not following the revealed law of Moses. Allah says:

---

[17] Qur'ān, 10:109.
[18] Qur'ān, 4:105.
[19] Qur'ān, 24:47–52.
[20] Qur'ān, 4:60.

أَلَمْ تَرَ إِلَى الَّذِينَ أُوتُوا نَصِيبًا مِنَ الْكِتَابِ يُدْعَوْنَ إِلَى كِتَابِ اللهِ لِيَحْكُمَ بَيْنَهُمْ ثُمَّ يَتَوَلَّى فَرِيقٌ مِنْهُمْ وَهُمْ مُعْرِضُونَ. [21]

Hast thou not regarded those who were given a portion of the Book, being called to the Book of God, that it might decide between them [in justice], and then a party of them turned away, in opposition [to the truth]?

It was a sign of hypocrisy not to submit to the revealed law. Allah says:

وَإِذَا قِيلَ لَهُمْ تَعَالَوْا إِلَى مَا أَنْزَلَ اللهُ وَإِلَى الرَّسُولِ رَأَيْتَ الْمُنَافِقِينَ يَصُدُّونَ عَنْكَ صُدُودًا [22]

And when it is said unto them: "Come unto that which Allah hath revealed and unto the Messenger," thou seest the hypocrites turn from thee in aversion.

3. Whoever does not follow the revealed law and does not judge according to it is counted an unbeliever. Whoever rejects the Divine revelation and acknowledges anyone but Allah as authorized to legislate is not a Muslim. Allah says:

وَمَنْ لَمْ يَحْكُمْ بِمَا أَنْزَلَ اللهُ فَأُولَئِكَ هُمُ الْكَافِرُونَ [23]

Whosoever judges not according to what Allah has sent down, they are the unbelievers.

This point is clarified by the following incident. 'Adī b. Ḥātim, a former Christian, heard the Prophet reciting:

اتَّخَذُوا أَحْبَارَهُمْ وَرُهْبَانَهُمْ أَرْبَابًا مِنْ دُونِ اللهِ وَالْمَسِيحَ ابْنَ مَرْيَمَ وَمَا أُمِرُوا إِلَّا لِيَعْبُدُوا إِلَهًا وَاحِدًا لَا إِلَهَ إِلَّا هُوَ سُبْحَانَهُ عَمَّا يُشْرِكُونَ

They have taken their rabbis and their monks as lords apart from Allah and the Messiah, Mary's son, and they were commanded to serve but One God; there is no deity but He; glory be to Him, above [all] that they associate [with Him].

When 'Adī b. Ḥātim heard this, he said that the Christians did not worship their monks. The Prophet's reply was, "Yes, they do, as they [the monks] forbade them what was lawful to them, and made for them lawful what was forbidden, and the Christians followed them in this matter, and that is the worship of those monks."[24]

The community was thus not to take disputes to whomever it liked. It had to go to the Prophet, whose judgments had undisputed and binding legal authority. But he had to judge according to what had been revealed to him.[25]

4. The revealed law is inalterable. No one had authority to alter the law.

---

[21] Qur'ān, 3:23.
[22] Qur'ān, 4:61.
[23] Qur'ān, 5:44.
[24] Ibn Kathīr, *Tafsīr*, 7 vols., Beirut, 1385/1968, Vol. 3, p.385; for the Qur'ānic Verse, see 9:31.
[25] Qur'ān, 10:109; see also 4:105; 5:48, 49.

Even the Prophet could not, of his own volition, alter the Divine revelation. Almighty Allah says:

وإذا تتلى عليهم آياتنا بينت قال الذين لا يرجون لقاءنا ائت بقرءان غير هذا أو بدله قل ما يكون لي أن أبدله من تلقاء نفسي أن أتبع إلا ما يوحى إلي أني أخاف إن عصيت ربي عذاب يوم عظيم. [26]

And when Our clear revelations are recited unto them, those who do not anticipate the meeting with Us say: "Bring a Qur'ān other than this or change it." Say [O Muḥammad]: "It is not for me to change it of my own accord. I only follow that which is revealed to me. Lo! if I were to disobey my Lord, I would fear the retribution of a terrible Day."

Hence, law can be seen to be an integral part of Islam. There was no aspect of behavior that was not intended to be covered by the revealed law, and this law was meant to be binding on all Muslims. The above verses indicate clearly that the concept of Islamic law (*Sharī'a*) was established during the life of the Prophet with the revelation of the Qur'ān and was not the product of a later period.

We turn now from the importance of law in Islam to the role of the Prophet in this legal system.

The Role of the Prophet in Islamic Law

The Qur'ān assigns the Prophet four distinct roles:

1. Expounder of the Qur'ān. The Prophet is the expounder of the Qur'ān and so appointed by Allah. Almighty Allah says:

وأنزلنا إليك الذكر لتبين للناس ما نزل إليهم ولعلهم يتفكرون. [27]

We have revealed unto thee the Remembrance [the Qur'ān], that you may explain to mankind that which has been revealed for them and in order that they may give thought.

Thus, the Qur'ān repeats — if we may take *ṣalāt* (prayer) as an example — orders for *ṣalāt* at numerous places, but does not prescribe in detail the manner of prayer. The responsibility for passing this on by practical demonstration, as well as orally, was entrusted to the Prophet.

2. Legislator. Almighty Allah, speaking about the legislative power of the Prophet, says:

ويحل لهم الطيبت ويحرم عليهم الخبئث ويضع عنهم أصرهم والاغلل التي كانت عليهم فالذين أمنوا به وعزروه ونصروه واتبعوا النور الذي أنزل معه أولئك هم المفلحون. [28]

He will make lawful for them all good things and prohibit for them only the foul, and will relieve them of their burden and the fetters which were set

---

[26] Qur'ān, 10:15.
[27] Qur'ān, 16:44.
[28] Qur'ān, 7:157; Chapter 1 also discusses legislative power.

upon them. Then those who believe in him, honor and help him, and follow the light which is sent down with him: they are the successful.

3. Muṭā' (مطاع), **"One to be obeyed."** There are many verses in the Qur'ān which order total obedience to the Prophet. For example, Allah says:

وما أرسلنا من رسول إلا ليطاع بإذن الله [29]

We have sent no Messenger save that he should be obeyed by Allah's leave.

He says further:

قل أطيعوا الله والرسول فإن تولوا فإن الله لا يحب الكافرين [30]

Say: "Obey Allah and the Messenger." But if they turn away, Allah loves not the unbelievers.

And again:

وأطيعوا الله والرسول لعلكم ترحمون [31]

Obey Allah and the Messenger, so that perhaps you will find mercy.

And:

يأيها الذين آمنوا أطيعوا الله وأطيعوا الرسول وأولي الأمر منكم فإن تنازعتم في شيء فردوه إلى الله والرسول إن كنتم تؤمنون بالله واليوم الآخر ذلك خير وأحسن تأويلا [32]

O believers, obey Allah, and obey the Messenger and those in authority among you. If you should dispute regarding anything, refer it to Allah and the Messenger, if indeed you believe in Allah and the Last Day. This is better and fairer in the issue.

One verse in particular explicitly states that to obey the Prophet is to obey Allah:

من يطع الرسول فقد أطاع الله ومن تولى فما أرسلناك عليهم حفيظا [33]

Whoever obeys the Apostle obeys Allah. But if any one turn away, we have not sent thee to watch over their [evil deeds].

4. The Model for Muslim Behavior. The Qur'ān refers to the life-pattern of the Prophet, saying:

لقد كان لكم في رسول الله إسوة حسنة لمن كان يرجو الله واليوم الآخر وذكر الله كثيرا [34]

You have in Allah's Messenger a noble model for all whose hopes are in Allah and the Last Day and who often call Allah to remembrance.

This means that Muslims should follow the example of the Prophet in

---

[29] Qur'ān, 4:64.
[30] Qur'ān, 3:32.
[31] Qur'ān, 3:132.
[32] Qur'ān, 4:59.
[33] Qur'ān, 4:80.
[34] Qur'ān, 33:21.

every aspect of life. His deeds were sanctioned by Allah as examples to all Muslims. The practices he initiated were later mentioned by the Qur'ān as the standard practice of the community — for example, the practice of *adhān*, to which the Qur'ān simply refers as the existing practice.[35]

Taken together, these verses show that for a Muslim no distinction can be made between the orders of Allah and the orders of the Prophet. Indeed, the total authority of the Prophet may be summarized in one verse of the Qur'ān. Allah says:

وما آتاكم الرسول فخذوه وما نهاكم عنه فانتهوا واتقوا الله إن الله شديد العقاب [36]

And whatsoever the Messenger gives you, take it. And whatsoever he forbids you, abstain from it and keep your duty to Allah. Lo, Allah is stern in reprisal.

Speaking about the judicial authority of the Prophet, Almighty Allah explicitly says:

فلا وربك لا يؤمنون حتى يحكموك فيما شجر بينهم ثم لا يجدوا في أنفسهم حرجا مما قضيت ويسلموا تسليما . [37]

But no, by thy Lord: They will not believe until they make you the judge regarding the disagreement between them; then they shall find in themselves no impediment touching thy verdict, but shall surrender in full submission.

From the above quotations it is clear that:

1. Law was an integral part of Islam. There was no aspect of behavior that was not intended to be covered by the revealed law and this law was to be binding on all Muslims; none had authority to alter it.
2. It was intended by Allah that His Prophet's whole life, decisions, judgments, and commands should have the force of law. The authority of the Prophet does not rest on the acceptance of the community or on lawyers and scholars, but on the will of Allah himself.

Schacht on Law in Islam and the Prophet's Role

It is against this background that Joseph Schacht would have us believe that law fell outside the sphere of religion. He says:

> Generally speaking, Muhammad had little reason to change the existing

---

[35] Qur'ān, 62:9.
[36] Qur'ān, 59:7. This verse was revealed in connection with sharing the spoils of war; its wording covers all other matters, as is the case in the implementation of the order of the Holy Qur'ān. Certain verses were revealed in a particular case, but it was a general order to everyone in a similar situation. The Prophet's explanation in this regard has been transmitted and recorded by many. See, for example, Ibn Ḥanbal, *Musnad*, vol I, pp. 352, 415. Cited hereafter as Ḥanbal; Ibn Kathīr, *Tafsır*, vol. 6, p. 604, etc.
[37] Qur'ān, 4:65.

customary law. His aim as a Prophet was not to create a new system of law; it was to teach men how to act, what to do, and what to avoid in order to pass the reckoning on the Day of Judgement and to enter Paradise.[38]

Speaking about the Prophet's authority, he says: "His authority was not legal but, for the believers, religious and, for the lukewarm, political."[39] He further says:

> During the greater part of the first century, Islamic Law, in the technical meaning of the term, did not as yet exist. As had been the case in the time of the Prophet, *law as such fell outside the sphere of religion*, and as far as there were no religious or moral objections to specific transactions or modes of behaviour, the technical aspects of law were a matter of indifference to the Muslims.[40]

It is not only Schacht who has argued that the Prophet had no role as a legislator; many Orientalists and their pupils in the East subscribe to this thesis. Anderson, for example, writes:

> It is evident that Muhammad himself made no attempt to work out any comprehensive legal system, a task for which he seems to have been singularly ill-suited; instead, he contented himself with what went little beyond *ad hoc* amendments to the existing customary law.[41]

Similar ideas are found in the writing of C. Snouck Hurgronje. He writes: "Mohammad knew too well how little qualified he was for legislative work to undertake it unless absolutely necessary."[42] Tyan holds the same view. He says: "When one glances through the work of Muhammad one is easily convinced that he did not intend to institute a new judicial system nor to introduce a new system of legislation."[43]

This position is echoed in the work of Fazlur Rahman. He says:

> Now, the overall picture of the Prophet's biography — if we look behind the colouring supplied by the medieval legal mass — has certainly no tendency to suggest the impression of the Prophet as a pan-legist neatly regulating the fine details of human life from administration to those of ritual purity. The evidence, in fact, strongly suggests that the Prophet was primarily a moral reformer of mankind and that, apart from occasional decisions, *which had the character of* ad hoc *cases, he seldom resorted to general legislation as a means of furthering the general Islamic cause.*[44]

He goes on:

> For one thing, it can be concluded *a priori* that the Prophet, who was, until

---

[38] *Introduction*, p. 11; see also *Origins*, Preface, p. v.
[39] *Introduction*, p. 11
[40] *Ibid.*, 19 (italics mine).
[41] J. N. D. Anderson, "Recent Developments in Sharī'a Law," *Muslim World*, 40 (1950), 245.
[42] C. Snouck Hurgronje, *Muhammadanism*, p. 60.
[43] E. Tyan, *Histoire de l'organisation judiciare en pays d'Islam*, (Leiden, 1960), p. 64.
[44] Fazlur Rahman, *Islamic Methodology in History*, (Karachi, 1965), p. 10 (italics mine).

his death, engaged in a grim moral and political struggle against the Meccans and the Arabs and in organising his community-state, could hardly have found time to lay down rules for the *minutiæ* of life.[45]

Perhaps Fazlur Rahman provides the fullest statement of the implications of this position. It denies the systematic legal activities of the Prophet, which consequently leads to the denial of the existence of the *sunna* of the Prophet, which in turn logically entails the rejection of the validity of whatever may have been described as the *sunna* of the Prophet.

Schacht himself has no hesitation in extending the theory this far. He writes:

> The Traditionists produced detailed statements or "traditions" which claimed to be the reports of ear- or eye-witnesses on the words or acts of the Prophet, handed down orally by an uninterrupted chain (*isnād*) of trustworthy persons. *Hardly any of these traditions, as far as matters of religious law are concerned, can be considered authentic*; they were put into circulation, no doubt from the loftiest of motives, by the Traditionists themselves from the first half of the second century onwards.[46]

A fundamental methodological error committed by Schacht is that he appears to have virtually ignored the evidence of the Qur'ān itself, as far as legalistic injunctions are concerned, in the formulation of his thesis.

Other Orientalists who have gone back to the Qur'ān have reached different conclusions from those of Schacht. Speaking about the nature of Islamic law, Fitzgerald says that Islam "regards God as the sole source of law and absolutely denies the power of any human authority to legislate."[47] And N. J. Coulson states that "the principle that God was the only Lawgiver and that His command was to have supreme control over all aspects of life was clearly established."[48]

S. D. Goitein concludes that in about the fifth year of Hijra it came to the mind of the Prophet "that even strictly legal matters were not irrelevant to religion, but were part and parcel of the divine revelation and were included in the heavenly book, which was the source of all religion."[49] He further argues that "the idea of the *Sharī'a* was not the result of post-Quranic developments, but was formulated by Muḥammad himself."[50]

Speaking about the Qur'ān as a legal document, Goitein says:

> In any case, if one condenses its subject matter to its mere essence, under five main headings of preaching, polemics, stories, allusion to the Prophet's life and legislation, one will reach the conclusion that proportionately *the*

---

[45] *Ibid.*, p. 11.
[46] *Introduction*, p. 34 (italics mine).
[47] Fitzgerald, S. V., "The Alleged Debt of Islamic to Roman Law," *Law Quarterly Review*, 67 (January 1951), 82.
[48] N. J. Coulson, *A History of Islamic Law* (Edinburgh, 1965), p. 20.
[49] S. D. Goitein, *Studies in Islamic History and Institutions*, pp. 129–30.
[50] *Ibid.*, p. 133.

Qur'ān does contain legal material not less than the Pentateuch, the Torah, which is known in world literature as "The Law."[51]

It is difficult to see how, in the face of all this evidence, Schacht can maintain that law fell outside the sphere of religion, that the Prophet did not intend to create a new system of law, and that his authority was religious and political but not legal. This chapter has attempted to show that this was most certainly not the case, at least according to the principles laid down in the Qur'ān. Schacht might have wanted to maintain that theory and principles are not always reflected in practice. The next chapter, therefore, will seek to show that the Islamic *Sharī'a* based on the Qur'ān and the *sunna* of the Prophet demanded a real departure from the pre-Islamic way of life and that this departure was reflected in the juridical activities of the first century A.H.

---

[51] *Ibid.*, p. 128 (italics mine).

Chapter Two

Islamic Law in the First Century A.H.

In his *Introduction to Islamic Law,* Schacht says categorically: "The first caliphs did not appoint Ḳāḍīs."[1] He later asserts that the Umayyads "took the important step of appointing Islamic judges or Ḳāḍīs."[2] This leads him to conclude that "during the greater part of the first century, Islamic law, in the technical meaning of the term, did not as yet exist."[3] This same position was expressed in *Origins of Muhammadan Jurisprudence,* where he says that: "The evidence of legal traditions carries us back to about the year 100 A.H. only; at that time Islamic legal thought started from late Umayyad administrative and popular practice, which is still reflected in a number of traditions."[4] He argues again: "It is safe to assume that Muhammadan law hardly existed in the time of the historical Shaʻbī,"[5] who died in 110 A.H.[6]

To accept Schacht's view is tantamount to arguing that there was a legal vacuum for one hundred years, a proposition which even Coulson, who believes Schacht's thesis to be "irrefutable in its broad essentials," finds necessary to reject. He writes:

"The Qur'ān itself posed problems which must have been of immediate concern to the Muslim community, and with which the Prophet himself, in his role of supreme political and legal authority in Medina, must have been forced to deal. When, therefore, the thesis of Schacht is systematically developed to the extent of holding that the evidence of legal traditions carries us back to about the year A.H. 100, [A.D. 719] only; and when the authenticity of practically every alleged ruling of the Prophet is denied, a void is assumed, or rather created, in the picture of the development of law in early Muslim society. From a practical standpoint, and taking the attendant historical circumstances into account, the notion of such a vacuum is difficult to accept."[7]

It is not only common sense and rational analysis that lead us to doubt

---

[1] *Introduction,* p. 16.
[2] *Ibid.,* p. 24.
[3] *Ibid.,* p. 19.
[4] *Origins,* p. 5.
[5] *Ibid.,* p. 230, *n.* 1.
[6] *Ibid.,* General Index, p. 347.
[7] Coulson, *A History of Islamic Law,* pp. 64–65.

Schacht; the historical evidence also demonstrates forcibly the weakness of his position. In the first century A.H., judges were appointed, legal codes were drawn up, and legal literature did make its appearance — all providing evidence that Islamic law did exist from the time of Prophet himself. The evidence on which these assertions are based will be presented in three sections: (1) the judicial activities of the Prophet; (2) legal codes and judgments based on the Prophet's judgments or examples; and (3) legal literature in the first century A.H.[8]

The Judicial Activities of the Prophet

The Qur'ān introduced new rules and regulations which in many cases contradicted earlier patterns of life and customs. These new regulations needed to be implemented. The Prophet, being the supreme authority of the newly born state, must have had to deal with matters of practical concern to all those he ruled.

Many of the Qur'ānic injunctions — such as those dealing with prayer, *zakāt*, *ḥajj*, usury, and other commercial transactions — needed careful explanation. The Prophet, as expounder of the Qur'ān, must have both explained them verbally and demonstrated them in practice. These explanations had the force of law and came under the heading of the *sunna* of the Prophet. Thus the *sunna* came into existence simultaneously with the revelation of the Qur'ān and were part of the process of the creation of an Islamic system of jurisprudence.

Much valuable information about the Prophet's *own* judgments can be derived from the writings of the fifth-century Spanish scholar, Ibn Ṭallāʿ [404–497 A.H.]. In his book *Aqḍīyat Rasūlillah* [*Judgements of the Prophet*][9] he collected cases reported in a variety of reliable sources which were compiled mostly in the second and third centuries. The book is by no means exhaustive, but it contains sufficient judgments made by the Prophet to give a clear indication of the importance of his judicial activities.[10]

If the Prophet had not made arrangements to dispense justice according to the new norms, he would have been breaching the law he himself had introduced. Thus we find him sending judges to different towns and

---

[8] The information furnished in the following three sections proves that the examples and evidences referred to were not fabricated in a later period by traditionists themselves in support of their own doctrines.
 The problem of the authenticity of *ḥadith* literature has been discussed in detail in my work, *Studies in Early Ḥadith Literature*, (Beirut, 1968) cited hereafter as *Studies*, pp. 212–268. The same subject has been discussed in this work, see below pp. 284–301, which proves beyond doubt the authenticity of *ḥadith* literature as a whole and the impossibility of mass fabrication as advanced by Schacht and others.
[9] Ibn Ṭallāʿ, *Aqḍīyat Rasūlillah*, ed. by Z. Al-Aʿzamī (Beirut, 1978).
[10] For further information and additional cases, see *ibid;* pp. 644–719.

provinces, and entrusting to them and to the local governors the administration of justice.[10a] Among his judges were:

1. 'Abdullah b. Mas'ūd[11]
2. Abū Mūsā al-Ash'arī[12]
3. 'Alī b. Abī Ṭālib[13]
4. 'Amr b. al-'Āṣ[14]
5. 'Amr b. Ḥazm[15]
6. 'Attāb b. Asīd[16]
7. Diḥya al-Kalbī[17]
8. Ḥudhaifa b. al-Yamān[18]
9. Ma'qal b. Yasār al-Muzanī[19]
10. Mu'ādh b. Jabal[20]
11. Ubai b. Ka'b[21]
12. 'Umar, the second caliph[22]
13. 'Uqbah b. 'Āmir al-Juhanī[23]
14. Zaid b. Thābit[24]

A further indication of the significance attached to judicial activities in the first century can be seen from the list of judges of just one city, Baṣra in Iraq.

1. 'Imrān b. Ḥuṣain[25]
2. Ayās b. Ṣubaiḥ, Abī Maryam[26]
3. Zurāra b. Abī Awafā[27]
4. 'Abdur Raḥmān b. Udhaina[28]

[10a] See M. Hamidullah, *al-Wathā'iq as-Sīyāsiya* (Beirut, 1968); p. 173; also Ziyaur Rahman al-A'zami, *A Critical Study and Edition of Ibn Ṭallā''s Work*, Doctoral thesis, al-Azhar University, 1396/97, (Beirut 1978), pp.23–35.
[11] Wakī', *Akhbār al-Quḍāt*, (Cairo, 1366) vol.1, p. 5.
[12] Wakī', *Ibid*, p. 100.
[13] See Ḥanbal, vol. 1, p. 88; Hamīdullah, *Wathā'iq Sīyāsīya*, No. 133, 80 D.
[14] Ḥanbal, vol. 2, p. 187; vol. 4, p. 205.
[15] Hamīdullah, *Wathā'iq Siyasiya*, No. 105.
[16] See Kattānī, *Trātīb*, (Beirut rep. N.D.)
[17] See Ibn Ṭāllā', *Aqḍiyat Rasūlillāh*, p. 34.
[18] Tha'ālabī, *al-Fikr as-Sāmī*, (Medina, 1977), vol. 1, p. 123.
[19] Ḥanbal, vol. 4, p. 26; Wakī', Akhbār al-Quḍāt, vol. 1, pp. 37–38.
[20] Khalīfa, *Tārīkh*, (Damuscus, 1968), vol. 1, p. 23.
[21] Kattānī, *Trātīb*, vol. 1, p. 258.
[22] *Ibid.*, p. 256.
[23] Dāraquṭnī, *Sunan* (Cairo, 1386) vol. 2, p. 2.
[24] Kattānī *Trātīb*, vol. 1, p. 208.
[25] Ibn Sa'd, *at-Ṭabaqāt al-Kabīr* (Leiden, 1904–1940), vol. 7, p. 91. Cited hereafter as Ibn Sa'd.
[26] Khalīfa, *Ṭabaqāt*, (Damascus), p. 475; Ibn Sa'd, *at-Ṭabaqāt al-Kabīr*, vol. 7, p. 91.
[27] Khalīfa, *Ṭabaqāt*, p. 467.
[28] Khalīfa, *Ṭabaqāt*, p. 469.

5. 'Abdullah b. Fuḍāla[29]
6. 'Umaira b. Yathrabī[30]
7. Ka'b b. Sūr[31]
8. Hishām b. Hubaira[32]
9. 'Abdul Mālik b. Ya'lā [judge in 103 A.H.][33]
10. Iyās b. Mu'āwiya[34]
11. Ḥasan al-Baṣrī[35]
12. Thumāma b. 'Abdulla[36]
13. Mūsā b. Anas[37]

Legal Codes and Judgments

The judges who were appointed were instructed to base their judgments on the law as revealed by Allah and the *sunna* of the Prophet. This basis is cited in many authorities — for example, in the letters of 'Umar to Abū Mūsā al-Ash'arī of Baṣra, Shuraiḥ of Kūfa and his general advice to the judges and governors,[38] and in the advice given by Ibn Mas'ūd.[39]

A particularly interesting example of the weight given to the authority of the Prophet is found in the disagreement between 'Umar and Sa'd about *tamattu'* *(performing ḥajj and 'Umra together in one journey)*. 'Umar argued that pilgrims should not perform *tamattu'* on the grounds that if it were discouraged, people would visit the house of Allah more frequently. Ḍaḥḥak b. Qais was in favor of 'Umar's decision in this regard. Once he said that only an ignorant person would perform *tamattu'*. Sa'd disagreed and said:

بئس ما قالت يا ابن أخي . . . قد صنعها رسول الله صلى الله عليه وسلم ، وصنعناها معه . [40]

What a bad thing you have said, O son of my brother. . . The Prophet performed it in this manner, and we performed it that way with him.

Nor was Ibn 'Umar in favor of 'Umar in his *tamattu'* decision. When it was argued by some people that 'Umar had prohibited *tamattu'*, he replied:

أفرسول الله أحق أن تتبعوا سنته أم سنة عمر . [41]

---

[29] Khalīfa, *Ṭabaqāt*, p. 451–452.
[30] Khalīfa, *Ṭabaqāt*, p. 455.
[31] Khalīfa, *Ṭabaqāt*, p. 477.
[32] Khalīfa, *Ṭabaqāt*, p. 452.
[33] Ibn Ḥajar, *Fatḥ al-Bārī*, (Cairo, 1380) vol. 13, p. 142.
[34] Khalīfa, *Tārīkh*, p. 468.
[35] Khalīfa, *Tārīkh*, p. 486.
[36] Khalīfa, *Tārīkh*, p. 486.
[37] Khalīfa, *Tārīkh*, p. 143.
[38] 'Abdur Razzāq al-Ṣan'ānī, *Muṣannaf*. (Beirut, 1390–92), vol. 11, pp. 324–325. Cited hereafter as *Muṣannaf*.
[39] *Muṣannaf*, vol. 8, p. 301.
[40] Mālik b. Anas, *Muwaṭṭā'* (Cairo, 1951) p. 344. Cited hereafter as *Muw*.
[41] Ḥanbal, vol. 2, p. 95.

Whose *sunna* deserves more to be observed by you, the *sunna* of the Prophet or the *sunna* of 'Umar?

Thus, although Ibn 'Umar used the word *sunna* for the judgments of both 'Umar and the Prophet, he reserved the ultimate authority for the latter. I should now like to cite further examples of judgments based directly on the *sunna* of the Prophet:

1. Abū Bakr (d.13 A.H.) told a grandmother who had asked for her inheritance share that, as far as he knew, no provision was made in such cases in the Qur'ān, and he knew nothing about it in the *sunna* of the Prophet. When Abū Bakr was informed by Mughīrah that the Prophet had said that the share to which a grandmother was entitled was one-sixth, he gave her the same.[42]
2. 'Umar, (d.23 A.H.) the second Caliph, was unclear about the Magians of Hajar and what to do in their case. When 'Abdur Raḥmān b. 'Auf informed him of the *ḥadīth* of the Prophet, 'Umar accepted *jizya* (protection tax) from them.[43]
3. 'Uthmān (d.35 A.H.) asked Furai'a what the Prophet had decided about her *ṭalāq* (divorce). He based his future decrees on it.[44]
4. Mu'ādh (d.18 A.H.) did not accept any *zakāt* on less than 30 cows. He said, "I did not hear anything about it from the Prophet (so I will not take anything on them) until I see him."[45]
5. Marwān wanted to cut off the hand of a slave who had stolen the pith of a palm tree. When he was informed about the *ḥadīth* of the Prophet that "the hand is not to be cut off for taking fruit or the pith of the palm tree," he freed the slave.[46]
6. 'Umar asked the pilgrims in Minā if anyone had any knowledge of the amount of blood money (*diya*) and Ḍaḥḥāk b. Sufyān told him that the Prophet had written to him ordering him to give the wife of Ashyam al-Ḍibābī the inherited share from her husband's *diya*, upon which 'Umar decreed accordingly.[47]

The caliphs and governors also used to ask the lawyers and scholars for advice on legal matters in terms of the *sunna* of the Prophet. Some brief examples follow (many more are available).

1. Marwān changes a decision.[48]
2. Marwān consults Ibn 'Abbās.[49]
3. 'Abdul Malik sanctions a decision given according to *sunna*.[50]

---

[42] *Muw, Farā'iḍ*, 4, p. 513.
[43] *Muw, zakāt*, 42, p. 278.
[44] *Muw, ṭalāq*, 87, p. 591.
[45] *Muw, zakāt*, 24, p. 259.
[46] *Muw, ḥudad*, 32, p. 839.
[47] *Muw*, p. 866.
[48] *Mu, Buyū'*, p. 40.
[49] Shaibānī, *Muwaṭṭā'*, p. 229. Cited hereafter as *Muw. Shaib*.
[50] *Muw, hiba*, p. 28.

4. Hishām asks the scholars of Medina, Mecca, Baṣra, and Kūfa about divorce and makes a decision according to the *sunna* of the Prophet.[51]

First-Century Legal Literature

Little remains extant of the first-century legal literature in its original form. Most was absorbed into later literature and some was lost altogether; and in most cases where early scholars refer to the authority, they quote by name rather than by the title of the book, thus leaving no trace of the book itself. Some references to actual books and writings have, however, come down to us. For example:

1. The judgments of Muʿādh (18 A.H.) were read and transmitted by Ṭā'ūs (23–101 A.H.) in Yemen.[52] (It is interesting to note that some of Muʿādh's legal decisions date to the year of the Farewell *Ḥajj* of the Prophet.[53])
2. ʿUmar's many official letters concerning legal matters are referred to Abū Mūsā al-Ashʿarī and others.[54]
3. The legal works of ʿAlī (d. 40 A.H.) are reported to have been in the possession of several scholars, including: Ibn ʿAbbās,[55] Ḥasan b. ʿAlī,[56] Ḥujr b. ʿAdī,[57] and Muḥammad.[58]
4. The works of Ibn Masʿūd (d. 32 A.H.)[59] are referred to by his son, ʿĀmir,[60] and ʿAbdur Raḥmān.[61]
5. Other first-century scholars whose legal writings are referred to in later works are:
    Zaid b. Thābit (d. 45 A.H.) and his book on inheritance (*Farā'iḍ*).[62]
    Jābir b. Zaid Al-Azdī (d. 93 A.H.).[63]
    ʿUrwa (d. 93 A.H.).[64]
    Ibrāhīm Nakhaʿī (d. 96 A.H.).[65]

---

[51] Azdī, *Tārikh Mauṣil* (Cairo, 1387) p. 42.
[52] *Muṣannaf*, vol. 8, p. 245; vol. 10, pp. 373–374.
[53] *Muṣannaf*, vol. 8, p. 245.
[54] For example, see *Muṣannaf*, vol. 1, pp. 206, 291, 295, 296, 535, 537, 552, 556; vol. 2, 104, 552; vol. 4, pp. 15, 16, 17, 40, 42, 62, 88, 163, 225, 394, 487, etc.
[55] *Mu.* pp. 13, 14.
[56] Ibn Ḥanbal, *'Ilal*, (Ankara, 1963) vol. 1, p. 104.
[57] Ibn Saʿd, vol. 6, p. 154.
[58] Ibn Ḥazm, *Muḥallā*, (Cairo, 1352), vol. 7, pp. 102–103.
[59] *Studies*, pp. 44–45.
[60] Ṭabarānī, *Muʿjam Kabīr*, vol. 5, pp. 97a–b.
[61] Fasawī, *Tārīkh*, vol. 3, pp. 215a.
[62] Fasawī, *Tārīkh*, vol. 2, p. 148b [vol. 1, p. 486 in Baghdad edition].
[63] Amr Ennami, *Studies in Ibadism*, (Beirut, 1392) pp. 39–40.
[64] Ibn Saʿd, vol. 5, p. 133.
[65] Nasaʿī, *Sunan*, vol. 2, p. 82 [Indian edition].

Abū Qilābah (d. 104 A.H.).[66]

Sha'bī (d. 103 A.H.) and his books on marriage, divorce, and inheritance[67] and on injury and compensation.[68]

Although these examples of first-century legal works by no means form a comprehensive list, they do show that there was much legal literary activity going on in various parts of the Muslim world at the time. Schacht's theory of Islamic law originating in the early second century would thus appear untenable. In the second part of this work, it will be shown that he was equally incorrect about the early bases of Islamic law.

---

[66] Nabia Abbot, *Studies in Arabic Literary Papyri*, (Chicago, 1967) vol. 2, p. 223; Ibn Ḥanbal, *'Ilal,* vol. 1, p. 295.
[67] Fasawī, *Tārīkh,* vol. 3, p. 252b.
[68] Khatīb, *Tārīkh Baghdād,* (Cairo, 1931) vol. 12, p. 232.

PART TWO
THE *SUNNA* OF THE PROPHET AND ISLAMIC LAW

The new legal theories that were discussed in Part One resulted in the community's making a clear break from pre-Islamic society: *Jāhilīya*. Schacht, however, might have sought to deny this by arguing that he had produced concrete examples to show that the legal theories of the ancient schools of law were based on "living tradition" rather than the traditions of the Prophet. He might furthermore have pointed to the evidence he claimed to have produced to suggest his contention that the mass fabrication of *ḥadīth* literature and the back-projection of the later statements into the mouth of the Prophet, accepting which automatically invalidates the *isnād* system as well. Part Two will therefore be devoted to a critical study of Schacht's methodology, and the examples he used to justify his conclusions will be critically analyzed.

CHAPTER THREE

THE *SUNNA:*
ITS MEANING AND CONCEPT

The Early Concept of the *Sunna*

According to Schacht, the early concept of *sunna* was that of the "living tradition" of the ancient schools of law, by which was meant customary or "generally agreed practice" (*'amal, al-amr al-mujtama' 'alaih*). This concept was unrelated to the Prophet.[1]

In his *Introduction to Islamic Law*, Schacht gives the following account:

> *Sunna* in its Islamic context originally had a political rather than a legal connotation; it referred to the policy and administration of the caliph. The question whether the administrative acts of the first two caliphs, Abū Bakr and 'Umar, should be regarded as binding precedents, arose probably at the time when a successor to 'Umar had to be appointed (23/644), and the discontent with the policy of the third caliph, 'Uthmān, which led to his assassination in 35/655, took the form of a charge that he, in his turn, had diverged from the policy of his predecessors and, implicitly, from the Koran. In this connexion, there appeared the concept of the "*sunna* of the Prophet," not yet identified with any set of positive rules but providing a doctrinal link between the "*sunna* of Abū Bakr and 'Umar" and the Koran. The earliest, certainly authentic, evidence for this use of the term "*sunna* of the Prophet" is the letter addressed by the Khārijī leader 'Abd Allāh ibn Ibāḍ to the Umayyad caliph 'Abd al-Malik about 76/695. The same term with a theological connotation, and coupled with the "example of the forebears," occurs in the contemporary treatise which Ḥasan al-Baṣrī addressed to the same caliph. It was introduced into the theory of Islamic law, presumably towards the end of the first century, by the scholars of Iraq.[2]

This exposition of the early concept of the *sunna* of the Prophet contrasts with the views of the early scholars. It is therefore necessary to begin our investigation of Schacht's thesis by looking at the various ways the word was used in pre-Islamic and early Islamic contexts.

According to Arabic lexicography, *sunna* means a way, course, rules, mode or manner of acting, or conduct of life.[3] The word has been used in

---

[1] *Origins*, p. 58.
[2] *Introduction*, pp. 17–18.
[3] See Ibn Manẓūr, *Lisān al-'Arab*, art; *sanan;* E.W. Lane, *Arabic English Lexicon (Edinburgh 1867)*, vol. 4, p. 1438.

pre-Islamic as well as in Islamic poetry with the same literary meanings. The pre-Islamic poet Khālid al-Hudhalī says:

فلا تجزعن من سنة أنت سرتها فأول راضٍ سنةٍ من يسيرها [4]

Do not manifest grief and agitate from a way (*sunna*) you have walked, because the first who agrees on a *sunna* is the one who initials it.

And Farazdaq says:

فجاء بسنة العمرين فيها شفاء للصدور من السقام

He brought the *sunna* of Abū Bakr and 'Umar which has the remedy for the heart from the disease.

The Word *Sunna*: Its Meaning and Usage

The word *sunna*, with its plural *sunan*, is used sixteen times in the Qur'ān in the sense of an established course or rule, a law, or a line of conduct.[6] For example, Almighty Allah says:

ولن تجد لسنة الله تبديلا [7]

Thou wilt not find for the *Law* of Allah (*sunna* of Allah) anything that can alter it.

And again:

قل للذين كفروا أن ينتهوا يغفر لهم ما قد سلف ، وإن يعودوا فقد مضت سنة الأولين . [8]

Tell those who are bent on denying the truth that if they desist, all that is past shall be forgiven them; but if they revert to their wrongdoing, let them remember what happened to the likes of them *(sunnat al awwalīn)* in times gone by.

The *ḥadīth* literature is replete with usage of this word, and it is used by the Prophet himself time after time. For example, Mālik quotes the following statements of the Prophet:

« تركت فيكم الأمرين لن تضلوا ما تمسكتم بهما ، كتاب الله وسنة نبيه . » [9]

I am leaving with you two things: you shall never go astray as long as you adhere to them: the Book of Allah and the *sunna* of His Prophet.

Some desert Arabs clad in woollen clothes came to Allah's Messenger (may peace be upon him). He saw them in a sad plight as they had been hard pressed by need. He [the Holy Prophet] exhorted people to give charity, but they showed some reluctance until [signs] of anger could be seen on his face. Then a person from the Anṣār came with a purse containing silver. Then came another person and then other persons followed them in succession

---

[4] *Al-Hudhalīyīn, Diwān* (Cairo, 1385) p. 157.
[5] Bevan, A. A., editor, (Beirut N.D.) p. 1013.
[6] See J. Penrice, *Dictionary and Glossary of the Koran* (London, 1875) pp. 72–73.
[7] Qur'ān, translated by Pickthal, p. 681; for the Qur'ānic Verses, see 33:62.
[8] Qur'ān, 8:38; translated by M. Asad, p. 320.
[9] *Muw.*, Qadr 3.

until signs of happiness could be seen on his face. Thereupon Allah's Messenger (may peace be upon him) said:

فقال رسول الله صلى الله عليه وسلم : من سن في الإسلام سنة حسنة فعمل بها بعده كتب له مثل أجر من عمل بها ولا ينقص من أجورهم شيء ، ومن سن في الإسلام سنة سيئة فعمل بها بعده كتب عليه مثل وزر من عمل بها ولا ينقص من أوزارهم شيء ،[10]

"He who establishes a good *sunna* [practice] in Islam which is followed after him [by people], will be assured a reward like that of the one who follows it, without their rewards being diminished in any respect. And he who establishes an evil *sunna* [practice] in Islam which is followed subsequently [by others], will bear the burden like that of the one who follows this [evil practice] without theirs being diminished in any respect.[10]

In all these quotations the word has been used in its literary meaning. This last *ḥadīth* implies that if anyone, of whatever standard he may be, consciously originates some act, good or bad, which is followed by others, it becomes his *sunna*.

Thus, we see that the word *sunna* was in continuous use from the pre-Islamic era, meaning way, law, mode or conduct of life. The expression "*sunna* of the Prophet" came into use during the life of the Prophet when Almighty Allah ordered the Muslims to obey the Prophet and to take his life as their model. The term was also used by the Prophet himself.[11] Sometimes the Arabic definite article *(al)* was affixed to the word to denote the *sunna* of the Prophet, while the general usage of the word continued for the *sunna* of others. Gradually the term became identified with the *sunna* of the Prophet, so that by the end of the second century it was used in legal books almost exclusively to mean norms set by the Prophet or deduced from his behavior or authentic *aḥādīth*.

Some Other Meanings of the Word *Sunna*

That the word was not used exclusively for the *sunna* of the Prophet, however, can be seen from the following quotations from *fiqh-Ḥadīth* literature.

١ قال عمر : « والله لو فعلتها لكانت سنة
٢ قال ابن عمر : إنها ليست سنة الصلاة وإنما أفعل هذا من أجل أني أشتكي
٣ قال مالك : إن من سنة المسلمين التي لا اختلاف فيها . . .
٤ قالت عائشة رضي الله عنها في تفسير قوله تعالى : وإن خفتم أن لا تقسطوا ، هي اليتيمة تكون في حجر وليها فيرغب في جمالها ومالها ويريد أن يتزوجها بأدنى من سنة نسائها . .
٥ قال مالك : فكانت تلك بعد سنة المتلاعنين
٦ قال مالك : وقد اعتكف رسول الله صلى الله عليه وسلم وعرف المسلمون سنة الاعتكاف

---

[10] *Mu. 'Ilm* 15.
[11] *Muw, Qadr*, 3.

٧ قال مالك : كتب ابن عمر إلى عبد الملك . . . « أقر لك بالسمع والطاعة على سنة الله وسنة رسوله فيما استطعت »

٨ ذكر الزهري في السيرة : خبيبا ، فقال : « فكان أول من سن الركعتين عند القتل »

٩ قال أبو بكر : « وما علمت لك في سنة رسول الله صلى الله عليه وسلم شيئا »

١٠ قال ابن عمر : « وسنة الله ورسوله أحق أن تتبع من سنة ابن فلان إن كنت صادقا »

1. 'Umar said: "By Allah, had I done that, it would have become a *sunna* (a norm)."[12]
2. Ibn 'Umar said: "This is not the *sunna* of Prayer, I simply do it this way because of pain (in my leg)."[13]
3. Mālik said: "The *sunna* of the Muslim Community regarding which there is no difference..."[14]
4. 'Ā'isha explained the meaning of the verse 4:3:

   وإن خفتم ألا تقسطوا

   [If you fear that you may not do justice], saying "this refers to the orphan girl living in the custody of a guardian who is attracted to her beauty and wealth and would like to marry her, but who desires to pay a dowry *(mahr)* less than the *sunna* of women of her rank."[15]
5. Mālik said: "It became afterward the *sunna* of the *Mutalā 'inīn*."[16]
6. Mālik said: "The Prophet and the Muslims knew the *sunna* of *I'tikāf*."[17]
7. Ibn 'Umar wrote to 'Abdul Mālik: "I agree to hear and to obey you according to the *sunna* of Allah and his Messenger, as far as I can."[18]
8. Zuhrī mentioned Khubaib in his book, saying: "He was the first who introduced the *sunna* of Praying two *rak'a* on the occasion of execution."[19]
9. Abū Bakr said: "I knew nothing (no share for a grandmother from inheritance) in the *sunna* of the Prophet."[20]
10. Ibn 'Umar said: "The *sunna* of Allah and his Messenger deserves to be more observed than the *sunna* of Ibn Fulān, if you are telling the truth."[21]

Thus we see that the word has been used in a variety of different contexts, such as:

The *sunna* of the Prophet.
The *sunna* of 'Umar (the Second Caliph).
The *sunna* of Muslims.
The *sunna* of Khubaib.
The *sunna* of women.

---

[12] *Muw*, p. 50.
[13] *Muw*, p. 89.
[14] *Muw*, p. 804.
[15] *Studies*, p. 144 (Arabic section).
[16] *Muw*, p. 567.
[17] *Muw*, p. 314.
[18] *Muw*, p. 983.
[19] *Muṣannaf*, vol. 5, p. 355.
[20] *Muw*, p. 513.
[21] *Ḥanbal*, vol. 2, p. 56–57.

The sunna of *Mutalā 'īnīn*.
The *sunna* of *ṣalāt* (prayer).
The *sunna* of *I'tikāf*.
The *sunna* of Ibn Fulān.

Not only was the word *sunna* originally not confined to the practices of the Prophet: its meaning also underwent changes. For example:

١ - قال الشيباني : « فقال بعضهم يعني صلاة الوتر سنة لا ينبغي تركها ؛ وقال بعضهم واجب » .

٢ - قال الشيباني : « والسنة أن الركعة الأولى أطول من الثانية » .

٣ - قال الشيباني : « من السنة أن يستقبل الناس الإمام يوم الجمعة إذا خطب . . . » .

٤ - قال الشيباني : « قال أبو حنيفة : السنة في الصلاة إذا أراد أن ينهض ، ينهض على صدور قدميه إن قدر ذلك » .

٥ - قال الشيباني : باب الإمارة ومن استن سنة حسنة عمل بها من بعده .

٦ - قال الشيباني : « قد جاءت السنة المعروفة أنه لا ينبغي لبس قميص ولا سراويل ولا قباء ولا خفين حتى يحل الرجل من إحرامه » .

٧ - قال مالك : الضحية سنة وليست بواجبة .

٨ - « . . . عن ابن شهاب : أنه كان يقول : من أدرك من صلاة الجمعة ركعة فليصل إليها أخرى ، قال ابن شهاب وهي السنة .
قال مالك : وعلى ذلك أدركت أهل العلم ببلدنا ، وذلك أن رسول الله صلى الله عليه وسلم قال : من أدرك من الصلاة ركعة فقد أدرك الصلاة » .

1. Shaibānī said: "Some of the scholars say that *witr* prayer is a *sunna* which ought not to be abandoned, while other scholars say it is compulsory."[22]
2. Shaibānī said: "The *sunna* is that the first *rak'a* (in prayer) is longer than the second one."[23]
3. Shaibānī said: "It is *sunna* that the people should face the *Imām* in the sermon of the Friday Prayer."[24]
4. Abū Ḥanīfa said: "The *sunna* in the prayer is that one should stand with the toes (extended and flat) when one wants to stand, if one can."[25]
5. Shaibānī said: "Chapter on *Imāra* (governorship) and one who introduces a good *sunna* which was followed by people later on."[26]
6. Shaibānī said: "It is in a well-known *sunna* that in *Iḥrām* (performing *ḥajj*) one should not wear the shirt, trousers, Qubā' or socks until the man comes out of his *Iḥrām*."[27]
7. Mālik said: "To sacrifice an animal (on the eve of *'Īd*) is *sunna* and not compulsory *(wājib)*."[28]
8. Ibn Shihāb said: "One who is able to join just one *rak'a* of *Jum'a* (Friday) prayer should pray one additional *rak'a* (after it). Ibn Shihāb said: "this is *sunna*." Mālik said: "I found the scholars of our city holding the same

---

[22] Shaibānī, *Ḥujja* (Hydrabad, 1385) I, 186.
[23] Ibid 1, 342.
[24] Ibid 1, 287.
[25] Ibid 1, 315.
[26] Shaibānī, *Āthār* (Karachi) 152.
[27] Shaibānī, *Ḥujja*, II, 399.
[28] *Muw*, p. 487.

opinion. It was so, because the Prophet said: 'Whoever prays a *rak'a* of the prayer with the *Imām* in congregation has not missed the prayer.' "²⁹

These quotations indicate that the word *sunna* was sometimes used for what had been deduced from the practice or the sayings of the Prophet, even though it was not stated or done by the Prophet in this way. In quotation 8, for example, Zuhrī says that if someone prays only one *rak'a* of *Jum'a* prayer with the *Imām*, instead of two, because he joined the prayer late, he should pray one additional *rak'a* when the *Imām* finishes his prayer. He adds that this is *sunna*. It is obvious that the Prophet never missed a *rak'a* of the *Jum'a* prayer, because he was always the *Imām*. Zuhrī deduced his doctrine from the saying of the Prophet that he who prays a *rak'a* (with the *Imām* in congregation), in fact has not missed the prayer (in congregation).³⁰ Now, a jurist when deducing a law or doctrine by using the process of analogy or other processes, properly speaking, only expounds (مظهر) the law and does not lay it down (لا يثبته);³¹ therefore, it was sometimes called *sunna*, meaning that it was established through the *sunna*.

A further example: *witr* prayer, according to the Hanafī school, is *wājib* (compulsory) according to the saying of Abū Ḥanīfa: ان الوتر سنة ("The *witr* prayer is *sunna*"). This means that its obligation was established through *sunna*.

In Muslim jurisprudence, every human act comes under one of five categories:

> When the communication from the law-giver assumes the form of a demand it may either be absolute or not. If the former, the demand may consist in requiring man to do something, in which case the act demanded is regarded as obligatory (*farḍ*, فرض), or it may require him to forbear or abstain from doing something, in which case the act to be forborne or abstained from is said to be forbidden (*ḥarām*, حرام); or, in other words, such a speech imposes duties of commission or omission. When the demand is not of an absolute character, the act to which it refers, if it be one of commission, is called commendable (*mandūb*, مندوب), and if it be one to be forborne or abstained from it is called condemned or abominable or improper (*makrūh*, مكروه). An act with respect to which the law-giver is indifferent is regarded as permissible (مباح)."³²

Mandūb has been divided into three categories:

1. If the emphasis is on carrying out the act with rebuke rather than punishment being the consequence for failing to do so, it is called *sunna mu'akkada* (سنة مؤكدة). The *Adhān* is an example.
2. If it is commendable, but the Prophet sometimes did it while having

---

²⁹ *Muw, Jum'a*, 11.
³⁰ Which means that he would be given the reward of praying in congregation.
³¹ Abdul Rahim, *Muhammadan Jurisprudence* (Lahore, 1968), p. 54.
³² *Ibid.*, p. 61.

at other times neglected to do it — such as fasting on Monday and Thursday in other than the month of *Ramaḍān* or certain *sunan* of ablution [*waḍū'*] — it is called *Al-nāfila*, or *Sunna Nāfila*.

3. If it is commendable, but a form of perfection for the follower — as with someone who follows the Prophet in his habit of dressing, eating, walking, and so on — it is called desirable (المستحب) or excellent (الفضيلة).³³ Thus we find that to refer to the acts of the third category *(mandūb)*, the word *sunna* has been used in the sense of an established religious practice without its being obligatory. For example, *'Id* prayer is *sunna* and not *wājib* (obligatory).³⁴ Sometimes it is used in the sense of السيرة العامة ("the complete conduct of life"). Every action of the Prophet relating to *dīn* — his sayings, deeds, and tacit approvals — are called *sunna*. And the sum total of all these actions are also called *sunna* or *sīra*. Whenever the expression الكتاب والسنة ("The Book and the *Sunna*") occurs, it means that the word has been applied in the sense of a complete conduct of life or, in other words, the Prophet's complete *sīra*.³⁵ We therefore sometimes find the words *sīra* and *sunna* being used interchangeably by scholars. Ibn Ḥanbal, for example, in the following case records the statement of 'Alī, transmitted by two narrators. The incident is the same, but one of them uses the word *sunna* while the other uses the word *sīra*.

١ - ﴿ . . . ﴾ مروان الفزاري ، أخبرنا عبد المالك بن سلع عن عبد خير ، قال سمعته يقول ، قام علي رضي الله عنه على المنبر ، فذكر رسول الله صلى الله عليه وسلم ، فقال ، قبض رسول الله صلى الله عليه وسلم واستخلف أبو بكر رضي الله عنه فعمل بعمله وسار بسيرته حتى قبضه الله عز وجل على ذلك ثم استخلف عمر رضي الله عنه على ذلك فعمل بعملهما وسار بسيرتهما حتى قبضه الله عز وجل على ذلك .

٢ - ﴿ . . . ﴾ ابن نمير عن عبد الملك بن سلع عن عبد خير ، قال سمعت عليا رضي الله عنه يقول : قبض الله نبيه صلى الله عليه وسلم على خير ما قبض عليه نبي من الانبياء عليهم السلام ثم استخلف أبو بكر رضي الله عنه فعمل بعمل رسول الله صلى الله عليه وسلم وسنة نبيه ، وعمر رضي الله عنه كذلك .

1. Marwān — 'Abdul Malik — 'Abd Khair said that he saw [the Caliph] 'Alī on the pulpit and then he mentioned the Prophet: "The Prophet died, and Abū Bakr succeeded [him] who acted according to the deed of the Prophet and pursued 'his conduct' *(sāra bi sīratihi)* سار بسيرته until Allah caused him to die. Then 'Umar succeeded him, who acted according to the acts of both [predecessors], and pursued the conduct of those two [*wa sāra bi sīratihimā*] وسار بسيرتهما until Allah made him die."³⁶
2. Ibn Numair — 'Abdul Malik — 'Abd Khair: He heard [the Caliph] 'Alī saying: "Allah caused His Messenger to die the best way any Messenger

---

³³ Khallāf, *'Ilm Uṣūl al Fiqh* (Kuwait) pp. 111–112.
³⁴ Thānawī, *A Dictionary of Technical Terms* (Calcutta, 1862), pp. 703–704.
³⁵ Yamānī, Mu'allimī, *Anwār Kāshifa* (Cairo, 1378) p. 20.
³⁶ Ḥanbal, I, 128.

of Allah was caused to die. Then Abū Bakr succeeded [him], who acted according to the deeds of the Prophet and his *sunna* [norm] and 'Umar in the like manner."³⁷

Conclusion

The word *sunna* literally means a way, rules, or conduct of life. It has been used in pre-Islamic poetry as well as in the Qur'ān in the same sense. Anyone can establish a *sunna*, good or bad, if it is followed by others. As the life of the Prophet was the model for all Muslims to follow, the expression "*sunna* of the Prophet" came into use in the life of the Prophet and was even used by him. Sometimes the norms drawn analogically from the practice or the sayings of the Prophet were also called *sunna*.

Before we move into a detailed study of Schacht's theory of the concept of *sunna*, certain points need to be emphasized. The first is that the source of legislation in modern constitutional states, the constitution, endorses the legislative authority and establishes its range of legislation. In Islam the legislative authorities have been fixed from the very beginning not by the lawyers but Almighty Allah. We have already seen that the legislative authority of the Prophet is laid down in the Qur'ān, where it is clearly shown that obedience to the Prophet is a Divine order and that the Prophet's legal authority therefore stems from Divine revelation.

The second point is that the Qur'ān never says that the source of law is *sunna* but specifically enjoins obedience to the Messenger of Allah and conformity with the examples he established. Thus, even if one were to agree with Schacht that Shāfi'ī was the first to use the term *sunna* exclusively for the *sunna* of the Prophet while earlier scholars used the word in a broader sense, this would in no way detract from the conceptual authority of the *sunna* of the Prophet. *The source of law is not the word itself but the concept, which derived its authority directly from the Qur'ān.*

This may appear merely a theoretical defense of the classical Muslim view. Let us therefore look at the evidence on which Schacht bases his theory.

Schacht's Theory of the Early Concept of the *Sunna*

A central part of Schacht's thesis hinges on the usage and the concept of the word *sunna*. Briefly, he contends that:

1. The early concept of *sunna* was that of the customary or generally agreed upon practice, what he calls the "living tradition." In coming to this conclusion he follows D. S. Margoliouth and cites Ibn Muqaffa', who, he says, found the term used in the early second century for the administrative regulations of the Umayyad government.³⁸

---

³⁷ *Idem*.
³⁸ *Origins*, pp. 58–59.

2. The concept of the *sunna* of the Prophet was of relatively late origin, coined by the Iraqis some time in the second century.[39]
3. Even the use of the term "*sunna* of the Prophet" does not mean the actual *sunna* originated by the Prophet; it was simply the "living tradition" of the school projected back into the mouth of the Prophet.[40]

In the first section of this chapter an exposition was given of the classical Muslim view of the meaning and usage of *sunna*, based on evidence from writings of the time recorded in works prior to Shāfi'ī.[41] In this section I will examine the examples Schacht brings forward to support his contentions.

To support his argument that the early concept of *sunna* was agreed upon in practice or the "living tradition," Schacht refers us to Margoliouth and Ibn Al-Muqaffa'. He writes: "Margoliouth has concluded that *sunna* as a principle of law meant originally the ideal or normative usage of the community and only later acquired the restricted meaning of the precedents set by the Prophet."[42] Let us look at Margoliouth's references to the different usages of the term *sunna* and see whether the deductions made from them are justifiable.

Schacht: Concept of *sunna* as described by Margoliouth:

1. *Known practice* as opposed to innovation.
    a. Conversation between 'Alī and 'Uthmān in 34 A.H.

    فأقام سنة معلومة وأمات بدعة متروكة [43]

    He established the known *sunna*, and decisively ended abandoned innovation.

    b. Saying of Ṭalḥah about the war against 'Alī in 36 A.H.

    هذا أمر لم يكن قبل اليوم فينزل فيه القرآن أو يكون فيه من رسول الله صلى الله عليه وسلم سنة . [44]

    This is a matter which did not happen before such, that a revelation in the Qur'ān might have sent down regarding it, or that there might have been some precedent from the Prophet regarding it.

    c. A speech of Ashtar.

    هؤلاء القوم لا يقاتلونكم إلا عن دينكم ليميتوا السنة ويحيوا البدعة ، ويعيدوكم في ضلالة . [45]

---

[39] *Ibid.*, p. 76.
[40] *Idem*.
[41] With the exception of the last example.
[42] *Origins*, p. 58.
[43] Ṭabarī, *Annales*, I, 2937. Paging according to De Geoje's edition.
[44] *Annales*, I, 3166.
[45] *Annales*, I, 3298.

Those people do not fight you except for the sake of your *dīn* (religion) in order to bring a decisive end to the *sunna* (norms) and allow innovation to flourish and push you back in error and misguidance.

    d. Ḥusain's saying to the Basrite in 60 A.H.

بعثت رسولي اليكم وأنا أدعوكم إلى كتاب الله وسنة نبيه . [46]

I have sent you my Messenger, and I am calling you to the book of Allah and the *sunna* of His Prophet.

    e. Conversation of Suwaid with Muṭarrif in 77 A.H.

وأن ندعوهم إلى كتاب الله وسنة نبيه . [47]

Whatever the case be, we call them only to the Book of Allah and the *sunna* of His Prophet.

2. *Past practice.*
Speech of 'Alī in 37 A.H., after the incident of *arbitration*.

فحكما بغير حجة بينة ولا سنة ماضية . [48]

They made their decision without any clear evidence or any early precedent of *sunna*.

3. *Good practice*, as opposed to bad practice.
The letter of 'Uthmān to Meccan in 35 A.H.

والسنة الحسنة التي استن بها رسول الله صلى الله عليه وسلم والخليفتان من بعده . . . [49]

The good norm [*sunna*] which has been initiated by the Prophet and the two Caliphs after him.

4. *Order*, as opposed to disorder.
Used in 64 A.H.

يأمر الناس بالسنة وينهى عن الفتنة . [50]

He enjoins people to act according to the *sunna* and forbids them from sedition.

5. *Practice*, without further definition.
    a. The argument of 'Alī against al-Khirrīt when he disagreed with the arbitration of 'Alī and wanted to leave 'Alī in 38 A.H.

هلم أدارسك الكتاب وأناظرك في السنن [51]

Come here and let me teach to you the Book of God and dispute with you regarding the *sunan*.

    b. The advice of Muhallab to his sons in 82 A.H.

---

[46] *Annales*, II, 240.
[47] *Annales* II, 984.
[48] *Annales*, I, 3368.
[49] *Annales*, I, 3044.
[50] *Annales*, II, 455.
[51] *Annales*, I, 3419.

عليكم بقراءة القرآن وتعلم السنن وآداب الصالحين .[52]

You are enjoined to recite the Qur'ān and to learn the *sunna* and the manners of the upright people.

6. *Ascribed to God, the Muslims, Islam.*
   a. A Law of Allah (38 A.H)[53] سنة الله
   b. Conduct of Muslims (36 A.H.).[54] سنة المسلمين
   c. Norms of Islam (34 A.H.).[55] سنة الاسلام

7. *Practice of the Prophet and the first two caliphs in 35 A.H.*

السنة الحسنة التي استن بها رسول الله والخليفتان من بعده[56]

The good norm [*sunna*] which has been acted upon by the Prophet and the two Caliphs after him.

8. *Something over and above the practice of the Prophet*
   (a conversation of Zaid b. 'Alī in 122 A.H.)

انما ندعوكم لكتاب الله وسنة نبيه ، وإلى أن السنن أن تحيى وإلى البدع أن تطفأ .[57]

We call you to the Book of Allah and the *sunna* of His Prophet, and to cause the *sunna* to flourish and to cause innovation to be extinguished.

9. *Practice taught by the Prophet.*
   Muhammad taught them practice, as it is described in a letter ascribed to 'Alī in 36 A.H.

فعلمهم الكتاب والحكمة والفرائض والسنن . . . ثم ان المسلمين استخلفوا به أميرين صالحين عملا بالكتاب والسنة وأحسنا السيرة ولم يعدوا السنة ألا وان لكم علينا العمل بكتاب الله وسنة رسوله .[58]

Then he taught them the Book, the wisdom, obligatory deeds and commendable deeds *(sunan)*. Later on, the Muslim community appointed as successors two pious rulers who acted according to the Book of Allah and the *sunna* (of the Prophet), whose conduct was excellent, and who did not deviate from the *sunna*. Indeed, it is your right over us that we act according to the Book of Allah and the *sunna* of His Prophet.

10. *Practice from the Qur'an.*
    In a letter, 129 A.H., by the founder of the Abbasids.

إن الله تعالى نزل عليه كتابه ، أحل فيه حلاله وحرم فيه حرامه وشرع فيه شرائعه وسنن فيه سننه .[59]

Allah revealed His Book to him, made lawful in it what is lawful and

---

[52] *Annales*, II, 1083.
[53] *Annales*, I, 3427.
[54] *Annales*, I, 3132, 3228.
[55] *Annales*, I, 2929.
[56] *Annales*, I, 3044.
[57] *Annales*, II, 1700.
[58] *Annales*, I, 3236.

prohibited what is forbidden. He set forth in it His various Laws *(sharā'i')* and established through it His *sunan*.[59]

From these references, Margoliouth deduces that:

> The practice of the Prophet in these stories is far commoner than any other phrase. The context in which these expressions are most frequently used is in reference to the third caliph, 'Uthmān, whose conduct was supposed to differ seriously from that of his predecessors; though the charges formulated against him are always somewhat vague. It seems clear that the second source of law was not yet anything quite definite, but merely what was customary, and had the approval of persons of authority, all of whom presently merged in the Prophet.[60]

It is extremely difficult to see how Margoliouth reaches these conclusions. First the only reference which mentions 'Uthmān is number 1, which has no bearing on the subject. Second, it is hardly logical to apply the "vagueness" of the charges he refers to — albeit without evidence from the text — into a vagueness regarding the definition of *sunna* itself. Would the authorities invite people to follow the *"sunna* of the Prophet" or promise to work according to it if it had not been clearly defined? Moreover one wonders how "it seems clear" that *sunna* was merely what was customary. Most of the documents, speeches, and charges refer specifically to the *"sunna* of the Prophet" and in a way that gives the phrase a fixed and definitive meaning (the genitive case is used): A definite personal practice of the Prophet is being spoken about and not a general practice of the community.

What is perhaps most damning, as far as Schacht's reliance on Margoliouth goes, is that most of Margoliouth's references are dated from the first half of the first century. If Schacht accepted these references as authentic, he would also have to accept the fact that the expression *"sunna* of the Prophet" was widely used a hundred years before he contended it was.

It is worthwhile to note here the excellent conclusions of M. M. Bravmann, whose work was first available to the me only when this book was going to press and which I have therefore not been able to draw on as heavily as might otherwise have been the case.[61] According to Bravmann:

> D. S. Margoliouth . . . assumes that the practice of the Prophet, which in the early times is most frequently mentioned in reference to 'Uthman, was not yet anything quite definite, but merely what was customary, that is: "the practice of the Muslims, or of the community. . . . " With respect to this theory it must be stated that the very specific term *Sīrat Rasūli-Ullāh* which is

---

[59] *Annales*, II, 1961.
[60] D. S. Margoliouth, *The Early Development of Mohammedanism* (London, 1914), pp. 69–70.
[61] See M. M. Bravmann, *The Spiritual Background of Early Islam: Studies in Ancient Arab Concepts* (Leiden, 1972).

used in 'Uthmān's oath of office (in al-Balādurī's report) for 'the practice and procedure of the Prophet' makes it perfectly clear that what is meant by the expression 'the practice of the Prophet' is the specific, personal practice of the Prophet himself and not the practice of the community. And it is the adherence to the personal practice of the Prophet, *Sīrat Rasūli-llāh*, that is specifically demanded from the candidate to be elected as 'Umar's successor. Obviously, the adherence to the law of the Qur'ān was a more or less self-understood duty for anyone aspiring to that office, or, for that matter, for any believer. It is evident that the Prophet had his specific, personal practice (consisting of concrete, single practices, procedures, which no less that the practice indicated in the Qur'ān, could, of course, in part have roots in earlier practices. . . .) But it is an important fact that the adherence to the personal practice of the Prophet was, in connection with the election of 'Umar's successor, declared to constitute a basic principle.[62]

Ibn al-Muqaffa'

According to Schacht, Ibn al-Muqaffa'

> realized that *sunna* as it was understood in his time, was based not on authentic precedents laid down by the Prophet and the first Caliphs, but to a great extent on administrative regulations of the Umaiyyad government. In contrast to Shāfi'ī, however, he did not fall back on traditions from the Prophet but drew the contrary conclusion that the Caliph was free to fix and codify the alleged *sunna*.[63]

Leaving aside the fact that Ibn al-Muqaffa' was neither a lawyer nor a theologian but an anti-Umayyad, indeed, charged with heresy,[64] it is simply not the case that he regarded the caliph as free to fix and codify the alleged *sunna*. Describing the role of the caliph, he says:

« فأما إثباتنا للإمام الطاعة فيها لا يطاع فيه غيره فان ذلك في الرأي والتدبير والأمر الذي جعل الله أزمته وعراه بأيدي الأئمة ، ليس لأحد فيه أمر ولا طاعة من غزو والقفول والجمع والقسم والاستعمال والترك والحكم بالرأي فيها لم يكن فيه أثر ، وامضاء الحدود والأحكام على الكتاب والسنة » .[65]

> In so far as our confirmation is concerned of obedience to the *Imām* [the ruler] in matters which none else ought to be obeyed, it pertains only to matters of *ra'y* [personal opinion] and of planning (*tadbīr*) and to those matters which God has placed under the authority of the *Imams*. No one else has the right to command or to be obeyed as regards setting out on or returning from combat, gathering and dividing troops, appointing and dis-

---

[62] Bravmann, *The Spiritual Background of Early Islam, op. cit.* (I have, however, certain objections to his methodology: (1) He apparently did not feel the necessity to check Margoliouth's references (2) His very limited use of the Qur'ān in determining the birth of the expression *Sirat Rasulillah* [*sunna* of the Prophet], a method common to almost every Orientalist).

[63] *Origins*, pp. 58–59.

[64] Ziriklī, *al-A'lām* (Cairo, 1373), vol. 4, p. 284.

[65] Ibn al-Muqaffa', *Itt.*, 349, published in *Āthār Ibn Muqaffa'* (Beirut, 1966).

missing governors, and giving judgment on the basis of *ra'y* [personal opinion] in matters for which there are no traditions (*āthār*) or in discharging punishments or rulings in accordance with the Book [of God] and the *sunna*.

Furthermore, he says,

ومن ذلك تعهد أدبهم في تعلم الكتاب والتفقه في السنة [66]

the caliph must attend carefully to seeing that they [the army] learn the Book [of God] and acquire knowledge of the *sunna*.

He says further:

« أما من يدعي لزوم السنة منهم فيجعل ما ليس له سنة حتى يبلغ ذلك به إلى أن يسفك الدم بغير بينة ولا حجة على الأمر الذي يزعم أنه سنة . وإذا سئل عن ذلك لم يستطع أن يقول : هريق فيه دم على عهد رسول الله أو أئمة الهدى من بعده . وإذا قيل له : أي دم سفك على هذه السنة التي تزعمون ؟ قالوا : فعل ذلك عبد الملك بن مروان أو أمير من بعض أولئك الأمراء » . [67]

As for those among them who claim to adhere to the *sunna*, they make that a *sunna* which it is not their right to do — even to the extent that they shed blood without evidence or proof in accordance with that which they deem the *sunna* to be. And if they are asked about it they cannot say that blood was shed in this case during the life of the Prophet or during the period of the rightly guided *Imāms* after him. If they are asked whose blood was shed according to this *sunna* which they claim, they would reply " 'Abdul Malik b. Marwān or one of those [Umayyad] governors did so.

It is evident that the writing of Ibn Muqaffa' is directed against the Umayyad period. We are not concerned here about whether his statement is right or wrong. What concerns us is only *his* concept of *sunna*. According to his report, there was much confusion, even within one city — Kūfa — and the judgments were not unanimous, so he advised that:

« فلو رأى أمير المؤمنين أن يأمر بهذه الأقضية والسير المختلفة فترفع اليه في كتاب ويرفع معها ما يحتج به كل قوم من سنة أو قياس ، ثم نظر في ذلك أمير المؤمنين وأمضى في كل قضية رأيه الذي يلهمه الله » . . . . [68]

Thus, if the Commander of the Believers should see fit to decree that these cases and different norms *(sīyar)* be brought before him in a book together with the explanation and argument of every scholar on the basis of the *sunna* or *qiyās* [analogy], the Commander of the Believers could examine them and give his decision in each case according to the inspiration (*ilhām*).

If the Ibn al-Muqaffa''s *Risālah fi aṣ-Ṣaḥābah* is taken as a whole, it is evident that in his opinion the caliph is bound to act according to the Qur'ān and the *sunna*, and that anything for which there is no precedent from the time of the Prophet or the rightly guided caliphs cannot be accepted as *sunna*. Moreover, the caliph is responsible for making

---

[66] *Ibid.*, 350.
[67] *Ibid.*, 353.
[68] Ibn al-Muqaffa', *Ṣaḥābah*, p. 354. published in *Athạr Ibn Muqaffa'*.

arrangements to teach the Qur'ān and the *sunna* to the people, for promulgating a law book based on the *sunna* and *Qiyās*, and for punishing offenders according to the Qur'ān and the *sunna*.

Not only does Ibn al-Muqaffa' give no indication that the caliph is free to fix the "alleged *sunna*," on the contrary, he states explicitly that the caliph must follow what has been established in the Qur'ān and the *sunna*. Moreover, his statements are specifically concerned with legal cases. It is difficult, therefore, to see how Schacht can deduce from these writings that law in the first century was not based on the Qur'ān and the *sunna*.

The Medinese School

Having stated his basic position, Schacht moves to a discussion of the ways in which the *sunna* was established in the Medinese school, attempting to show that the concept refers not necessarily to the Prophet but to the agreed-upon doctrine of the authorities of the school. He concludes that, for the Medinese, *sunna* was the "practice" or "living tradition" of the school.

In support of his view, Schacht refers to the discussion between Shāfi'ī and Rabī' in *Ikhtilāf Mālik*, where it is pointed out that the Medinese establish *sunna* in two ways:

1. Authorities among the Companions hold an opinion that agrees with the doctrine in question.
2. Men do not disagree about it.[69]

In this discussion there is no reference to the Prophet himself as an authority for establishing *sunna*, a point which Schacht clearly considers significant. But if we examine the evidence, we find that there is very little that can be used here as the basis for a valid theory regarding the Medinese school. First of all, these opinions about how the Medinese established *sunna* are those of an opponent of the Medinese school. In the context of this statement of Rabī', and in support of the alleged Medinese concept of *sunna* and its way of establishing the *sunna*, Schacht cites the case of preemption:

> For instance, *Muw.* iii. 173., where Mālik quotes a *mursal* tradition on pre-emption, on the authority of the Successors Ibn Musaiyib and Abū Salama b. 'Abdalrahmān from *the Prophet*, and adds: "To the same effect is the *sunna* on which there is no disagreement amongst us." In order to show this, he mentions that he heard that Ibn Musaiyib and Sulaimān b. Yasār were asked whether *there was a sunna [that is, a fixed rule] with regard to pre-emption*, and both said yes, and gave the legal rule in question.[70]

Here is the original text:

حدثنا يحيى عن مالك عن ابن شهاب عن سعيد بن السيب وعن أبي سلمة بن عبد الرحمن بن

---

[69] *Origins*, p. 61.
[70] *Origins*, p. 61 (italics mine).

عوف أن رسول الله صلى الله عليه وسلم قضى بالشفعة فيما لم يقسم بين الشركاء ، فاذا وقعت الحدود بينهم فلا شفعة فيه .
قال مالك : وعلى ذلك السنة التي لا اختلاف فيها عندنا .
قال مالك : إنه بلغه أن سعيد بن المسيب سئل عن الشفعة هل فيها من سنة ؟ فقال : نعم الشفعة في الدور والأرضين ولا تكون إلا بين الشركاء . [71]

Ibn Shihāb informed us that Saʿīd b. al-Musayyab and Abū-Salama b. ʿA. ʿAuf [both Successors] reported that the Prophet made a ruling on the basis of pre-emption regarding an estate which had not been divided among the partners. But if there was *ḥudūd* [partitions] between them, there would be no pre-emption.

Mālik says this is the *sunna* regarding which there is no difference of opinion among us.

Mālik stated that he had been informed that Ibn Al-Musayyab was asked about pre-emption, "Is there any *sunna* concerning it?" He replied, "Yes. Pre-emption pertains to houses and lands and only to properties held among partners."

It is crucial to emphasize here that this text totally undermines Schacht's case. Schacht is attempting to demonstrate — in support of Rabīʿ's statement — that:

1. The *sunna* was established by the Medinese authorities because the Companions held an opinion that agreed with the doctrine in question.
2. The said opinion has no reference to the Prophet.
3. Men did not disagree about it.

However, the above-mentioned points cannot be established with the reference to Schacht's text, because:

1. The authorities mentioned are Successors, not Companions.
2. There is an explicit ruling of the Prophet involved which has been recorded in this case by the Medinese scholars and even mentioned by Schacht — a fact which demolishes Schacht's entire approach. To establish his point, Schacht needs a precedent where the Prophet must not have been mentioned. To choose an example where the basis for their agreement is a well-known tradition of the Prophet, quoted by those scholars, indicates, perhaps, the absence of a more telling example.

However, Schacht commits a few more mistakes in this citation.

1. In the Arabic text clear reference is made to *sunna* and Schacht translates it as "a fixed rule," which is wholly unacceptable unless he means a fixed rule established by the Prophet.
2. He mentions the name of Sulaimān b. Yasār, who, however, has not been mentioned in the text referred to.

---

[71] *Muw*, pp. 713–714.

After quoting the case of preemption recorded by Mālik, Schacht says that "the wording here and elsewhere implies that *sunna* for Mālik is not identical with the contents of traditions from the Prophet."[72] To prove this, he cites five examples. Each will be examined in detail, and it will be shown that, to establish his case, Schacht has had to distort the evidence, take arguments out of context, and suppress the facts.

EXAMPLE 1

In *Origins* Schacht says:

> In *Muw.* iii, 181 ff., Mālik establishes the *sunna* by a tradition from the Prophet and by reference to the opinions of 'Umar b. 'Abdal'azīz, Abū Salama b. 'Abdalraḥman, and Sulaimān b. Yasār. He adds systematic reasoning because "one wishes to understand', but he returns to the *sunna* as decisive: 'the *sunna* is proof enough, but one also wants to know the reason, and this is it." It does not occur to Mālik to fall back on the tradition from the Prophet as such, as the decisive argument, a thing which Shāfi'ī does in *Tr. iii*, 148 (p. 249).[73]

Here is the background of the argument:

1. Any tradition contradicting the Qur'ān cannot be a genuine tradition, a rule accepted by all scholars.
2. The Qur'ān (ii, 282) demands two witnesses to establish legal rights.
3. A tradition narrated by Mālik and followed by him shows that the Prophet made rulings based on a single witness and the oath of the plaintiff.

The opponent's argument is that this tradition apparently goes against the Qur'ān. Therefore, it is unacceptable. Mālik argues that it does not contradict the Qur'ān. He shows further that even the opponent accepts a single witness for the verdict in certain cases.

Schacht appears to admit that Mālik "returns to the *sunna* as decisive"; but he immediately qualifies this because Mālik in his argument with his opponents seeks to justify the *sunna* on rational grounds rather than on the grounds that it came from the Prophet. This leads Schacht to argue that it is the logical justifiability of the *sunna* which is important to Mālik, not its origin. "It does not occur to Mālik to fall back on the tradition of the Prophet as such, as the decisive argument." He hopes accordingly to extrapolate the conclusion that for Mālik it is neither sufficient nor necessary that a *sunna* should come from the Prophet to be valid.

This can only be done by ignoring the context in which Mālik made his remarks. The problem which Mālik was addressing was what branches of law could make a valid judgment based on one witness and the oath of the plaintiff. Mālik records the judgment of the Prophet and the opinions of the Medinese scholars, showing that this ruling of the Prophet was not

---

[72] *Origins*, p. 61.
[73] *Origins*, p. 62.

abrogated; he shows that the Qur'ānic rules concerning witnesses and the above-mentioned tradition are not in conflict. The point at issue is that Mālik's opponent believes the ruling to be against the injunctions of the Qur'ān; Mālik goes into considerable detail to show that the ruling has a sound basis in reason and does not in fact conflict with the Qur'ān.

It is because of the need to convince his opponent that Mālik seeks rational proof for his acceptance of the particular *sunna*, not because he himself feels the inadequacy of accepting the *sunna* as *sunna*. Indeed, after discussing several similar problems, Mālik says:

... فان أقر بهذا فليقرر باليمين مع الشاهد وان لم يكن ذلك في كتاب الله عز وجل وانه ليكفي من ذلك ما مضى من السنة ، ولكن المرء قد يحب أن يعرف وجه الصواب وموقع الحجة ، ففي هذا بيان ما أشكل من ذلك ان شاء الله تعالى . [74]

If he [the opponent] should admit to [handing down judgments based on a single witness in certain cases] then he must admit to [the validity of] an oath with one witness, although it is not mentioned in the Book of Allah. What has been laid down in the established *sunna* is sufficient yet one may desire to understand the reason and to know what is right and the basis of argument. Therefore, in this, if God — may He be exalted — is willing, there is sufficient clarification of that.

EXAMPLE 2

Schacht says, "In *Muw.* i. 196, Mālik quotes a decision of Zuhrī, ending with the words: 'this is the *sunna*'; and Mālik adds that he has found this to be the doctrine of the scholars of Medina."[75] Here is the passage:

« مالك عن ابن شهاب أنه كان يقول : من أدرك من صلاة الجمعة ركعة فليصل اليها أخرى ، قال ابن شهاب : وهي السنة . قال مالك : وعلى ذلك أدركت أهل العلم ببلدنا وذلك أن رسول الله صلى الله عليه وسلم قال : من أدرك من الصلاة ركعة فقد أدرك الصلاة » [76]

Zuhrī said, "Whoever joins in at least one *rak'a* of the Friday prayer [in congregation] should pray one additional *rak'a* with it [after the completion of congregational prayer]. Zuhrī said, "This is the *sunna*." Mālik said, "I found the scholars of our city of the same opinion. This was so because the Prophet said, 'He who joins in praying a single *rak'a* of the prayer [with the *Imām*] has partaken of the prayer.

What Schacht argues from this particular example is that Zuhrī used the term *sunna* to describe a decision of his own about Friday prayer and that Mālik not only approved of this procedure but added that this was the doctrine of Medinese scholars.[77]

Examination of a larger section of the passage quoted by Schacht makes it clear that what Zuhrī describes as *sunna* was not based on

---

[74] *Muw*, pp. 724–725.
[75] *Origins*, p. 62.
[76] *Muw.*, vol. 1, p. 196.
[77] *Origins*, p. 61.

personal discretion but on well-known *hadīth* of the Prophet. Indeed, Mālik himself quotes the *hadīth* after quoting the decision of Zuhrī. He says that the Prophet said:

وذلك أن رسول الله صلى الله عليه وسلم قال : من أدرك من الصلاة ركعة فقد أدرك . ⁷⁸

This is because the Messenger of Allāh, may Allāh bless him and grant him peace, said, "Whoever joins in a single *rakʿa* of the prayer has partaken of the prayer.

The same *hadīth* has been recorded separately by Mālik through Zuhrī. Here is the original text:

حدثني يحيى عن مالك عن ابن شهاب عن أبي سلمة بن عبد الرحمن عن أبي هريرة أن رسول الله صلى الله عليه وسلم قال : من أدرك ركعة من الصلاة فقد أدرك . ⁷⁹

Ibn Shihāb Zuhrī reported on the authority of Abū Salama from Abū Huraira that the Prophet said, "He who joins in a single *rakʿa* of the prayer [with the *Imām*] has partaken of the prayer."

What this means is that Mālik's approach to Zuhrī's decision in this case was based directly on a *hadīth* of the Prophet; in the same way, he approves of the doctrines of the scholars of Medina precisely because they were acting according to a *hadīth* of the Prophet. It is only by partial citation of his example that Schacht is able to present this argument.

In case it may be argued that what is deduced from the *hadīth* or *sunna* of the Prophet is also *sunna*, it should be remembered that this has been the usual practice. Not only in the pre-Shāfiʿī period but even today, jurists use the same terminology. (Chapter 3 discusses this matter under the heading "Other Meanings of the Word *Sunna*.") It may be shown, therefore, that Schacht's deduction about Example 2 is invalid — if for no other reason than that the totality of the text he is relying on to make his case contradicts the citation he has given.

EXAMPLE 3

Schacht says: "In *Muw.* iii. 110, Mālik speaks of the *sunna* in the past (*madat al-sunna*) on a point of doctrine on which there are no traditions."⁸⁰ Here is the original text:

قال مالك : « ولا يصلح التسليف في شيء من هذا يسلف فيه بعينه إلا أن يقبض المسلف ما سلف فيه عند دفعه الذهب إلى صاحبه يقبض العبد أو الراحلة أو المسكن . . لا يصلح أن يكون في شيء من ذلك تأخير ولا أجل .
قال مالك : وتفسير ما كره من ذلك أن يقول الرجل للرجل أسلفك في راحلتك فلانة أركبها في الحج وبينه وبين الحج أجل من الزمان . . . فانه إذا صنع ذلك كان إنما يسلفه ذهبا على أنه إن وجد تلك الراحلة صحيحة لذلك الأجل الذي سمي له فهي له بذلك الكراء ، وإن حدث بها حدث من موت أو غيره رد عليه ذهبه وكانت عليه على وجه السلف عنده .

---

⁷⁸ *Ibid.*
⁷⁹ *Muw.*, p. 10.
⁸⁰ *Origins*, p. 62.

قال مالك : وإنما فرق ما بين ذلك ، القبض ، من قبض ما استأجر أو استكرى فقد خرج من الغرر والسلف الذي يكره ، وأخذ أمرا معلوما . وإنما مثل ذلك أن يشتري الرجل العبد أو الوليدة فيقبضهما وينقد أثمانهما ، فان حدث بهما حدث من عهدة السنة أخذ ذهبه من صاحبه الذي ابتاع منه . فهذا لا بأس به ، وبهذا مضت السنة في بيع الرقيق .[81]

Mālik said: It is invalid to give an amount of [money] in advance for a particular thing except in the case where the moneylender takes hold of the material for which he has given gold to its owner and then takes hold of it, such as [in buying] a slave, a riding animal, a dwelling . . . It is invalid if delivery is late or if a later date was fixed for delivery.

Mālik explained: An illustration of that which is reprehensible in this case is that one man says to another, "I will give you advanced payment for such-and-such a riding camel of yours which I will use in performing the pilgrimage," while there is still a considerable time between that [agreement] and the pilgrimage.

In this case if he does so he is lending the money on condition that if he find that particular camel in perfect order at that time which has been fixed, then it is for his use at that stipulated amount, but if there has been any mishap by way of death or anything else, his gold will be returned to him, and the money will be counted as a loan.

Mālik stated that the difference between [what is valid and invalid in the cases under discussion] is in taking possession [of the object]. Anyone who takes possession of what he has taken on a rental basis *is out of danger of risk (gharar)*,[82] and also out of the range of the cases of advance money which are invalid, because he has possession of fixed [and agreed-upon] articles. This resembles the case of someone who buys a male or female slave and holds possession of him/her and pays the price. Thus if something happens to the slave within the year, he would receive back his money from the seller on the basis of a year's warranty.[83]

There is nothing wrong in this. And such as this has the *sunna* been established in the past regarding selling of slaves.[84]

Again it is clear that Schacht has failed to place the example in its proper context. Mālik does not base his doctrine on some *sunna* unrelated to and/or predating the Prophet; he deduces it in the light of the Prophet's prohibition of any sale which contains an element of risk. He refers to this by the word *al-gharar*, and quotes the *ḥadīth* of the Prophet concerning *gharar* (risk). We have already shown (in Chapter 1 and in Example 2) that jurists sometimes use the term *sunna* to express what has been deduced from the *sunna* or *ḥadīth* of the Prophet.

EXAMPLE 4

In a further attempt to show that to establish the *sunna*, reference to the

---

[81] *Muw. Buyū'*, p. 629–30.
[82] *gharar* means peril, hazard, or risk. See Lane, *Arabic English Lexicon*, p. 2239.
[83] *Muw.*, pp. 629–630.
[84] Mālik quotes a tradition from the Prophet (see *Muw.*, p. 664) forbidding any sale containing the danger of risk, uncertainty *(gharar)*:

« إن رسول الله صلى الله عليه وسلم نهى عن بيع الغرر »

Prophet was not primary, Schacht says, "*Mud*. 1. 115 establishes the practice of Medina as *sunna* by two traditions transmitted by Ibn Wahb, which Mālik had as yet ignored and by references to the first four Caliphs and to other old authorities."[85] Here is the original text:

قال مالك : يجمع بين المغرب والعشاء في الحضر وإن لم يكن مطر إذا كان طين وظلمة ويجمع أيضاً بينهما إذا كان المطر .

قال ابن وهب . . . ابن قسيط حدثه أن جمع الصلاتين بالمدينة في ليلة المطر المغرب والعشاء سنة ، وأن قد صلاها أبو بكر وعمر وعثمان على ذلك ،

قال ابن وهب : وقال عبد الله بن عمر ، وسعيد بن المسيب ، والقاسم ، وسالم ، وعروة بن الزبير ، وعمر بن عبد العزيز ، ويحيى بن سعيد ، وربيعة وأبـو الأسود مثله .

قال سحنون : وان النبي صلى الله عليه وسلم جمعها جميعا .[86]

Mālik said: *Maghrib* and *'Ishā'* prayers can be prayed together while in the city, even if there is no rain but on condition that there is mud and darkness, and they can also be prayed together if there is rain.

Ibn Wahb reported . . . [that] Ibn Qusaiṭ reported to him that praying *Maghrib* and *'Ishā'* together in Medina on rainy nights is *sunna*. [The Caliphs] Abū Bakr, 'Umar, and 'Uthmān all prayed accordingly.

Ibn Wahb said: This was the doctrine of 'Abdulla b. 'Umar, S'aīd b. Musayyib, al-Qāsim, Sālim, 'Urwa b. Zubair, 'Umar b. 'Abdul 'Azīz, Yaḥyā b. Sa'īd, Rabī'a and 'Abul Aswad. Saḥnūn said: And the Prophet also prayed them together.

Schacht is incorrect in saying that Mālik ignored the tradition. Here is the original text from Mālik's own writing:

« عن مالك عن أبي الزبير المكي ، عن سعيد بن جبير ، عن عبد الله بن عباس ، أنه قال : صلى رسول الله صلى الله عليه وسلم الظهر والعصر جميعا ، والمغرب والعشاء جميعا في غير خوف ولا سفر .

قال مالك : أرى ذلك كان في مطر .

وحدثني عن مالك عن نافع أن عبد الله بن عمر كان إذا جمع الأمراء بين المغرب والعشاء في المطر جمع معهم .

"Mālik . . . reported on the authority of Ibn 'Abbās that the Prophet prayed *Ẓuhr* and *'Aṣr* as well as *maghrib* and *'ishā'* together without being in any fear of war or on a journey.

Mālik said, "In my opinion this was because of rain." Mālik reported on the authority of Nāfi' that when the governors *(umarā')* of Medina would

---

[85] *Origins*, p. 62.
[86] Saḥnūn, *Mudawwana*. (Cairo, 1323) vol. 1, p. 115, cited hereafter as *Mud*. The point at issue is the praying of the two prayers of *Magrib* and *'Ishā'* together if there was rain. Ibn Wahb reported the opinion of Mālik that the two prayers might be prayed together if there was rain, darkness, or mud. Later he reported the statement of Ibn Qusaiṭ that this was *sunna* and was practiced by the three caliphs, and himself added the names of Ibn 'Umar and a few other authorities. Saḥnūn says that the Prophet prayed these two prayers together in the circumstances mentioned above, thus providing the documentation for the above mentioned *sunna*.

pray *maghrib* and *'ishā'* together in times of rain, Ibn 'Umar would join them in prayer.[87]

It is clear in the light of the writings of Mālik that he himself recorded what was reported about the practice of the Prophet and what he understood about that practice. Furthermore, he explains that it was a continuous practice, not having been abrogated. He, therefore, reports the practice of Ibn 'Umar (d. 74 A.H.) to assert his point, and he formulates his own doctrine accordingly.

The author of the *Mudawwana*, Saḥnūn, records the practice of the Prophet in this case. Schacht refers to the same passage in the *Mudawwana* and quotes the first few caliphs and other old authorities, but omits the explicit reference to the Prophet. In the same way he totally ignores the writings of Mālik and contrary to fact, contends that Mālik is ignorant of these traditions.

EXAMPLE 5

Schacht says, "In *Mud*. v. 163, Ibn Qāsim says: 'So it is laid down in the traditions *(āthār)* and *sunnas* referring to the Companions of the Prophet.[88] Here is the original text:

قلت : أرأيت لو أن حربية خرجت الينا مسلمة أتنكح مكانها ؟
قـال : لا
قلت : فيصنع ماذا ؟
قـال : تنتظر ثلاث حيض ، فان أسلم زوجها في الحيض الثالث كان أملك بها ، وإلا فقد بانت منه ، وكذلك جاءت الآثار والسنن في أصحاب النبي صلى الله عليه وسلم . وكذلك ذكر مالك أن من أسلم منهم قبل أن تنقضي عـدة امراته ، وقد أسلمت فهاجرت فأسلم زوجها في عدتها كان أحق بها .

Saḥnūn:	What is your opinion regarding a [married] woman from enemy territory who has migrated to us after embracing Islam: Can she or can she not be [re-] married [immediately]?
Ibn Qāsim:	No.
Saḥnūn:	Then what should be done?
Ibn Qāsim:	She would wait for three menstrual periods to pass. If her husband accepts Islam before the third monthly period, he would take her to himself; otherwise she would be divorced from him.

It is in accordance with this that the reports *(āthār)* and *sunan* have been transmitted in [the cases] of the Companions of the Prophet, may God bless him and give him peace.

Likewise Mālik explained that whoever accepted Islam during the *'idda* period of his wife[89] after she had accepted Islam and migrated to live with the

---

[87] *Muw.*, *Qaṣr*, 3–5, pp. 144–145.
[88] *Origins*, p. 62.
[89] Saḥnūn *Al-Mudawwana* (Cairo, 1323), vol. 5, p. 163. (In translating I have supplied the names instead of "he said" and "I said").

Muslims had the greatest right to her.⁹⁰

Schacht attempts by this example to argue that the Companions created their own independent *sunna* and that these could be appealed to in settlement of disputes. In fact, this interpretation is based on a misreading of the Arabic text. Ibn Qāsim did not say that it was the Companions who established the *sunna*. He does not say سنة الصحابة (*"sunna* of the Companions"), but والسنن في أصحاب النبي صلى الله عليه وسلم (the *sunan* among the Companions of the Prophet"), or in other words the *sunna* which was followed by the Companions of the Prophet.⁹¹ There is no textual justification for the assumption that the *sunna* in question originated with the Companions; if anything, this example indicates that the *sunna* was identical with the injunctions of the Prophet. Indeed, all five of the examples we have analyzed either make explicit reference to the Prophet or to norms deduced from the practice or the orders of the Prophet.

The Syrian School

In discussing the concept of *sunna* in the Syrian school, Schacht has this to say:

> Auzā'ī knows the concept of "*Sunna* of the prophet" . . . but does not identify it with formal traditions. He considers an informal tradition without *isnād*, concerning the life-story of the Prophet, sufficient to establish a "valid *sunna*" . . . and an anonymous legal maxim sufficient to show the existence of a *sunna* going back to the Prophet."⁹²

The contention that Auz'ī does not identify *sunna* with formal traditions, however, is based on no explicit statement by Auzā'ī himself. If Schacht is deriving it from the writing of Abū Yūsuf, he must show whether what Abū Yūsuf has recorded is the original and complete writing of Auzā'ī or whether it has been abridged for the sake of refutation. This he does not do. What is clear is that in the writings of Fazzārī (d. 188), a student of Auzā'ī and contemporary of Abū Yūsuf (d. 182), we have positive evidence of the importance Auzā'ī attached to *isnād*.⁹³

One must also take into account the probability that on the occasions Auzā'ī fails to provide *isnād, it may well be because he felt a particular*

---

⁹⁰ The *'idda* period refers to the three menstrual periods which, in certain cases, a woman has to wait after divorce before she may marry again.

⁹¹ The problem under discussion is whether a woman who converts to Islam and migrates from enemy territory *(Dār-al Ḥarb)* to Muslim territory is able to remarry. Ibn Qāsim gives the opinion that if her husband joins her within three menstrual periods and becomes a Muslim, the woman would return to him. *Āthār* and *sunan* from the Companions of the Prophet are quoted to this effect. Similar situations were faced by many women who migrated to Medina and left their husbands behind during the life of the Prophet. If their husbands embraced Islam and came to Medina within the required period, their wives were returned to them.

⁹² *Origins*, p. 70.

⁹³ See Fazzārī, *Siyar*, (Fez Library, MS. 139) e.g. Fo. 19, 22, 23, 28, 30, 31, 33, 34, 38, 62, 64,

sunna was so unanimously held to be authentic that further verification of its origin was superfluous.⁹⁴ On the point at issue, in fact, it is sufficient that he refers to the precedent set by the Prophet.

What Schacht refers to as the "Life Story of the Prophet" is in fact his wars, peace treaties, the management of conquered lands, and the distribution of booty — clearly matters at the very heart of international law. Schacht's statement that an "anonymous legal maxim" is sufficient for Auzā'ī to establish a valid *sunna* is contrary to the facts. Auzā'ī states clearly that the practice began with the Prophet. He explicitly says:

مضت السنة عن رسول الله صلى الله عليه وسلم من قتل علجا فله سلبه .

> The *sunna* which has been established from the past on the authority of the Prophet is that he who kills an enemy in a battle has the right to his spoils.⁹⁵

Morever, the "legal maxim" is in fact the wording of the Prophet himself, recorded by scholars and biographers of the Prophet prior to Auzā'ī,⁹⁶ a fact that Schacht chooses to ignore.

The Iraqian School

On the Iraqian school, Schacht states that "the Iraqians, in their view of *sunna*, no more think it necessarily based on traditions from the Prophet than do the Medinese."⁹⁷ He uses two quotations to support this view. It should be noted from the outset that neither quotation is from the original writings of Iraqians; both are summaries made by Shāfi'ī, one of their opponents. "Thus in *Tr. II*, 4 *(f)*," says Schacht, "in a tradition from 'Alī, representing an 'unsuccessful' Iraqian doctrine, *sunna* occurs in the sense of 'established' religious practice.' ' And he goes on:

> And *Tr. III*, 148 . . . makes the Iraqian say: 'We do this on account of the *sunna* [i.e. they give judgment on the defendant's refusal to take the oath when the plaintiff can produce no legal proof, and they do not demand from the plaintiff a confirmatory oath as do the Medinese]. There is no mention of the oath, or of the refusal to take it, in the Koran. This is a *sunna* which is not in the Koran, and it does not come into the category of evidence from witnesses [which is provided for by Koran ii. 282]. We hold that the Koran orders us to give judgment on the evidence of witnesses, either two men or one man and two women, and the refusal to take the oath does not come under this.⁹⁸

His overall conclusion from these quotations is: "The essential point is

---

⁹⁴ It ought to be noted that the use of *isnād* is only to prove the authenticity of the tradition and its correct attribution to the Prophet, not its authority.
⁹⁵ For a detailed discussion on the مضت السنة see Bravmann, *The Spiritual Background of Early Islam*, pp. 139–151.
⁹⁶ Ibn Hishām, *Sīra*, (Cairo 1955) iii, 448.
⁹⁷ *Origins*, p. 73.
⁹⁸ *Origins*, p. 73.

that the Iraqians use *sunna* as an argument, even when they can show no relevant tradition."⁹⁹

Here are the original texts of the above-mentioned cases. The first case:

١ - أخبرنا الربيع ، قال أخبرنا الشافعي قال أخبرنا ابن علية عن ليث عن الحكم عن حنش بن المعتمر أن عليا رضي الله عنه قال : صلوا يوم العيد في المسجد أربع ركعات . ركعتان للسنة ، وركعتان للخروج الأم : ٧ : ١٥٥ .

'Alī said: Pray four *rak'a* on the occasion of '*Īd* in the mosque. Two *rak'a* for the sake of the *sunna* and two *rak'a* for not having gone outside the mosque to pray [as is normally done].

The second case:

٢ - قال الشافعي . . . والذين يخالفونكم في اليمين مع الشاهد يقولون نحن أعطينا بالنكول عن اليمين فبالنسبة أعطينا ، ليس في القرآن ذكر يمين ولا نكول عنها ، وهذا سنة ، غير القرآن وغير الشهادات . زعمنا أن القرآن يدل على أن لا يعطي أحد من جهة الشهادات ، إلا بشاهدين أو شاهد وامرأتين ، والنكول ليس في معنى الشهادات . الأم ٧ : ٢٤٩ .

Shāfi'ī said to Medinese: Those who differ with you in the case of making rulings on the basis of a single witness and an oath, say that they give judgment on the basis of the defendant's refusal to take the oath [saying], "We do this on account of the *sunna*." But the Qur'ān mentions neither this matter of a single oath nor the refusal to take it. This is *sunna* [or, rather, a rule derived from *sunna*]. It is not derived from the Qur'ān, nor does it come under the procedure of giving witness [which has been mentioned by the Qur'ān ii, 282]. We believe that the Qur'ān demands that no one should be given [his claim] on the basis of a single witness but only with two male witnesses or one male witness and two female witnesses. And refusal to take an oath *(nukūl)* [in the court on the part of defendant] does not come in the category of witness.¹⁰⁰

As far as the first quotation is concerned, it has been noted earlier that the term *sunna* is used in different contexts, one of them being an established religious practice instituted by the Prophet which is not compulsory *(wājib* or *farḍ)*. For example, five daily prayers and the Friday prayers are *farḍ* (obligatory). These prayers were instituted by the Prophet, but the Prophet himself offered other prayers, either in solitude or in congregation. He prayed *Tahajjud* late at night, the '*Īd prayer*, twice a year, and superogatory prayers every day before or after the congregational prayer of *Fajr, Zuhr, Maghrib,* or '*Ishā*'. All these prayers are called *sunna* — a fact known to every Muslim child. In this sense, the word means a practice established by the Prophet that is not compulsory.

---

⁹⁹ *Idem.*
¹⁰⁰ *Umm* (Cairo, 1321) vol. 7, p. 249, cited hereafter as *Umm*. If the plaintiff can produce no witness, and asks the defendant to take an oath, who in turn refuses, the case would be decided in the favor of the plaintiff.

53

Thus the *'Īd* prayer is *sunna*, and not *wājib* or *farḍ*. When 'Alī mentioned the practice of praying two *rak'as* for *'Īd* prayer, referring to it by the term *sunna,* he was referring to a practice well known to every Muslim. The *sunna* in *'Īd* prayer is that the Prophet used to pray it outside the city. 'Alī asked the people to pray two *rak'as* as *sunna* after the manner of the *'Īd* prayer and two additional *rak'as* because of having been unable to go outside the city.

Schacht says that it was used in the sense of "established religious practice." But the question then arises of who first instituted the *'Īd* prayer practice. Is it a pagan practice which was followed by the Companions such as 'Alī, or was it initiated and established by the Prophet or someone else? I do not think that anyone would claim that the *'Īd* prayer was originated by anyone other than the Prophet. Thus *sunna* here refers to the practice of the Prophet. It is, therefore, clearly wrong to use this as an example of the Iraqians using the term *sunna* when they can show no relevant tradition.

The same is true of the second example. The term here is used in the sense of a norm proved by the means of *sunna* — *one of the four adilla*. In this case, the Iraqian opponent actually refers to a well-known tradition from the Prophet [101] البينة على المدعي واليمين على من أنكر which means that the burden of proof rests upon the plaintiff and the oath on the defendant. Thus, the Iraqians say that their doctrine is derived from a well-known *ḥadīth* or, rather, *sunna*.

Moreover, Schacht has mistranslated the passage. The Iraqians did not say: "This is a *sunna* which is not in the Koran." No one claims that the Qur'ān is the repository of the *sunna*. What Schacht has done is to join two sentences with "which," thus changing the sense. The original text is: وهذا سنة غير القرآن وغير الشهادات . which means: "This is a *sunna* [i.e. a ruling derived from the *sunna*] and is neither derived from the Qur'ān nor does it come under the category of bearing witness" [which is mentioned in Qur'ān ii, 282].

Schacht has, therefore, failed to prove his point that the concept of *sunna* in the ancient schools of law was not identical with the content of traditions from the Prophet. While the word *sunna* was certainly used for the acts of other people, in the majority of cases it denoted the *sunna* of the Prophet and not the "living tradition." Moreover, the *sunnas* of the Prophet were given binding authority over any other legal precedents or opinions.

We turn now to an examination of Schacht's contention that the ancient schools of law based their jurisprudence on the "living tradition" and that the *sunna* of the Prophet was fabricated by these schools and incorporated into their body of law.

---

[101] For detail, see Ibn Ḥajar, *Fatḥul Bārī*, v, 282–283, quoting Ṭabarānī, Baihaqī, and Bukhārī with different wordings.

Chapter Four

The Living Tradition Is More Authoritative Than the *Sunna* of the Prophet

Schacht calls the ancient schools of law the Medinese, the Syrians, and the Iraqians. It is important to note here that these names are misleading. There were many law schools in the early days of Islam, the most famous in the first two centuries being those of Medina and Kūfa, and in both cities there were many scholars whose opinions on law differed. Schacht has based his views on the writings of only a few scholars from these geographical areas: Mālik b. Anas of Medina, Abū Yūsuf and Shaibānī of Kūfa (the Ḥanafī school) and, primarily, the polemical writings of Shāfi'ī during his last, Egyptian phase. Although Schacht himself says that "it would be a mistake to generalize, even within the circle of the Kufians, the uniformity of doctrine,"[1] he nevertheless makes broad generalizations on the basis of the writings of a single scholar of a single school of Kūfa and extends them to the whole of Iraq; similarly he generalizes on Mālik's work and applies his generalizations to all the scholars of Medina.

To put the theories of the ancient schools of law into perspective, these schools themselves should be precisely identified. Thus, instead of Medinese, Iraqians, and Syrians, we should speak of the school of Mālik, the school of Abū Ḥanīfa, the school of Auzā'ī, and so on. It is then clear that their opinions represent only their own school and not necessarily the whole of Medina, Iraq, or Syria. Nevertheless, in the discussion that follows we shall — in order to avoid confusion about what is being discussed — follow Schacht's terminology.

Before embarking on a detailed discussion of the points he raises, it is necessary to clarify the issue of the term "practice." It is not common to all the ancient schools of law. Mālik often used it and similar terms in his *Muwaṭṭa'*, but nothing like it is found in the writings of Auzā'ī. Abū Yūsuf, indeed, condemns the concept, saying:

---

[1] *Origins*, p. 242.

One should not decide a question regarding what is lawful *(Ḥalāl)* and unlawful [*Ḥarām*] by contending that "the people always did such things," because most of what the people have always done is not lawful and ought not to be done. There are cases which I could mention, where the great mass of the people [*'āmma*] act against a prohibition of the Prophet. In these cases one has to obtain the knowledge or order from the *sunna* of the Prophet and [from the *Fatwā* of] the first generations from among his Companions and from legal scholars *(al-sunna 'an rasūl Allah wa'an al-salaf min aṣḥābih wa min qaumin fuqahā').*[2]

Since "practice" played a greater role in Medina than in other schools, our discussion will center mostly on the writings of Mālik. Schacht's views on the so-called Syrians and Iraqians will be dealt with later.

The Medinese and the Living Tradition

Traditionally, the Medinese "practice" held a privileged place in the eyes of most scholars. We know that when the Prophet was in Mecca, his followers met with much hardship and were often forced to migrate to Ethiopia and later to Medina. No government could be established in Mecca at that time, but when the Prophet migrated to Medina he was able to establish the first Islamic state. Thus the people of Medina were the first to receive legislation under Islamic law. Generally speaking, all the laws of the Qur'ān as well as the *sunna* of the Prophet were first put into practice here. Thus the practice that began from the time of the Prophet in Medina had the value of transmitting a law of the Qur'ān or the *sunna* of the Prophet through continuous practice from generation to generation.

This fact conferred a special privilege on practices originating from the earliest days of Islam in Medina. If a tradition of the Prophet transmitted by only one narrator was found in opposition to established practice in Medina, the Medinese practice was preferred and regarded as being more authoritative. Thus, Abū Yūsuf, for example, changed a number of his opinions when he learned that the practices of Medina were contrary to what he had been holding as valid.[3]

Not all the practices of Medina, however, had their origin in the time of the Prophet or even in that of the rightly guided caliphs. Practices which originated later, either in the late first century or in the second century are called *al-'amal al-muta'akhkhir* ("the late practice"). There is also another type of practice called *al-'amal al-istidlālī* ("practice based on legal deduction"). These two types of practices were found in Medina but were disputed and not accepted by other schools. Even some of the

---

[2] *Auzā'ī*, p. 76. Schacht himself quotes this passage (*Origins*, p. 75), although he has unfortunately mistranslated it.
[3] For details, see Aḥmad Noor Saif, *'Amal ahl al-Medīna'* (M.A. thesis, Sharia College, Mecca), p. 92.

Malikites did not regard them as binding, especially if they were in conflict with the traditions of the Prophet.

Now let us look at Schacht's views on this. He says, "The element of 'practice' in the Medinese 'living tradition' is expressed by terms such as *'amal* 'practice', *al-'amal al-mujtama' 'alaih* 'generally agreed practice', *al-amr 'indanā* 'our practice' . . ."[4] and then makes the following main points:

1. The practice "existed first and traditions from the Prophet and from Companions appeared later."[5]
2. The Medinese contrasted "practice" with traditions.[6]
3. Practice is "explicitly identified" with those traditions which the Medinese accepted.[7]
4. The practice of the Medinese "does not simply reflect the actual custom, it contains a theoretical or ideal element."[8] It sometimes was used as a device to propose changes in the doctrine of the schools with varying degrees of success.[9]

It should at once be noted that Schacht has based his theories about the Medinese on the statements of Rabī' — an anti-Medinese scholar. Many instances of Schacht's views about the dishonesty of the scholars of the time and the way authorities were fabricated to support doctrines have already been cited in the present work. For example, he says, "By the time of Ibn 'Abdalbarr, spurious information regarding old Medinese authorities had been put into circulation, so as to bring their doctrine into line with the tradition . . ."[10] Given such suspicions, one would have thought that he would be wary of using any source other than the writings of Mālik himself to deduce Mālik's doctrines. But here, as in other parts of his book, Schacht seems determined to use only anti-Medinese sources — so long as they support his theories — and to discount evidence that does not advance his case, even though this may be a far more direct source.

We now turn to a detailed examination of the different parts of Schacht's argument.

1. Practice Predating Traditions from the Prophet. Schacht's first startling claim is that the practice existed first and traditions from the Prophet and Companions appeared later. In his own words:

> That the "practice" existed first and traditions from the Prophet and from Companions appeared later, is clearly stated in *Mud.* iv. 28, where Ibn Qāsim gives a theoretical justification of the Medinese point of view. He

---

[4] *Origins*, p. 62.
[5] *Origins*, p. 63.
[6] *Origins*, p. 63.
[7] *Origins*, p. 66.
[8] *Origins*, p. 68.
[9] *Origins*, p. 66.
[10] *Origins*, p. 65.

says: "This tradition has come down to us, and if it were accompanied by a practice passed to those from whom we have taken it over by their own predecessors, it would be right to follow it. But in fact it is like those other traditions which are not accompanied by practice. [Here Ibn Qāsim gives examples of traditions from the Prophet and from Companions.] But these things could not assert themselves and take root *(lam tashtadd wa-lam taqwa)*, the practice was different, and the whole community and Companions themselves acted on other rules. So the traditions remained neither discredited [in principle], nor adopted in practice [*ghair mukadhdhab bih wa-lā ma'mūl bih*], *and actions were ruled by other traditions which were accompanied by practice.*

These traditions were passed on from the Companions to the Successors, and from these to those after them, without rejecting or casting doubt on others that have come down and have been transmitted. But what was eliminated from practice is left aside and not regarded as authoritative, and only what is corroborated by practice is followed and so regarded. Now the rule which is well established and is accompanied by practice is expressed in the words of the Prophet . . . and the words of Ibn 'Umar to the same effect . . ."[11]

Schacht's immediate comment on this quotation is that "the Medinese thus oppose 'practice' to traditions."[12] In footnotes on the same page, he adds, "This lip-service paid to traditions shows the influence they had gained in the time of Ibn Qāsim" and "It deserves to be noted that Ibn Qāsim relies on 'practice' although he might have simply referred to the tradition from the Prophet."

The fact is, however, that, not for the first time, Schacht has chosen a passage to justify his theories which not only does not help him but, indeed, contradicts his basic postulates. Ibn Qāsim's whole discussion is based on the point that there are two sorts of traditions related on the authority of the Prophet: one group that is accompanied by the practices of Companions and Successors and another group that is not accompanied by any sort of practice. In the case of a conflict, the tradition accompanied by practice should be adopted. Nowhere does Ibn Qāsim say, or even imply, that the practice existed first and traditions from the Prophet appeared later.

Moreover, Ibn Qāsim explicitly refers to the traditions from the Prophet and says that the tradition that is supported by the continuous practice of the community is the one that should be adopted. In the face of this, it is difficult to see how he can be accused of simply paying "lip-service" to the tradition, or how Schacht can say he relies on practice, although he "might have simply referred to the tradition from the Prophet." Because he has made the *a priori* assumption that "practice" has nothing to do with traditions from the Prophet, Schacht necessarily fails to analyze correctly the meaning of the text.

---

[11] *Origins*, p. 63 (italics mine).
[12] *Origins*, p. 63.

2. Practice Opposed to Traditions. Schacht's second conclusion from the same text is that the Medinese preferred practice against traditions from the Prophet. We have already seen that Ibn Qāsim's words refute this theory, since the "practice" referred to is the continuous practice of a tradition from the Prophet. Schacht refers also to the Annales of Ṭabarī, iii, 2505, in support of his case. Thus, whenever Muḥammad b. Abū Bakr gave a judgment against a tradition his brother used to raise objections, and Muḥammad would reply, "What of the practice?" Schacht comments, " . . . meaning the generally agreed practice in Medina, which they regarded as more authoritative than a tradition."[13]

One way of refuting this would be simply to use Schacht's methodological reasoning to work against him. The statement is found in a fourth-century work and is not quoted in second-century literature. According to Schacht, the fourth-century work must, therefore, be spurious. More seriously, however, the special status accorded to the practice in Medina has already been explained, namely, that the early Medinese practice was considered more authoritative than those traditions which were narrated only by a single narrator, and that there was a variety of opinions about the validity of later Medinese practice.

Let us now examine the three examples Schacht cites to prove his theory that the Medinese preferred "practice" over traditions from the Prophet.

EXAMPLE 1

He says:

> Mālik (*Muw.* iii, 134, 136; *Mud.* x. 44) and Rabī' (*Tr.* iii, 48) admit the sale of bales by specification from a list, because it is the current practice in the past and present by which no uncertainty (*gharar*) is intended (Mālik), or because men consider it as valid (Rabī'). *Mud.* x. 44 considers Mālik's statement as authoritative (*ḥujja*), particularly because he states the practice, and finds it confirmed by traditions (*āthār*) — not from the Prophet but from authorities such as Yaḥyā b. Saʿīd who establishes the same practice. "Practice" therefore decides the extent to which the general prohibition of *gharar*, incorporated in a tradition from the Prophet, is to be applied.[14]

There seems here to be a marked difference between what Schacht sets out to prove and the conclusion he reaches. There is no indication in the text that Mālik preferred a practice to a tradition from the Prophet. He is simply trying to clear up the meaning of an ambiguous term, *gharar*, used in the tradition by analyzing how the community that learned the tradition from the Prophet acted upon it and how the jurists and scholars of law in the community understood it. We must bear in mind that in the eyes of the Muslim community these scholars were God-fearing and would not

---

[13] *Origins*, p. 64.
[14] *Origins*, p. 64.

transgress the law; Mālik and other scholars referred to their practice in order to understand the real implications of the tradition from the Prophet.

EXAMPLE 2

Schacht says: Mālik [*Muw.* iii, 136] and Rabī' [*Tr. iii*, 47] declare, against a tradition from the Prophet which gives the parties to a sale the right of option as long as they have not separated: "We have no fixed limit and no established practice for that."[15]

We know that there was considerable controversy on this case between the Malikites and others, and the generally held opinion has been that Mālik did not accept this tradition. But recent research proves this to be wrong. Mālik does not deny the *Khiyār Majlis* itself. Under the heading "Chapter on *Khiyār Majlis*" باب بيع الخيار he quotes the tradition and says: وليس لهذا عندنا حدّ معروف ، ولا أمر معمول به فيه "There is no limit known to us for the period of *Khiyār*, and no established practice for that." Had he denied *Khiyār Majlis*, he would have said, ليس عليه العمل عندنا "There is no such practice." The case has been discussed in detail by Aḥmad Noor Saif.[16] However, if Schacht had used Mālik's work to establish Mālik's doctrines rather than the accusations of Shāfi'ī and other scholars, he would not have been led to declare that Mālik opposed a tradition from the Prophet.

EXAMPLE 3

Schacht states that: "Mālik in *Muw.* iii, 219 ff. prefers the practice, 'What people used to do,' as expressed in a statement ascribed to Qāsim b. Muḥammad and a concurring action reported from Ibn 'Umar to a tradition related from the Prophet."[17] Later on he quotes a detailed argument from the writings of Shāfi'ī, who attacks Mālik for not following this tradition from the Prophet.

Elsewhere, Schacht has charged Shāfi'ī with making unjustified assumptions, arguing arbitrarily, and misrepresenting and exaggerating the opinions of his opponents. He provides a few dozen examples of this,[18] and yet he is content in this particular case to accept Shāfi'ī's charges. If we look more closely at the text of Mālik and at Shāfi'ī's comments, however, we find that Shāfi'ī did not pay proper attention to Mālik's wording. Here is the text:

حدثني مالك . . . ان رسول الله صلى الله عليه وسلم قال : ايما رجل أعمر عمرى له ولعقبه فانها للذي يعطاها لا ترجع إلى الذي أعطاها أيضاً .
قال القاسم بن محمد : « ما أدركت الناس إلا وهم على شروطهم في أموالهم وفيما أعطوا » ،

---

[15] *Origins*, p. 64.
[16] See Aḥmad Noor Saif, *('Amal ahl al-Medīna,)* pp. 234–241.
[17] *Origins*, p. 65.
[18] Origins, p. 321 ff.

قال يحيى ، سمعت مالكا يقول : وعلى ذلك الأمر عندنا ان العمرى ترجع إلى الذي أعمرها إذا لم يقل : هى لك ولعقبك ، (ط الا قضية ٣٧)

Mālik reported the Prophet saying:

If any man designates an *'Umra* to another man *for him and his posterity* [i.e., if he should say to someone else that this house or land or a certain camel or anything of that sort were for *him and his children*], then it would belong completely to the man to whom it had been given and would never revert to the man who gave it. Al-Qāsim b. Muḥammad said that he likewise only found people to be bound by the stipulations they make in their contracts in financial dealings as well as in the gift they give. Yayḥā said that he heard Mālik say: "Hence, in our opinion, the *'Umrā* gift would return to the donor if he had not said: 'It is for you and *for your posterity*."[19]

According to the Arabic lexicographer Lane, *'Umrā* means a man's saying to another, of a house or of lands or of camels, "It is yours for your life."[20]

Thus Mālik distinguishes between two types of *'Umra* — one where the donor explicitly states that it is for the man and his successors and the other where the man's posterity are not mentioned. In the second case, Mālik's view is that ownership would revert to the donor.

The tradition of the Prophet quoted by Mālik refers to the first situation but not to the second. Mālik confirms his understanding by reference to the practice of Ibn 'Umar and the statement of Qāsim. This is clearly not a case of preferring practice to a tradition from the Prophet. Mālik is simply elucidating the tradition with reference to how it has been implemented and what the decision ought to be in a case not covered by the *ḥadīth* of the Prophet.

Thus, none of the examples quoted by Schacht proves his point that "practice" was preferred to traditions from the Prophet. We might have expected Schacht to analyze the traditions quoted by Mālik to see how many he neglected in favor of practice. Had he done so he would have seen that of the nine hundred or so traditions from the Prophet and roughly the same number of reports from other authorities that Mālik quotes in the *Muwaṭṭa'*, no more than ten are neglected in favor of practice or for other reasons.[21] This is hardly a sufficient basis from which to argue that the Medinese considered practice more authoritative than the traditions of the Prophet.

3. Practice Identified with Tradition Accepted by the Medinese.

Schacht's third conclusion is that "practice is explicitly identified with those traditions which the Medinese accept."[22] Yet if we examine the

---

[19] *Muw.* iii, 219 (italics mine).

[20] E.W. Lane, *Lexicon* (Edinburgh, 1867), p. 2155.

[21] The reasons are discussed further in Chapter 5 under the heading "Schacht on the Medinese School." For the numbers of rejected traditions, see notes 55 and 56 in Chapter Six.

[22] *Origins*, p. 66.

traditions accepted by Mālik, we find hundreds of examples of his accepting traditions from the Prophet and the Companions without any further reference to practice.[23]

Moreover, we have positive evidence that Mālik went against some earlier practices. Schacht himself quotes Shāfi'ī reprimanding the Medinese for not following Ibn 'Umar's opinion,[24] and Mālik explicitly describes instances of this in his *Muwaṭṭā'*. For example, it was the opinion of Ibn 'Umar that if a man prayed behind an *Imām* he should not recite the Qur'ān, the recitation of the *Imām* being sufficient for them both; this was the practice of Ibn 'Umar as well.[25] But Mālik disagrees with Ibn 'Umar, arguing that when the *Imām* does not recite loudly, the *ma'mūm* [i.e., the praying behind the *Imām*] should recite the Qur'ān to himself.[26] Another example: Mālik recorded that 'Umar prostrated himself after reciting *Sūrat al-Najm*.[27] But Mālik records his own opinion contrary to this practice.[28]

These examples make it clear that Mālik does not always quote practice when he accepts traditions from the Prophet, neither does he always follow the practice he describes.

4. Practice Falsely Ascribed to Early Authorities to Bring About Change. Schacht's fourth point is that practice was falsely ascribed to early authorities "to justify doctrines which reflected the current 'practice' *or which were meant to change it.*"[29] Schacht, in common with many Orientalists, is very prolific in producing theories of this sort. We may justifiably ask why this theory does not fit in the case of Mālik himself. In the preceding section we have seen that Mālik records the practice of Medinese authorities and then diverges from it, and also records their opinions and opposes them.

Rather than modify his theory to fit the evidence, Schacht goes into further realms of speculation to resolve this contradiction. He says:

> After the first legitimization of doctrine by reference to Companions of the Prophet had been achieved, the further growth of traditions from Companions and also from the Prophet went partly parallel with the further elaboration of doctrine within the "living tradition" of the ancient schools, but partly also represented the means by which definite changes in the accepted doctrine of a school were proposed and supported. These efforts were sometimes successful in bringing about a change of doctrine, but often not, and we find whole groups of "unsuccessful" Medinese and Iraqian doctrines expressed in traditions.[30]

---

[23] See, for example, *Muw.*, pp. 15–20.
[24] See *Origins*, p. 26.
[25] *Muw.*, *Ṣalāt* 10, p. 86.
[26] *Muw.*, p. 86.
[27] *Muw.*, p. 206.
[28] *Muw.*, p. 207.
[29] *Origins*, p. 66 (italics mine).
[30] *Origins*, p. 66.

In other words, many of the opinions ascribed to ancient authorities in the works of Mālik, Abū Yūsuf, and Shaibānī are fabricated. Leaving aside the inherent improbability of such wholesale invention, let us take the case of Mālik as a way of testing the validity of Schacht's theory.

According to Schacht: "As the groups of pious specialists grew in numbers and in cohesion, they developed, in the first few decades of the second century of Islam, into the 'ancient schools of law.' "[31] Thus the birth of the ancient schools of law occurred in the early decades of the second century. It is believed that Mālik was born in the last decade of the first century, which means that he witnessed the birth of the ancient school of law in Medina when he was in his twenties or thirties.

Mālik records the opinions of his immediate teachers, such as Nāfi', Zuhrī, and Rabī'a, as well as the opinions of first-century scholars such as 'Umar, Ibn 'Umar, Ibn al-Musayyab, and 'Urwah. In Schacht's view, the doctrines ascribed to these early authorities cannot be taken as genuine, but are only a device used "in order to justify doctrines which reflected the current 'practice' or which were meant to change it."[32] He further notes that "these efforts were sometimes successful in bringing about a change . . . but often not."[33]

It might be theoretically possible to accept this view if the Medinese always followed the early authorities, but, as we have seen, Mālik was sometimes in agreement and sometimes in disagreement with the authorities he quoted. If he were falsely ascribing doctrines to these authorities to bring about changes in the doctrine of the school, he would not then contradict what he had himself just fabricated. Was he perhaps under some kind of pressure that would not allow him to formulate his own doctrines as he wished but would make him want to pass on the relevant information to later authorities? There is no evidence that this kind of situation existed, and, in fact, there is abundant evidence to the contrary. We find many scholars changing their decisions whenever the weight of evidence indicates that they may have been wrong in the first place. Mālik himself changed his doctrine continuously as, for example, regarding his opinion about *al-Mash 'ala al-Khuffain*.[34]

Similarly, we know Abū Yūsuf differed from the opinions of Abū Ḥanīfa in almost a third of the cases they ruled upon. Two examples are the problems of the shares allotted to the horse and the soldier[35] and of usury between a Muslim and non-Muslim in enemy territory.[36] Abū Yūsuf likewise changed many of his own opinions. See, for example, his early opinion about the number of horses that ought to be given as shares

---

[31] *Introduction*, p. 28.
[32] *Origins*, p. 66.
[33] *Idem*.
[34] Shaibānī, *Al-Ḥujja* (Hydrabad, 1385), vol. 1, pp. 23–47. Cited hereafter as *Ḥujja*.
[35] Abū Yūsuf, *Al-Radd 'alā Siyar al-Auzā'ī* (Cairo, 1357), p. 21. Cited hereafter as Auzā'ī.
[36] *Ibid.* p. 97.

in the booty of war.³⁷ Shāfiʿī, also, is famous for his "old doctrine" and his "new doctrine" *(al-qaul al-qadīm* and *al-qaul al-jadīd)*.

These are but a few of the very many examples which could be adduced to show that scholars were free from outside coercion in the formulation of their doctrines. So we return to the problem of why Mālik first falsely ascribed doctrines to early authorities and then did not follow them. If he were really trying to change the doctrine of the school, then he weakened his case by not following them. All the evidence points to the fact that he reported doctrines and opinions of earlier scholars honestly, according to the best of his knowledge.

The discussion of Schacht's theories about the "living tradition" in the Medinese school may be summarized as follows:

1. Schacht claimed that it is clearly stated in the *Mudawwana* that practice existed first and the traditions from the Prophet came later. This has been proved to be contrary to the statement recorded in the *Mudawwana*.
2. He adduced three examples to show that the Medinese opposed practice to traditions from the Prophet. Each one of these examples in fact contradicts his claim.
3. His theory that practice is explicitly identified with those traditions accepted by the Medinese has been proved wrong by reference to the number of traditions that were not identified with practice and the variety of practices that existed.
4. His final claim that doctrines were falsely ascribed to earlier authorities to justify doctrines that reflected the practice or were meant to change has been shown to have no basis.

We now examine Schacht's assertions about the "living tradition" in what he calls the Syrian and Iraqian schools.

The Syrians and the Living Tradition: Auzāʿī

Speaking about Auzāʿī, Schacht says:

> His idea of "living tradition" is the uninterrupted practice of the Muslims, beginning with the Prophet, maintained by the first Caliphs and by later rulers, and verified by the scholars. The continuous practice of the Muslims is the decisive element, reference to the Prophet or to the first Caliphs is optional, but not necessary for establishing it. Examples occur in almost every paragraph of *Tr. IX*.³⁸

If we examine the treatise Schacht refers to, which comprises 50 cases, we find the following:

    a. 9 cases: practices of the Prophet and followed by Muslims (1, 3, 4, 5, 7, 8, 10, 13, 31)

---

³⁷ Compare Auzāʿī, p. 41, with Abū Yūsuf, *Kharāj*, p. 19. Cited hereafter as *Kharāj*.
³⁸ *Origins*, p. 70.

b. 10 cases: practice of the Prophet, with no mention of continuous practice (17, 23, 26, 34, 36, 39, 47, 48, 49, 50)
c. 3 cases: traditions of the Prophet (2, 20, 38)
d. 1 case: "the established *sunna*" (37)
e. 1 case: order of the first caliph, Abū Bakr, and accepted by Muslim leaders (28)
f. 1 case: prohibition by Abū Bakr (29)
g. 1 case: practice of 'Umar (22)
h. 1 case: practice of 'Alī b. Abū Ṭālib (42)
i. 1 case: practice of 'Umar b. 'Abdul 'Azīz (25)
j. 6 cases: based on the practice of Muslims and their leaders (6, 9, 14, 19, 24, 32)
k. 2 cases: Auzā'ī's deduction from the Qur'ān (16, 21)
l. 13 cases: his personal analogy (11, 12, 15, 18, 27, 30, 33, 35, 41, 43, 44, 45, 46)
m. In case 40, no opinion of Auzā'ī is recorded.

In only 15 of the 50 cases, therefore, does Auzā'ī refer to the continuous practice of the Muslims,[39] and only nine of these are related to the Prophet.[40] Given that 22 cases contain reference to traditions from the Prophet[41] and 13 of these are not supported by any reference to practice,[42] it is highly disputable to say that "continuous practice is the decisive element" or that "reference to the Prophet ... is optional."

Auzā'ī was very precise in referring to his authorities to the best of his knowledge. Sometimes he refers to the Prophet, sometimes to the early caliphs, sometimes to the practice of the Muslims, and in almost a third of the cases he simply gives his own opinion. This itself is enough to refute Schacht's claim that Auzā'ī is "inclined to project the whole 'living tradition', the continuous practice of the Muslims, as he finds it, back to the Prophet and to give it the Prophet's authority, whether he can adduce a precedent established by the Prophet or not."[43]

Moreover, we may note that a practice established in the time of 'Umar, even though it was established by 'Umar himself, has no authority in the doctrine of Auzā'ī. Schacht refers to the same case but distorts the evidence, using it to show that "Auzā'ī opposes the fictitious constant usage of the Prophet and of the caliphs to the actual administrative practice."[44]

We may conclude that Schacht's statements regarding the "living tradition" of the Syrian school have no basis and that his conclusions are based

---

[39] See a and j above.
[40] See a above.
[41] See a, b, and c above.
[42] See b and c above.
[43] *Origins*, pp. 72–73.
[44] *Origins*, p. 70.

on assumptions rather than on exact analysis of Auzā'ī's writings. Auzā'ī's own writings, in fact, tend to refute Schacht' thesis.

The Iraqians and the Living Tradition

The Iraqians, says Schacht,

> hardly use the term *'amal*, "practice", even where their doctrine endorses actual administrative procedure ... We have seen Abū Yūsuf inveigh against Auzā'ī's concept of practice, although his own idea of *sunna* comes down to the same. Shāfi'ī's Basrian opponent, when charged with making "practice" prevail over traditions from the Prophet, replaces this term in his own answer by *sunna*.[45]

This is simply not true. The Basrian opponent was not charged with making practice prevail over traditions, neither did he replace the term practice with *sunna*.[46] Schacht goes on to say:

> However it be formulated, the Iraqian idea of "living tradition" is essentially the same as that of the Medinese, and Shāfi'ī can say, addressing the Egyptian Medinese: "Some of the Easterners have provided you with an argument and hold the same views as you" (*Tr. iii*, 148, p. 242). This "living tradition" is meant when an Iraqian opponent of Shāfi'ī says that there would be nothing to choose between two doctrines, each of which is represented by a tradition, "if there were nothing to go by but the two traditions" (*Ikh.* 158f). It corresponds to the accepted doctrine of the school, and a scholar from Kufa, presumably Shaibānī himself, can comment on the fact that a well-authenticated tradition from the Prophet is not acted upon because "all people" have abandoned it, saying: "By 'people' I mean the muftis in our time or [immediately] before us, not the Successors"; he specifies the people of Hijaz and Iraq; for Iraq, he can only mention Abū Ḥanīfa and his companions, and he is aware that Ibn Abī Lailā holds a different opinion which, however, "we do not share"; he knows nothing about the muftis in Baṣra (*Ikh.* 336 f). The Iraqians, therefore, like the Medinese, take their doctrine "from the lowest source." The scholars of Kufa in particular find this doctrine expressed in the opinions ascribed to Ibrāhīm Nakha'ī.[47]

This passage raises many issues which are not relevant to our discussion here; however, much of it bears upon the problem of the "living tradition." First, it is an unreasonable assumption to say that it is the living tradition that is meant when the Iraqian opponent of Shāfi'ī comments on the choice between two doctrines supported by a tradition. There is no evidence in the text for this and no basis for assuming that anything other than traditions from the Prophet are being cited.

Schacht tells us that the "living tradition" is composed of two elements:

---

[45] *Origins*, p. 76.
[46] Chapter Six discusses this further under the heading "Was the *Sunna* of the Prophet Imposed on the Old Idea of *Sunna*?"
[47] *Origins*, pp. 76–77.

(1) customary or "generally agreed" practice which (2) should coincide with the accepted doctrine of the school. Given this definition, we may note that one of these essential elements — i.e., practice — is lacking in the school of Abū Yūsuf, or as Schacht calls it, the Iraqian school. Abū Yūsuf attacks Auzāiʻī severely on this issue, saying:

> One should not decide a question of *Ḥarām* and *Ḥalāl* this way, saying that people always did so. Because most of what people always did is not allowed and ought not to be done. There are cases which I could mention, where the great mass acts against a prohibition of the Prophet. In these cases one has to obtain the knowledge or order from the *sunna* of the Prophet and from the [*Fatwā*] of forbears from his Companions and from the lawyers.[48]

Schacht quotes this passage himself (in *Origins*, p. 75) noting that "the Iraqians hardly use the term . . . 'practice,' even where their doctrine endorses actual administrative procedure."[49] Yet he continues to maintain that the Iraqian idea of living tradition is essentially the same as that of the Medinese.

On this important point, Schacht adduces only one example, that of *Ḥadīth muṣarrāt*, which says that if a man sells a goat and the buyer wants to return it, he should return also a quantity of dates, since he has had the use of the goat's milk. But what Schacht quotes here is the polemical writing of Shāfiʻī — and the inadequacy of using anything other than the original writings of the party concerned has already been commented on at length. Where Shāfiʻī says that Abū Ḥanīfa did not act on this *ḥadīth*, Abū Yūsuf quotes the same *ḥadīth* as the reasoning of Abū Ḥanīfa in making *Khiyār baiʻ* for three days only,[50] which means that this *ḥadīth* was accepted by Abū Ḥanīfa and even used in other legal cases.

The second element in the "living tradition" is that it should coincide with the accepted doctrine of the school. In the case in question we find little to show that there was an accepted doctrine. This is the opinion of Abū Ḥanīfa, as quoted by Shaibānī, which was not even shared by Ibn Abī Lailā, who, as a judge, would have given judgments accordingly if he concurred. Abū Ḥanīfa was not a judge and has no forebears who shared his opinion. Clearly this was not the opinion of all the Kūfans, let alone all the Iraqians.

We may conclude that Schacht's theory of a "living tradition" in Iraq flies in the face of all the available evidence. Abū Yūsuf inveighs strongly *against* using practice to decide legal cases, and there is no evidence to suppose that there was any "accepted doctrine" in the Iraqian school: In fact, there was no Iraqian school as such.

The aim of this chapter has been to show that the living tradition, existing before the traditions from the Prophet, is largely a figment of Schacht's imagination. In the majority of cases, as we have seen, the

---

[48] *Tr. ix*, 24; Shāfiʻī *Umm*, (Cairo, 1321), vol. 7, p. 320.
[49] *Origins*, p. 76.
[50] Abū Yūsuf, *Ikhtilāf Abī Ḥanīfa* (Cairo, 1957), p. 16. Cited hereafter as Ibn Abī Lailā.

"practice" referred to is in fact practice based on a tradition from the Prophet. The following chapter will seek to take the refutation a stage further and show the untenability of Schacht's view that traditions from the Prophet, all fabricated, gradually supressed this "living tradition" in the second century as a result of factional infighting among the so-called "ancient schools of law" and the traditionists.

Chapter Five

The Authority of the *Sunna* of the Prophet in the Ancient Schools of Law

In Part One of this book the status of the Prophet as far as the Qur'ān is concerned was discussed. It was shown there that he was to be seen as the expounder of the Qur'ān, as a legislator, and as a model for Muslim behavior. The possibility always exists, of course, that practice may fall short of what was commanded; let us therefore analyze exactly how strong the commitment of the early lawyers to the *sunna* of the Prophet was. For this purpose we shall discuss the attitudes of the Medinese, the Syrians, and the Iraqians, respectively.

The Attitudes of the Medinese, Syrian, and Iraqian Schools

In the *Muwaṭṭa'*, Mālik records the statement of the Prophet: "I leave with you two things after my death, if you hold on fast to them you can never go astray: They are the Book of Allah and the *sunna* of the Prophet."[1] Although the mere recording of the statement is not evidence that the Medinese actually used the traditions of the Prophet to support their judgments,[2] we have quoted earlier Mālik's saying "The *sunna* is proof enough," and this statement explicitly describes the Medinese doctrine concerning the *sunna* of the Prophet. Moreover, if we study the *Muwaṭṭa'* more closely we find numerous instances of Mālik basing his

---

[1] *Muw.*, *Qadr* 3, p. 899.
[2] After quoting this statement of the Prophet from *Muw.*, *Qadr* 3, Schacht claims that "this use of *sunna* is not part of Medinese legal reasoning proper" (*Origins*, p. 62) and that in the generation before Shāfi'ī the Medinese supported their arguments with references to practice, rather than to traditions from the Prophet. Although in fact basing his conclusions on a misunderstanding of the text (as discussed in Chapter Six in the first example), Schacht uses this reference as an exception that does not prove the rule.

judgments *explicitly* on the Prophet's orders.[3] These examples, while not exhaustive, are surely sufficient to show that the use of *sunna* of the Prophet was an essential part of Medinese doctrine.

The statement of Auzā'ī in *Tr. ix* 4 is an excellent demonstration of the authority given to the *sunna* of the Prophet by the Syrians. Abū Ḥanīfa maintained that a soldier's share of the spoils of war should be determined according to his registration category. If he was listed as a *rājil* — a foot soldier without horse — he should have the share of a *rājil* even if he obtained a horse and entered battle on it. Auzā'ī objected to this judgment, saying that the system of registration began in the time of 'Umar, while in the time of the Prophet there was no register and a soldier's share was determined according to the extent of his real contribution to the war. His refusal to accept Abū Ḥanīfa's view was based entirely on a precedent from the Prophet.

Of the Ḥanafī school, which Schacht calls the Iraqian school, we have some of the books written by Abū Yūsuf and Shaibānī — two of the most distinguished companions of Abū Ḥanīfa. Books such as *Āthār* by Abū Yūsuf and *Āthār*, *Muwaṭṭa'*, and *al-Ḥujja 'alā ahl-al-Madīna* by Shaibānī are filled with traditions from the Prophet.

Abū Yūsuf and the *Sunna* of the Prophet

Let us first examine some of Abū Yūsuf's statements.

وأما أرض الحجاز ومكة والمدينة وأرض اليمن وأرض العرب التي افتتحها رسول الله صلى الله عليه وسلم فلا يزاد عليها ولا ينقص منها ، لأنه شيء قد جرى عليه أمر رسول الله صلى الله عليه وسلم وحكمه ، فلا يحل للإمام أن يحوله إلى غير ذلك .[4]

As for the land of the Ḥijāz, Mecca, Madina, Yemen and those Arab territories which have been conquered by the Prophet, there should be no *increase or decrease* in [land tax] because upon them the order of the Prophet has been implemented. Therefore, the Caliphs are not allowed to divert it to something else.

إن رسول الله صلى الله عليه وسلم أقطع لاناس من مزينة أو جهينة أرضاً فلم يعمروها ، فجاء قوم فعمروها فخاصمهم الجهنيون أو المزنيون إلى عمر بن الخطاب رضي الله تعالى عنه ، فقال : لو كانت مني أو من أبي بكر لرددتها ولكنها قطيعة من رسول الله صلى الله عليه وسلم .[5]

The Prophet awarded a piece of land to some people of the tribe of Muzaina or Juhaina, but they did not utilize it. Some other people came and used it. The Muzanī or Juhanī people complained to the Caliph 'Umar. 'Umar said:

---

[3] See pp. 92–93, 105, 124, 145–146, 248, 263–264, 274, 283, 313–314, 323, 325, 337, 340, 342, 414, 514, 644, 649, 663, 706, 725, 720, 761, 773, 779, 782, 789, 805, 833, 853–854, 859, 870, 879, 892, 912, 950, 983, 993, etc. There are many hundreds of cases in the *Muwaṭṭa'* alone where Mālik deducts his doctrines from the traditions of the Prophet.

[4] *Kharāj*, p. 58; also 60.

[5] *Kharāj*, p. 61.

"Had the land been granted by Abū Bakr or myself, I should have taken it back, but it was granted by the Prophet [so I cannot change it.]'

﴿ وسألت يا أمير المؤمنين عما يجب في الصدقة .... فمر يا أمير المؤمنين العاملين عليها بأخذ الحق وإعطائه من وجب له وعليه ، والعمل في ذلك بما سنه رسول الله صلى الله عليه وسلم ثم الخلفاء من بعد . ﴾ [6]

Amīrul Mu'minīn you have asked about the *zākat*. . . . *Amīrul Mūminīn* you should order the officers [appointed for its collection] to collect the rights and to give it to whom it is due and [to collect it] from whom it is due and to work in this case after the manner of the *sunan* established by the Prophet and then the Caliphs after him."

The first quotation shows that no one has the authority to change what has been fixed by the Prophet, and the second shows that 'Umar followed this view. One of the Prophet's orders was that any man awarded a piece of land should use it within three years or have it taken away from him. In the case in question, the man left the land unused and other people began to use it. Given the general injunction of the Prophet, 'Umar should have transferred the land to those who were using it, but he did not do so and excused himself by saying: "Had the land been granted by Abū Bakr or myself, I should have taken it back, but it was granted by the Prophet."

In the third quotation, Abū Yūsuf advises the caliph that he should instruct the governors to collect *zakāt* and dispense it according to the *sunna* of the Prophet and that which has been laid down by the caliphs.

Finding contradictions in some of the *aḥādīth*, Abū Yūsuf chooses one which has more weight than others. Speaking about the partnership in farming he says:

﴿ قال أبو يوسف : فكان أحسن ما سمعنا في ذلك ـ والله أعلم ـ إن ذلك جائز مستقيم ، اتبعنا الأحاديث التي جاءت عن رسول الله صلى الله عليه وسلم في مساقاة خيبر ، لأنها أوثق عندنا وأكثر وأعم مما جاء في خلافها من الأحاديث . ﴾ [7]

The best we have heard in this case — And Allah knows the best — is that it is allowed and right [to do so]. We have followed the traditions which came down from the Prophet regarding the partnership of the Land of Khaibar. For these traditions are more trustworthy and more in [number] and general [in rules] than the traditions which have been related against these [traditions].

These quotations clearly show the overriding authority attached by Abū Yūsuf to the *sunna* of the Prophet.

Shaibānī and the *Sunna* of the Prophet

In Shaibānī's *Muwaṭṭa'*, as well as in *Āthār*, in almost every chapter and often more than once he writes:

وبهذا كله نأخذ وهو قول أبي حنيفة رحمه الله

---

[6] *Kharāj*, p. 76.
[7] *Kharāj*, p. 89.

"All of this we follow: And it is Abū Ḥanīfa's opinion." This characteristic, which has also been recorded by Schacht,[8] is in itself sufficient to show the authority of the *sunna* of the Prophet in the Ḥanafī school. The explicit statement of the Iraqi scholar لا حجة في أحد مع النبي صلى الله عليه وسلم "that no one has any authority when placed alongside the Prophet"[9] may also be cited. Taking this together with Abū Yūsuf's explicit statements quoted above and their practical adherence to the traditions from the Prophet, there seems no room for doubt that the *sunna* of the Prophet had overriding authority. Schacht does not and, indeed, cannot attempt to deny the existence of the many references to the authority of traditions from the Prophet. But he takes passages such as *Muw., Shaib.*, 357, where Shaibānī insists on the decisive role of a decision of the Prophet,[10] and asks us to treat them skeptically on the grounds that the argument that the opinion of the opponent is not based on traditions from the Prophet is common to the Iraqians and Medinese in their polemics against one another.[11] The point here, however, is surely that this argument would hardly have been used in polemics unless both schools accepted the overriding authority of the *sunna* of the Prophet, in theory at least; without this acceptance, accusations that the opponent's arguments were not based on traditions from the Prophet would have been meaningless. We must conclude, therefore, not on the basis of the polemical writings of Shāfi'ī but on the basis of the explicit statements of Abū Yūsuf and Shaibānī, that the doctrine of the Ḥanafī school was based on the overriding authority of the Prophet's *sunna*.

The Attitudes of the Ancient Schools According to Schacht

In the preceding pages examples have been cited from the writings of Mālik of Medina, Auzā'ī of Syria, and Abū Yūsuf and Shaibānī of Kūfa to show the attitude of the early caliphs, governors, lawyers, and judges towards the *sunna* of the Prophet. The examples have been deliberately chosen from scholars and literature prior to Shāfi'ī to show that that was the attitude of ancient schools of law toward the *sunna* of the Prophet, prior to Shāfi'ī. Let us see what Schacht says on these topics in his two books on the subject. In *An Introduction to Islamic Law*, Schacht states that "as the groups of pious specialists grew in numbers and in cohesion, they developed, in the first few decades of the second century of Islam, into the 'ancient schools of law.' "[12] He goes on to say that the ancient schools of law, while differing in many details, shared a common legal

---

[8] See *Origins*, p. 306.
[9] *Umm*, vii, 292; see also *al-Ḥujja*, i, 45, 204.
[10] *Origins*, p. 28.
[11] *Ibid.*, p. 27.
[12] *Introduction*, p. 28.

theory: "The central idea of this theory was that of the 'living tradition of the school' as represented by the constant doctrine of its authoritative representatives."[13] A little farther on, he writes:

> The movement of the Traditionists . . . in the second century of the *hijra*, was the natural outcome and continuation of a movement of religiously and ethically inspired opposition to the ancient schools of law . . . The main thesis of the Traditionists, as opposed to the ancient schools of law, was that formal "traditions" . . . deriving from the Prophet superseded the living tradition of the school . . . The Traditionists produced detailed statements or "traditions" which claimed to be the reports of ear- or eye-witnesses on the words or acts of the Prophet, handed down orally by an uninterrupted chain *(isnād)* of trustworthy persons. Hardly any of these traditions, as far as matters of religious law are concerned, can be considered authentic; they were put into circulation, no doubt from the loftiest of motives, by the Traditionists themselves from the first half of the second century onwards.[14]

"Initially the ancient schools of law, the Medinese as well as the Iraqians, offered strong resistance to the disturbing element represented by the traditions which claimed to go back to the Prophet,"[15] says Schacht in the same book, while in his *Origins of Muhammadan Jurisprudence* he states that "the hostility towards traditions . . . was the natural reaction of the early specialists on law against the introduction of a new element, traces of which survive in the attitude of the ancient schools of law."[16]

"In the time of Shāfi'ī," he claims, "traditions from the Prophet were already recognized as one of the material bases of Muhammadan law. Their position in the ancient schools of law was . . . much less certain."[17] Shāfi'ī, according to Schacht, identifies two groups of antitraditionists:

1. Those who rejected the traditions altogether, the Mu'tazila.
2. Those who rejected the *khabar al-khāṣṣa*, that is, the traditions based on the authority of individual transmitters only. "It was Shāfi'ī who, for polemic reasons, applied this name to them . . . and they do not, in fact, reject the *khabar al-khāṣṣa* on principle; . . . they are identical with the followers of the ancient schools of law, who prefer the 'living tradition' of the school to individual traditions from the Prophet."[18]

Schacht's Concept of the Antitraditionists

Although Schacht claims that Shāfi'ī knew of two groups of antitraditionists, Shāfi'ī names only one group: Those who rejected the traditions from the Prophet altogether. We know nothing of them from their own writ-

---

[13] *Introduction*, p. 29.
[14] *Introduction*, p. 34.
[15] *Introduction*, p. 35.
[16] *Origins*, p. 40.
[17] *Idem*.
[18] *Origins*, p. 41.

ings but only from Shāfi'ī's discussion in *al-Umm*. They were, therefore, a very minor group, known only to few scholars. Their attitude is totally contrary to the Qur'ān, where the faithful are enjoined to follow the law given by the Prophet and the life patterns established by him,[19] and for the following reasons it is highly questionable to identify them with the Mu'tazila:

1. The Mu'tazila did not develop any legal school in the early centuries. Their activities were concentrated entirely on theological problems, a fact admitted by Schacht himself.[20]
2. There were many great *traditionists* who belonged to the Mu'tazila. Among them were Ḥasan al-Baṣrī (d. 110 A.H.), Qatādah (d. 117 A.H.), Sa'īd ibn Abī 'Arūba (d. 155 A.H.), 'Auf b. Abū Jamīla (d. 146 A.H.), and Maṭar b. Ṭahmān (d. 125 A.H.). These Mu'tazila scholars, who were the pioneers in the field of traditions, belong to the first half of the second century A.H.[21]
3. Early Mu'tazila writings and theories recorded by Khayyāṭ before 300 A.H. contradict this antitraditionist hypothesis, as do later authorities such as Qāḍī 'Abdul Jabbār and Abul Ḥusain, whose book *al-Mu'tamad* contains a wealth of information confirming our statements.[22] Khayyāṭ, for example, quotes a statement of Wāsil b. 'Aṭā' (d. 131 A.H.) on a theological problem. In his opinion, where scholars disagree, they should produce evidence from the Book of Allah and the *sunna* of the Prophet.[23] There are many other clear references in the same vein.[24] However, all these explicit statements of Mu'tazila writers — the parties concerned — have been rejected by Schacht as it "certainly does not represent the doctrine of the ancient Mu'tazila."[25]

Schacht's only basis for identifying the *ahl al-Kalām* with the Mu'tazila is the evidence of the anti-Mu'tazila writer Ibn Qutaiba of the late third century, who ascribes antitraditionist attitudes to some of the Mu'tazila. This would hardly appear to be sufficient for his purposes, although this still does not deny that there was a small, albeit relatively unimportant, sect of antitraditionists who did exist. We shall now examine Schacht's evidence for the existence of what he calls "moderate antitraditionist" groups in the Medinese, Iraqian, and Syrian schools.

Before going into a detailed discussion of this group, it may be men-

---

[19] Chapter One discusses this point in detail under the heading "The Role of the Prophet in Islamic Law."
[20] *Origins*, p. 258.
[21] See Ibn al-Murtaḍā, *Ṭabaqāt* Mu'tazila, pp. 133–140, which contains a lengthy list of Mu'tazila traditionists. Though some of the names are disputed, many remain authentic.
[22] Abu al Ḥusain, *al-Mu'tamad*, (Damascus, 1964) 337–87; 566–687.
[23] Al-Khayyāṭ, *al-Intiṣār*, (Beirut, 1957) p. 118.
[24] See al-Khayyāṭ, *al-Intiṣār*, pp. 68, 75 and 118.
[25] *Origins*, p. 259.

tioned briefly that it is wrong to label them antitraditionists; their contentions pertained to the documentation and authentication of certain traditions, not to the question of the authority of traditions *per se*. One cannot act according to a decree until it is proved to be authentic.

In the opinion of these people, a narrator relating something on the authority of the Prophet needed another witness to corroborate his statement, as is the case with witnesses in an Islamic court of law. One witness is insufficient to prove the case. The same parallel was drawn here. These people, however, do not belong to well-known schools of Medina, Kūfa, or Syria as we shall see.

By "moderate antitraditionists" Schacht means those groups who rejected the validity of the *khabar-khāṣṣah* (a tradition reported by a single narrator), and identifies them as the followers of the ancient schools of law. [26]

In Chapter 6 of his *Origins of Muhammadan Jurisprudence*, "Arguments For and Against Traditions," Schacht goes into some detail about the devices used by the "antitraditionists." Much of the discussion is repeated from Chapter 4, "Traditions in the Ancient Schools of Law." Both chapters will therefore be treated together to avoid unnecessary overlapping of arguments.

Schacht cites 12 different devices used by the antitraditionist to "disparage" traditions from the Prophet:

1. Saying that traditionists reject some *ḥadīth* as unacceptable, and that if it is possible to do this with one *ḥadīth* it is possible to do it with all.[27]
2. Asserting that many traditions are contrary to reason and observation and therefore absurd and ridiculous.[28]
3. Rejecting traditions by comparing them with the Qur'ān. Schacht maintains that "This kind of argument drawn from the Koran against traditions from the Prophet is familiar to the Iraqians . . . [though] Shāfi'ī and the Iraqians [are] on common ground against 'those who follow the outward meaning of the Koran and disregard the traditions.' "[29]
4. Saying that the Qur'ān repeals traditions.[30]
5. Minimizing the importance of traditions from the Prophet by: (a) unwillingness to relate traditions; (b) insistence on their small numbers; and (c) warning against careless attribution of traditions

---

[26] *Origins*, pp. 41, 51.
[27] *Origins*, pp. 44–45, based on *Ikh.*, p. 366 ff. and Ibn Qutaiba, p. 10.
[28] *Origins*, p. 45.
[29] *Origins*, p. 46.
[30] *Origins*, p. 46, based on Schacht's understanding of Shāfi'ī, *Ikhtilaf al-Ḥadīth* p. 48. Cited hereafter as *Ikh*.

to the Prophet. Schacht claims that these arguments were especially popular in Iraq.[31]

6. Searching for contradictions between traditions and subsequently rejecting one of them.[32]
7. Explaining away a tradition by the assumption of repeal.[33]
8. Maintaining that an injunction was for a particular case and not meant as a general rule.[34]
9. Claiming that the practice was the personal privilege of the Prophet and not the general rule.[35]
10. Saying that it was the personal taste of the Prophet.[36]
11. Arguing that Companions could not be unaware of the *sunna* of the Prophet and would know it best.[37]
12. Asserting that "isolated" traditions — that is, a tradition transmitted by a single individual *(khabar al-wāḥid, khabar al-infirād)*, cannot be accepted as well authenticated.[38] "The disparagement of the *khabar al-wāḥid* was, in fact, so typical of the ancient schools of law that Shāfiʿī, using a synonym, could refer to them as 'those who reject the *khabar al-khāṣṣa*'. . . . According to them, it is ignorance to accept the *khabar al-infirād*."[39]

The Weaknesses in Schacht's Thesis

Before going into detail about the specific attitude of each of the ancient schools of law to the *sunna* of the Prophet, the mode of research which Schacht used to reach these conclusions will be examined. In particular, it will be argued that he made arbitrary use of source material, tended to overgeneralize, and allowed internal inconsistencies to remain in his thesis.

1. The Arbitrary Use of Source Material. Most of Schacht's arguments about the position of the *sunna* of the Prophet in the doctrines of the ancient schools of law derive from the writings of Shāfiʿī; they are based either on Schacht's own deductions from those writings or the accusations of Shāfiʿī against his opponents. This would hardly seem a reliable method, given that Schacht himself quotes dozens of examples of Shāfiʿī's lack of objectivity. He says in so many words: "He (Shāfiʿī) often misrepresents the Iraqian doctrine," and: "Shāfiʿī often misrepresents the

---

[31] *Origins*, p. 47, referring to Dārimī, *Sunan*.
[32] *Origins*, p. 47, based on his understanding of *Ikh.*, p. 328.
[33] *Origins*, p. 47, citing *Muw., Shaib.* 142; *Tr.*, IX., 29.
[34] *Origins*, p. 49, quoting *Muw.*, iii, 89.
[35] *Origins*, p. 49, based on *Muw., Shaib.* Even Shāfiʿī accepts personal privilege; see *Umm*, vii, 329.
[36] *Origins*, p. 49, based on *Muw., Shaib.*, 280.
[37] *Origins*, p. 50.
[38] *Idem*.
[39] *Origins*, p. 51.

Medinese doctrine," and he provides a few dozen examples.[40] He also gives several examples of Shāfi'ī's biased editing of his opponents' texts.[41]

Clearly, we are obliged to believe in the light of Schacht's findings that Shāfi'ī is an unreliable source for tracing the doctrines of the ancient schools of law, and yet Schacht is content to base his own theories on Shāfi'ī's polemical writings. Moreover, Schacht apparently uses and discards Shāfi'ī's assertions at will. Shāfi'ī's accusations that opponents have departed from certain *hadīth* of the Prophet are expanded into a general principle regarding the ancient schools of law. But when Shāfi'ī and his opponent explicitly admit that they are unanimous in recognizing the overriding authority of the *sunna* of the Prophet, Schacht accepts neither the claims of Shāfi'ī nor those of the ancient scholars, the parties concerned.

Similarly, we seldom find Schacht referring to the original texts to formulate the doctrines of the ancient schools of law. The Medinese doctrine on the authority of the *sunna* of the Prophet, for example, is not traced in the *Muwaṭṭa'* of Mālik. Whenever Schacht finds explicit statements of Mālik which run counter to his arguments, he denigrates their importance, preferring to refer to Rabī', the pupil of Shāfi'ī and "self-appointed" solicitor of the Medinese.[42] This abuse of source material is hardly consonant with sound scholarship, and it is therefore not surprising that the conclusions Schacht reaches are so wildly inaccurate.

2. Overgeneralization. Schacht's imprecision in his naming of the ancient schools of law has been commented on earlier. It will be remembered that Schacht assumes the school of Mālik b. Anas to be representative of the whole of Medina, and he generalizes the doctrines of the Ḥanafī school of Kūfa to cover the whole of Iraq. This he does *against the background of his own acknowledgment* that "it would be a mistake to generalize, even within the circle of the Kufians, the uniformity of doctrine . . . "[43]

We are not concerned here simply with a matter of misnaming schools; for it is central to Schacht's thesis that there *was* a uniformity of doctrine among the ancient schools of law, particularly with regard to their resistance to traditions from the Prophet.

3. Internal Inconsistences. Although Schacht purports to advance a coherent and comprehensive theory to explain the development of Islamic law, inconsistencies and contradictory statements abound, not simply between the theories advanced in his two books but within *Origins of Muhammadan Jurisprudence* itself.

For example, at one point Schacht says, "Traditions from the Prophet

---

[40] *Origins*, pp. 321–332.
[41] See *Origins*, pp. 87 and 109–2.
[42] See, for example, *Origins*, pp. 22–23.
[43] *Origins*, p. 242.

had to overcome a *strong opposition on the part of the ancient schools of law*, let alone the *ahl al-kalām*, before they gained general acceptance."[44] But elsewhere we read, "The best way of proving that a tradition did not exist at a certain time is to show that it was not used as a legal argument in a discussion which would have made reference to it imperative, if it had existed."[45] If the ancient schools of law were hostile to traditions from the Prophet, then how could it have been imperative for them to refer to them?

Another example is his argument to prove the inferior position of the traditions from the Prophet in the ancient schools of law compared to other traditions. After saying "The first striking fact is that the traditions from the Prophet are greatly outnumbered by those from Companions and Successors,"[46] he then provides the following statistics:

	Mālik's Muwaṭṭa'	Muw. Shaib.	Āthār A.Y.	Āthār Shaib.
From the Prophet	822	429	189	131
From Companions	613	628	372	284
From Successors	285	112	549	550
From later authorities	—	10	—	6

In the *Muwaṭṭa'* of Mālik (d. 179 A.H.), the number of traditions from the Prophet are almost equal to those transmitted on the authority of Companions and Successors together, and more in number than those of any single group. In the *Muwaṭṭa'* of Shaibānī (d. 189 A.H.), the number of traditions from the Prophet is about half of the others. In *Āthār* Abū Yūsuf, the ratio is about 1 to 5, and for *Āthār* Shaibānī, about 1 to 6.

The implications, in Schacht's view, are that traditions from the Prophet were less important at the time of Shaibānī than in the time of Mālik, who died ten years earlier. Yet we find Schacht asserting the contrary when he says:

> Being later, he [Abū Yūsuf] is subject to a stronger influence from traditions going back to the Prophet and Companions than Abū Ḥanīfa . . . Shaibānī's technical interest in traditions is attested to by his edition of Mālik's *Muwaṭṭa'*, and his habitual formula "We follow this" shows the degree to which he is, at least formally, under the influence of traditions.[47]

Traditions from the Prophet either became more important as time went on, or they became less important — but Schacht cannot ask us to believe in both views.

One final example should serve to illustrate the inherent contradictions on which this section of Schacht's thesis is based. In *An Introduction to*

---

[44] *Origins*, p. 57 (italics mine).
[45] *Origins*, p. 140.
[46] *Origins*, p. 22.
[47] *Origins*, pp. 33–34.

Islamic Law, he says: "An important aspect of the activity of the ancient schools of law was that they took the Koranic norms seriously for the first time."⁴⁸ Later, writing about the ancient schools of law and their attitude to traditions from the Prophet, he says: "Initially the ancient schools of law, the Medinese as well as the Iraqians, offered strong resistance to the disturbing element represented by the traditions which claimed to go back to the Prophet."⁴⁹ In *Origins of Muhammadan Jurisprudence*, speaking about Shāfi'ī, Schacht says: "Shāfi'ī bases his unquestioning acceptance of traditions from the Prophet on the Koranic passages which make it a duty to obey the Prophet."⁵⁰

The injunction of Almighty Allah to obey the Prophet is mentioned in the Qur'ān dozens of times. If the ancient schools of law took the Qur'ānic norms seriously, then they must surely have followed the traditions from the Prophet; yet Schacht wants us to believe that they offered strong resistance to them.

The aim of this discussion has been to demonstrate the weak foundations on which Schacht's theories of the position of *sunna* of the Prophet are based. The following account of his assertions about the doctrines of each of the schools he names should be viewed in that context.

Schacht on the Medinese School

Schacht's broad view of the position of traditions from the Prophet among the Medinese can be summarized in a few quotations. On one page he says: "Mālik enjoins that traditions be followed. . . [He] "harmonizes an old-established tradition from the Caliph Abū Bakr with historical traditions from the Prophet."⁵¹ Yet on the next page, Schacht maintains that Mālik is far behind Shāfi'ī in accepting traditions from the Prophet.⁵² Earlier, he says,

> The Medinese, then, and the ancient schools of law in general, had already used traditions from the Prophet as the basis of *many* decisions, but had *often* neglected them in favour of the reported practices or opinion of his Companions, not to mention their own established practice.⁵³

Let us first examine his use of these two words "many" and "often." He has provided the following figures for the number of traditions in the *Muwaṭṭa'* of Imām Mālik:

Traditions from the Prophet – 822
Traditions from the Companions – 613
Traditions from Successors – 285 ⁵⁴

---

⁴⁸ *Introduction*, p. 29.
⁴⁹ *Ibid.*, p. 35..
⁵⁰ *Origins*, p. 16.
⁵¹ *Origins*, p. 22.
⁵² *Ibid.*, p. 23.
⁵³ *Ibid.*, p. 13 (italics mine).

If we look at Mālik's treatment of these traditions, we find that he accepted 819 of the traditions from the Prophet and rejected only three.[55] Of the 613 traditions from Companions, he rejected 10[56] and challenged the authenticity of one other.[57] It is difficult to see how three rejections out of 822 traditions from the Prophet can be the basis for the assertion that they were "often neglected." On the contrary, it seems clear that Mālik was firm in his acceptance of the overriding authority of traditions from the Prophet.

Schacht, however, details a variety of means which he argues were used by the Medinese to get rid of or to minimize the importance of traditions from the Prophet. They can be listed as follows:

1. They chose freely among the traditions from the Prophet and from others.
2. They even rejected both kinds altogether.
3. They put reason and analogy before traditions.
4. Traditions from the Prophet were often superseded by traditions from Companions.
5. Traditions from the Prophet were disregarded for no apparent reason.
6. They were regularly interpreted in the light of tradition from Companions, on the assumption that the Companions knew the *sunna* of the Prophet best.
7. Opinions of a Companion prevailed over what the same Companion might relate from the Prophet.
8. Traditions from the Prophet were interpreted restrictively unless they were justified by traditions from Companions.[58]

Schacht concludes: "On the whole we can say that the Medinese give preference to traditions from Companions over traditions from the Prophet. This attitude, which is reflected in an anecdote on Zuhrī and Ṣāliḥ b. Kaisān in Ibn Sa'd . . . is of course unacceptable to Shāfi'ī."[59]

If we examine each of the "rules" in the above list in turn, we find that there is little basis for any of Schacht's assertions.

"Rules" 1 and 2. The Medinese (1) "chose freely among the traditions from the Prophet and from others," and (2) "even reject both kinds altogether." Rabī' says explicitly: "Our doctrine is to authenticate only

---

[54] *Ibid.*, p. 22.
[55] See *Muw.*, pp. 387, 486, and 617.
[56] *Ibid.*, pp. 86, 125, 206, 396, 449, 472, 608, 748, 826, and 851.
[57] *Ibid.*, p. 576.
[58] *Origins*, pp. 23–24.
[59] *Origins*, p. 24.

those traditions that are agreed upon by the people of Medīna, to the exclusion of other places (*Tr. iii*, 148, p. 242)."[60]

Rabī''s statement does not logically lead to Schacht's conclusion. Rabī''s statement means that they had doubts about traditions related by those other than the Medinese — i.e., they challenged their *authenticity*, not the authority. He himself uses the word "authenticate." But challenging their authenticity does not constitute "choosing freely"; on the contrary, it implies that there were rigid rules to validate the authenticity of traditions.

But even if we were to accept Schacht's interpretation, we are again confronted with the fact that this is not the writing of an accredited Medinese scholar but of an opponent. Rabī' was not Medinese by birth, nor did he follow the Medinese school. His biographers describe him as a follower of Shāfi'ī.[61] No one mentioned that he was a Medinese who was subsequently converted by Shāfi'ī — which is what Schacht suggests.[62] Thus we can hardly accept him as the spokesman for the Medinese.

"**Rule**" 3. "In the opinion of the Medinese, sound reason and analogy supersede traditions (*Tr. iii*, 145 [a])."[63] It should again be noted that this statement is based on Shāfi'ī's writing, not on Mālik's. Even so, it is falsely based. Shāfi'ī does not make this assertion. In fact, Shāfi'ī says that Mālik related a decision of Ibn 'Umar — not a tradition from the Prophet[64] — but gave a decision somewhat different from that of Ibn 'Umar. Shāfi'ī criticizes Mālik for rejecting Ibn 'Umar's opinion, saying what Mālik holds is even against sound reasoning and analogy.[65] He says:

« وتتركون ما شئتم بغير حجة فيما أخذتم ولا ماتركتم »

"And you abandon whatever you wish, without a sound argument for what you have accepted or for what you have rejected." There is no basis here for supposing that reasoning and analogy supersede traditions from the Prophet. Rather, the reverse is the case: Reasoning and analogy were used to show the weakness of an *athār* which was not followed by Mālik.

"**Rules**" **4 and 5.** Schacht has given us no evidence to support his assertion that traditions from the Prophet were often superseded by those from Companions and even disregarded for no apparent reason. We have

---

[60] *Origins*, p. 23. Since Schacht did not bring forward any argument concerning rule 2, it has been left without any discussion.
[61] See, for example, Nawāwī, *Tahdbīb Asmā'* (Reprinted in Beirut), vol. 1, pp. 188–189.
[62] *Origins*, General Index, p. 347.
[63] *Origins*, p. 23.
[64] It ought to be noted that Schacht is discussing the position of the traditions of the Prophet, thus he should not mention this example here.
[65] See *Tr*. iii, 145 (a), referring to *Umm* vii, 218, line 33.

already analyzed Mālik's treatment of traditions from the Prophet and from Companions."[66]

"Rules" 6, 7, and 8. The last three points deal with essentially the same subject — the relative weight given to the traditions from Companions as against those from the Prophet. Schacht claims that traditions from the Prophet were interpreted in the light of traditions from Companions, that opinions of a Companion prevailed over what the same Companion might relate from the Prophet, and that traditions from the Prophet were minimized or interpreted restrictively unless justified by traditions from Companions.

To clarify the misunderstandings underlying these assertions, we need to examine the special position accorded to the Companions. All scholars, even Shāfi'ī, grant them a special position. Schacht has criticized Shāfi'ī for this, saying that there is no theoretical basis for accepting the opinions of the Companions and it is only a remnant of the early doctrine of *sunna*.[67] There is, of course, both a theoretical and a practical basis for according them a privileged position.

First, one must consider the honor conferred on them by Allah. Thus, we read in the Qur'ān that Almighty Allah says:

وكذلك جعلناكم أمة وسطا لتكونوا شهداء على الناس ويكون الرسول عليكم شهيدا ، (سورة البقرة ١٤٣) [67]

Thus we have appointed you a middle nation that ye may be witness against mankind, and that the Messenger may be a witness against you.

Allah, speaking about the Muslims, of whom the Companions were the first, says:

كنتم خير أمة أخرجت للناس تأمرون بالمعروف وتنهون عن المنكر وتؤمنون بالله . [68]

Ye are the best community that hath been raised up for mankind. Ye enjoin right conduct and forbid indecency; and ye believe in Allah.

Speaking about the Companions, Almighty Allah says:

والسابقون الأولون من المهاجرين والانصار . والذين اتبعوهم بإحسان رضي الله عنهم ورضوا عنه ، وأعد لهم جنات تجري تحتها الأنهار خالدين فيها أبدا ذلك الفوز العظيم . [69]

And the first to lead the way, of the *Muhājirīn* and the *Anṣār*, and those who followed them in goodness — Allah is well pleased with them and they are well pleased with Him. . . .

Allah comforting His Messenger says:

---

[66] Chapter Five analyzes Mālik's treatment under two headings, "The Attitudes of the Medinese, Syrian, and Iraqian Schools" and "Schacht on the Medinese School."
[67] Qur'ān, 2:143.
[68] Qur'ān 3:110.
[69] Qur'ān, 9:100.

يا أيها النبي حسبك الله ومن اتبعك من المؤمنين . [70]

O Prophet! Allah is sufficient for thee and those who follow thee of the believers.

Elsewhere Allah's attitude to the Companions is described as follows:

لقد رضي الله عن المؤمنين إذ يبايعونك تحت الشجرة فعلم ما في قلوبهم فأنزل السكينة عليهم وأثابهم فتحا قريبا (سورة الفتح ١٨) . [71]

Allah was well pleased with the believers when they swore allegiance unto thee beneath the tree, and He knew what was in their hearts, and He sent down peace of reassurance on them and hath rewarded them with a near victory.

And the Qur'ān draws the following picture of the Muslim community of Medina and their sacrifices:

والذين تبوؤا الدار والايمان من قبلهم يحبون من هاجر اليهم ولا يجدون في صدورهم حاجة مما أوتوا ويؤثرون على أنفسهم ولو كان بهم خصاصة ومن يوق شح نفسه فأولئك هم المفلحون (الحشر ٩) [72]

And those who made their dwelling in the abode of *Hijra* and who were firm in belief, before them, they love whosoever has immigrated to them, not finding in their breasts any need for what they have been given, and preferring others above themselves, even though poverty be their portion. And who so is guarded against the avarice of his own soul, it is those who attain ultimate success.

These few verses show the position granted to the Companions in the Qur'ān. If one looks at their historical deeds, one finds further reason for according them a special place in Islam. They helped the Prophet when he was forced to migrate to Medina, and devoted all they had to the cause of Islam. In their generation, the Muslim faith was spread from India to Morocco, and in this endeavor they sacrificed not only their property but often their own lives and the lives of their families.

The third factor that explains the special position accorded to the Companions is that it was they who witnessed the birth of the Islamic state. In the life of the Prophet, all the rules and regulations of Islam were implemented through them, primarily in Medina. Some were appointed judges and governors by the Prophet, while others were made teachers and judges by the early caliphs. The Companions were thus among the first administrators of Islamic law. Clearly, then, they would have the closest understanding of Islamic jurisprudence in theory and practice, based on their experience of the life and teachings of the Prophet. Thus their opinions were given due weight in cases where the Prophet's statements needed interpretation.

---

[70] Qur'ān, 8:64.
[71] Qur'ān, 48:18.
[72] Qur'ān, *al-Hashr*, 59:9.

For all these reasons, the schools of law in the Muslim community accepted their position. It was therefore natural and logical for Shāfi'ī to attack the Iraqians and Medinese for not following the opinions of the Companions, just as he attacked them for not following certain traditions from the Prophet. The special status accorded to the Companions cannot properly be used as evidence of opposition to or neglect of traditions from the Prophet, since this status was granted because of their services to the Prophet in the course of Islam. It was unthinkable to the Muslim community that a Companion would knowingly go against a clear order of the Prophet. Thus, if he related something on the authority of the Prophet, and later came to hold a different view, it was believed that he had learned that the tradition he had originally related had been abrogated.

Schacht's overall conclusion is that "the Medinese give preference to traditions from Companions over traditions from the Prophet."[73] Let us examine the anecdote of Zuhrī and Ṣāliḥ b. Kaisān to which he refers. The latter was a contemporary of Zuhrī [51–124 A.H.], who was born a little earlier but studied with him in Medina. Here is the original text.

قال معمر : أخبرني صالح بن كيسان ، قال : « اجتمعت أنا والزهري ونحن نطلب العلم فقلنا نكتب السنن ، قال : وكتبنا ماجاء عن النبي صلى الله عليه وسلم ، قال ثم قال : نكتب ماجاء عن الصحابة فانه سنة ، قال قلت أنه ليس بسنة فلا نكتبه ، قال : فكتب ولم أكتب ، فأنجح وضيعت » (ابن سعد ٢/٢ : ١٣٥). [74]

Ṣāliḥ says: I met with Zuhrī, while we were both seeking knowledge. Thus we said, "Let us write down the *sunna*." We wrote down what was related from the Prophet. Then he [Zuhrī] said, "Let us write down what is related on the authority of the Companions, for it is [also] *sunna*." I told him that it is not *sunna*, therefore, we should not write it down. Zuhrī wrote it down, and I did not write it. He attained success, while I met with failure.

Does this really prove that the Medinese gave preference to traditions from the Companions? The two scholars *agreed* that what was related on the authority of the Prophet was *sunna* but differed on whether what was related on the authority of the Companions was also. Zuhrī's theory was clearly new and not commonly accepted. Ṣāliḥ's final comment — that Zuhrī succeeded whereas he failed — on which Schacht apparently rests his case, could mean no more than that Zuhrī had more knowledge than Ṣāliḥ. Even if it did mean that traditions related on the authority of the Companions eventually were regarded as *sunna*, we should note that Zuhrī clearly gives such traditions second place to the *sunna* of the Prophet, as he recorded first what was related on his authority.

An interesting final comment on the issue is that this example refutes another of Schacht's most important theories. He holds that all the traditions from the Prophet were fabricated in the second and third centuries. Yet here he quotes a scholar's statement which belongs most

---

[73] *Origins*, p. 24.
[74] Ibn Sa'd, vol. ii, part 2, p. 135.

probably to the third quarter of the first century and in whose time much information was recorded about traditions from the Prophet.

We may conclude that Schacht's theories about the Medinese view of the authority of the *sunna* of the Prophet are unfounded. I have shown that Mālik's view was that traditions from the Prophet had overriding authority, and that Schacht's mistaken ideas are based primarily on his use of polemical writings, on overgeneralization from them, and the arbitrary conclusions he draws from them. In the next two sections I shall demonstrate that he is similarly mistaken about the doctrines of the so-called Iraqians and the Syrians.

Schacht on the Iraqian School

Schacht's overall conclusion about the Iraqians is that

> the attitude of the Iraqians and of the Medinese to legal traditions is essentially the same, and differs fundamentally from that of Shāfiʿī. *Ikh.* 30 ff. shows that both the Iraqians and the Medinese neglect traditions from the Prophet in favour of systematic conclusions from general rules, or of opinions of the Companions; Shāfiʿī argues first (pp. 30 ff.) against the Medinese from the point of view of the Iraqians, and then (pp. 34 ff.) in turn against these; he says: "These same arguments apply to you when you follow the same method with regard to other traditions from the Prophet"; he states that both groups of opponents use the same arguments, and that his own arguments against both are the same, and he uses each party in order to refute the other.[75]

It must yet again be emphasized that these conclusions are based entirely on Shāfiʿī and not on the writings of the parties concerned — an objection that will by now be familiar to the reader. A further point of note, however, is the illogicality of the underlying assumption that both schools use the same methods in neglecting traditions from the Prophet. Were this the case, then they would have always been in agreement about accepting or rejecting certain traditions. But Shāfiʿī points out that this is not the case — sometimes the Iraqians were with him and the Medinese against him and at other times the reverse was the case. Clearly, there was considerable disagreement. In fact, Schacht himself seems to accept that there were basic differences in attitudes and approaches when he says: "The interpretation by the ancient Iraqians of those traditions which they accept, confirms that their decisive criterion is the previously established doctrine."[76]

Let us now look more closely at the "general rules" and arguments which Schacht claims the Iraqians used to restrict the use of traditions from the Prophet. He cites the following patterns:

---

[75] *Origins*, p. 21.
[76] *Origins*, p. 30.

1. Rejection of irregular tradition.[77]
2. Subordinating traditions from the Prophet to those from the Companions.[78]
3. Rejecting traditions because they disagreed with the Qur'ān or because the rule expressed in them was not mentioned in the Qur'ān or in parallel traditions from the Prophet or because nothing was said about them by the four caliphs who carried out the divine command after the Prophet.[79]
4. Arguing that "everyone has abandoned it."[80]
5. Saying that the general opinion was different and the tradition from the Prophet to the contrary could be explained away or considered repealed.[81]
6. Looking for contradictions in traditions and rejecting one of those that were in contradiction.[82]
7. Being unwilling to relate traditions from the Prophet, insisting on their small number and warning against careless attribution of traditions to the Prophet.[83]

1. Irregular traditions. This "general rule" is easily explained. The rejection of irregular *(shādhdh)* traditions was not confined to the Iraqians. They were universally rejected[84] in order to ensure that genuine traditions from the Prophet were not adulterated by spurious traditions — a matter which I shall go into in greater detail in the next two chapters.

2. Preference for Traditions from the Companions. Schacht says: "The Iraqian thesis of the overruling authority of traditions from the Prophet is definitely relegated to a subordinate place by the importance which the Iraqians attach, in theory and practice, to traditions from Companions. We find this principle explicitly formulated in many places, for instance, *Tr. I*, 89."[85] Here is the text:

قال الشافعي رحمه الله : وهم يزعمون أنهم لا يخالفون الواحد من أصحاب النبي صلى الله عليه وسلم ، وقد خالفوا حكم عمر . ويزعمون أنهم لا يقبلون من أحد ترك القياس ، وقد تركوه ، وقالوا فيه قولا متناقضا .[86]

Shāfi'ī said: They [Abū Ḥanīfa and his School] claim that they never differ from anyone of the Companions of the Prophet, yet they opposed the ruling of 'Umar. And they [also] claim that never accept from anyone to violate

---

[77] *Origins*, p. 28, quoting Abū Yūsuf.
[78] *Origins*, p. 29.
[79] *Origins*, pp. 21, 28, 30, and 46.
[80] *Ibid.*, p. 30.
[81] *Idem.*
[82] *Origins*, p. 47.
[83] *Idem.*
[84] See Suyūṭī, *Tadrīb*, (Cairo, 1379), vol. i, pp. 232-236.
[85] *Origins*, p. 29.
[86] *Umm*, vol. vii, p. 111. (*Tr.* 1, 89).

analogy, yet they themselves violated analogy, and brought forward contradicting opinions.

Here we have a perfect example of Schacht's arbitrary, self-contradictory use of his source material. The reference is to Shāfi'ī quoting Abū Ḥanīfa's claim that he never differs from any of the Companions of the Prophet, nor does he violate analogy. But Shāfi'ī points out that this is not so, since Abū Ḥanīfa in a particular case opposed the ruling of 'Umar. Shāfi'ī even accuses the Iraqians of violating analogy. Nowhere is there any indication that traditions from the Companions are preferred over those from the Prophet — the entire discussion centers on the Companions themselves. Therefore, Schacht's reference does not help in this regard. I have already explained at some length the reasons for the special status accorded to the Companions.[87] What must be remembered is that they gained this status because they had responsibilities as the guardians and transmitters of Prophetic knowledge. Their authority thus springs from the Prophet himself, so it is hardly likely that any scholar would accord them more importance than the Prophet.

To prove his point successfully, Schacht would need to show first that the Companions differed from the Prophet knowingly and second that Abū Ḥanīfa in the majority of those cases preferred the opinions of the Companions rather than the traditions from the Prophet. This he has not done.

3. Comparison with the Qur'an. Schacht says:

> The Iraqians reject traditions from the Prophet, because the tradition in question disagrees with the Koran [*Ikh.* 345 f.]; or because the rule expressed in it is not mentioned in the Koran [here Schacht notes in a footnote that Mālik argues against this reasoning of the Iraqians in *Muw.*, iii, 183] or in parallel traditions from the Prophet, and nothing similar to it is related from the four Caliphs who carried out the divine command after the Prophet [*Tr.* iii, 10] . . .[88]

As far as nonconformity with the Qur'ān is concerned, the two instances used by Schacht are in fact one case — that is, the judgment of an issue based on one witness and the oath of the plaintiff. Mālik enters into a lengthy discussion to show that this tradition is not in disagreement with the Qur'ān, where two witnesses have been required for judgment. Mālik, since he clearly accepts the rule that what contradicts the Qur'ān cannot be *sunna*, goes into great detail to prove his point to the Iraqians. All the scholars, including Shāfi'ī, agree that what contradicts the Qur'ān cannot be *sunna*.[89]

Schacht's inference that traditions were rejected on the grounds that

---

[87] Chapter Five discusses the Companions' status under the heading "Schacht on the Medinese School."
[88] *Origins*, p. 30.
[89] Shāfi'ī, *Risāla*, (Cairo, 1940) p. 228.

they contradicted parallel traditions or the actions of the four caliphs is similarly unfounded. His reference is to a difference of opinion between Abū Ḥanīfa or Ibrāhīm Nakha'ī and other scholars concerning *zakāt* on agricultural produce, though he does not quote the complete discussion. Nakha'ī and Abū Ḥanīfa consider every product liable to taxation, while others consider products of less than five *wasaq* (a unit of measurement) to be exempt. It seems that Abū Ḥanīfa considered three factors:

1. The divine order to take *zakāt* from everything.[90]
2. A tradition from the Prophet that demands one-tenth of all production, if it was irrigated by rainwater only.[91]
3. Another tradition from the Prophet that there is no *zakāt* on production below five *wasaq*.[92]

Abū Ḥanīfa considers factors 1 and 2 to reinforce each other, and therefore challenges the authenticity of 3. In support of this challenge, a spokesman for Abū Ḥanīfa comments to Shāfi'ī that *zakāt* has been collected by the central government since the time of the Prophet but that he has seen no letter of the Prophet written for this purpose which may support the doctrine otherwise, nor has he knowledge of any instruction about the matter from the four caliphs.

Schacht's statement is clearly misleading. As far as Abū Ḥanīfa is concerned, the choice is between a tradition supported by a divine order and a tradition supported by no other evidence. This is hardly proof that traditions were rejected wholesale because they were not supported by the deeds of the four caliphs. Moreover, three other Iraqians — Al-Thaurī of Kūfa,[93] Abū Yūsuf,[94] and Shaibānī[95] — all disagree with Abū Ḥanīfa and Nakha'ī. The weight of evidence, therefore, indicates that more Iraqians accepted than rejected the traditions, favoring no *zakāt* on less than five *wasaq*. Therefore, Schacht's conclusion is invalid.

4. General Disuse. The argument that traditions were rejected on the grounds that "everyone has abandoned it" is based on Shāfi'ī's record *Ikh.* 336 relating to the Iraqian attitude. Sources prior to Shāfi'ī reject this statement. Ibn Abī Lailā, for example, did not accept it, and the very *ḥadīth* Schacht refers to is quoted by Abū Ḥanīfa who deduced certain rules from it.[96] Ṭaḥāwī tells us of Abū Yūsuf's opinion, which agrees with the *ḥadīth*;[97] and although it is not so well known as Abū Yūsuf's opinion, Abū Yūsuf's own writing tends to support Ṭaḥāwī's statement. Given

---

[90] Qur'ān, 6:141.
[91] See *Kharāj*, p. 54.
[92] *Idem.*
[93] See *Muṣannaf*, iv, 142; Thaurī [97–161 A.H.] was a contemporary of Abū Ḥanīfa.
[94] See *Kharāj*, p. 53.
[95] See *Muw. Shaib.*, p. 169.
[96] Ibn Abī Lailā, 16–17.
[97] Ṭaḥāwī, *Sharaḥ Ma'ānī al-Āthār* (Cairo), 18, 19.

these disagreements among the Iraqians, it is wrong to say that they typically used this device to discredit or disregard traditions from the Prophet. All that can be said is that this particular *ḥadīth* was rejected by certain Iraqi scholars and accepted by certain others.

5. General Opinion and Repeal. For the next device — that general opinion was different and the tradition from the Prophet to the contrary could be explained away or considered repealed — Schacht takes as his source *Muw. Shaib.* 142. This concerns the reciting of the Qur'ān in an evening prayer, at which time, according to a tradition from the Prophet, the shortest *sūras* are preferred. *Sūrat Ṭūr* is lengthy, and Shaibānī gives a different interpretation for this *ḥadīth*. This does not, however, mean that "general opinion" was given precedence over a *ḥadīth* from the Prophet. The sunset prayer is said all over the Muslim world, and people learned this through daily practice from the time of the Prophet as well as through verbal *aḥādīth* from the Prophet. Shaibānī interpreted this tradition in the light of these facts.

6. Contradictions. Schacht's assertions that the Iraqians sought to find contradictions in two traditions and then reject one of them is again based on Shāfi'ī (*Ikh.* 328) rather than on explicit or implicit statements by the Iraqians. There are, no doubt, *aḥādīth* that contradict each other and others that appear to be contradictory. Few scholars achieved Shāfi'ī's success in harmonizing these apparent contradictions and, in the passage cited, Shāfi'ī is simply teaching his opponent the art of reconciliation.

7. Reticence and Conservation. Schacht says:

> The antitraditionist attitude showed itself further in (1) unwillingness to relate traditions from the Prophet, (2) insistence on their small number, (3) warning against careless attribution of traditions to the Prophet, and similar considerations which were especially popular in Iraq.[98]

But Schacht does not appear to have paid sufficient attention to the heading of the chapter. Dārimī calls it باب من هاب الفتيا which means "chapter on those who were afraid of giving judicial opinion [*fatwā*]," and the chapter contains 27 *āthār*, primarily on this subject. Clearly, a Muftī would be conscious of his responsibility to give correct opinions and show the right way to Allah's *Sharī'a*. He could hardly be considered antitraditionist if he preferred to be certain that his opinions were based on authentic traditions and warned others to do the same. To stigmatize this protection of the purity of traditions as antitraditionist is tantamount to calling a mathematics teacher who advises his pupils to follow the rules carefully an "antimathematician," or to say that every government with a department to check on counterfeit currency is "antimoney." This is obviously an absurd conclusion.

---

[98] *Origins*, p. 47. Schacht's reference is to Dārimī, *Sunan, bab man hāb al-futyā.*
[99] See Dārimī, *Sunan*, vol. I, pp. 50–64.

Schacht does not tell us how many traditions were rejected by the Iraqians as a result of these numerous "general rules" and how this number compared with those that were accepted. In fact, only a handful were rejected as against thousands that the Iraqians as a whole accepted. Scholars will always disagree, finding traditions unacceptable on the grounds of lack of documentation or some other reason. Even Shāfi'ī, who is the champion of the cause of *sunna*, according to Schacht, has been charged by Ibn 'Abdul Ḥakam of neglecting the Qur'ān and the *sunna* of the Prophet in a work entitled *al-Radd 'alā ash-Shāfi'ī fimā Khālufa fīhi al-kitāb was sunna*.[100]

If we were to believe every scholar's accusations against his fellows, few would be found who were total adherents of the Qur'ān and the *sunna* of the Prophet. This indicates that we should formulate the doctrine of a school only on the basis of its own explicit statements, and not on the basis of opponents' texts. But, as we have seen, Schacht has often overlooked or disregarded explicit statements by those he calls the Iraqians, preferring to rely on conclusions based on Shāfi'ī's polemics. It may therefore be instructive at this point to quote statements by Abū Yūsuf and Shaibānī that show conclusively the position of the *sunna* of the Prophet among these scholars. Abū Yūsuf says: "That has been fixed by the Prophet, thus it is not allowed for the Caliph to change it."[101] Shaibānī echoes him with "No one has authority besides the Prophet."[102] These are not isolated sentiments but are repeated in hundreds of other examples throughout their books.

Schacht on Auzā'ī's Attitude

According to Schacht, "Auzā'ī is the only representative of the Syrians on whom we have authentic information in *Tr. IX* and in Ṭabarī, and his attitude to traditions is essentially the same as that of the Medinese and the Iraqians."[103]

On this, at least, we may agree with Schacht. Auzā'ī *is* in agreement with the other scholars, who are unanimous in their view of the overriding authority of the traditions from the Prophet, as has been shown. Schacht's view of the attitude of the Iraqians and the Medinese is, however, fundamentally different, as we have seen. Let us look at his evidence. To support his case, Schacht says:

> Auzā'ī states, quoting Koran xxxiii. 21, that "the Prophet is a good example" (*Tr.* IX. 23), and that "the Prophet deserves most to be followed and to have his *sunna* observed" (#50), but in order to establish the practice of the

---

[100] See Subkī, *Ṭabaqāt al-Shāfa 'īya al-Kubrā*, (Cairo, 1964), vol. 2, p. 69.
[101] See Chapter One for discussion of the Medinese and Syrian concepts of the Living Tradition. See also *Kharāj*, p. 58.
[102] See *Al-Ḥujja*, i, pp. 45, 204.
[103] *Origins*, p. 34.

Prophet he refers to "what happened at the time of the Prophet and afterwards" (#26 and elsewhere). He refers to Ibn 'Umar beside the Prophet (#31), and to Abū Bakr, 'Umar, and the Umaiyad Caliph 'Umar b. 'Abdal'azīz by themselves.[104]

From this the reader is doubtless meant to infer that the Prophet's words or practice could not stand alone and required the support of others' actions, while others stood for themselves. If this supposition is correct, we need only refer to Auzā'ī's treatise to refute it. In this work, Auzā'ī cited actions of the Prophet that were later followed by Muslims, 10 times; actions of Muslims and their *Imāms,* six times; actions of the Prophet alone, nine times; traditions from the Prophet, three times; and practices of others, five times — Abū Bakr twice and 'Umar, 'Alī b. Abī Ṭālib, and 'Umar b. 'Abdal'azīz once.[105]

Thus we find 12 references to the Prophet alone and 22 references to the Prophet's actions in total, as against 11 references to others alone. Add to this Auzā'ī's own assertion, quoted by Schacht, that "the Prophet deserves most to be followed."[106] This fact explicitly contradicts Schacht's assumption. We can only conclude that Auzā'ī's attitude to the authority of the *sunna* of the Prophet is the same as that of the rest of the scholars. He conforms with the Divine order: Obey Allah and Obey the Messenger.[107]

Further Questions on the Methods of the Antitraditionists

Before going on to the next chapter, specific devices of the antitraditionists, as cited by Schacht,[108] a few cases remain for discussion.

Schacht's citation number 1:
". . . traditionists reject some *ḥadīth* as unacceptable on certain grounds and that if it is possible to reject some it is possible to reject all."[107]

First, it ought to be noted that this is simply a hypothesis and does not indicate that the argument was used in rejecting *ḥadīth*. Second, it is hardly possible to prove that the said scholar belongs to an ancient school of law. Furthermore, even if he belongs to one of the schools he might not have been able to reconcile the problem in the face of the problem he mentioned. Therefore, his statement cannot be taken as a device to get rid of the traditions of the Prophet. Abū Ḥātim Al-Rāzī [d. 275 A.H.], one of the most famous critics of *ḥadīth*, says that one of the lawyers brought a

---

[104] *Origins*, p. 34.
[105] For more detail, see the discussion of the Syrian and Iraqian concepts of the Living Tradition in Chapter One.
[106] *Origins*, p. 34.
[107] See, Tr. *IX*, #50.
[108] See *Origins*, pp. 44–45.

book to him containing *aḥādīth*. After going through it, Rāzī declared that some of them were authentic and some weak and unacceptable. The lawyer objected to his judgment, asking "Has the author of the book informed you that he committed certain mistakes or that he told a lie in certain other *ḥadīth*?"[109] Imām Muslim also records the objection of some people on the statements of *Muḥaddithīn* that a certain *ḥadīth* is correct and a certain other one is wrong, i.e., that this amounted to claiming unseen knowledge, impossible to obtain: مدع علم غيب لا يوصل إليه [110]

Can we assume from these two statements that this was the trend of *Muḥaddithīn*, that they thought it was impossible to differentiate between correct *ḥadīth* and false ones? As far as this objection is concerned, Imām Shāfi'ī has provided a very sound answer. He explains the case giving an example of a judge who accepts the evidence of a witness whom he knows to be reliable, rejects one whose character is objectionable, and reserves judgment on the evidence of a third whose status he does not know.[111] Likewise, if one challenges a tradition, it does not mean that all the traditions should be challenged.

Schacht's citation number 2:
". . . many traditions are contrary to reason [*naẓar*] and observation and therefore absurd and ridiculous."

Schacht ascribes this to the *ahl al-kalām*, saying: "It is worth noticing that this kind of reasoning which occurs continuously in Ibn Qutaiba, is not discussed by Shāfi'ī."[112]

It ought to be noticed that this sort of objection is mentioned by the *ahl-kalām*, who, after all, were not lawyers (*fuqahā'*); therefore, this device should not be mentioned by Schacht as representative of the ancient schools of law. Furthermore, as Schacht notices this sort of objection is frequently mentioned in Ibn Qutaiba (d. 276 A.H.) and not discussed by Shāfi'ī (d. 204 A.H.) It indicates that this is a later trend after the death of Shāfi'ī; otherwise he would most likely have discussed it. Therefore it is a post-Shāfi'ī development and not pre-Shāfi'ī.

Schacht's citation number 4:
". . . the Qur'ān repeals traditions."

It ought to be noted that there are verses in the Qur'ān which were abrogated by Almighty Allah. He says:

(ما ننسخ من آية أو ننسها نأت بخير منها أو مثلها . ألم تعلم أن الله على كل شيء قدير) . [113]

For whatever verse we abrogate or cast into oblivion to be forgotten, we

---

[109] Ibn Abī Ḥātim al-Rāzī, *Introduction*, (Hydrabad, 1360), pp. 349–351.
[110] Muslim, *Tamyīz*, (Riyadh, 1395), p. 123.
[111] *Ikh.*, pp. 366–368.
[112] *Origins*, p. 45.
[113] Qur'ān, 2:106.

bring a better in its stead or the like of it. Knowest thou not that God is powerful over everything.

There are differences of opinion as to whether or not the Qur'ān can be abrogated by *sunna*. Some of the scholars maintain that the Qur'ān can be abrogated by the *sunna*.[114] Would it be rational to suppose that those scholars who hold the later doctrine are antiQur'ān? How can a Muslim be labelled as antiQur'ān? If one is antiQurān then one would no longer remain a Muslim. The same could be applied in this case.

Schacht citation number 8:
". . . an injunction was for a particular case and not meant as a general rule."

Here Schacht says: "Another easy method of disposing of traditions from the Prophet by interpretation was to represent them as particular commands, applicable only to the occasion on which they were given."[115] By way of illustration he cites the example of "artificial creation of foster-parentship between adults [*Muw*. iii. 89]. According to it, 'Ā'isha made a habit of this practice, but the other wives of the Prophet regarded his ruling as a special one for the benefit of the individual in question.[116] Schacht comments:

> The argument is meant to invalidate the tradition related from 'Āisha in favour of the *practice*. The antitraditionist argument in its turn was met by two counterarguments. According to one, 'Ā'isha referred, against her fellow wife Umm Salama, to the example of the Prophet . . . According to the second the other wives of the Prophet were engaged in the same practice.[117]

The explanation of this case as an attack and a counterattack seems to me out of the question. We find judges sitting on the same bench, hearing the same case, having the same written law, possessing the same academic degree, yet differing widely on their judgments in many cases. Are such disagreements then genuine? Scholars often agree and on other occasions disagree honestly. Or do they reflect underlying pro- and anti-law attitudes on the part of the men involved? If scholars often honestly disagree today, then why should it not also be the case with these early scholars that they disagreed honestly and sincerely on certain issues, one of them mentioned above. If Schacht wanted us to believe otherwise, he ought to have proved that this rule cannot be applied to those scholars.

Let us discuss the case on his own terms. First, the Qur'ān refers to the practice of foster-parentship.[118] Furthermore, it mentions the period of

---

[114] See al-Bihārī, *Musallam ath-thubūt*, vol. i, p. 349.
[115] *Origins*, p. 48.
[116] *Idem*.
[117] *Idem* (italics mine).
[118] Qur'ān, 4:23.

nursing, or in other words feeding by breast for two years.[119] Thus the scholars are unanimous on this sort of parentship, if the baby was fed within two years of age. However, there is disagreement about the quantity: i.e., whether it ought to be fed several times or whether it is sufficient for it to have had just one nursing.[120] But the case under discussion pertains to adults: Can foster-parentship be established even in adulthood? The case referred to concerns a grownup boy. 'Ā'isha alone took it as a precedent, while others thought it a personal concession. Against this background, let us check Schacht's arguments:

According to Schacht, the argument was made by an antitraditionist to invalidate the tradition of 'Ā'isha and was met by two counterarguments by traditionists. A few points may be noted here:

1. Both traditions have been recorded by traditionists[121] and they did not perceive any "antitraditionist feeling."
2. If the traditionists transmitted two arguments in favor of 'Ā'isha against the counterargument of an antitraditionist, then why they did not formulate their own doctrine in accordance with the tradition of 'Ā'isha? They unanimously held the opposite view.[122]
3. According to Schacht, the second counterargument of the traditionists in favor of 'Ā'isha's doctrine was that other wives of the Prophet were engaged in the same practice. However, this is contrary to the text cited. The original text is: وهو صغير يرضع ("He was a baby under nursing").[123] And in another one: وهو يوم أرضعته صغير يرضع ("And when she fed him by her breast, he was a baby under nursing").[124] The meanings are the same. Thus it is out of context, because there is no difference of opinion in the case of the child under two years of age.

It has been argued in this chapter that, both in theory and practice, Schacht was wrong to assert that the ancient schools of law offered strong resistence to traditions from the Prophet, although a small group of uninfluential antitraditionists (who ought not to be confused with the Mu'tazila sect as Schacht has done) did exist. Rather than hostility and resistance, the schools of Mālik, Abū Ḥanīfa, and Auzā'ī evidence strong adherence to the traditions from the Prophet. It has also been demonstrated that Schacht's misconceptions about these schools arise from arbitrary use of source material and a tendency to generalize from a few examples.

---

[119] Qur'ān, 2:233.
[120] Zurqānī, *Commentory on Muwaṭṭā* (Cairo, 1310), iii, 242–243. Cited hereafter as Zurqānī or *Muw.*, giving the volume and page numbers.
[121] See *Mus., Riḍā'a,* p. 29.
[122] Zurqānī, iii, 247.
[123] Zurqānī, iii, 242.
[124] *Muw. Shaib,* 272.

In the following chapters we turn to an examination of Schacht's theories on how the traditions from the Prophet imposed themselves on the old idea of the *sunna*, and how scholars of the ancient schools of law projected their sayings back to the Prophet.

Chapter Six

The *Sunna* of the Prophet in Transition

Was the *Sunna* of the Prophet Imposed on the Old Idea of *Sunna*?

Given the thesis that the *sunna* of the Prophet came into existence at a late stage, and that the "living tradition" was the basis for legal judgments in the formative period of Islamic law, Schacht needs to show how the *sunna* of the Prophet came to achieve its ultimate status in Islamic law.

He infers from the writing of Ibn Muqaffaʿ that the early scholars' definition of *sunna* was different from that of Shāfiʿī. Although it has already been shown that this inference is erroneous, let us, nonetheless, follow Schacht along his chosen path. In his own words: "The early texts contain numerous traces of the process by which traditions from the Prophet imposed themselves on the old idea of *sunna* and thereby prepared the ground for Shāfiʿī's identification of *sunna* with them."[1] He uses three examples in support of this.

Example 1

Schacht says:

> In *Ikh.* 284, the Iraqian opponent points out that Shāfiʿī's reasoning, which starts from traditions, is new compared with that of Shāfiʿī's companions, the Medinese, who base themselves on practice. Shāfiʿī replies: "I have told you before that practice means nothing, and we cannot be held responsible for what others say; so stop arguing about it."[2]

Schacht's main point here is that the Medinese reasoning used to start from practice while Shāfiʿī introduced a new methodology — arguing from traditions from the Prophet.

The case at issue is that of speaking during prayer. Shāfiʿī reported a well-known tradition from Ibn Masʿūd, who said:

> We used to give *salāms* to the Prophet, even if he was praying, and he used to answer our greeting *(salām)*, but when I came back from Ethiopia [where he

---

[1] *Origins*, p. 59.
[2] *Origins*, p. 59.

migrated in the early years of the Meccan period] I gave *salām* to the Prophet while he was praying, and he did not return my *salām*. After praying, the Prophet informed him that Allah had decreed it forbidden to speak with anyone while praying.³

Another related tradition is transmitted by several Companions who prayed with the Prophet in Medina. The Prophet inadvertently ended the prayer without completing it, praying only two *rak'as* instead of four. One of them asked the Prophet whether it had been reduced to two or whether he had forgotten to pray four. The Prophet replied neither. The other Companions confirmed that he had prayed only two *rak'as*, upon which the Prophet prayed two more *rak'as* and thus completed the four. This tradition is known as the tradition of Dhul Yadain.

These two traditions have given rise to differences of opinion among scholars about the validity of prayer interrupted by speaking in the case referred to above. Shāfi'ī's view is that if the man spoke without realizing that he had not finished his prayer and then he realized that he had not done so, the earlier part of the prayer was valid and he only needed to complete his prayer. However, if he became aware that he had not finished, yet nonetheless spoke, then he would have to repray. The second view is that if the man realized that he had not completed the prayer and even then he spoke about that prayer itself, the earlier prayer was valid and he needed to complete his prayer. This is the Medinese view.

However, the Iraqian view is that the prayer is invalid *(fāsid)* if one speaks without completing the prayer, whether one has spoken intentionally or inadvertently. The opponent charged Shāfi'ī with deviating from tradition in certain cases (see *Ikh*. 278). Shāfi'ī denied the charge.

Both Shāfi'ī and his opponents considered their own views to be backed by traditions from the Prophet. The following is the last portion of the dialogue:

(باب الخلاف في الكلام في الصلاة)

[ناقش الشافعي مخالفه وكان يزعم مخالفه ان الشافعي يخالف حديث ذي اليدين وجرى بينهما الحديث التالي :

قال مخالفه للشافعي]فأسألك حتى أعلم أخالفته أم لا ؟ : قلت

فسل .

ما تقول في إمام انصرف من اثنتين فقال له بعض من صلى معه قد : قال انصرفت من اثنتين ، فسأل آخرين ، فقالوا : صدق .

أما المأموم الذي أخبره والذين شهدوا أنه صدق ـ وهم على ذكر من أنه لم : قلت يقض صلاته ـ فصلاتهم فاسدة .

فأنت تروي أن النبي صلى الله عليه وسلم قضى ، وتقول : قد قضى معه : قال من حضر وإن لم تذكره في الحديث .

---

³ See *IKH*, p. 275.

قلت :	أجل .
قال :	فقد خالفته .
قلت :	لا . ولكن حال أمامنا مفارقة حال رسول الله .
قال :	فأين افتراق حاليهما في الصلاة والإمامة ؟
قال ، فقلت له :	إن الله كان ينزل على رسوله فرضا بعد فرض فيفرض عليه مالم يكن فرضه عليه ويخفف عنه بعض فرضه .
قال :	أجل .
قلت :	ولا نشك نحن ولا أنت ولا مسلم أن رسول الله لم ينصرف إلا وهو يرى ان قد أكمل الصلاة .
قال :	أجل .
قلت :	فلما فعل لم يدر ذو اليدين أقصرت الصلاة بحادث من الله ، أم نسي النبي وكان ذلك بينا في مسئلته إذ قال : أقصرت الصلاة أم نسيت ؟
قال :	أجل .
قلت :	ولم يقبل النبي من ذي اليدين إذ سأل غيره .
قال :	....
قلت :	ولما سأل غيره احتمل أن يكون سأل من لم يسمع كلامه فيكون مثله ، واحتمل أن يكون سأل من سمع كلامه ولم يسمع النبي رد عليه ، فلما لم يسمع النبي رد عليه كان في معنى ذي ـ اليدين من أنه لم يسمع النبي رد عليه كان في معنى ذي ـ اليدين من أنه لم يستدل النبي بقوله ، ولم يدر أقصرت الصلاة أم نسي النبي ، فأجابه ، ومعناه معنى ذي اليدين من أن الفرض عليهم جوابه ، ألا ترى أن النبي لما أخبروه فقبل قولهم لم يتكلم ولم يتكلموا حتى بنوا على صلاتهم . فلما قبض الله رسوله تناهت فرائضه فلا يزاد فيها ولا ينقص منها أبدا .
قال :	نعم .
فقلت :	هذا فرق بيننا وبينه .
فقال من حضره :	هذا فرق بين لا يرده عالم لبيانه ووضوحه .
فقال :	فإن من أصحابكم من قال : ما تكلم به الرجل في أمر الصلاة لم يفسد صلاته . قال فقلت له : إنما الحجة علينا ما قلنا لا ما قال غيرنا .
قال الشافعي وقال :	قد كلمت غير واحد من أصحابك فما احتج بهذا ولقد قال : العمل على هذا ، فقلت له : قد أعلمتك أن العمل ليس له معنى ، ولا حجة لك علينا بقول غيرنا .
قال :	أجل .
قلت :	فدع ما لا حجة لك فيه .

أنظر الأم جـ ٧ ص ٢٨٢-٢٨٤ :[4]

Opponent: May I ask you a question to know whether or not you have deviated [from the Prophet's tradition]?

Shāfi'ī: Ask.

Opponent: What do you say regarding an *Imām* who left the prayer having performed two [*rak'a* instead of three or four *rak'a*] and who was told by a follower who prayed behind him that he prayed

---

[4] See margin of *Umm*, vol *VII*, pp. 282–284.

	only two *rak'a*? He [*Imām*] asked others from the congregation and they said that the man told the truth.
Shāfi'ī:	As for the follower who informed him and the others who bore witness that he told the truth — all knowing that the *Imām* did not complete the prayer — their prayer is invalid *(fāsid)*.
Opponent:	You transmit that the Prophet made up for his incomplete prayer [in a similar case] and hold that those present with him in the prayer did the same though you do not mention that in the tradition?
Shāfi'ī:	I do [accept your statement].
Opponent:	Then you have deviated.
Shāfi'ī:	No. But the position of our *Imām* is different from that of the Messenger of Allah.
Opponent:	Where is the difference between them concerning the prayer and *imāma* [the leading of prayer]?
Shāfi'ī:	Allah revealed unto his Messenger obligations one after the other, commanding him new obligations not revealed before or reducing previous obligations.
Opponent:	Yes.
Shāfi'ī:	And neither we nor you or any other Muslim doubts that the Prophet ended the prayer in the full conviction that he had completed it.
Opponent:	Yes.
Shāfi'ī:	When he did, Dhul Yadain [the man who informed the Prophet that he did not complete the prayer] did not know whether the prayer was shortened by a command from Allah or whether the Prophet had forgotten, and that was clear from his question [to the Prophet]: "Has the prayer been shortened or have you forgotten?"
Opponent:	Yes.
Shāfi'ī:	And the Prophet did not accept Dhul Yadain's statement, since he asked others.
Opponent:	Yes.
Shāfi'ī:	And when he asked others, then it is possible that he asked someone who did not hear his previous conversation, thus he would be like him [Dhul Yadain]. And it is [also] possible that he asked someone who heard Dhul Yadain's enquiry but did not hear the reply of the Prophet. When he did not hear the reply of the Prophet to Dhul Yadain, he was like him, that the Prophet did not accept his statement, and did not know whether the prayer was shortened or the Prophet forgot it. Then he replied to the Prophet. His case is similar to that of Dhul Yadain, and it was obligatory upon them to reply to the Prophet. Do you not notice that when they informed the Prophet, and he accepted their statements, he did not speak, nor did they, until they completed their whole prayer.
	And when Allah called back his Messenger, Allah's obligations were completed, never to be added to or decreased later on by anyone else.
Opponent:	Yes.

Shāfi'ī:	This is the difference between us and the Prophet.
People present:	This is such a clear difference that no knowing person would oppose it because of its clarity.
Opponent:	But some of your fellows said that if the man spoke about the prayer [the act of speaking] it did not invalidate his prayer.
Shāfi'ī:	Verily our responsibility is for what we have said and not for what we have not said.
Opponent:	I have spoken to more than one of your fellows and they did not reason as you did but said that the practice was thus.
Shāfi'ī:	I have informed you that the practice has no meaning and you have no argument against us because of the statement of other persons.
Opponent:	Yes.
Shāfi'ī:	Then leave that for which you have no argument.

Schacht uses this example to try to show how traditions from the Prophet supplanted the old idea of *sunna* — in this case defined as Medinese "practice." His conclusions, however, are based on false premises. It is important to note that both parties are arguing from traditions from the Prophet; their differences revolve around interpretation only. Shāfi'ī is defending himself against the accusation that he opposes a tradition from the Prophet which he narrated himself. Thus the case reverses — far from imposing a tradition from the Prophet that runs counter to pragmatic reasoning, he is in fact applying his rational faculty to a tradition from the Prophet and nullifying its effect.

Moreover, while the Medinese used the word "practice" to explain their doctrine in this case, they were actually referring to this well-known tradition, that is, a practice which started from the Prophet.

EXAMPLE 2

Schacht says: "Similarly, in *Tr. III*, 148 (p. 243), Shāfi'ī addresses a Baṣrian opponent: If you answered consistently with your principle, you ought to hold that men are obliged to act, not according to what is related from the Prophet, but according to a corresponding practice or lack of practice after him." The opponent replies: "I do not hold that." But this refers only to the negative consequence which Shāfi'ī forces on him, as appears from his further reply: "There can be no *sunna* of the Prophet on which the caliphs have not acted after him."[5]

As in the first example, it is difficult to see how this quotation can be used to prove that traditions from the Prophet imposed themselves on the old idea of *sunna*. The point at this issue is not "practice" as opposed to traditions from the Prophet, but rather the procedure for the establishment of *sunna* of the Prophet. Because of the possibility of a tradition being abrogated, or some mistake being made in its transmission, some

---

[5] *Origins*, p. 59.

scholars from Baṣra held that a tradition was only to be accepted if the caliphs had acted upon it. Again, both parties accept the overriding authority of traditions from the Prophet; their disagreement is only on how these *sunna* are established. Let us look more closely at the discussion:

المحادثة بين الشافعي ومخالفه
(يعمل بالخبر الواحد إذا عمل به إمام من قبل)

قال الشافعي : قلت له أرأيت الفرض علينا وعلى من قبلنا في اتباع سنة رسول الله صلى الله عليه وسلم أليس واحدا ؟

قال : بلى

فقلت : إذا كان أبو بكر خليفة النبي صلى الله عليه وسلم والعامل بعده فورد عليه خبر واحد عن النبي صلى الله عليه وسلم . وأبو بكر لا مدة بينه وبين النبي صلى الله عليه وسلم يمكنه فيها أن يعمل بالخبر فلا يترك ، ما تقول فيه ؟

قال أقول : انه يقبله ويعمل به .

فقلت : قد ثبت إذا الخبر ولم يتقدمه عمل من أحد بعد عن النبي صلى الله عليه وسلم يثبته لأنه لم يكن بينهما إمام فيعمل بالخبر ولا يدعه وهو مخالف في هذا حال من بعده .

قال الشافعي : فقلت : أرأيت إذا جاء الخبر في آخره ولا يعمل به ولا بما يخالفه في أول عمره وقد عاش أكثر من سنة يعمل ، فما تقول فيه ؟

قال : يقبله .

فقلت : فقد قبل خبرا لم يتقدمه عمل .

قال الشافعي : لو أجبت إلى النصفة على أصل قولك يلزمك أن لا يكون على الناس العمل بما جاء عن النبي صلى الله عليه وسلم إلا بأن يعمل به من بعده أو يترك العمل لأنه إذا كان للإمام الأول أن يدعه لم يعمل به كان جميع من بعده من الأئمة في مثل حاله لأنه لابد أن يبتديء العمل به الإمام الأول أو الثاني أو من بعده .

قال : فلا أقول هذا .

قال الشافعي : فما تقول في عمر ـ وأبو بكر إمام قبله ـ إذا ورد عليه خبر الواحد لم يعمل به أبو بكر ولم يخالفه ؟

قال : يقبله .

قلت : أيقبله ولم يعمل به أبو بكر ؟

قال : نعم ولم يخالفه .

قلت : أفيثبت ولم يتقدمه عمل ؟

قال : نعم .

قلت : وهكذا عمر في آخر خلافته وأولها ؟

قال : نعم

قلت : وهكذا عثمان ؟

قال : نعم .

قلت : زعمت ان الخبر عن النبي صلى الله عليه وسلم يلزم ولم يتقدمه عمل قبله وقد ولي الأئمة ولم يعملوا به ولم يدعوه .

قال :   فلا يمكن أن تكون للنبي صلى الله عليه وسلم سنة إلا عمل بها الأئمة بعده [6].

Shāfi'ī: Do you agree that we as well as those before us are equal in obligation to follow the *sunna* (traditions) of the Prophet?
Opponent: Of course.
Shāfi'ī: If Abū Bakr was the successor of the Prophet and the one who was in charge [of the community] after him came to know about a tradition from the Prophet, although there is no time gap between Abū Bakr and the Prophet, he would be able to act upon it and thus not abandon it; what do you say about this *sunna*?
Opponent: He would accept it and act accordingly.
Shāfi'ī: The tradition is thus confirmed although nobody after the Prophet acted upon it to confirm it because there was no *Imām* (Caliph) between them [the Prophet and Abū Bakr] to act on it or abandon it. In this way Abū Bakr is different from those after him.

Now, suppose that the tradition was known in the last days of [Abū Bakr] and he neither acted upon it nor acted contrary to it in his early days and he lived working for more than one year [after the Prophet]; what do you say?
Opponent: He would accept it.
Shāfi'ī: Then he would have accepted a tradition not preceded by an action. If you are fair to your principal statement you will have to accept that people are not obliged to act according to a tradition of the Prophet except when such a tradition was acted upon or it should be abandoned because if the first *Imām* could abandon it then all following *Imāms* would be in the same situation, as action must be started by the first, the second, or the succeeding *Imām*.
Opponent: I do not say so.
Shāfi'ī: What do you say then about 'Umar [and Abū Bakr preceded him as *Imām*] if he received a tradition not acted upon by Abū Bakr nor contradicted by him?
Opponent: He should accept it.
Shāfi'ī: Should he accept it although it was not acted upon by Abū Bakr?
Opponent: Yes. He [Abū Bakr] did not act contrary to it.
Shāfi'ī: Would it be confirmed though it was not preceded by an action?
Opponent: Yes.
Shāfi'ī: And so with 'Umar in the beginning and the end of his Caliphate?
Opponent: Yes.
Shāfi'ī: And so with 'Uthmān?
Opponent: Yes.

---

[6] *Umm*, vol. *VII*, p. 243.

Shāfi'ī: You claimed that a tradition of the Prophet is obligatory even when not preceded by an action nor when the *Imāms* have passed without acting accordingly or contrary to it.

Opponent: There would not be a tradition of the Prophet but it was something acted upon by the *Imāms* who followed him.

It is clear from this argument that in the opinion of the opponent of Shāfi'ī, for a *ḥadīth* to be a valid *sunna* of the Prophet, it is necessary that the caliph or caliphs had acted according to it. This practice of the caliphs based on the reported *sunna* of the Prophet produces confidence in the said *sunna* in two ways: (1) that the said *sunna* was not abrogated, and (2) that its narrator did not commit a mistake while transmitting it.

Moreover, in the whole discussion there is nothing such as "practice" opposing the tradition of the Prophet. Indeed, the very practice referred to is in itself based on the traditions narrated on the authority of the Prophet. Thus the practice was based not on the act of the community or caliphs but on the statement of the Prophet. Therefore, Schacht's evidence to show how the traditions from the Prophet imposed themselves on the old idea of *sunna* fails to prove it.

EXAMPLE 3

In Schacht's third example he says: "In *Ris.* 58, commenting on a tradition which makes 'Umar change his decision when a decision of the Prophet to the contrary became known to him, Shāfi'ī says: 'A tradition from the Prophet must be accepted as soon as it becomes known, even if it is not supported by any corresponding action of a Caliph.' " He goes on to say: "The opponent acknowledges that if this were correct, it would prove that the *sunna*, in Shāfi'ī's sense, superseded all contrary practice, that one could not pretend that validity of the *sunna* required confirmation by evidence of its subsequent application, and that nothing contradictory to the *sunna* could affect it in any way. This shows what the actual doctrine of the opponents is."[7]

Here is the text:

(إن حديث رسول الله يثبت بنفسه لا بعمل غيره بعده)

فان قال قائل : فادللني على أن عمر عمل شيئا ثم صار إلى غيره بخبر عن رسول الله .
قلت : فان أوجدتكه .
قال : ففي ايجادك إياي ذلك دليل على أمرين أحدهما : أنه قد يقول من جهة الرأي إذا لم توجد السنة والآخر أن السنة إذا وجدت وجب عليه ترك عمل نفسه ووجب على الناس ترك كل عمل وجدت السنة بخلافه وإبطال أن السنة لا تثبت إلا بخبر بعدها وعلم أنه لا يوهنها شيء إن خالفها .[8]

---

[7] *Origins*, p. 59.
[8] Shāfi'ī, *Risāla*, p. 425.

To paraphrase in English:

> If someone said: "Give me an example indicating that 'Umar changed his practice when a tradition from the Prophet became known to him, [Shāfi'ī] replied, [What will be the advantage of] my giving you one?" He said, "Such an example will establish two rules: First, that opinion may be accepted in case there is no *sunna*. Second, that if the *sunna* reveals that one must do a certain thing, one must abandon what he [previously] had been doing [if it was contrary to it]. For one must discard practices contrary to the *sunna*. One must also abandon [the idea that] the *sunna* is *confirmed* only by a narrative that has preceded it, for he should know that it is not vitiated by anything that contradicts it."[9]

Lengthy discussion of this example is unnecessary, since the subject matter is the same as in the second example. In the time of Shāfi'ī there were some scholars, not belonging to the known schools of Medina, Syria, and Iraq, who held the opinion that a mere narrative on the authority of the Prophet was not sufficient but needed also to be *confirmed* by subsequent actions by the Companions and early Muslims in accordance with it. It is interesting to note that both Schacht and Majid Khaddurī, the translator of Shāfi'ī's *Risālah*, used the word "confirmation" and "confirmed" respectively.

Again, this is not a problem of the authority of the *sunna* of the Prophet, but a question of its documentation and confirmation. Shāfi'ī precedes this paragraph with a discussion of the difference between witness, narration of *ḥadīth*, and the judgment of the judge, going into considerable detail on the difference between witnesses and the narration of *ḥadīth*. Some people held that two witnesses were required, and a *ḥadīth* transmitted by a single narrator was only one witness. To compensate for this, some scholars decided that such *ḥadīth*, to be valid, must be followed by action on the part of the early caliphs or by others.[10] Clearly, this discussion by Shāfi'ī in no way supports Schacht's contention that traditions from the Prophet gradually superseded or imposed themselves on the old idea of *sunna*; that is, "generally agreed practice."

The main point of this section may be summarized as follows: The idea that traditions from the Prophet imposed themselves on the old idea of *sunna* is an imaginary construct made necessary only by the earlier theories and disproved by the evidence.

Having argued that Schacht's concept of the meaning and usage of the term *sunna* and its authority in the ancient schools of law is untenable, we shall move on to discuss his theory that the ancient schools of law simply renamed their "living tradition" under the aegis of the Prophet and called it the *sunna* of the Prophet.

---

[9] See Majid Khaddurī, *Islamic Jurisprudence* (Baltimore, 1961), p. 263 (italics mine).
[10] See *Umm*, vol. *VII*, p. 243; *Ris*. p. 424 (Shākir's edition).

Was the Living Tradition Projected Back into the Mouth of the Prophet?

In this section of the chapter we examine Schacht's argument that the concept of the *sunna* of the Prophet was coined by the Iraqi school sometime in the second century A.H.[11] and that the *sunna* of the Prophet is therefore, "simply the 'living tradition' of the school put under the aegis of the Prophet."[12] In other words, the second-century scholars projected back their theories and judgments into the mouth of the Prophet to add authority to them.

We have seen, however, that the Qur'ān describes the life of the Prophet as the model that ought to be followed, and that the word *sunna* has been used in the Qur'ān in several places.[13] Clearly, then, the term "*sunna* of the Prophet" must have been in use in the time of the Prophet himself — and this is further proved by the hundreds of *aḥādīth* containing this usage which were current in the time of the Prophet.

Schacht, in fact, contradicts his own theory. Although he wants to argue that the concept "*sunna* of the Prophet" is a second-century accretion, he quotes Goldziher, whose opinion is that the term *sunna* was originally a pagan term that was adapted by Islam.[14] It is difficult to see how the term could be current in the pre-Islamic era, used frequently in the Qur'ān, and then not be used again by scholars or by the community at large until the middle of the second century.

Leaving aside Schacht's cynical view of human nature that underlies the assumption of dishonesty and collusion on a massive scale among second- and third-century scholars[15] (never mind the logistics of mounting such a deception), let us nonetheless analyze the examples Schacht brings from the writings of the Iraqian and Syrian schools in support of his thesis.

Opinions of Companions Allegedly Ascribed to the Prophet

In his attempt to show that the opinions of the Companions were ascribed to the Prophet, Schacht refers to Ibn Mas'ūd. He says:

> It was claimed that their [the Companions] opinions were likely to coincide with the decisions of the Prophet: 'Ibn Mas'ūd was asked about a problem [concerning dowry, etc.]; he replied: "I am not aware of any decision of the

---

[11] *Origins*, p. 76: "In any case, it was the Iraqians and not the Medinese to whom the concept of '*sunna* of the Prophet' was familiar before the time of Shāfi'ī."
[12] *Origins*, p. 76.
[13] Meaning norms, line of conduct and course, etc.
[14] *Origins*, p. 58.
[15] Chapter Eight discusses this topic under the heading "Arbitrary and Careless Creation of Isnāds."

Prophet on this"; asked to give his own opinion *(ra'y)*, he gave it; thereupon one of the men in his circle declared that the Prophet had given the same decision, and Ibn Mas'ūd was exceedingly glad that his opinion coincided with the decision of the Prophet.'[16]

Later, Schacht says, "We have seen that the opinion of Ibn Mas'ūd was supposed to coincide with the decision of the Prophet."[17] But is this what the text really shows? A man like Ibn Mas'ūd who lived in the service of the Prophet for some 20 years, a period sufficient to make him understand the mind of the Prophet, gave a decision. According to the testimony, his decision coincided with the decision of the Prophet. Does this really imply a false projecting back? Even if it *is* a false ascription, this is only one incident which Schacht stretches to cover the life and legal activities not only of Ibn Mas'ūd but of all the tens of thousands of Companions.

The Syrian School: Auzā'ī. Speaking of Auzā'ī, Schacht says that "he is inclined to project the whole 'living tradition,' the continuous *practice* of the Muslims, as he finds it, back to the Prophet and to give it the Prophet's authority, whether he can adduce a precedent established by the Prophet or not. He has this feature in common with the Iraqians."[18]

In fact, Auzā'ī refers to the practice of the Prophet and the Muslims in only nine cases out of 50. In six cases, he refers to the practice of the Muslims but does not refer to the practice of the Prophet. In five cases, he refers to authorities such as Abū Bakr, 'Umar, and so on and not to the Prophet.[19] Thus, Schacht's statement that he projects back "the whole living tradition" to the Prophet does not tally with the real references of Auzā'ī.

Moreover, although Abū Yūsuf disagrees with Auzā'ī in the majority of cases, we find him in agreement with Auzā'ī in his references to the Prophet and some early authorities. For example, Abū Yūsuf agrees with Auzā'ī on the authentication of traditions on the authority of the Prophet in 14 cases (Nos. 1–5, 20, 26, 34, 38–39, and 47–50) and other authorities in four cases (Nos. 22, 25, 28, and 29) and challenges the authenticity or correctness of the information in only five cases (Nos. 7, 9–12).

If Auzā'ī were merely projecting back the practices of his time into the mouth of the Prophet, we would be unlikely to find Abū Yūsuf — an opponent — agreeing with him. Although he agrees with Auzā'ī on the authenticity of 14 traditions from the Prophet, he mostly disagrees on their interpretation. Had the two been in agreement on the interpretations, it might have been possible to say that their "living tradition" was similar and that they had projected their traditions back to the Prophet

---

[16] *Origins*, p. 29.
[17] *Origins*, p. 32.
[18] *Origins*, pp. 72–73.
[19] For more detail, see Chapter Four's discussion of the Syrian and Iraqian Living Traditions.

and accidentally tallied with each other — which was, as a matter of fact, impossible. Their agreement on the authenticity of the traditions while differing about their implications means that those traditions originally belonged to a common stock far from the inventions of the schools. That common stock is the personality of the Prophet.

The Iraqi School: Abū Yūsuf. Let us look at a second example from the same source. Schacht says: "In *Tr. IX,* 18, Abū Yūsuf applies the term '*sunna* of the Prophet' to a case in which nothing to the contrary is known on the authority of the Prophet and of the Companions."[20] Later he says: "The ancient schools of law shared the old concept of *sunna* or 'living tradition' as the ideal practice of the community, expressed in the accepted doctrine of the school. It was not yet exclusively embodied in traditions from the Prophet, although the Iraqians had been the first to claim for it the authority of the Prophet, by calling it the '*sunna* of the Prophet.'"[21]

The case being referred to is that of a slave who ran away from his master and was later recaptured. Auzā'ī said that if the slave was non-Muslim his punishment would depend on the decision of the *Imām*, who might behead him or crucify him. Abū Yūsuf objects to this *fatwā* (decision) of Auzā'ī, saying that there is no *sunna* of the Prophet to this effect.

Schacht seems to be trying either to give the impression that Abū Yūsuf applied the term "*sunna* of the Prophet" to a case when no *sunna* existed or that it was sufficient for *sunna* to be established if nothing contrary was reported. In fact, the point Abū Yūsuf raised was that there was no *sunna*, and that punishments of this type ought to be based on precedent from the Prophet. Abū Yūsuf says:

وأما قوله في الصلب فلم تمض بهذا سنة عن رسول الله ولا عن أحد من أصحابه فيما نعلم .

("However, his [Auzā'ī's] decision concerning crucifixion, there is no executed *sunna* from the Prophet to this effect, neither from anyone of his Companions as well, according to our knowledge.") This is hardly convincing proof that doctrines were falsely projected back to the Prophet; rather, it is a vindication of the classical view that scholars faithfully followed the Prophet to the best of their knowledge and ability, although Schacht has altered the evidence from negative to positive.

Shaibānī. Schacht ascribes the same kind of dishonesty to Shaibānī. "The degree to which Shaibānī puts the doctrine of the Iraqians under the aegis of the Prophet," he says, "becomes clear from *Muw. Shaib.* 361, where he calls it 'something we have heard on the authority of the

---
[20] *Origins,* p. 75.
[21] *Origins,* p. 80.

Prophet'; but his whole evidence for this consists in statements of Zuhrī and 'Aṭā' on a change of a practice in Umaiyad times."[22]

The case referred to is a point of the law of evidence — whether or not one witness and one oath are a sufficient basis for a verdict. Mālik transmitted a *ḥadīth* in its favor. Shaibānī says, "We heard something from the Prophet against it." Then he quotes the statement of Zuhrī and 'Aṭā' that the first to accept one witness and one oath were Mu'āwiya and 'Abdul Malik.

The most one can say in this case is that although Shaibānī claimed to have heard something on the authority of the Prophet against the *ḥadīth*, he had, nevertheless, failed to report it. It would be false to say that he put the doctrines of the Iraqians under the aegis of the Prophet, because he ascribed to the later authorities what he knew about them, and did not ascribe the statements or verdicts of later authority to the Prophet. Moreover, it was common practice among Abū Yūsuf, Shaibānī, and others to mention the existence of *aḥādīth* and *āthār* on the subject without recording them in their books.[23]

We have thus seen that Schacht's accusation that the Syrians and Iraqians projected their own doctrines back to the Prophet is baseless and contrary to the evidence he himself adduces. However, we have seen that the examples provided by Schacht to prove his theory of projecting back the others' statements to the Prophet have hardly any bearing on his claim. The natural result of Schacht's theory of back projection would be the "growth of *ḥadīth* literature." Schacht has devoted an entire chapter to this. We will now examine his treatment of this theme.

---

[22] *Origins*, pp. 75–76.
[23] For example, see Auzā'ī, p. 21; *Ḥujja*, vol. 1, p. 269.

Chapter Seven

On the Growth of Legal Tradition

Earlier in this book the position of the *sunna* of the Prophet in the light of the verses of the Qur'ān has been discussed. The way in which the ancient schools of law used the *sunna* of the Prophet as a binding and original source for the deduction of Islamic norms has also been indicated in some detail. The *aḥādīth* of the Prophet are repositories for the *sunna* of the Prophet and the sole source of knowledge about it. Hence it is natural that all possible steps should have been taken to preserve and diffuse the *aḥādīth* from the time of the Prophet.

The Diffusion of *Aḥādīth*

The Prophet himself gave explicit instructions about this when he said: "Pass on information from me even if it is only one verse."[1] And in the same tone at the farewell *Ḥajj* ceremony: "Let those who are present convey the information to those who are absent."[2] Elsewhere, we find the same order, but in the form of prayer: "Allah fills with light a man who hears what I say, preserves it carefully in memory, and passes it on to others."[3] Deputations coming to Medina were ordered to teach their people about the *aḥādīth* on their return.[4] Mālik b. al-Ḥuwairith is a specific example of someone thus ordered by the Prophet; the same order was given to the other delegates.[5] When the deputation of 'Abdul Qais visited the Prophet, they asked him to teach them how they might best convey his message and teach the people after them.[6]

Various practical arrangements were made for the diffusion of the *sunna*. We find the Prophet teaching the *sunna* himself.[7] To facilitate memorization and understanding, he used to repeat important things three times.[8] After teaching, he used to listen to his Companions reciting

---

[1] Bukhārī, *Saḥīḥ* (printed with Fatḥul Bārī, Cairo, 1380) Anbīyā, 50 cited hereafter as Bu.
[2] *Bu, 'Ilm*, 9, 10, 37; *Mu, Ḥajj* p. 446.
[3] Tirmidhī, *Jām', 'Ilm* 7; (Cairo, 1936) Ḥanbal, 1, p. 437.
[4] *Bu, 'Ilm*, 25.
[5] *Bu, 'Ilm*, 25; Ibn Sa'd, vol. vii, pp. 29–30.
[6] *Bu, Manāqib*, 5.
[7] See al-Khāṭīb, *al-Faqīh* (Riyadh) vol. ii, p. 124.
[8] *Bu, 'Ilm*, 30.

what they had learned.[9] Deputations arriving from outlying areas were given into the custody of the Medinese, not only to be accommodated but also for education in the Qur'ān and the *sunna*. The Prophet asked them questions to discover the extent of their learning.[10]

Method of Learning *Aḥādīth*

The Companions used to listen to every word of the Prophet with the utmost care, learning the Qur'ān and the *sunna* from him, mostly in the mosque. When the Prophet left them for any reason, they immediately began to go over what they had learned. This practice was described well by Mu'āwīya[11] and is also found in the statements of Abū Al-Dardā',[12] culminating in the statements of Anas, the servant of the Prophet. He says: "We sat with the Prophet, maybe 60 persons in number, then the Prophet taught them *Ḥadīth*. Later on, if he went away for any work then we used to memorize it among ourselves, and by the time we left, it had been cultivated in our hearts."[13]

The Companions had the same obligations of daily life as everybody else. So it was not practically possible for all of them to attend the circle of the Prophet on every occasion. Those who were absent therefore used to learn from those who had been present.[14] This has been well described by the Companion Barā' b. 'Āzib.[15] This was the order of the Prophet, as we have seen earlier. It therefore became a common practice among them to inform absentees about the Prophet's sayings and deeds. Some of them came to an agreement between themselves to attend the circle of the Prophet in rotation.[16]

After the Prophet's death, the pattern of transmission remained much the same. 'Umar, the second caliph, entrusted his governors with the duty of teaching the Qur'ān and the *sunna* of the Prophet.[17] He used to send out many teachers for this purpose.[18] Memorization of *ḥadīth* was conscientiously performed, just as it had been when the Prophet was alive. Abū Hurairah used to divide the night into three portions: one third for sleeping, one third for prayer, and one third for the memorization of *ḥadīth* of the Prophet.[19]

'Umar and Abū Mūsā al-Āsh'arī would also memorize *ḥadīth* until the

---

[9] *Bu, Wuḍūa'*, 75.
[10] Ḥanbal, vol. iv, p. 206.
[11] See M.A. Al-Ḥākīm, *al-Mustadrak* (Hyderabad), vol. i, p. 94.
[12] Ḥanbal, vol. vi, p. 443.
[13] 'Ayād al-Qāḍī, *al-Ilmā'* (Cairo, 1970) p. 142; al-Khaṭīb, *al-Jāmi'*, 43a, Ms. Alexandria Municipal Library.
[14] Al-Ḥākim, *al-Mustadrak*, vol. i, p. 95.
[15] *Ibid.*, vol. i, p. 127, 95; Ibn Ḥanbal, *al-'Ilal*, 96b.
[16] Bu, *'Ilm*, 25; Ibn Sa'd, vol. viii, p. 136.
[17] Ḥanbal, vol. i, p. 48.
[18] Sa'īd b. Manṣūr, *Sunan* (Malegaon, 1967), vol. iii, Part i, p. 1.
[19] Dārimī *Sunan* (Damuscus, 1349), vol. i, p. 82; al-Khaṭīb, *al-Faqīh*, vol. ii, p. 128.

morning,[20] as did Ibn 'Abbās and Zaid b. Arqam.[21] Ibn Buraidah reports a similar situation in Ḥims with Mu'āwīya.[22]

Many of the Companions themselves advised the Successors on the memorization of ḥadīth — notably 'Alī b. Abī Ṭālib,[23] Ibn Mas'ūd,[24] Ibn 'Abbās,[25] and Abū Sa'īd al-Khudrī.[26] They used to memorize ḥadīth either in groups[27] or individually,[28] and they passed on the same kind of advice to their students.

The official recording of ḥadīth may be said to begin with the letters sent by the Prophet to kings, rulers, chieftains, and governors. There are many of these covering a wide range of legal matters, zakāt taxation, forms of worship, and so on. The extent of this activity may be seen from the number of scribes — as many as 65 — who wrote for the Prophet at one time or another.[29] Recordings of the aḥādīth dictated by the Prophet to various Companions, notably 'Alī b. Abū Ṭālib and 'Abdullāh b. 'Amr b. al-'Āṣ, may be called official. But there must have been many more unofficial recordings. Several of the Companions kept aḥādīth in written form, although it is not always possible to tell whether these were committed to writing during the life of the Prophet or later. This problem is covered in more detail in my book *Studies in Early Ḥadīth Literature*.

Precautions Against Errors and Forgeries

Although the early scholars took extensive precautions against the possibility of human error entering the memorization and copying of aḥādīth, and themselves continuously revised what they had written down and advised their students to do likewise, errors did inevitably find their way into the body of ḥadīth literature. Scribes made mistakes, memories failed, and there were deliberate forgeries. We now turn to a discussion of the rigorous tests to which aḥādīth were subjected before they were accepted as valid. There were basically three methods of testing: (1) the character of the narrator, (2) textual comparisons, and (3) rational criticism.

1. The Character of the Narrator. The first of these tests was that of the character of the narrator. A reliable narrator needed to be *'Adl* — that is, acceptable within the Islamic code of ethics. The scholar Ibn al-Mubārak

---

[20] Khaṭīb, *al-Faqīh*, 132a.
[21] Ḥanbal, vol. iv, p. 374.
[22] Al-Ḥākim, *al-Mustadrak*, vol. i, p. 94.
[23] Dārimī, *Sunan*, vol. I, p. 150.
[24] Dārimī, *Sunan*, vol. i, p.150.
[25] Khaṭīb, *Shraf Aṣḥāb al-Ḥadīth*, Ms. 56a.
[26] Abū Zur'ah, *Tārīkh* (Fātih Ms. 4210, Istanbul) 95b: al-Ḥākīm, *al-Mustadrak*, vol. 1, p. 94.
[27] See, for example, Abū Khaithamah, *'Ilm*, 127; Dārimī, *Sunan*, vol. i, p. 149.
[28] See, for example, Abū Khaithamah, *'Ilm* 126; Dārimī, *Sunan*, vol. i, p. 148.
[29] See Azamī, *Kuttāb an-Nabī*, pp. 25–112, read with Bāqillāni, al-Intiṣār (Bayazit Ms. No. 18671, Istanbul) Fol. 132.

(118–181 A.H.) defines the reliable narrator as one who prays in congregation, does not drink *nabīdh*,[30] is not lawless in his life, does not lie, and suffers from no mental defect.[31] A man may be a great scholar, but if his morals are suspect, then a *ḥadīth* related by him is not acceptable.

All scholars, apart from the Companions themselves, whose characters had never been doubted, were measured against this yardstick. In most cases, however, it must be admitted, one has to rely on contemporary authorities for evidence.

2. Textual Comparisons. The second test, or series of tests, was to make cross-comparisons between *aḥādīth*, for example:
  Comparing the *aḥādīth* of different students of the same scholar.
  Comparing statements made at different times by the same scholar.
  Comparing oral with written versions.
  Comparing a *ḥadīth* with a related text in the Qur'ān.
Some examples of these methods are given below.

A. Comparing *aḥādīth* of different students of the same scholar. This method was approved by early scholars. Ayyūb al-Sakhtīyānī, a Successor (68–131 A.H.) says: "If you wish to know the mistakes of your teacher, then you ought to sit down with others as well."[32] Similarly, Ibn al-Mubārak (118–181 A.H.) says: "To reach an authentic statement one needs to compare the words of scholars with each other."[33]

The method itself is illustrated by the work of the third-century scholar Ibn Ma'īn (d. 233 A.H.). He visited 18 of the pupils of the great scholar Ḥammād b. Salamah to read their versions of his books. When questioned about his purpose in doing so, he replied:

> Ḥammād b. Salamah committed mistakes, and his students added some more mistakes. So I want to distinguish between the mistakes of Ḥammād and those of his students. If I find all the students of Ḥammād committing a certain mistake unanimously, then the source of the mistake is Ḥammād. If I find the majority of the students of Ḥammād say something, and some of them go against them, then this mistake was committed by those particular students. In this way, I make a distinction between the mistakes of Ḥammād and those of his students.[34]

This method allowed Ibn Ma'īn not only to identify mistakes, but also to grade Ḥammād's students according to their accuracy. The method was not, of course, invented by Ibn Ma'īn, nor was he the first to apply it — we find it operating from the time of the first caliph, Abū Bakr.

Another example comes from Muslim, the student of al-Bukhārī. Ibn

---

[30] A drink usually made by dates or raisins into a pot and pouring water on them. If the mixture was left, it fermented and became alcoholic.
[31] Khaṭīb, *al-Kifāya*, (Hydrabad, 1357), p. 79.
[32] Dārimī, *Sunan*, vol. i, p. 153.
[33] Khaṭīb, *al-Jāmi'*, folio 5a.
[34] Ibn Ḥibbān, *al-Majrūḥīn'* (Aya Sofiya Ms. 496, Istanbul) 11a.

'Abbās once spent a night in the room of his aunt Maimūna. After a time, according to his statement, the Prophet stood up, performed the ablution, and began to pray. Ibn 'Abbās did the same, and after performing the ablution went and stood at the left of the Prophet, upon which the Prophet moved him from his left and made him stand at his right. This incident was also narrated by one of the scholars, Yazīd b. Abū Zinād, on the authority of Kuraib, from Ibn 'Abbās; but in his version Ibn 'Abbās stood at the right of the Prophet and later on he was made to stand at his left.

To determine which was the correct version, Muslim applied the following method: He gathered all the statements of the colleagues of Yazīd, the students of Kuraib, who unanimously agreed that Ibn 'Abbās first stood at the left of the Prophet. Then he gathered all the statements of the colleagues of Kuraib, the students of Ibn 'Abbās, who unanimously agreed that Ibn 'Abbās first stood at the Prophet's left. He next collected reports of occasions when a Companion had prayed with the Prophet alone. In all these cases it was confirmed that the other man stood at the right of the Prophet. The weight of evidence served to prove that what was related by Yazīd b. Abū Zinād was a mistake.[35]

B. Comparing statements made at different times by the same scholar.
'Ā'isha once told her nephew 'Urwah to go to 'Abdullāh b. 'Amr and ask him about the *aḥadīth* of the Prophet, as he had learned a lot from the Prophet. One of the *aḥadīth* 'Urwah learned from him was about the way knowledge will be taken away from the earth. He reported to 'Ā'isha what he had learned, and she became disturbed about this particular *ḥadīth*. After a year or so, she sent 'Urwah back to 'Abdullāh b. 'Amr to ask him about the same *ḥadīth*. 'Urwah reported that 'Abdullāh b. 'Amr repeated the *ḥadīth* once again exactly as he had reported before. Upon which she said, "I cannot but think him correct, as he has neither added anything to it nor shortened it."[36]

C. Comparing orally transmitted *aḥadīth* with written versions. There are many examples of the use of this method, but two will suffice. Muḥammad b. Muslim and al-Faḍl b. 'Abbād were learning *ḥadīth* in the presence of Abū Zur'ah. Muḥammad transmitted a *ḥadīth* which was not accepted by al-Faḍl, and they argued together, then asked Abū Zur'ah to say who was right. Abū Zur'ah referred to a book to find the said *ḥadīth*, where it became clear that Muḥammad b. Muslim was mistaken.[37]

A *ḥadīth* was transmitted by Sufyān through Ibn Mas'ūd, regarding the raising of the hands while going into *Rukū'*. Yaḥyā b. Ādam said that he checked the book of 'Abdullāh b. Idrīs, and could not find the sentence in

---

[35] Muslim, *Tamyīz* (Riyadh, 1395) pp. 136–138.
[36] *Mu. 'Ilm.* 14.
[37] Ibn Abī Ḥātim, *Introduction*, p. 337.

question. Commenting on this, Bukhārī commends the practice because a book is more accurate [*Aḥfaẓ*] in the eyes of scholars.[38]

D. Comparing the *ḥadīth* with related verses of the Qur'ān: We find that this method was used by 'Umar in rejecting the *ḥadīth* of Fāṭima bint Qais concerning maintenance money for divorced women.[39] 'Ā'isha also applied the same method in several cases.[40]

3. Rational Criticism. The two tests described above were applied to ascertain the validity of narrators or chains of narrators, but rationality ['*Aql*] was also given its proper place. According to al-Mu'allāmī al-Yamānī, it was applied at every stage — in learning *ḥadīth*, in teaching *ḥadīth*, in judging narrators, and in evaluating the authenticity of *ḥadīth*.[41]

According to Ibn Abī Ḥātim al-Rāzī, the essential rational test is that the *ḥadīth be worthy of the Prophet*. He says:

> The goodness of a *dinār* is known when it is measured against another. Thus if it differs in redness and purity, it will be known that it is counterfeit. A diamond is evaluated by measuring it against another one. If it differs in brilliance and hardness, it will be known to be glass. The authenticity of a *ḥadīth* is known by its coming from reliable narrators and the statement itself must be worthy of being the statement of Prophethood.[42]

Ibn al-Qayyim adduced several general rules for recognizing a false *ḥadīth* without going into *isnād* criticism. Some of the features he considers indicative of false *aḥādīth* are:

1. Fanciful statements that the Prophet could not have made. For example, a false *ḥadīth* attributed to the Prophet was: "Whoever pronounces *La ilāha ill Allah*, God creates from this sentence a bird with seventy thousand tongues . . ."
2. Statements that can be shown to be false empirically.
3. Nonsensical kinds of attribution.
4. Contradiction of well-known *sunan*.
5. Statements claimed to have been made by the Prophet in the presence of many Companions, but which are reported by none of them.
6. Statements that bear no resemblance to other statements of the Prophet.
7. Phraseology that resembles that of sufis or medical practitioners.
8. Contradiction of the Qur'ān.
9. Inadequacy of style.[43]

---

[38] Bukhārī, *Raf' al-Yadain* (Delhi, 1299), p. 9.
[39] Mu. *Ṭalāq.*, 46, versing the Qur'ān, *Ṭalāq*, vol. i.
[40] See A'zami, Introduction to *Tamyīz*, pp. 47–48.
[41] See Muslim, *Tamyīz*, pp. 66–67.
[42] See Muslim, *Tamyīz*, Introduction, pp. 68–69.
[43] For details, see *Muslim, Tamyīz*, Introduction, pp. 69–70.

These are only a few tests out of many that were applied by scholars to evaluate *aḥādīth* on a rational basis. Supplemented by *isnād* criticism,[44] these tests of rationality served to ensure that *ḥadīth* literature was transmitted in as pure a form as possible, with every effort made to eliminate suspect material.

A Critique of Schacht's View Regarding *Aḥādīth*

Schacht's central contention is that the *ḥadīth* literature was fabricated by scholars in the second and third centuries who sought to justify their own views by tracing origins back to the Prophet. His opinion is that "generally speaking, the living tradition of the ancient schools of law, based to a great extent on individual reasoning, came first, that in the second stage it was put under the aegis of Companions, [and] that traditions from the Prophet himself [were] put into circulation by traditionists towards the middle of the second century A.H."[45] He concludes: "We shall find that the bulk of legal traditions from the Prophet known to Mālik originated in the generation preceding him, that is in the second quarter of the second century A.H., and we shall not meet *any legal tradition from the Prophet which can be considered authentic.*"[46]

He further repeats the same conclusion in his *Introduction to Islamic Law,* where he says: "The traditionists produced detailed statements or 'traditions' which claimed to be the reports of ear- or eye-witnesses on the words or acts of the Prophet, handed down orally by an uninterrupted chain [*isnād*] of trustworthy persons. Hardly any of these traditions, as far as matters or religious law are concerned, can be considered authentic. . ."[47]

In short, Schacht appears to have believed that the entire body of *aḥādīth* literature is a confidence trick perpetrated by unscrupulous scholars throughout the Muslim world.

Briefly, the classical viewpoint, as has been described earlier, is that there exists an authentic corpus of information that has been traced back to the Prophet. Spurious and questionable additions were made to this core in succeeding generations, but scholars made every attempt to verify what was authentic and found the great majority of *aḥādīth* to be valid and traceable back to the Prophet.

Given such a fundamental departure from the accepted view of Muslim scholars, it is necessary to examine in the greatest detail the evidence Schacht adduces to support his argument. Before doing so, it is important to note that his thesis is based on the *e silentio* principle, which assumes that if one scholar at any given time was ignorant of a particular *ḥadīth* or

---

[44] See below, Chapter Eight.
[45] *Origins*, p. 138.
[46] *Ibid.*, p. 149 (italics mine).
[47] *Introduction*, p. 34.

failed to mention it or, rather, that if it was not mentioned by later scholars that earlier scholars used that particular *ḥadīth*, then the *ḥadīth* did not exist at that time. If the *ḥadīth* is first found with incomplete *isnād*, and, later, with complete *isnād*, then the *isnād* has been "improved," in other words, fabricated. In a *reductio ad absurdum*, this argument would mean that if one writer in the Middle East failed to mention London as one of the major cities in the world, then all other writers who mentioned it later would be guilty of collusion in creating a fictional city. Even allowing for the fact that Schacht did not have available to him many important source books, he quotes from those that were available in a way which sometimes appears to accept and reject authorities arbitrarily and to ignore certain political and geographical realities.

Schacht devotes the whole of Chapter 2 of Part II of his *Origins of Muhammadan Jurisprudence*, entitled "The Growth of Legal Traditions in the Literary Period. . . ," to the defense of his thesis. Careful scrutiny of his examples and repeated reference to the original source material, however, reveals inconsistencies both within the theory itself and in the use of source material, unwarranted assumptions and unscientific method of research, mistakes of fact, ignorance of the political and geographical realities of the time, and misinterpretation of the meaning of the texts quoted, and misunderstanding of the method of quotation of early scholars. In the following pages, these five assertions will be justified, making reference to half of the nearly 50 examples Schacht uses to support his case. Difficult as it may seem, it is necessary to go into this level of detail to refute a false theory that threatens to divert the proper course of Islamic scholarship.

Here is the list of the cases discussed by Schacht. When examining them, I shall refer to them by number.

1. A difference of opinion between Abū Ḥanīfah and Mālik concerning certain injuries and their compensation (not related on the authority of the Prophet.)
2. An alleged letter of Ḥasan Baṣrī to 'Abdul Malik (not from the Prophet).
3. Prostration after reciting certain verses of the Qur'ān.
4. The position of a woman in congregational prayer.
5. Imprecation against enemies in the prayer.
6. The best time for morning prayers.
7. Regarding the sanctity of Mecca.
8. Regarding fasting.
9. Tooth injury.
10. Spoils belong to the killer.
11. Those who join a people belong to it.
12. Stealing by a slave from the booty.
13. Running away of a slave to enemy territory (not from the Prophet).
14. False testimony (not from the Prophet).

15. Agricultural tithes.
16. About exchange (prohibition of sale of food grain before its possession).
17. *Tayammum* (an act of ritual purification).
18. *Zakāt* on orphans' property.
19. The share of a boy who took part in war (age of maturity).
20. Ritual purity.
21. Certain transactions.
22. Prostrations in the Qur'ān.
23. Sanctity of Mecca and the killing of snakes there.
24. Prohibition against destroying the property of the enemy in war (tradition from Abū Bakr, not from the Prophet).
25. A person who has more than four wives when he becomes a Muslim.
26. Taking a bath for Friday prayer.
27. The rate of exchange between gold and silver.
28. The cleaning of a pot that has been licked by a dog.
29. The sale of animals.
30. Ablution three times and once.
31. Eating lizards.
32. The black dog is a devil.
33. Triple divorce.
34. The witness of Jews against Christian and vice versa.
35. Saying '*Āmīn* out loud.
36. Reading something other than *Fātiha* in prayers.
37. Reciting certain *Sūrahs* in *Fajr* Prayer.
38. The use of perfume before *Hajj Ihrām*.
39. *Werqeld* for a Jew or Christian.
40. Wiping over one's socks (ritual purification).
41. Covering one's face during pilgrimage (not from the Prophet).
42. The Prophet's resting in Muhassab in pilgrimage.
43. Making a vow to go to the Ka'ba on foot.
44. Paying *Zakāt al-fitr* before the end of *Ramadān*.
45. Hajāmah[48] in the case of a fasting man.
46. Cutting off the hand of one who denies what he has borrowed.
47. "I was given the Qur'ān and *ahādīth* similar to it."

Inconsistencies Both in Theory and in the Use of Source Material

Schacht restricts himself to "legal traditions" in the title of the chapter, and states explicitly, after discussing 47 examples from different periods, "So far we have discussed the growth of legal traditions *from the Prophet*

---

[48] Cupping – a method of drawing the blood to the surface of the body in the treatment of certain diseases.

only."⁴⁹ In fact, examples 1, 2, 13, 14, and 24 out of 24 discussed do not come from the Prophet, and the great majority of *aḥādīth* are not legal by his definition, but ritual (examples 2–8, 15, 17, 18, 20, 22, and 23); the only legal traditions related on the authority of the Prophet, in 24 cases discussed below, are numbers 9–16, 19, and 21. In other words, only one quarter of the material is relevant to the heading of the chapter.

In the classical Muslim view, since all facets of life are ruled by Islam, no distinction can be drawn between ritual and legal *aḥādīth*. But as this distinction is central to Schacht's thesis, we may legitimately ask why he has filled the chapter with ritual *aḥādīth* rather than restricting himself to legal matters. At best, his definitions are applied inconsistently; a more skeptical reading might be that the ritual *aḥādīth* were added to give apparent weight to a shaky argument.

Unwarranted Assumptions and Unscientific Research Methods

Schacht's basic premise is that if a *ḥadīth* was not referred to in a legal discussion at one time and a later scholar utilized it in his legal argument, then it must have been fabricated in the interim between the two scholars. In his own words: "The best way of proving that a tradition did not exist at a certain time is to show that it was not used as a legal argument in a discussion which would have made reference to it imperative if it had existed."[50]

In earlier chapters of the same books, Schacht argues: (1) that two generations before Shāfiʿī, reference to the *aḥādīth* of the Prophet were the exception[51]; and (2) that all the ancient schools of law offered strong resistance to the *aḥādīth* of the Prophet.[52] If we accept these statements as true, it is clearly untenable to assert that a tradition could not have existed if it was not used in a legal argument, since those resisting the traditions would hardly have been likely to have used them. So Schacht's use of the *e silentio* argument is condemned by Schacht himself.

However, if we ignore this contradiction and examine Schacht's argument on its own merits, the following points need to be proved:

a. That if a certain *ḥadīth* was not mentioned by a certain scholar, it is proof of that scholar's ignorance of that *ḥadīth*.
b. That all the works of the early scholars have been printed and nothing is missing, so that we possess all that they compiled.
c. That one scholar's ignorance of a particular *ḥadīth* is sufficient proof that the *ḥadīth* did not exist.
d. That knowledge known to one scholar at a particular time must

---

⁴⁹ *Origins*, p. 150 (italics mine).
⁵⁰ *Ibid.*, p. 140.
⁵¹ *Ibid.*, p. 3.
⁵² *Ibid.*, p. 57.

have been known to all his contemporaries in that branch of knowledge.
e. That when a scholar writes on a subject, he uses *all* the evidence available to him at that time.

Pure reason, not to mention knowledge of the practices of the time, is sufficient to demonstrate the absurdity of these assumptions. The burden of proof rests with Schacht, and he has failed to prove any one of these points.

The absurdity of the assumption that anything not found in early works but found in later sources must have been fabricated in the interim can be demonstrated by turning the method upside down, that is, by testing *aḥādīth* found in early works that are not found in later works.

Take, for example, Shaibānī and Mālik.[53] Shaibānī, as we know, was younger than Mālik and prepared an edition of Mālik's *Muwaṭṭa'*. A comparison of the two works reveals many omissions in the latter work, as the following list shows:

a. The section on timings of the prayers in *Muw.* (p. 3 ff) is contained in all 30 *aḥādīth*; only three of these are mentioned in *Muw. Shaib.* (p. 42 ff).
b. The disagreement between the Kūfans and Medinese about the time of the morning prayer is well known. The Medinese were in favor of praying early, while it was still dark, while the Kūfans were of the view that prayer should preferably be held when there was some light. *Muw. Shaib* (p. 42) mentions this doctrine of the Kūfans, but makes no mention of a *ḥadīth* from the Prophet that supports it, although one is mentioned in *Muw.* (p. 4 ff).
c. On the question of whether touching of the genital organs necessitated fresh ablution, *Muw.* (p. 42 ff) has six *aḥādīth*, of which *Muw. Shaib.* (p. 50) records only two. The omitted *aḥādīth* include one from the Prophet and another from Ibn 'Umar.
d. On the question of *ghusl* owing to *Janābah*, *Muw.* (p. 44 ff) quotes four *aḥādīth*, only one of which is found in *Muw. Shaib.* (p. 70 f). The omitted *aḥādīth* include two *aḥādīth* from the Prophet.
e. The section "*ghusl al-mar'ah idhā ra'at fi al-manām*" *Muw.* (p. 51 ff) contains two *aḥādīth*, while *Muw. Shaib.* (p. 79) contains only one, omitting one recorded in *Muw.* (p. 51 ff) as a *ḥadīth* from the Prophet with the *isnād*: Mālik – Hishām – his father – Zaynab bint Abū Salmah – Umm Salamah – Umm Sulaym – the Prophet.
f. The entire section entitled "*al-wudū' min al-qublah*" in *Muw.* (p. 43 ff), is not found in *Muw. Shaib.*

---

[53] I am indebted to Professor Z. I. Anṣārī for this fundamentally important point and for allowing these examples to be cited. See *"The Early Development of Fiqh in Kūfah"* (doctoral thesis, McGill University, 1966), pp. 237–241.

g. The whole section entitled *"al-ṭuhūr fi al-mā'"* (*Muw.* p. 22 ff) is not found in *Muw. Shaib.*
h. The sections on *"al-Bawl qā'iman"* and *"al-siwāk"* (p. 64 ff) are not found in *Muw. Shaib.*
i. The section *"al-nidā' fī al-ṣalāh"* (*Muw.* p. 67 ff), if compared with the corresponding section in *Muw. Shaib.* (p. 82 ff), shows that several *aḥādīth* of *Muw.* (see numbers 1, 3, 5 – 7, and 9) are not found in *Muw. Shaib.*
j. The section entitled *"Kafan al-mayyit"* *Muw.* (p. 223 ff) contains three *aḥādīth*, of which *Muw. Shaib.* (p. 162) quotes only one (number 7 in *Muw.*), a *ḥadīth* from 'Abd Allāh b. 'Amr b. Al'Āṣ; of the two omitted *ḥadīth*, one reports the manner in which the Prophet was wrapped in the coffin.
k. The section on *zakāt al-fiṭr* in *Muw. Shaib.* (p. 176) does not contain the *ḥadīth* from Ibn 'Umr found in *Muw.* (p. 283].
l. The *aḥādīth* contained in the sections of *Muw.* entitled *"Man lā tajib 'Alayh Zakāt al-fiṭr"* (p. 285), *"Makilat zakāt al-fiṭr"* (p. 284), and *"Man tajib 'alayh zakāt al-fiṭr"* (p. 283) are not found at all in *Muw. Shaib.*
m. In the section on *Isti'dhān al-bikr wa al-ayyim*, three *aḥādīth* are found in *Muw.* (p. 254 ff) while only one is found in *Muw. Shaib* (p. 239). Those missing include a *ḥadīth* from the Prophet.
n. The section on *Li'ān* in *Muw. Shaib.* (p. 262) omits several *aḥādīth* found in the corresponding section in *Muw.* (p. 566 ff).
o. The section on the prohibited forms of the sale of dates in *Muw. Shaib.* (p. 330 ff) contains only one of the three *aḥādīth* mentioned in *Muw.* (p. 623 ff), even though all three go back to the Prophet.

These omissions alone should be sufficient to demonstrate that scholars did not necessarily quote *all* the *aḥādīth* known to them — one of Schacht's basic assumptions. Nor is this particular comparison an isolated example. The same point can be illustrated by comparing the works of Abū Yūsuf and Shaibānī — particularly *Āthār A.Y.* and *Āthār Shaib*.

a. *Āthār A.Y.* 845, a *ḥadīth* from Ibn Mas'ūd on *Muḍārabah*, is not found in *Āthār Shaib*.
b. *Āthār A.Y.* 830, a *ḥadīth* from the Prophet regarding disagreement on the price between the buyer and the seller, is not found in *Āthār Shaib*.
c. *Āthār A.Y.* 666, a *ḥadīth* from 'Umar occurring in the section on divorce and *'iddah*, is not found in *Āthār Shaib*.
d. On the question *nafaqah* and *sukna*, *Āthār, A.Y.* embodies several *aḥādīth* (592, 608, 726, and 728). These are not found in *Āthār Shaib*.
e. *Āthār A.Y.* 704, 707, and 709, which are related to *li'ān*, are not found in *Āthār Shaib*.

f. *Āthār A.Y.* 492, 692, and 696, which deal with *ẓihār*, are not found in *Āthār Shaib*.
g. *Āthār A.Y.* 857, a *ḥadīth* from Sālim on *muzāra'ah*, is not found in *Āthār Shaib*.
h. *Āthār A.Y.* 779 and 780, which refer to *farā'iḍ*, are not found in *Āthār Shaib*.
i. *Āthār A.Y.* 399, 401, 597, and 607, on miscellaneous subjects, are not found in *Āthār Shaib*.

There is no reason to suppose that Shaibānī was ignorant of the *aḥādīth* he omitted. In fact, reference to other published sources proves that he *did* know some of the *aḥādīth* he omitted, but simply did not record them in his own work. In Mālik's *Muwaṭṭa'*[54] we find reference to the letter of 'Umar to his governor Abū Mūsā al-Ash'arī, instructing him on the times of daily prayer. Mālik quoted three *aḥādīth* on this matter. Shaibānī omitted all three in his version of *Muwaṭṭa'*[55] but later refers to one of them to support his doctrine in his polemical book against the Medinese.[56]

A typical pattern among scholars seems to have been to quote more *aḥādīth* in support of their doctrines than against them. But even then, few scholars quote *all* the relevant evidence. In discussing the differences of opinion on the best time for morning prayer, for example, Shaibānī says: "There are many different *aḥādīth* supporting both views but we prefer *Isfār*." After this statement he gives only one *ḥadīth* in favor of dusk prayer, but quotes five *aḥādīth* in support of his own doctrine.[57] Similarly, in a disagreement between Abū Yūsuf and Abū Ḥanīfah about the share of a horse used on the battlefield, Abū Yūsuf records two *aḥādīth* in favor of his doctrine that it should be given double the share of a warrior. He adds: "The *aḥādīth* and *āthār* in favor of giving a horse double share and a man a single share are more numerous and more authentic."[58] In other words, he knows other *aḥādīth* that support his point, but contents himself with quoting only two.

In another place Abū Yūsuf says:

وما جاء في هذا من الأحاديث كثيرة لولا طول ذلك لكتبت لك شيئا كثيرا .[59]

There are many *aḥādīth* concerning this. Had I not been afraid of making this book too lengthy, I would have mentioned very many.

It would be tedious to enumerate all of Schacht's examples whose validity is challenged by the simple recognition that scholars did not feel the need to cite *all* the *aḥādīth* available to them. His assumption that they

---

[54] *Waqūt*, 6–8.
[55] See *Bāb Waqūt aṣ-Ṣalāt*, pp. 42–45.
[56] *Al-Ḥujjah 'alā Ahl al-Madīna*, vol. 1, p. 7.
[57] *Ḥujja*, vol. 1, p. 1; for further examples see *Ḥujja*, vol. 1, pp. 457–462.
[58] *Kharāj*, p. 19.
[59] *Auzā'ī*, p. 38.

did feel this need is the basis on which his theory rests – and the rock against which it founders.

Mistakes of Fact

Many of the examples Schacht cites to demonstrate the fabrication of *aḥādīth* can be invalidated by reference to other sources that give evidence that contemporary or earlier scholars were aware of the *aḥādīth* in question. For this we may refer to examples 4, 6, 7, 10, 17, 19, 23, and 24.

Ignorance of Political and Geographical Realities

Schacht asks us to believe that a massive confidence trick was perpetrated by scholars throughout the Muslim world in the second century A.H. This in itself may strain our credibility, given any belief in human rectitude and honesty.

There is no way of proving to a cynic that scholars do not deliberately falsify records, but we may suggest that the political and geographical realities of the time militated against collusion on such a wide scale. Are we really to believe that without the benefit of telephone, telegraph, or modern methods of transportation, scholars were able to communicate so well that the same *aḥādīth* grew up in such widely disparate areas?[60]

Misunderstanding of the Quotation Methods of Early Scholars

Schacht's methodological errors are compounded by basic misunderstandings and misinterpretations of the methods of early scholars in their writing and *fatwā*. Let us scrutinize some of his examples to determine how a careful scholar could have fallen into this error. In discussing these cases, almost the same pattern set by Schacht will be followed and almost always only the same sources will be used. (Had classical collections of *ḥadīth* been used, it would have been much easier to demonstrate the errors). The cases will be referred to by number.

An Examination of Schacht's Examples

EXAMPLE 1: COMPENSATION FOR INJURIES[61]

Schacht seems to be using this as an example of the fabrication of *ḥadīth* by the Iraqians. The case in point is a difference of opinion between Abū Ḥanīfah and Mālik about compensation for various injuries. In his discussion, Schacht justifies his approach thus:

> The evidence collected in the present chapter has been chosen with particular regard to this last point [that it is proof that a *ḥadīth* did not exist at a given time if it was not cited in a legal discussion that demanded reference to it],

---

[60] For a full discussion, see Chapter Eight, "Beginning and Development of the *Isnād* System."
[61] My title, deduced from Schacht's arguments.

and in a number of cases one or the other of the opponents himself states that he has no evidence other than quoted by him, which does not include the tradition in question. This kind of conclusion *e silentio* is furthermore made safe by *Tr. VIII*, 11, where Shaibānī says: "[This is so] unless the Medinese can produce a tradition in support of their doctrine, but they have none, or they would have produced it."[62]

Commenting on this statement, Schacht says: "We may safely assume that the legal traditions with which we are concerned were quoted as arguments by those whose doctrine they were intended to support, as soon as they were put into circulation."[63] Here is the original text:

« قال أبو حنيفة كل شيء يصاب به العبد من يد أو رجل ... فهو من قيمته على مقدار ذلك ... وقال أهل المدينة في موضحة العبد نصف عشر ثمنه .. فوافقوا أبا حنيفة في هذه الخصال الأربعة وقالوا فيها سوى ذلك ما نقص من ثمنه . قال محمد بن الحسن : كيف جاز لأهل المدينة أن يتحكموا في هذا فيختاروا هذه الخصال الأربعة من بين الخصال ... فينبغي أن ينصف الناس ولا يتحكم فيقول : قولوا بقولي ما قلت من شيء إلا أن يأتي أهل المدينة فيما قالوا من هذا بأثر فننقاد له . وليس عندهم في هذا أثر يفرقون به بين هذه الأشياء ، فلو كان عندهم جاءونا به فيها سمعنا من آثارهم فاذا لم يكن هذا فينبغي الانصاف فإما أن يكون هذا على ما قال أبو حنيفة ... »[64]

Abū Ḥanīfa said: If any slave's hand or leg were afflicted by an accident, the compensation for it would be from his price [meaning the difference in his price before and after the injury].

The Medinese says: In case of *Mūḍiḥa* [65] injury the compensation would be five percent of his value. They agreed with Abū Ḥanīfa in four types [cases] of injury, but in other cases they said that the compensation would be as much as his value has been decreased. Shaibānī objects, saying: How is it legitimate for the Medinese to make arbitrary decisions? So in different types of injury they picked up only four types of injury . . . People ought to be just, and should not say things arbitrarily, saying "Do as I say." In cases where *the Medinese bring traditions to this regard showing different sorts of compensation for different injuries, we will follow them.* But they have no tradition in this regard to make differentiation in compensation. Had they some traditions we would have learned them from them. Therefore, if they have nothing of this sort, they must be fair in treatment. Therefore, the right decision would be what Abū Ḥanīfa has decided.[66]

The first striking fact in the discussion is that there is neither a reference to a *ḥadīth* from the Prophet nor to any other authority. The discussion concerns the decision [*fatwā*] of Abū Ḥanīfa about compensation for certain kinds of injuries to slaves. The Medinese scholars agree with Abū Ḥanīfa in some cases and disagree in others. Al-Shaibānī thinks the

---

[62] *Origins*, p. 140.
[63] *Ibid.*, pp. 140–141.
[64] *Umm*, vol. vii, p. 288.
[65] "A wound in which the head or face is broken that shows the whiteness of the bone." – E.W. Lane, *Arabic English Lexicon* (Edinburgh, 1867), p. 2947.
[66] *Umm.* vol. vii, p. 288.

Medinese attitude illogical and asks them the reason for their discrimination in certain matters. He wants to know why they agree with Abū Ḥanīfah's decision only halfway and if they have any *Āthār* to this effect. If they had, the Iraqians would follow them in their discrimination.

In the whole discussion there is no reference to any *ḥadīth*, nor was any higher authority quoted; yet Schacht was able to discover a forged *ḥadīth* from the Prophet in it.

EXAMPLE 2: THE ALLEGED LETTER OF HASAN BAṢRĪ

Under the heading "Traditions Later Than Ḥasan Baṣrī," Schacht says:

> Although the dogmatic treatise ascribed to Ḥasan Baṣrī is not concerned with matters of law, it is appropriate to begin with it, because it shows that even dogmatic traditions which are, generally speaking, earlier than legal ones, hardly existed at the time of its composition towards the end of the first or in the very early years of the second century A.H. There is no trace of traditions from the Prophet, and the author states explicitly: Every opinion which is not based on the Koran, is erroneous.[67]

To understand the treatise we have to look at its background. According to its writer, 'Abdul Mālik asked Ḥasan Baṣrī about his doctrine of free will, whether he had learned it from the Companions of the Prophet, whether it was his personal opinion, or whether there was any argument in its favor from the Qur'ān, for he had not heard anyone speak on the subject before Ḥasan. He explicitly says:

« والأمر الذي به تأخذ عن رواية عن أحد من أصحاب رسول الله صلى الله عليه وسلم أم عن رأي رأيته أم عن أمر يعرف تصديقه في القرآن . فانا لم نسمع في هذا الكلام مجادلا ولا ناطقا قبلك .

> This opinion which you hold, is it based on something that has been related on the authority of any one of the Companions of the Prophet or is it your opinion which you think [right] or is it something which could be verified by the Qur'ān? Because we did not hear this opinion, neither in arguments nor simply in the [personal] statements of anyone before you.

In his reply, Ḥasan reports that the early scholars, who followed the *sunna* of the Prophet and were capable of true understanding of the Qur'ān, did not believe in predestination. They spoke neither in its favor nor against it. When people later began to discuss the subject and to wrongly interpret the Qur'ān, he spoke on the subject to clear the issue. He says:

انما أحدثنا الكلام فيه حيث أحدث الناس النكرة له . . . وحرفوا كتاب الله . . .

> We initiated argumentation in this matter only insofar as the people initiated the custom of denying it . . . and altered [the meaning of] the book of Allah.

Once again, the treatise repeats the same accusation. It reads:

---

[67] *Origins*, p. 141.

ولقد خالف القوم يا أمير المؤمنين كتاب الله وحرفوه . . . .

O Commander of the Believers, these people have gone against the Qur'ān and altered its [meaning].

We know that there are verses in the Qur'ān which have been used to support the doctrine of predestination and other verses which have been used to support the doctrine of free will. The treatise explains some of the verses quoted in support of predestination, showing that it was not the right interpretation. After discussing the interpretation of a few verses in this regard, Ḥasan says:

وجميع ما في القرآن من اشباه ذلك يظن الجاهلون انه ينهاهم عن قضائه وقدره .

And all verses in the Qur'ān similar to this are construed by the ignorant as forbidding them [from free actions] by virtue of His Decree and His predetermination.

As Schacht did not find in this treatise any tradition quoted on the authority of the Prophet on the matter of creeds, he concludes that any tradition recorded anywhere on the subject of creed must be later than the compilation of the treatise, which "cannot be," according to Schacht, "later than the very early years of the second century."[68]

Before accepting this conclusion, there are some serious questions that ought to be resolved. First, Schacht himself doubts the attribution of the work to Ḥasan[69]: therefore, it is highly questionable to put it under the aegis of Ḥasan. Secondly, Schacht did not provide any basis for his assumption that the treatise cannot be dated later than the early second century A.H. There is, however, positive reason to believe that this treatise did not belong to Ḥasan or any author of early centuries of Islam, because Ḥasan Baṣrī was a traditionist. In his period, anything which was written must have been transmitted through the *isnād* system. Furthermore, any treatise which was written by the scholars of that time must have a reading certificate in the beginning of the book, at the end of the book, and even in the margins here and there. This was the procedure followed for many centuries.[70] But the printed text of the treatise does not contain any *isnād* at the beginning or anywhere else. On these grounds, anyone who is acquainted with the style of the period finds it difficult to attribute it to Ḥasan Baṣrī or to date its origin early in the second century.

But let us assume that it is the work of Ḥasan Baṣrī. Earlier, I have explained the background of the treatise based on its own contents.[71] Its main theme is to prove the error of those scholars who based their doctrine of predestination on the certain verses of the Qur'ān, and to explain the correct method of interpretation of those verses. Schacht notices that "the author states explicitly: 'Every opinion which is not

---

[68] *Ibid.*, p. 74.
[69] *Idem.*
[70] See my *Ḥadīth Methodology and Literature* (Indianapolis, 1977), p. 22.
[71] See above, pp. 221–223.

based on the Koran is erroneous.' "[72] However, this comment does not appear to be in its proper context. The author was not writing the treatise to explain the sources of creeds, because the opponent of the author had already quoted so many verses from the Qur'ān in the favor of the doctrine, a fact which was recorded by the author of the treatise himself. Therefore, the main issue, in the view of the author, is the correct method for the interpretation of the Qur'ān, not the source of the creed. Therefore, the author does not quote any tradition in this regard. However, the enquiry of 'Abdul Malik to Ḥasan Baṣrī as to whether or not he had learned this doctrine from the Companions of the Prophet and Ḥasan's reply that the Companions did not speak on the subject for or against it, are indication of the importance of the traditions of the Prophet.

EXAMPLE 3: THE MAKING OF PROSTRATIONS AFTER RECITING *SŪRAT ṢĀD* IN THE QUR'ĀN

Schacht says, under "Traditions Originating Between 'Ibrāhīm Nakha'ī [d. 95 A.H.] and Ḥammād' [d. 120 A.H.]":

> *Āthār A.Y.* 206: Abū Ḥanīfa – Ḥammād – Ibrāhīm – Ibn Mas'ūd did not follow a certain practice. *Āthār Shaib.* 37: Abū Ḥanīfa – Ḥammād – Ibrāhīm did not follow it; the same is related from Ibn Mas'ūd. But there is a tradition from the Prophet to the contrary. *Āthār A.Y.* 207: Abū Ḥanīfa – Ḥammād – 'Abdalkarīm – with an *isnād* going back to the Prophet, that he did follow it. *Āthār Shaib.* 37: Shaibānī – 'Umar b. Dharr Hamdānī – his father – Sa'īd b. Jubair – Ibn 'Abbās – Prophet: a tradition in favour of the practice, polemically directed against the other opinion. The same tradition with another Iraqian *isnād* occurs in *Tr. II*, 19 *(t)*.
>
> It will be shown that the name of Ibrāhīm Nakha'ī is often a label for the ancient Iraqian doctrine. This and the then recently produced tradition from the Prophet to the contrary were transmitted by Ḥammād to Abū Ḥanīfa, and the tradition from the Prophet soon acquired better *isnāds*.[73]

Schacht's argument may be summarized as follows: It is quoted by Abū Yūsuf, through Abū Ḥanīfa, Ḥammād, and Nakha'ī, that Ibn Mas'ūd did not prostrate himself after reciting *Sūrat Ṣād*; the same is ascribed to Nakha'ī, as quoted by Shaibānī.

However, Schacht mentions three other traditions which show the practice of the Prophet was contrary to the practice of Ibn Mas'ūd. These chains are:

1. Abū Ḥanīfa – Ḥammād – 'Abd al-Karīm – the Prophet.[74]
2. Ibn 'Uyaynah – Ayyūb – 'Ikrimah – Ibn 'Abbās – the Prophet.[75]
3. 'Amr – His father – Ibn Jubair – Ibn 'Abbās – the Prophet.[76]

---

[72] *Origins*, p. 141.
[73] *Ibid.*, p. 141.
[74] *A.Y.*, 207.
[75] *Umm.* vol. vii, p. 174.
[76] Shaibānī, *Āthār*, p. 111.

Schacht asks us to believe that these *aḥādīth* were fabricated between the period of Nakhaʿī and Ḥammād. It should be pointed out here that there are other traditions on the subject, recorded either by the same authorities Schacht quoted or by authorities older than Shāfiʿī [150 – 204 A.H.] and Shaibānī [135 – 189 A.H.] such as ʿA. Razzāq [127 – 207 A.H.]. Additional traditions from the Prophet in this regard include:

Abū Yūsuf – Abū Ḥanīfa – Ḥammād – ʿAbdul Karīm – the Prophet.[77]

Shaibānī – ʿUmar – Abih – Ibn Jubair [d. 93] – Ibn ʿAbbās [d. 68] – the Prophet.[78]

ʿA. Razzāq – ʿUmar – Ibn Jubair – Ibn ʿAbbās – the Prophet.[79]

ʿA. Razzāq – Maʿmar – Ayyūb – ʿIkrima [d. 107] – Ibn ʿAbbās – the Prophet.[80]

Shaibānī – Ibn ʿUyayna – Ayyūb – ʿIkrima – Ibn ʿAbbās – the Prophet.[81]

Shāfiʿī – Ibn ʿUyayna – Ayyūb – ʿIkrima – Ibn ʿAbbās – the Prophet.[82]

Ḥumaidī – Ibn ʿUyayna – Ayyūb – ʿIkrima – Ibn ʿAbbās – the Prophet.[83]

Shaibānī – Misʿar – ʿAmr – Mujāhid [d. 105] – Ibn ʿAbbās – the Prophet.[84]

Shaibānī – Sallām – Laith – ʿAṭāʾ [d. 117] – Ibn ʿAbbās – the Prophet.[85]

Ibn Wahb – Hafs – Zaid – ʿAṭāʾ – Ibn ʿAbbās – the Prophet.[86]

Ibn Wahb – Hishām – Zaid – ʿAṭāʾ – Ibn ʿAbbās – the Prophet.[87]

Shaibānī – Thaurī – Suddī – Abū Mālik – the Prophet.[88]

ʿA. Razzaq – Thaurī – Suddī – Abū Mālik – the Prophet.[89]

Ibn Wahb – ʿAmr – Saʿīd – ʿAyāḍ [b. 100] – Abū Saʿīd Khudrī [d. 74] – the Prophet.[90]

ʿA. Razzāq – Ibn ʿUyayna – ʿĀṣim – Bakr [d. 106] – the Prophet.[91]

Further traditions regarding the subject are related on the authority of other than the Prophet:

---

[77] *A.Y.*, 207.
[78] Shaibānī, *Āthār*, p. 111, *Ḥujja*, I, 109.
[79] *Muṣannaf*, vol. iii, p. 337.
[80] *Muṣannaf*, vol. iii, p. 337.
[81] *Ḥujja*, I, 109.
[82] *Umm*, VII, 174.
[83] Ḥumaidī, *Musnad* (Karachi, 1963), *Ḥadīth*, 477.
[84] *Ḥujja*, I, 110.
[85] *Ḥujja*, I, 111–113.
[86] Ibn Wahb, *Jāmiʿ* (Cairo, 1939), 43b.
[87] Ibn Wahb, *Jāmīʿ*, 43b.
[88] *Ḥujja*, I, 110.
[89] *Muṣannaf*, vol. iii, p. 337.
[90] Ibn Wahb, *Jāmiʿ*, 43a.
[91] *Muṣannaf*, vol. iii, p. 337.

'A. Razzāq – Ibn 'Uyayna – 'Ubaidullah [40 – 126] – Ibn 'Abbās.[92]
'A. Razzāq – M'amar – Abū Jamara [d. 128] – Ibn 'Abbās.[93]
'A. Razzāq – b. Juraij b. Khālid – Ibn Jubair [d. 93] – Ibn 'Abbās.[94]
'A. Razzāq – Ma'mar – Zuhrī – Sā'ib – 'Uthmān.[95]
Shaibānī – Ya'qūb – Ḥusain – Mujāhid [d. 105] – Ibn 'Abbās.[96]
'A. Razzāq – b. Juraij – Sulaimān – Mujāhid – Ibn 'Abbās.[97]
'A. Razzāq – Ibn 'Uyayna – 'Abdah – Ibn 'Umar.[98]
'A. Razzāq – b. Juraij – Sulaimān – Mujāhid – Ibn 'Abbās – 'Umar.[99]
Shaibānī – Mis'ar – 'Amr – Mujāhid – Ibn 'Abbās.[100]
Shaibānī – Ibn 'Uyayana – 'Abdah – Ibn 'Umar.[101]

We may summarize the above by saying that against the act of Ibn Mas'ūd and Nakha'ī, the practice of the Prophet has been reported through several Companions. The practice of Ibn 'Abbās, Ibn 'Umar, 'Uthmān, and 'Umar has been similarly reported.

As these *aḥādīth* are contrary to the view of Ibn Mas'ūd and Nakha'ī Schacht argues that they must have been fabricated between Nakha'ī and Ḥammād. Again, Schacht fails to prove the following points: First, that every scholar has a complete knowledge of his subject and cannot be ignorant of anything in his field; and second, that one scholar's ignorance of a particular *ḥadīth* invalidates the positive knowledge of other scholars. Moreover, it seems that Schacht did not keep in mind what he had written earlier in his book and thus contradicted himself. This can be seen by referring to his opinion about Ibn Mas'ūd and whether or not it can be reconciled with his conclusion in this particular *ḥadīth*.

There is an additional issue to be covered here. As part of his discussion of this example, Schacht says, "The name of Ibn Mas'ūd is usually an indication of the prevailing doctrine of the school of Kufa . . .,"[102] and later, "Ibn Sa'd (vi. 232) identified Ḥammād's own doctrine with what Ḥammād put under the aegis of Ibrāhīm . . ."[103] In this case, however, the *ḥadīth* runs counter to the prevailing doctrine of the Kūfians[104] school and their sponsors, Ibn Mas'ūd and Nakha'ī. Are we expected to believe that second-century Iraqi scholars fabricated a *ḥadīth* simply for the purpose of rejecting it? Surely, they would be more likely to attribute to

---

[92] *Ibid.*, vol. iii, p. 337.
[93] *Ibid.*, 335–336.
[94] *Ibid.*, 335.
[95] *Ibid.*, 337.
[96] *Ḥujja*, vol. i, p. 111.
[97] *Muṣannaf*, vol. iii, p. 336.
[98] *Ibid.*, 338.
[99] *Ibid.*, 336.
[100] *Ḥujja*, vol. i, p. 110.
[101] *Ibid.*, p. 111.
[102] *Origins*, p. 232.
[103] *Ibid.*, pp. 238–239.
[104] *Ḥujja*, vol. i, p. 109.

their sponsor statements supporting their doctrine. If they were as unscrupulous in exploiting the names of earlier scholars as Schacht would have us believe, would they not have suppressed evidence that ran counter to their doctrine and fabricated evidence in support of the doctrine? Moreover, how were these Iraqians able to persuade their opponents, that is, traditionists from Mecca, Medina, and Egypt, as well as the followers of the Medinese and Egyptian schools of law to fabricate evidence for the benefit of Iraqians? Far from proving Schacht's point, the existence of opposing *aḥādīth* serves to illustrate the scholars' good faith in recording the material they learned. Thus the positive knowledge of many cannot be invalidated by the misinformation of a single man.

EXAMPLE 4: POSITIONS IN CONGREGATIONAL PRAYER

In discussing the *ḥadīth* concerning the arrangement of people standing behind the *Imām* for prayers under the heading "Traditions Originating Between Ibrāhīm Nakha'ī' and Abū Ḥanīfah," Schacht comments that the *ḥadīth* was "unknown to Ibrāhīm (*Āthār Shaib.* 22), known to Abū Ḥanīfah without *isnād* (*Āthār A.Y.* 251), and appears with a full *isnād* in *Muw.* i. 275; *Muw. Shaib*, 122; *Tr. II.* 19 *(g)* and in the classical collection."[105] From this he concludes that: (a) the *ḥadīth* was fabricated between the time of Ibrāhīm Nakha'ī and Abū Ḥanīfah; (b) it was known to Abū Ḥanīfa without *isnād*; and (c) it appeared with full *isnād* in *Muw.*

It is interesting to note Schacht's use of the words "known" and "unknown." Ibrāhīm Nakha'ī did not say explicitly that he did not know this *ḥadīth*. All that can be said is that Abū Yūsuf or Shaibānī did not record this *ḥadīth* through Nakha'ī in *Al-Āthār*, and we have already established that Abū Yūsuf or Shaibānī, like other scholars, did not usually quote all the evidence available to them.[106] Contrary to Schacht's claim, we find Nakha'ī reporting the practice of Ibn Mas'ūd and 'Umar, and preferring the practice of 'Umar, which corresponds to the said *ḥadīth*.[107] Thus he differed from the opinion of Ibn Mas'ūd, who is, however, in the view of Schacht, the aegis under which the Iraqian school developed. This deviation of Nakha'ī implies that he might have known the practice of the Prophet as reported in this *ḥadīth*.

Even if Nakha'ī did *not* know the *ḥadīth*, this is hardly sufficient proof that it did not exist. It would be safer to believe that all the *aḥādīth* were not known to every individual scholar. In fact, this same *ḥadīth* was known to scholars earlier than Nakha'ī – notably Anas b. Mālik (d. 93 A.H.), Jābir b. Zaid (d. 93 A.H.),[108] and Isḥāq. It would be comforting to believe that Schacht's oversight in this regard was due to his inability to

---

[105] *Origins*, p. 141.
[106] See the discussion in this chapter under the heading "Unwarranted Assumptions and Unscientific Research Methods."
[107] Shaibani, *Āthār*, p. 70, *ḥadīth* 93.
[108] See Rabī', *Musnad* (Damascus, 1388), p. 54.

obtain source material. But evidence that these scholars knew the *ḥadīth* is found in the same sources that Schacht cites to prove Nakhaʿī's ignorance.[109] This point proves the illogicality of assuming that the ignorance of one scholar "proves" the nonexistence of the *ḥadīth* in question. There is no proof in this case that Ibrāhīm Nakhaʿī was ignorant of the *ḥadīth*, and Schacht himself seems not to accept the positive knowledge of other scholars as proof of its existence.

This example also serves to illustrate Schacht's arbitrary application of his thesis. Typically, when he finds a *ḥadīth* in an early collection with incomplete *isnād* and the same *ḥadīth* with complete *isnād* in a later collection, he concludes that there was an "improvement," i.e., fabrication of the *isnād*. In other words, he starts from the earlier available records and bases his discussion on them. In this example, however, it is the earlier source, the *Muwaṭṭaʾ* of Mālik, that contains the full *isnād*; the later source, *ʿĀthār A.Y.* 251, gives no *isnād*. Rigorous application of Schacht's theory at this point would tend to prove rather than disprove the validity of *ḥadīth* and *isnād* system. Schacht chooses to ignore the discrepancy.

EXAMPLE 5: IMPRECATION AGAINST ENEMIES

Schacht places this case under "Traditions Originating Between Ibrāhīm Nakhaʿī and Abū Ḥanīfa."[110] Earlier, he says: Ibrāhīm is aware that the imprecation against political enemies during the ritual prayer is an innovation introduced only under ʿAlī and Muʿāwīyah some considerable time after the Prophet. He confirms this by pointing out the absence of any information on the matter from the Prophet, Abū Bakr, and ʿUmar. It follows that the tradition, which claims the Prophet's example for this addition to the ritual and which Shāfiʿī of course accepts, must be later than Ibrāhīm.[111] Here are the quotations:

٣٤٩ - عن أبي حنيفة عن حماد عن ابراهيم عن النبي صلى الله عليه وسلم أنه لم يقنت في الفجر إلا شهرا واحدا حارب حيا من المشركين قنت يدعو عليهم ، لم ير قانتا قبلها ولا بعدها .[112]

٣٥٠ - عن أبي حنيفة عن حماد عن ابراهيم عن علقمة عن عبد الله رضي الله عنه عن النبي صلى الله عليه وسلم مثله .[113]

---

[109] See *Muw. Safar*, 31.
[110] *Origins*, p. 141.
[111] *Ibid.*, p. 60.
[112] Abū Yūsuf, *Āthār* (Cairo, 1355), Ḥadīth numbers 349, cited hereafter as *A.Y.*
[113] *A.Y.*, 350.

٣٥١ - عن أبي حنيفة عن حماد عن إبراهيم أن أبا بكر رضي الله عنه لم يقنت حتى لحق بالله تعالى . [114]

٣٥٢ - عن أبي حنيفة عن حماد عن إبراهيم أن عليا رضي الله عنه قنت يدعو على معاوية رضي الله عنه حين حاربه فأخذ أهل الكوفة عنه ، وقنت معاوية يدعو على علي فأخذ أهل الشام عنه . [115]

349. Abū Ḥanīfa – Ḥammād – Ibrāhīm. The Prophet did not imprecate in dawn prayers except for one month; when he was fighting some polytheist tribes, he imprecated against them. He was seen imprecating neither before nor after that.
350. Abū Ḥanīfa – Ḥammād – Ibrāhīm – 'Alqama – Abdullah. The Prophet, as above [mentioned].
351. Abū Ḥanīfa – Ḥammād – Ibrāhīm. Abū Bakr never imprecated during his whole life.
352. Abū Ḥanīfa – Ḥammād – Ibrāhīm. 'Alī imprecated against Mu'āwiya when he was fighting, so the Kūfans took it from him, and Mu'āwiya imprecated against 'Alī, and the Syrians took it from him.

In this text, *Nakha'ī* narrates two *aḥādīth*, one with complete *isnād* and another with imperfect *mursal isnād*, describing the practice of the Prophet. It is difficult to see how Schacht deduces from this that the imprecation against enemies is an innovation introduced some considerable time after the Prophet unless he complete disregarded the text or misunderstood it.

EXAMPLE 6: TIME OF MORNING PRAYER

Schacht: ("Traditions Originating Between Ibrāhīm Nakha'ī and Mālik"):

> *Āthār A.Y.* 98: Ibrāhīm says: 'There is nothing with regard to prayer on which the Companions of the Prophet agreed so fully as saying the morning prayer in full daylight.' This seems to be an authentic statement of Ibrāhīm. Later than this and in favour of saying it in early dawn are traditions from 'Alī and Ibn Mas'ūd (ibid.) and from the Prophet (first in *Muw.* i. 19).[116]

Mālik reported the practice of the Prophet, and Abū Yūsuf is silent on the matter. Mālik quoted a letter of Caliph 'Umar to his army commanders concerning prayer times. The letter was reported by Ṣafīya, wife of Ibn 'Umar,[117] and quoted by Nāfi' (d. 117 A.H.) in his book,[118] as well as

---

[114] *A.Y.*, 351.
[115] *A.Y.*, 352.
[116] *Origins*, p. 142.
[117] See Ibn Ḥajar, *Tahdhīb al-Tahdhīb* (Hydrabad, 1325), vol. 12, pp. 430–431. Cited hereafter as *Tahd.*
[118] See Al-A'ẓamī. *Studies in Early Ḥadīth Literature* (Beirut 1968), p. 117 Arabic section.

reported by Mālik b. Abū 'Āmir (d. 74 A.H.)[119] and 'Urwa [d. 95 A.H.].[120] Furthermore, this letter was accepted as authentic by Shaibānī, who utilized part of it to support his doctrine.[121] Thus, scholars earlier than Nakha'ī [d. 96 A.H.] and sources much earlier than *Āthār* Abū Yūsuf contain information contrary to the report of Nakha'ī. The most one can say is that Nakha'ī reported what he knew to the best of his knowledge but was mistaken, as has been shown.

Thus early positive information cannot be invalidated by the silence of later scholars or negative information from them. But for the purpose of proving "fabrication of *ḥadīth*," Schacht chose to believe that the statement made by Ibrāhīm Nakha'ī is authentic, even against the evidence of *Muwaṭṭā*' and other sources. He knew that most scholars were of the opinion that Nakha'ī had no direct contact with any of the Companions[122] and thus had no firsthand information. Schacht himself rejects statements of Nakha'ī elsewhere although documented through the same channels of *isnād* as this statement which he accepts.[123] He impugns the *isnād* as spurious in that discussion yet chooses to accept it here. One may ask on what grounds Schacht accepts Nakha'ī's statement in this case as an authentic one.

Furthermore, there is no tradition from Ibn Mas'ūd in favor of saying the *fajr* prayer in early dawn. Thus the impression which Schacht wanted to create, that this *ḥadīth* of Ibn Masu'ūd was fabricated later, is unfounded and falsely ascribed.

EXAMPLE 7: REGARDING THE SANCTITY OF MECCA

According to Schacht "Tradition Originating Between 'Aṭā' and Shāfi'ī' ":

> *Tr. I*, 181: Abū Yūsuf refers to and follows the opinion of 'Aṭā', which he heard personally from Ḥajjāj b. Arṭāt. It is likely that this opinion goes back not even to 'Aṭā' himself but only to Ḥajjāj. But in Shāfi'ī's time it was expressed in a tradition from the Prophet.[124]

In the Qur'ān, the sanctity of Mecca has a unique position.[125] The Qur'ān recorded the order to fight in the cause of Allah, but prohibited it in the

---

[119] *Tahd.*, X, 19.
[120] For detail see *Muw. Waqūt*, 6–8.
[121] *Ḥujja*, I, 7.
[122] See *Tahd*, vol. 1, pp. 177–179.
[123] Schacht says, "*Āthār A.Y.* is a largely coextensive collection of Ibrāhīm's *alleged* opinions and traditions, made by Abū Yūsuf" (*Origins*, p. 86, italics mine). However, in the first 50 *aḥādīth* recorded by Abū Yūsuf in his book *Āthār*, the following have been recorded through the *isnād* Abū Ḥanīfa – Ḥammād – Ibrāhīm; 6, 7, 9–13, 15, 19–23, 25–29, 33–34, 36–39, 42, 44, 46, and 48 – that is, 29 out of 50. See also *Ḥadīth* Barīra in *A.Y. 141* by the same *isnād*, which Schacht has stigmatized as spurious (*Origins*, p. 174).
[124] *Origins*, p. 142.
[125] See Qur'ān, 2: 125, 3: 97, and 5: 97.

sanctuary of Mecca unless it was begun by polytheists.[126] In view of the unique status of Mecca, there was a difference of opinion among scholars about grazing animals on the grass of Mecca and cutting down its trees. Abū Yūsuf reported their views as follows:

> Abū Ḥanīfa disliked grazing or cutting down of trees in Mecca.
> Ibn Abū Lailā allowed both grazing and cutting.
> Ḥajjāj b. Arṭāt (d. 145 A.H.) reported the opinion of 'Aṭā: he allowed grazing but not cutting down of trees.[127]

Schacht finds it likely that this opinion goes back "not even to 'Aṭā' himself but only to Ḥajjāj."[128] He further says in this case that Ḥajjāj "must be suspected of putting into circulation recently forged traditions."[129]

Schacht, however, fails to justify his conclusion that this opinion could not be ascribed even to 'Aṭā'. Pilgrims were coming to Mecca for the *Ḥajj*, even in the pre-Islamic era. They had to sacrifice animals, which had to be fed. Both pilgrims and scholars faced this practical problem in the very early days of Islam. There does not seem, therefore, to be any situational or historical reason to reject the argument that the problem was discussed in the earliest Islamic days.

Schacht's claim that this opinion was only expressed in a fabricated tradition from the Prophet in Shāfi'ī's time may be refuted by referring to the *Sīra* of Ibn Isḥāq (d. 151 A.H.)[130] at the birth of Shāfi'ī (150 – 204 A.H.), the Ibadi scholar Rabī' bin Ḥabīb [d. 160 A.H.],[131] and Wāqidī (d. 207 A.H.), a contemporary of Shāfi'ī.[132] The same *ḥadīth* has also been recorded by Shiite scholars.[133]

EXAMPLE 8: REGARDING FASTING

According to Schacht, this *ḥadīth* was not known to Ibn Abī Lailā [d. 148] but known to Abū Ḥanīfa (d. 150 A.H.) with imperfect *mursal isnād* and with the suspected transmitter 'Aṭā' Khurāsānī in the *isnād*, and known with uninterrupted *isnād* at the time of Mālik. Schacht therefore assumes that it was invented between Ibn Abī Lailā and Abū Ḥanīfa and that the *isnād* was "improved" during Mālik's time.

In fact, Mālik records the *ḥadīth* from two chains:[134] Zuhrī – Ḥumaid – Abū Hurairah – the Prophet; and 'Aṭā' Khurāsānī – Ibn al-Musayyab –

---

[126] Qur'ān, 2: 191 – 192.
[127] Ibn Abī Lailā, p. 138.
[128] *Origins*, p. 142.
[129] *Ibid.*, p. 250.
[130] *Sīra* (Cairo, 1375) vol. 3, pp. 415–416.
[131] Rabī', *Musnad*, p. 105.
[132] Wāqidī, *Magāzī* (London, 1966) p. 835–836.
[133] A.J. Ya'qubī, *Tarikh al-Ya'qūbī*, vol. 2, p. 59.

the Prophet.¹³⁵ Abū Yūsuf reports its *isnād* as Abū Ḥanīfa – 'Aṭā' b. Abī Rabāḥ – Ibn al-Musayyab – the Prophet.¹³⁶ Thus, Mālik reported this *ḥadīth* on the authority of Zuhrī (d. 124 A.H.) and 'Aṭā' Khurāsānī (d. 136 A.H.), and Abū Ḥanīfa narrated it on the authority of Aṭā' b. Abū Rabāḥ (d. 114 A.H.).

If we suppose that these chains are genuine, it would imply that this *ḥadīth* was known to Ibn al-Musayyab (d. 93 A.H.), Ḥumaid (d. 95 A.H.), and Abū Hurairah (d. 59 A.H.), who, of course, were much older than Ibn Abī Lailā (d. 148 A.H.). But if Schacht suspected that the *isnād* was "improved," then at least he had to accept the statement of Mālik and Abū Ḥanīfah, ascribing the knowledge of this *ḥadīth* to 'Aṭā' and Zuhrī. The only reasonable assumption would appear to be that Ibn Abī Lailā was not aware of this *ḥadīth*, while his contemporaries and earlier scholars knew it.

One more point needs to be made about this example. According to Schacht, early lawyers offered strong resistance to accepting *aḥādīth* from the Prophet.¹³⁷ In this example, as well as in almost all the other examples of this chapter, it is implied that Ibn Abī Lailā or other lawyers *would have followed* the *ḥadīth* if they had known it. Since Ibn Abī Lailā was a lawyer and judge, we would expect him – according to Schacht – to have resisted the *ḥadīth*, and yet – according to Schacht – he would have followed it had he known it.

Other mistakes of fact can be found in the same example. Schacht brands Khurāsānī as a suspect transmitter, when in fact he is well authenticated.¹³⁸ He is also mistaken in saying that Abū Ḥanīfah transmitted through Khurāsānī.¹³⁹ He is further mistaken in saying that Abū Ḥanīfah knew this *ḥadīth* with imperfect *isnād* and that it was known with uninterrupted *isnād* at the time of Mālik. Mālik recorded it with the same imperfect *isnād* as used by Abū Ḥanīfa, as quoted above.

Although it may be argued that these are only minor errors with little impact on the overall thesis, they do serve as examples of a lack of rigorous analysis that makes one immediately skeptical of the validity of other, more important arguments. The problem of *isnād* and its interruption will be discussed in detail later.¹⁴⁰

EXAMPLE 9: COMPENSATION FOR TEETH

According to Schacht, Ibn Abī Lailā is ignorant of a *ḥadīth* from the Prophet that appears in Abū Ḥanīfa (or Abū Yūsuf), Shāfi'ī, and the

---

[134] *Origins*, p. 142.
[135] *Muwaṭṭa'*, *Ṣaum*, 9.
[136] *A.Y.* 795.
[137] See *Origins*, p. 57.
[138] See *Tahd.* vii, 212–215.
[139] See *Origins*, p. 142.
[140] Chapter Eight discusses the *isnād* system in detail.

classical collections. Schacht assumes that this means the *ḥadīth* was invented between Ibn Abī Lailā and Abū Ḥanīfa.[141]

His contention may again be refuted by reference to earlier sources, one of whom, 'Aṭā', was some 50 years older than Ibn Abī Lailā. The *ḥadīth* was recorded by Ibn Juraij (80 – 150 A.H.) on the authority of 'Aṭā' b. Abū Rabāḥ (27 – 114 A.H.) from Ya'lā b. Umayyah – his father – the Prophet.[142] It was also recorded by Thaurī (97 – 161 A.H.) from Ḥumaid (d. 130 A.H.) – Mujāhid – the servant of Ya'lā b. Umayyah – the Prophet, almost with the same wording as reported by Abū Ḥanīfa.[143] Thus the *ḥadīth* was known to Thaurī, Abū Ḥanīfah, Ḥumaid, 'Aṭā' and many others in the lifetime of Ibn Abī Lailā. Some of them were older than Ibn Abī Lailā by 50 years.

EXAMPLE 10: SPOILS BELONG TO THE ONE WHO KILLS HIS OPPONENT

In "Tradition Originating Between Auzā'ī and Mālik,"[144] Schacht implies that:

1. The legal maxim which Auzā'ī in paragraph 13 takes as a proof of "valid *sunna* going back to the Prophet" does not say that this is related on the authority of the Prophet.
2. Abū Yūsuf does not know it to be a *ḥadīth* from the Prophet, otherwise he would have mentioned it.
3. The first time it appeared was in the *Muwaṭṭa'* of Mālik.
4. In later sources some additional authorities were mentioned.[145]

He further comments: "Whereas this calls for caution in the use of the argument *e silentio*, it also shows that the tradition was not widely known in the time of Mālik."[146] This statement of Schacht contains mistakes of fact as well as misunderstandings of the text.

1. The saying of Auzā'ī is:

مضت السنّة عن رسول الله صلى الله عليه وسلم من قتل علجا فله سلبه .

The *sunna* which has been executed by the Prophet is that whoever kills [in the battlefield] an infidel, his spoils belong to the killer...

It means this practice was established by the Prophet. Auzā'ī did not relate it with the *isnād*. This was the method of early lawyers, as will be seen in the next chapter. Furthermore, it is not an original writing by Auzā'ī, but most likely an abridgement by Abū Yūsuf. We do not know whether or not Auzā'ī related it with *isnād*. It is simply a quotation or reference.

---

[141] *Origins*, p. 142.
[142] *Muṣannaf*, IX, 354–355.
[143] *Ibid.*, IX, 355.
[144] *Origins*, p. 142, referring to *ibid.*, p. 70.
[145] See *Origins*, pp. 70–71.
[146] *Ibid.*, p. 142.

2. We cannot say whether Abū Yūsuf knew it or not. The most one can say is that the few books of Abū Yūsuf which are extant do not mention it. Abū Yūsuf most probably did know it. His objection was not about the authenticity of the *hadīth* but about the method of applying it. Moreover, the *hadīth* was recorded by Ibn Isḥāq,[147] whose work was well known to Abū Yūsuf who quoted from it time after time.[148]

3. Schacht's claim that it appeared for the first time in the *Muwaṭṭa'* of Mālik is wrong. It was recorded by Ibn Isḥāq (80 – 115 A.H.), who was earlier than Mālik (91 – 179 A.H.), and recorded by Auzā'ī (88 – 158 A.H.) who was also older than Mālik. Moreover, Schacht cannot give us a list of works that were compiled earlier than *Muwaṭṭa'* and still exist in their original form. When Schacht says that it appeared for the first time in *Muwaṭṭa'*, he implies that he has consulted a number of books prior to Mālik and all lacked this particular *hadīth*. But he does not give references.

Schacht's comment that his argument *e silentio* needs to be used with caution is, of course, applicable not only here but in all the other examples we have dealt with above and those to follow.

EXAMPLE 11: WHOEVER JOINS A PEOPLE BELONGS TO IT

Schacht claims that this lawyers' maxim originates between Auzā'ī and Ibn Sa'd.[149] He refers to the statement of Auzā'ī:

من تولى قوما فهو منهم

"Whoever joins a people belongs to it" and in a footnote he states that "it appears as a tradition from the Prophet only in a somewhat different form from Ibn Sa'd onwards."

What he does not seem to have taken into consideration is that many lawyers used the wordings of a *hadīth* in their writings without explicitly ascribing them to the Prophet. For example, in a difference of opinion about *zakāt* on vegetables Shaibānī says:

وأما قولنا فليس في الخضر صدقة ... حتى يبلغ خمسة أوساق .[150]

"In our opinion there is no *zakāt* on a vegetable till it reaches five *wasaq*."

He did not record any *hadīth* of the Prophet. But Mālik, who was 40 years older than Shaibānī and happened to be Shaibānī's teacher, recorded the *hadīth* of the Prophet in almost identical words:

(ليس فيما دون خمسة أوسق صدقة)[151]

"There is no *zakāt* on less than five *wasaqs*."

---

[147] Ibn Hishām, *Sīra* I, vol. 3, p. 448.
[148] See Auzā'ī, pp. 7, 32–33, 38, 43, 48, 85, 90, etc.
[149] *Origins*, p. 142, referring to *ibid.*, 180, n.1.
[150] Shaibānī, *Āthār*, p. 143.
[151] *Muw. zakāt*, 1 – 2.

The same *hadīth* is also recorded by Shaibānī.[152]

This indicates that the *hadīth* is genuine and that Shaibānī considered it authentic and well established enough to use it without referring to the Prophet to prove its validity. Given this habit, it is more logical to assume that nonreference to a *hadīth* coming down from the Prophet is proof of conviction in its validity rather than to assume, as Schacht does, that the *hadīth* in question does not exist.

Furthermore, to err is human. Scholars do make mistakes. *Muhaddithīn* were quite aware of this fact. It was quite possible that a certain scholar might have ascribed to the Prophet a statement from a later authority. *Muhaddithīn* themselves criticized scholars who made mistakes of this sort, and we find arguments along these lines among scholars from the second century of Hijra – a further proof of their credibility, sincerity, and honesty.[153]

EXAMPLE 12: STEALING OF SLAVES FROM THE SPOILS OF WAR

Schacht considers this *hadīth* to have originated between Abū Hanīfah and Abū Yūsuf: "*Tr. IX*, 42: Abū Yūsuf adduces a tradition with an imperfect *isnād*, not through Abū Hanīfah who obviously did not yet know it, but through an anonymous sheikh. Several similar cases occur in *Āthār A.Y.*"[154]

There is not enough evidence to show whether or not Abū Hanīfa knew this *hadīth*. The most that can be said is that Abū Yūsuf did not quote it through Abū Hanīfah. We know early scholars used to give decisions (*fatwā*) without mentioning the basis of their decisions. For example, Shāfi'ī gives his *fatwā* (*Umm, VII*, 133) for fasting two months without mentioning the relevant *hadīth* of the Prophet, while it is recorded by Mālik in *Muw.*,[155] a book well known to Shāfi'ī. However, I could not trace the *hadīth* in discussion in later works except in *Musannaf*,[156] where 'Abdur Razzāq reported it on the authority of 'Abdullah b. Muharrir, a contemporary of Abū Hanīfa who died between 150 and 160 A.H.[157] He is a very weak *(Matrūk)*, unreliable narrator, which implies that the *hadīth* was known in the life of Abū Hanīfa but not acceptable to scholars, and thus had no legal value. Moreover, it shows the honesty of scholars in ascribing and naming the authorities. If they had been engaged in wholesale fabrication, Abū Yūsuf would surely have named Abū Hanīfa as his authority in this *hadīth*.

---

[152] *Muw. Shaib*, 169, for a further example see *Musannaf*, vol. viii, p. 52.
[153] For examples, see: Ibn Abī Hatim al-Rāzī, *Al-Jarh wa al-Ta'dīl*, vol. 2, part 1, p. 279; Al-Dhahabī, *Mīzān*, (Cairo, 1382), vol. 1, p. 23; Dāraqutnī, *Sunan* (Anṣārī Press, Delhi, 1310), p. 198 (in the commentary).
[154] *Origins*, p. 143.
[155] See Zurqānī, vol. 2, pp. 171–174.
[156] *Musannaf*, X, 212.
[157] See *Tahd.*, V, 390.

EXAMPLE 13: RUNNING AWAY OF A SLAVE IN ENEMY TERRITORY

He claims that:

a. There was a common ancient doctrine on slaves captured by the enemy and recaptured by the Muslims, a subject for which Auzā'ī and Abū Ḥanīfa did not yet know a tradition.
b. The tradition from the Prophet on the subject appears for the first time in Abū Yūsuf in *Tr. IX.* 18 as a ruling in general form. The version is improved, and a further personal touch is added in the versions in Dāraquṭnī (d. 385 A.H.) and Baihaqī (d. 458 A.H.).
c. Ḥasan b. 'Umāra in the generation preceding Abū Yūsuf is the lowest common link in the three *isnāds* of the above-mentioned *ḥadīth*, and he or a person using his name must have been responsible for the creation of this tradition.
d. Ibn 'Umāra was a weak narrator and was discredited; it was alternatively related on the authority of 'Abdul Malik b. Maisara, who was also considered weak.
e. The same doctrine was expressed in two Medinese traditions with first-class *isnāds*, Abū Yūsuf – 'Ubaidulla – Nāfi' – Ibn 'Umar. Both were quoted for the first time by Abū Yūsuf in *Tr. IX*, 18 and *Kharāj*, 123. The first gives it as the general ruling while the second purports to describe the loss by Ibn 'Umar of a slave and a horse to the enemy.
f. This anecdote was recorded by Mālik in its older form without *isnād* and without the reference to the Prophet. None of it is genuine.
g. The Prophet is made directly responsible for the ruling in a later version by Bukhārī (see footnote Nos. 2, 3, p. 158, *Origins*).[158]

Let us analyze these points in the same sequence.

a. Schacht's use of the argument that certain scholars knew so much only or even did not know has been commented on several times already.
b. It is also difficult to appreciate the claim that it was quoted for the first time by Abū Yūsuf, because there is little extant which was compiled prior to Abū Yūsuf in its original form. Even using Schacht's methodology, we may conclude that this *ḥadīth* was well known before Abū Yūsuf.
c. According to Schacht, Ḥasan b. 'Umāra is the lowest commmon link in the three *isnāds*, and he or a person using his name must have been responsible for the creation of this tradition and the fictitious higher part of the *isnād*. Thus Schacht asks us to accept that Abū Yūsuf, who was so accurate that he did not transmit this

---

[158] *Origins*, p. 143, referring to *ibid.*, p. 158.

ḥadīth through Abū Ḥanīfah – as he most probably did not learn it from him – failed to recognize the man from whom he learned it, calling him Ḥasan while he was actually someone else. But this man was the chief justice in the Caliphate of Hārūn al-Rashīd. It is highly questionable that someone might have used Ḥasan b. 'Umāra's name fraudulently and that Abū Yūsuf would have accepted him as Ḥasan.

In addition, there are not three *isnāds*, but two – those of Miqsam and Ṭā'ūs:

1. Abū Yūsuf – Ḥasan – Ḥakam – Miqsam – Ibn 'Abbās – the Prophet.[159]
2. Yazīd – Ḥasan – 'Abdul Malik – Ṭā'ūs – Ibn 'Abbās – the Prophet.[160]
3. Qāsim – Ḥasan – 'Abdul Malik – Ṭā'ūs – Ibn 'Abbās – the Prophet.[161]
4. Mis'ar – Abdul Malik – Ṭā'ūs – Ibn 'Abbās – the Prophet.[162]

It is also evident that the lowest common link is 'Abdul Mālik and not Ḥasan. 'Abdul Malik died, according to Bukhārī, in the second decade of the second century.[163] Accepting Schacht's own theory of the common lowest link, therefore, would lead one to conclude that this *ḥadīth* was known at the very beginning of the second century.

    d. Schacht's claim here is very interesting. But his conclusion is confusing, for 'Abdul Mālik b. Maisara is unanimously well authenticated and trustworthy.[164] But let us suppose, as Schacht claims, that Ḥasan was a weak narrator and that someone wanted to improve the *isnād* and fabricated a new one with 'Abdul Malik b. Maisara. This person would not have chosen another weak narrator.

Moreover, Ḥasan himself is one of the narrators from 'Abdul Malik, as is evident from my quotations in which he is referred to by Schacht. If it was a case of fabrication to improve the value of *isnād*, why did they produce the weak authority of 'Abdul Malik – according to Schacht, a weak narrator – and insert the name of Ḥasan once again in this newly fabricated *isnād*? Were these fabricators so blind that they did not even notice whether or not their fabrication served their cause?

    e. Schacht's argument here is based on the point that since Abū Yūsuf did not quote a *ḥadīth* on the subject through Abū Ḥanīfah, Abū Ḥanīfah did not know it. Suppose Schacht is right: he says that the doctrine was expressed in two Medinese traditions with first-class *isnād*: Abū Yūsuf – 'Ubaidulla – Nāfī – Ibn 'Umar. Both were

---

[159] *Tr., IX*, 18.
[160] Dāraquṭnī, *Sunan* (Cairo, 1386) vol. 4, pp. 114–115.
[161] Baihaqī, *Sunan*, (Hydrabad, 1344) vol. 9, p. 111.
[162] *Ibid.*, vol. 9, p. 111, margin.
[163] *Tahd*, vi, 426.
[164] *Tahd.*, vi, 426.

quoted for the first time by Abū Yūsuf. The question that arises here is that of lack of documentation by Abū Yūsuf through Abū Ḥanīfah being proof of the nonexistence of the said *ḥadīth*: Why is the positive recording of Abū Yūsuf through 'Ubaidullah not evidence *for* its existence?

'Ubaidullah died in 145 A.H.,[165] five years before the death of Abū Ḥanīfah and thirteen years before Auzā'ī's, which indicates that this *ḥadīth* was known in the lifetime of Abū Ḥanīfah and Auzā'ī. Even if it could be established that Abū Ḥanīfah and Auzā'ī did not know it, other scholars must have known it.

Schacht also contends that the doctrine expressed in the *ḥadīth* of Ḥasan b. 'Umāra is being expressed in two Medinese traditions with a first-class *isnād*. Abū Yūsuf – 'Ubaidullah b. 'Umar – Nāfi – Ibn 'Umar.[166] However, there are fundamental differences between the narrations of Ḥasan and 'Ubaidullah. Here is the original text:

١ - الحسن بن عمارة ، عن الحكم بن عتيبة ، عن مقسم ، عن ابن عباس عن رسول الله صلى الله عليه وسلم في عبد وبعير ، أحرزهما العدو ثم ظفر بهما ، فقال رسول الله لصاحبهما « إن أصبتهما قبل القسمة فهما لك » .

٢ - حدثنا عبد الله بن عمر عن نافع عن ابن عمر أن عبداً له أبق وذهب له بفرس فدخل في أرض العدو فظهر عليه خالد بن الوليد فرد عليه أحدهما ـ وذلك في حياة رسول الله صلى الله عليه وسلم ـ ورد الآخر بعد وفاة رسول الله صلى الله عليه وسلم (الخراج ٢٠٠) .

٣ - حدثنا عبيد الله بن عمر عن نافع عن ابن عمر رضي الله عنهما في عبد أحرزه العدو فظفر به المسلمون فرده على صاحبه .[167]

1. Ḥasan – Ḥakam – Miqsam – Ibn 'Abbās reported that the Prophet was asked about a slave and a camel, both of which belonged to a Muslim but were captured by enemy but were then recaptured by Muslims. The Prophet said to their owner, "If you have taken possession of them before the booty was distributed then they are yours."
2. A slave of Ibn 'Umar ran away and took away his horse and entered into enemy territory. Khālid b. Walīd conquered them, and returned one of them to Ibn 'Umar. It was during the life of the Prophet, and the other one was returned to Ibn 'Umar after the death of the Prophet.
3. 'Ubaidulla – Nāfi' – Ibn 'Umar stated that the enemy captured the slave, then the Muslims recaptured him, and then he was given back to his owner.

According to Ḥasan's version, if the owner of the slave found him

---

[165] *Tahd*, vii, 40.
[166] *Kharāj*, p. 200. The same *ḥadīth* is repeated by Abū Yūsuf in his two books with slightly different wording. Schacht has counted it two *aḥādīth*.
[167] Auzā'ī, pp. 58–59.

recaptured by Muslims before the booty was distributed, he had the right to take him back without paying for him; but if the owner found him after distribution of the booty, he had to pay. This ruling was a direct injunction of the Prophet.

'Ubaidullah did not give this detail. He reported that the horse of Ibn 'Umar was returned to him by Khālid after having been recaptured (without involving the authority of the Prophet).

There are different legal opinions in this matter. These are: (1) as related above in the *hadīth* of Ḥasan; (2) that he had no right to receive his property back (the decision of 'Alī, Zuhrī, and others)[168]; and (3) that he had the right to regain his property without paying, whether or not booty had been distributed.

Schacht appears unable to differentiate between the implications of these two *aḥādīth*, but if one supposes that there is no difference between the versions of Ḥasan and 'Ubaidullah (d. 145 A.H.), the implication is that this *hadīth* was known to scholars in the life of Abū Ḥanīfa.

f. Schacht's point that this anecdote was recorded by Mālik without *isnād* is correct. But his objection arises from lack of knowledge of the methodology of the early lawyers. His claim that "none of this is genuine" is simply a statement, not an argument. We are justified in asking for reasons. Were there, for example, no wars between Muslims and non-Muslims in that period? Were or were not horses used on the battlefield? Could or could not a slave or horse run away and be recaptured? Was booty distributed or not? Were Ibn 'Umar and Khālid real persons or not?

g. Reference to Bukhārī refutes Schacht's claims that "the Prophet is made directly responsible for the ruling in a later version in Bukhārī" and that "another version in Bukhārī . . . dates it to the time of Abū Bakr."[169]

Here are the original texts:[170]

١ - حدثنا عبد الله بن عمر عن نافع عن ابن عمر أن عبدا له أبق وذهب له بفرس فدخل في أرض العدو فظهر عليه خالد بن الوليد فرد عليه أحدهما ـ وذلك في حياة رسول الله صلى الله عليه وسلم ـ ورد الآخر بعد وفاة رسول الله صلى الله عليه وسلم . [171]

٢ - حدثنا عبيد الله بن عمر عن نافع عن ابن عمر رضي الله عنهما في عبد أحرزه العدو فظفر به المسلمون فرده على صاحبه . [172]

٣ - عن مالك أنه بلغه أن عبدا لعبدالله بن عمر أبق وأن فرسا له عار فأصابها المشركون ثم غنمهما المسلمون فردوا على عبد الله بن عمر وذلك قبل أن تصيبهما المقاسم . [173]

---

[168] *Muṣannaf*, vol v, pp. 193–194.
[169] *Origins*, p. 158 (n.).
[170] For translation of *Ḥadīths* 1 and 2, see page 140, numbers 2 and 3.
[171] *Kharāj*, p. 200.
[172] Auzā'ī, pp. 58–59.
[173] *Muw.* p. 452

٤ - وقال ابن نمير : حدثنا عبيد الله عن نافع عن ابن عمر رضي الله عنهما ، قال ذهب فرس له فأخذه العدو فظهر عليه المسلمون فرد عليه في زمن رسول الله صلى الله عليه وسلم ـ وأبق عبد له فلحق بالروم فظهر عليه المسلمون فرده عليه خالد بن الوليد بعد النبي صلى الله عليه وسلم .[174]

3. Mālik reported that he was informed that a slave of Ibn 'Umar ran away, and his horse also ran away. They were captured by the enemy, then they were recaptured by the Muslims and were returned to Ibn 'Umar. This happened before the booty was distributed.
4. It was reported that a horse of Ibn 'Umar ran away, which was taken by the enemy. Then the Muslims recaptured it, and it was returned to him. This happened during the life of the Prophet. His slave also ran away and joined the Byzantines, then the Muslims got him back. Then Khālid b. Walīd [the commander] returned him to Ibn 'Umar. This happened after the death of the Prophet.

No difference exists between the versions of Bukhārī and Abū Yūsuf, nor is there any direct reference to the Prophet or Abū Bakr.

Other sources which were not consulted by Schacht tell us that the *hadīth* of Ibn 'Umar was recorded by Ibn Juraij of Mecca [80 – 150 A.H.] and by Ayyūb of Baṣra (68 – 131 A.H.). This *hadīth* was thus known to scholars of Medina, Mecca, and Baṣra on the authority of Nāfi' (d. 117 A.H.).[175] It therefore goes back to Nāfi'.[175] Even if we suppose that Nāfi' was a liar and fabricated it, we must acknowledge the fact that he died some 33 years before Abū Ḥanīfa. But not even Schacht's methodology can lead to his conclusion that the *hadīth* originated between Abū Ḥanīfa and Abū Yūsuf. Clearly, it was in existence before Abū Ḥanīfa started his legal career, when he took leadership of his circle after the death of Ḥammād (d. 120 A.H.).

EXAMPLE 14: PUNISHMENT FOR FALSE TESTIMONY

To quote "Traditions Originating Between Abū Ḥanīfa and Shaibānī":

> *Tr. II*, 18(y): Abū Ḥanīfah, for a rule of penal law, can refer only to a tradition from Sha'bī. Shaībanī gives a tradition from the Prophet, not through Abū Ḥanīfah but through another transmitter. The underlying doctrine was not yet acknowledged by Ibn Abī Lailā (see *Tr. I*, 112). Similar cases occur in *Āthār Shaib*.[177]

The case mentioned concerns *Ta'zīr*; there is no reference either to Abū Ḥanīfah or Sha'bī. Going through *Tr. I*, 112, one finds the case concerns

---

[174] *Bu. Jihād*, 187.
[175] See *Muṣannaf*, V, 193 – 194.
[176] One reaches the conclusion even following Schacht's methodology – that is, the theory of the lowest common link.
[177] *Ibid.*, p. 143.

Ta'zīr on false testimony. Schacht's statement implies that Abū Ḥanīfah did not know a *hadīth* on the subject of false testimony and that later Shaibānī transmitted a *hadīth* to this effect from the Prophet.

Here are the original texts quoted in sequence, in addition to the relevant chapter from *Āthār Shaib*:

١ - « رجل عن شعبة ، عن الأعمش ، عن القاسم بن عبد الرحمن ، عن أبيه ، عن عبد الله أنه وجد امرأة مع رجل في لحافها على فراشها ، فضربه خمسين ، فذهبوا فشكوا ذلك إلى عمر رضي الله عنه ، فقال : لم فعلت ذلك ؟ قال : لأني أرى ذلك . قال : وأنا أرى ذلك .

وأصحابنا يذهبون إلى أنه يبلغ بالتعزيز هذا وأكثر منه إلى ما دون الثمانين بقدر الذنوب وهم يقولون : لا يبلغ بالتعزيز في شيء أربعين ، فيخالفون ما رووا عن عمر وابن مسعود رضي الله عنهما » . الأم ٧ : ١٧٠

٢ - وقال أبو يوسف :
« وكان أبو حنيفة لا يرى على شاهد الزور تعزيراً غير أنه يبعث به إلى سوقه ان كان سوقيا وإلى مسجد قومه ان كان من العرب . فيقول : القاضي يقرئكم السلام ، ويقول : انا وجدنا هذا شاهد زور فاحذروه وحذروه الناس . وذكر ذلك أبو حنيفة عن القاسم عن شريح .

وكان ابن أبي ليلى يقول : عليه التعزير ولا يبعث به ، ويضربه خمسة وسبعين سوطاً ، قال أبو يوسف : أعزره ولا أبلغ به أربعين سوطا ويطاف به وقال أبو يوسف بعد ذلك أبلغ به خمسة وسبعين سوطاً » .

ابن ابي ليلى ٧٥ - ٧٦ ، الأم ٧ : ١١٦ - ١١٧

٣ - محمد قال أخبرنا أبو حنيفة عن الهيثم بن أبي الهيثم عمن حدثه عن شريح قال اذا أخذ شاهد زور فان كان من أهل السواد قال للرسول قل لهم أن شريحا يقرئكم السلام ويقول إنا أخذنا هذا شاهد زور فأحذروه وان كان من العرب أرسل به إلى مسجد قومه اجمع ما كانوا ، فقال للرسول مثل ما قال في المرة الأولى .

قال محمد وبهذا كان يأخذ أبو حنيفة ولا يرى عليه ضربا . واما في قولنا فانا نرى عليه مع ذلك التعزير ولا يبلغ به أربعين سوطاً .

محمد قال أخبرنا أبو حنيفة قال حدثني رجل عن عامر الشعبي أنه كان يضرب شاهد الزور ما بينه وبين أربعين سوطاً . قال محمد وبه نأخذ .

آثار محمد ٢٨٤

1. A man – Shu'ba – A'mash – Qāsim b. 'Abdur Raḥmān – his father, Ibn Mas'ūd: A man was found with a woman in her bed under her blanket. Ibn Mas'ūd punished him fifty [lashes], upon which his people went to the Caliph 'Umar and complained to him. 'Umar asked Ibn Mas'ūd: "Why did you do

that?" He replied, "Because it is my opinion [legal decision]." He ['Umar] said, "I am of the same opinion."

In the views of our fellows one can punish in *ta'zīr* this much or even more, but less than eighty [lashes], according to the crime.

They say: In *ta'zīr* punishment one should not reach the limit of forty [lashes] and thus diverge from what they have related of the opinions of 'Umar and Ibn Mas'ūd.[178]

2. Abū Yūsuf said that Abū Ḥanīfa was of the opinion that there is no *ta'zīr* on the false witness, except that he should be sent to the marketplace, if he is a merchant, or to the *masjid*, if he belongs to some Arab tribes, and there it would be declared thus: "The *Qāḍī* sends you his greetings [*salāms*] and says we found this man guilty of false witness, to beware of him, and warn others about him. Abū Ḥanīfa ascribed this opinion to Shuraiḥ."

2a. Ibn Abī Lailā was of opinion that he [the one who gives false witness] must be punished by the way of *ta'zīr*, and may be flogged up to seventy-five lashes. Abū Yūsuf later on was of the opinion that he may be flogged up to seventy-five.[179]

Abū Ḥanīfa – Haitham – some narrators – Shuraiḥ [the judge]: That if he caught someone from the rural area who was guilty of false witness, he would send him [to his locality] and say to the messenger: Tell them, Shuraiḥ sends his greetings to you and says, "We have caught this man bearing false witness, thus be aware of him." If he belonged to some Arab tribes, he would send him to the *masjid* of the tribe when the people were in great gathering, and say to the messenger as has been reported earlier.

3a. Muḥammad Shaibānī says: The same was the opinion of Abū Ḥanīfa, in whose opinion there was no flogging. However, in my own opinion he should be beaten on the basis of *ta'zīr* but it would not exceed forty lashes.

3b. Abū Ḥanīfa reported on the authority of a man that the judge Sha'bī used to flog the man guilty of false witness up to forty lashes.

Shaibānī says that he follows this opinion.[180]

It is evident from the above that Abū Yūsuf recorded different precedents from the early judges. Some of them used to denounce the man in his locality, while others punished him directly. On punishment, they differed about whether he should be beaten less than forty lashes or up to eighty. Schacht, however, fails to provide a reference in Shaibānī's work for a *ḥadīth* from the Prophet on the subject. This, in fact, is precisely because no *ḥadīth* from the Prophet on the subject is recorded by Shaibānī at all.[181]

EXAMPLE 15: AGRICULTURAL TITHES

The following is the background to this example, given by Schacht as a "Tradition Originating Between Abū Ḥanīfah and the Classical Collections."[182]

---

[178] *Umm*. vol. vii, p. 170.
[179] Ibn Abī Lailā, pp. 75–76; *Umm*, vii, 116–117.
[180] Shaibānī, *Āthār*, p. 284.
[181] Shaibānī, *Āthār*, p. 284, numbers 628–629, recorded above.
[182] *Origins*, p. 143.

There are differences of opinion regarding *zakāt* on farm produce based on (a) the kind of the produce and (b) the quantity. Some scholars think that *zakāt* is due on wheat, barley, dates, and so on but that green vegetables are exempt. Many believe that the minimum quantity on which *zakāt* can be levied is five *wasaqs* (about 600 kg). Abū Ḥanīfah disagreed with both points. He imposes *zakāt* on every kind of farm product and has no minimum weight for its application. Abū Ḥanīfah says that this is the doctrine of Ibrāhīm An-Nakha'ī as well, but he does not mention any *ḥadīth* on the subject. In Schacht's view, any *ḥadīth* which supports Abū Ḥanīfa's doctrine must have been fabricated later.

There are two relevant *aḥādīth* from the Prophet:

١ - قال رسول الله صلى الله عليه وسلم : فيها سقت السهاء والعيون والبعل العشر وفيها سقى بالنفح نصف العشر .

٢ - ليس فيها دون خمسة أوسق من الثمر صدقة .

1. The Prophet said: [*Zakāt* on the produce of] land which has been irrigated by rain, spring, or natural water supply would be one-tenth, and on land which has been watered by irrigation would be one-twentieth.[183]
2. There is no *zakāt* on less than five *wasaqs* of dates.[184]

Abū Ḥanīfah interpreted the first order of the Prophet as including all kinds of farm produce without exemption on the basis of quantity. Other scholars restricted the general injunction of the first *ḥadīth* in the light of the second *ḥadīth*.

However, let us see what Schacht records:

Tr. I, 169: Abū Ḥanīfah can refer only to Ibrāhīm Nakha'ī [also in *Kharāj*, *Āthār A.Y.*, and *Āthār Shaib.*] traditions from the Prophet to the same effect appear in the classical works and, with a fictitious *isnād* in which Abū Ḥanīfah himself appears, in a late version of the *Musnad Abī Ḥanīfah*.[185]

This can be easily disproved, since the *ḥadīth* in question is recorded by Mālik (93 – 179 A.H.)[186] and Abū Yūsuf (d. 183 A.H.),[187] which means that the *ḥadīth* was well known in the life of Abū Ḥanīfa and he, apparently, deduced his doctrine from this *ḥadīth* without mentioning it. The same *aḥādīth* are recorded by Ibn Juraij (80 – 150 A.H.) and Ma'mar (97 – 153 A.H.) who read them in the letters of the Prophet to different chiefs.[188] Schacht might say that neither Nakha'ī nor Abū Ḥanīfah mentioned this *ḥadīth* and deduce from this that it was fabricated. But as has already been pointed out, scholars did not always refer their legal decisions to *aḥādīth* or to a particular verse of the Qur'ān. In *Muwaṭṭa' Shaib.*, 114, we

---

[183] See *Muw.*, *zakāt* 33; *Kharāj*, p. 54.
[184] See *Muw.*, *zakāt* 1; *Muw. Shaib.* p. 169.
[185] *Origins*, p. 143.
[186] *Muwaṭṭa'*, *Zakāt*, 33.
[187] *Kharāj*, 54.
[188] See *Muṣannaf*, iv, 133, 134, and 136.

find Shaibānī recording the *ḥadīth* that there is no *zakāt* due on less than five *wasaqs* of produce. In *Āthār*,[189] however, he mentions it as his legal decision without mentioning the *ḥadīth* from which it was derived. The same is true in the case of Abū Yūsuf. He says:

ليس في البقول والخضروات عشر ... إلا الحنطة والشعير والحبوب ، وليس فيه شيء حتى يبلغ خمسة أوسق .[190]

> There is no *zakāt* on the herbs and green vegetables except wheat, barley, and dry grains, and it must reach in quantity five *wasaqs*.

He uses almost the same wording of the *ḥadīth* as recorded by Mālik but does not mention the *ḥadīth*.

EXAMPLE 16: ABOUT EXCHANGE

To quote Schacht's "Tradition Originating Between Mālik and Shaibānī":

> Mālik (*Muw. iii*, 129) knows a tradition only from Ibn 'Abbās in a short version which he interprets restrictively, in keeping with his own doctrine. But Shaibānī (*Muw. Shaib*. 331, without *isnād*) and Shāfi'ī (*Tr. III*, 95 with full *isnād*) know a fuller version which implicates the Prophet and is followed by Ibn 'Abbās's own extensive interpretation.[191]

The implications are that the statement of Ibn 'Abbās was put into the mouth of the Prophet in the time of Shaibānī, and that the task of completing *isnād* was achieved in the time of Shāfi'ī.

Schacht's argument rests on a misunderstanding of the text. The main subject under discussion is the Prophet's prohibition of the sale of food grain before taking possession of it. The *aḥādīth* to this effect were recorded by Mālik through the following chains: (1) Mālik – Nāfi' – Ibn 'Umar – the Prophet; (2) Mālik – Ibn Dīnār – Ibn 'Umar – the Prophet. In this *ḥadīth*, the Prophet orders that one who buys food grain should not sell it until he has taken full possession of it.[192] There follows: (3) Mālik – Nāfi' – Ḥakīm b. Ḥizām – ruling of 'Umar, as above;[193] and (4) Mālik – Zaid b. Thābit and another Companion of the Prophet – that is, Abū Huraira – and their objection to certain buying and selling against the above-mentioned *ḥadīth* and Marwān's order to cancel those transactions.[194]

The *ḥadīth* on the subject was thus recorded by Mālik on the authority of Ibn 'Umar from the Prophet, the ruling of 'Umar, the protest of 'Zaid

---

[189] p. 143.
[190] Ibn Abī Lailā, 125.
[191] *Origins*, p. 143.
[192] *Muw., Buyū'*, 40; *Muw. Shaib.*, 331; *Studies*, 131, Arabic section.
[193] *Muw., Buyū'*, 43.
[194] *Muw., Buyū'*, 44.

and another Companion, and Marwān's order in accordance with it. The *aḥādīth* on the subject were therefore well known.

Mālik is silent about the *ḥadīth* of Ibn 'Abbās. He recorded only Ibn 'Abbās's legal decision, which is based on the above-mentioned *ḥadīth* and is intended to be general in its application. Ibn 'Abbās holds that the Prophet's prohibition of the selling of food grain until the buyer had taken full possession of it is a general order applicable to all goods, even clothes, and so on, while Mālik is of the opinion that it should be restricted to food grain only.

However, it is quite clear that the *aḥādīth* on the subject were well known. Mālik did not record a *ḥadīth* on the topic through Ibn 'Abbās as he had recorded it from several other Companions; hence there was no need of "fabrication." The *ḥadīth* of Ibn 'Abbās has been recorded by Ibn 'Uyayna with full *isnād*,[195] and Ibn 'Uyayna was older than Abū Yūsuf and Shaibānī and preceded Shāfi'ī by 43 years. It was also recorded by 'Abdur Razzāq on the authority of Ma'mar (d. 153 A.H.),[196] who was even older than Mālik. Schacht's claim runs counter to the historical evidence.

EXAMPLE 17: *TAYAMMUM*

There is a *ḥadīth* concerning *Tayammum* which Schacht considers to have originated between the time of Mālik and Shāfi'ī, because of "*Tr. II*, 2 (g): Neither the Iraqians who refer to the consensus of the scholars as against a tradition from Ibn Mas'ūd nor the Medinese (*Muw.* i., 100; *Mud.* 1.31) know traditions from the Prophet on the problem in question. Only Shāfi'ī gives a tradition from the Prophet."[197]

There is much evidence to the contrary. Even if Mālik had not recorded the *ḥadīth*, many earlier scholars did, both in Iraq and Hijāz, and it is even referred to in the Qur'ān (4:44). The *ḥadīth* was transmitted by Abū Ḥanīfa via Ḥammād – Ibrāhīm – the Prophet.[198] Abū Ḥanīfa was older than Mālik, and died at about the time of the birth of Shāfi'ī.

The same *ḥadīth* was recorded by Ibn 'Uyayna, who was forty-three years older than Shāfi'ī,[199] and several *aḥādīth* on the subject were recorded by the *Ibāḍī* scholar Rabī' b. Ḥabīb (d. 160 A.H.), the contemporary of Mālik.[200]

It was also recorded by Abū Qilābah of Baṣra (d. 104 A.H.),[201] whose book came into the hands of Ayyūb, (d. 131 A.H.), and from Ayyūb it was transmitted by Ma'mar[202] and Ibn Juraij (d. 150 A.H.) of Mecca.[203] That

---

[195] Ḥumaidī, *Musnad* (Karachi, 1963), vol. I, p. 236.
[196] See *Muṣannaf*, vol. viii, p. 38.
[197] *Origins*, p. 143.
[198] See A.Y. 77, Ḥumaidī, *Musnad*, I, 79; *Ḥadīth*, 144.
[199] Rabi', *Masnad*, 46 – 47; see also *Muṣannaf*, i, 226–227, 230, 236, and 238.
[200] See *Muṣannaf*, i, 236 – 270.
[201] *Studies*, 63.
[202] *Muṣannaf*, i, 237.
[203] *Ibid.*, i, 239.

Mālik did not record the *ḥadīth* does not prove that he did not know it. Even if he did not know it, there were several scholars who did. Any "ignorance" on the part of Mālik cannot contradict the positive knowledge of others.

EXAMPLE 18: *ZAKAT* ON ORPHAN'S PROPERTY

Schacht considers this *ḥadīth* to have originated between Mālik and Shāfi'ī. He says: "The recommendation to invest the property of orphans, so that the *zakāt* tax may not consume it, is known to Mālik (*Muw.* ii, 49) only as a saying of 'Umar, but to Shāfi'ī already as a saying of the Prophet with full *isnād*."[204]

In fact, it was recorded by 'Abdur Razzāq, a student of Ibn Juraij, with the *isnād*. Ibn Juraij (80 – 150 A.H.) – Yūsuf b. Māhik – the Prophet.[205] In Shāfi'ī the following *isnād* has been recorded: 'Abdul Majīd – Ibn Juraij – Yūsuf b. Māhik – the Prophet.[206]

Thus this *ḥadīth* was transmitted by Ibn Juraij, who was older than Mālik and died in the year Shāfi'ī was born. Schacht's claim that it was not known to Mālik – even if this is the case – does not prove its nonexistence during the life of Mālik. His argument about the origination of the *ḥadīth* between Mālik and Shāfi'ī can therefore have no basis. Schacht makes another minor mistake when he says that this *ḥadīth* appeared in Shāfi'ī with full *isnād*. As a matter of fact it is a *mursal* one, in which the Companion has not been mentioned.[207]

EXAMPLE 19: SHARE OF A BOY WHO PARTICIPATED IN WAR

Another of Schacht's "Traditions Originating Between Mālik and Shāfi'ī" is as follows:

> *Tr. IX*, 10: Auzā'ī had referred to an "historical" tradition from the Prophet, without *isnād*, but Abū Yūsuf had rejected it as not acceptable to specialists and referred to a tradition from Ibn 'Abbās in favour of his own, different doctrine, shared by Mālik and Shāfi'ī. It was therefore imperative for Mālik to mention a tradition from the Prophet, if he knew one, but he adduces only the alleged opinion of the ancient Medinese scholars Qāsim b. Muḥammad and Sālim (*Mud.* iii, 34), and *Mud.* adds only a circumstantial but certainly spurious tradition which is set in the time of the Companions. The classical tradition from the Prophet on the problem in question, through Nāfi' – Ibn 'Umar, was still unknown to Mālik and appears for the first time in Shāfi'ī. It is added that Nāfi' related this tradition to 'Umar b. 'Abdal'azīz who gave instructions accordingly; this expresses the attitude of the traditionists.[208]

---

[204] *Origins*, p. 143.
[205] *Muṣannaf*, iv, 66.
[206] *Umm*, vii, 175; see also *Ḥujja*, I, 457–462, where Shaibānī mentions *aḥādīth* to this effect without recording them.
[207] See *Tahd*, xi, 421; Yūsuf is a Successor.
[208] *Origins*, pp. 143 – 144.

There is no argument by Mālik in *Mud.* on the subject under discussion. Mālik did not discuss this problem in *Muwaṭṭa'*. Even in *Mud.* iii, 34, the whole discussion is connected with Ibn Wahb (125 – 197 A.H.), who reported the opinions of Qāsim and Sālim. It is difficult to see how Schacht can attribute Ibn Wahb's argument to Mālik and later on claim that Mālik did not know a *ḥadīth* on the subject that was recorded for the first time in Shāfi'ī, and that consequently it was fabricated between the period of these two scholars. As we have seen, Mālik is totally silent on the subject. However, that is not a conclusive proof of his ignorance; as we have already shown, many chapters of early works were not quoted by later authors.[209] Schacht also errs when he says that this *ḥadīth* was recorded for the first time in Shāfi'ī; it was recorded by Abū Yūsuf[210] who was 40 years older than Shāfi'ī. Moreover, Shāfi'ī recorded the same *isnād*, Nāfi' – Ibn 'Umar, which had been recorded by Abū Yūsuf.

EXAMPLE 20: *TAYAMMUM* (RITUAL PURIFICATION)

Schacht also cites in "Traditions Originating Between Mālik and Shāfi'ī": "*Ikh.* 96: a tradition from the Prophet on an important point of ritual purity, the sound *isnād* of which Shāfi'ī commends, is still unknown to and not followed by Mālik (*Muw.* i, 100: *Muw-Shaib.* 76)."[211]

Mālik did not quote a *ḥadīth* from the Prophet to this effect. But he quoted the practice of the Companion Ibn 'Umar accordingly, which confirms the *ḥadīth* recorded by Shāfi'ī. Thus Mālik most probably knew it. Mālik also follows the doctrine stated by Shāfi'ī,[212] hence Schacht's claim is contrary to the writings of Mālik.

EXAMPLE 21: CERTAIN CONTRACTS

Schacht claims that this *ḥadīth* originated between the time of Mālik and the classical collections:

> *Muw.* iii. 134: Mālik adds to the text of a tradition from the Prophet his own definition of the aleatory contracts *mulāmasa* and *munābadha;* the same definition appears as a statement of Mālik, not in connexion with any tradition, in *Mud.* x. 37 f. It is, in fact, a current Medinese formula, ascribed to Rabī'a in *Mud.* x. 38, and also occurring as an explanatory addition to the text of two parallel versions of the same tradition, where Mālik does not appear in the *isnād* (*ibid.*). But this interpretation has become part of the words of the Prophet in Bukhārī and Muslim (see Zurqānī, iii, 134); at the same time, Bukhārī and Muslim relate the same tradition without the interpretation, and in Nasā'ī where the addition is slightly longer, it is clearly separated from the text.[213]

---

[209] See the section entitled "Unwarranted Assumptions and Unscientific Research Methods" earlier in this chapter.
[210] *Kharāj*, p. 175.
[211] *Origins*, p. 144.
[212] *Muw.* i, 56.
[213] *Origins*, p. 144.

Bukhārī has given the exact *ḥadīth* transmitted by Mālik without any additional material from Mālik's commentary. Here is the original text.

The version of Muw:

حدثنا يحيى عن مالك عن محمد بن يحيى بن حبان ، عن أبي الزناد ، عن الاعرج ، عن أبي هريرة ان رسول الله صلى الله عليه وسلم نهى عن الملامسة والمنابذة .²¹⁴

Yaḥyā – Mālik – Muḥd – Abū Zinād – A'raj – Abū Huraira, the Prophet forbade selling by *mulāmasa* and *munābadha*.

The version of Bukhārī:

حدثنا اسماعيل ، قال حدثني مالك عن محمد بن يحيى بن حبان عن أبي الزناد عن الاعرج ، عن أبي هريرة رضي الله عنه ان رسول الله صلى الله عليه وسلم نهى عن الملامسة والمنابذة .²¹⁵

Ismā'īl — Mālik-Muḥd — Abū Zinād — A'raj-Abū Huraira, the Prophet forbade selling by *mulāmasa* and *munābadha*.

It is clear that the wording recorded by Bukhārī is exactly the same as in *Muw.* of Mālik. However, additional material similar to Mālik's statement is furnished in a *ḥadīth* transmitted by 'Uqail – Ibn Shihāb – 'Āmir b. Sa'd – Abū Sa'īd al-Khudrī: "The Prophet forbade selling by *munābadha*, that is, to sell one's garment by setting a price for it to the buyer without giving him a chance to see or examine it. [Similarly] he forbade selling by *mulāmasa*, that is, to buy a garment by merely touching it, and without looking at it."²¹⁶ Here is the original text:

« حدثنا سعيد بن عفير ، قال حدثني الليث ، قال حدثني عقيل : عن ابن شهاب قال : أخبرني عامر بن سعد أنّ أبا سعيد رضي الله عنه أخبره أن رسول الله ـ صلى الله عليه وسلم ـ نهى عن المنابذة ـ وهي طرح الرجل ثوبه بالبيع إلى رجل قبل أن يقلبه أو ينظر اليه ـ ونهى عن الملامسة ـ والملامسة لمس الثوب لا ينظر اليه » .

Commentators on the books have discussed this sentence, collecting all the material relevant to this *ḥadīth*. Some scholars describe it as the wording of Ibn 'Uyaynah. But Ibn Ḥajar argues that is the commentary of Abū Sa'īd al-Khudrī,²¹⁷ from whom Mālik himself might have taken this definition. As early scholars themselves have differentiated this portion from the *ḥadīth* of the Prophet, it is hardly justifiable for Schacht to impugn it for this sort of discrepancy.

The early scholars were aware of this sort of discrepancy and discussed it theoretically in *uṣūl* books, quoting individual cases in commentaries. In every *Uṣūl al-Ḥadīth* work one finds a chapter on *Mudraj*,²¹⁸ meaning

---

²¹⁴ *Muw.* iii, 134.
²¹⁵ *Bu.*, Buyū', 63.
²¹⁶ *Ibid.*, 62.
²¹⁷ Ibn Ḥajar, *Fatḥul Bārī*, (Cairo, 1380), vol. 4, p. 360.
²¹⁸ See, for example, Suhyūtī, *Tadrīb*, (Cairo, 1379), vol. I, p. 268.

original texts containing a gloss by one of the transmitters, where problems of this sort are discussed.

EXAMPLE 22: PROSTRATIONS IN THE QUR'ĀN

According to Schacht in "Traditions Originating Between Mālik and the Classical Collections":

> Tr. III, 22: Mālik's own words, technically formulated (*Muw.* i, 372; *Mud.* i, 109) and repeated by Rabī' in a discussion which turns on the traditional authority for the doctrine in question, without any suggestion that these words are part of a tradition, have become a tradition from the Prophet in Ibn Māja's collection (quoted *Comm. Muw. Shaib.* 148, n. 3, also in Ṭaḥāwī, 1. 207).[219]

Ibn Māja's version:

١ - عن أم الدرداء قالت حدثني أبو الدرداء أنه سجد مع النبي صلى الله عليه وسلم احدى عشرة سجدة منهن النجم .

٢ - حدثتني عمتي أم الدرداء عن أبي الدرداء قال : سجدت مع النبي صلى الله عليه وسلم احدى عشرة سجدة ليس فيها من المفصل شيء » .

Tahawi's version:

٣ - « . . . عمن أخبره ، عن أبي الدرداء ، قال : سجدت مع النبي صلى الله عليه وسلم ـ احدى عشرة سجدة منهن النجم » (الطحاوي ١ : ٣٥٣) .

1. Umm al-Dardā' transmitted on the authority of Abū ad-Dardā' that he prostrated with the Prophet eleven times (in the reciting of the complete Qur'ān); one of the prostrations was in *sūrat at Najm*.
2. Abū ad-Dardā' reported that he prostrated with the Prophet eleven times in (the recitation of the whole Qur'ān) but there was no prostration *(sajda)* in the portion of the Qur'ān called the *mufaṣṣal*.[220]
3. Abū ad-Dardā' reported that he prostrated with the Prophet eleven times; one of the prostrations was in *sūrat at Najm*.[221]

The traditions above contain the statement of Abū Dardā', a companion of the Prophet (d. 35 A.H.) Although the *isnād* is not sound, there is other evidence which proves that the wording was known in the life of the Companions. The following traditions make this clear:

---

[219] *Origins*, p. 144.
[220] Ibn Māja, *Sunan* (Cairo, 1373), *Iqāmat Salāt*, 71.
[221] Ṭaḥāwī, *Ma'ānī Āthār*, 1, 353. The Qur'ān has been divided into four portions with four names: (a) *al-sab'a al-Ṭūl*, that is, seven longer, *sūra's*, from the second to the eighth; (b) *Ma'īn*, that is, the *sūras* containing about 100 verses; (c) Mathānī, with less than 100 verses (read more frequently); and (d) *Mufuṣṣal*, small *sūras*. For detail see suyūṭī, *Itqān* (Cairo, 1967), II, pp. 179–180.

> ابن جريج قال أخبرنا عكرمة بن خالد أن سعيد بن جبير أخبره أنه سمع ابن عباس وابن عمر يعدان كم في القرآن من سجدة ... وحم السجدة احدى عشرة ، (المصنف ٣ : ٣٣٥).[222]

Sa'īd b. Jubair reported that he heard both Ibn 'Abbās and Ibn 'Umar counting the numbers of prostrations in the Qur'ān; [they counted] eleven prostrations [Sajdās].

> « عبد الرزاق عن معمر عن أبي جمرة الضبعي قال سمعت ابن عباس يقول في القرآن احدى عشرة سجدة فعدهن كما ذكره ابن جريج عن عكرمة عن سعيد بن جبير » . (المصنف ٣ : ٣٣٦).[223]

Abū Jamara said that he heard Ibn 'Abbās saying that there were eleven prostrations [Sajdās] in the Qur'ān, and he counted them as they have been explained in the report of Sa'īd b. Jubair.

Here Ibn Juraij (d. 150 A.H.) quotes through 'Ikrima-Sa'īd b. Jubair (d. 93 A.H.) that Ibn 'Abbās (d. 68 A.H.) and Ibn 'Umar (d. 74 A.H.) both counted eleven *Sajdās* in the Qur'ān. Since it is a problem of ritual, Ibn 'Umar and Ibn 'Abbās must have learned it from the Prophet. The statement of Abū Dardā' also sheds some light on the subject.

However, it is certain that in the first century – most probably in the middle of it – it was known at least to be the statement of Ibn 'Umar and Ibn 'Abbās. Mālik is not the originator of this statement, which Schacht falsely ascribes to him, because it was known one hundred years before Mālik's death. It was recorded by authors such as Ibn Juraij and Ma'mar, the latter of whom died a quarter of a century earlier than Mālik.

Mālik must, therefore, have heard something from the earlier authorities and based his doctrine on them. It has been shown that scholars used to deduce doctrines, record them, and inform their students about them without referring to the relevant verses of the Qur'ān and *ḥadīth* of the Prophet. This is the case here also.[224]

EXAMPLE 23: KILLING OF SNAKES BY A PILGRIM

Schacht says: "Mālik had to rely on a *mursal* tradition from 'Umar, and on a subsumption which Shāfi'ī refutes as contrary to Arabic usage. There are two traditions from the Prophet with Medinese *isnāds* in Muslim's collection (quoted by Zurqānī II, 196)."[225]

The *ḥadīth* concerns the killing of snakes by pilgrims. Schacht cites this as an example of a *ḥadīth* originating between Mālik and the classical collections. In fact, it was mentioned earlier by Abū Ḥanīfah on the authority of Ibn 'Umar, which was transmitted from the Prophet.[226] Moreover, permission to kill snakes by the *Muḥrim* is also reported by

---

[222] *Muṣannaf*, iii, 335.
[223] *Ibid.*, iii, 336.
[224] See, for instance, examples II and 15 above.
[225] *Origins*, p. 144.
[226] *Shaibānī, Āthār*, p. 166.

Muḥammad b. Abī Yaḥyā (d. 147 A.H.) through Ḥarmala – Ibn al-Nusayyab – the Prophet.[227]

Since Ibn Abī Yaḥyā died some 30 years before Mālik, Schacht's assumption that the *ḥadīth* about snakes was fabricated between Mālik and Shāfi'ī must be considered baseless.

EXAMPLE 24: NOT DESTROYING THE PROPERTY OF THE ENEMY IN WAR

Schacht refers to this as a tradition originating between Abū Yūsuf and Shaibānī:

> *Tr. IX*, 29: Auzāī refers to the alleged instruction of Abū Bakr not to lay waste the enemy country . . . Abū Yūsuf has the countertradition (on the authority of Ibn Isḥāq) that Abū Bakr instructed one of his commanders to lay waste to every village where he did not hear the call to prayer . . . The original instruction of Abū Bakr was interpreted away (a) by making Abū Bakr say that Syria would certainly be conquered (so that there was no point in laying it waste) (*Siyar*, i. 35) – this can be dated between Abū Yūsuf and Shaibānī – and (b) by *mursal* traditions regarding the instructions which the Prophet gave to the leader of an expedition sent against Syria (Ibn Wahb in *Mud*. iii, 8).[228]

Let us analyze this example. First, the Qur'ān allows the laying waste of enemy property in war.[229] The practice of the Prophet and instructions of Abū Bakr to Khālid b. Walīd are both in agreement with the provision of the Qur'ān. Auzā'ī records another instruction of Abū Bakr which prohibits the laying waste of enemy property. Apparently, it goes against the Qu'ān. Auzā'i wants to say that Abū Bakr understood the Qur'ān better than Abū Ḥanīfah. Therefore, when Abū Bakr gave this order it could not be contradictory to the Qur'ān. Abū Yūsuf did not deny the genuineness of Abū Bakr's instructions, and explained them in a way that would reconcile them with his doctrine. That is, as Abū Bakr knew that this country was going to come into the possession of Muslims, there was no point in laying it waste. How Abū Bakr knew this was not disclosed by Abū Yūsuf.

Shaibānī referred to the Prophet's prophecy that the Muslims would capture the treasures of Caesar and Kisra, the King of Persia. This leads Schacht to conclude that these words of the Prophet were fabricated between Abū Yūsuf and Shaibānī. But these words of the Prophet are recorded by Ibn Isḥāq,[230] who was 30 years older than Abū Yūsuf and some 53 years older than Shaibānī, and died when Shaibānī was only 17 years old.

---

[227] *Muṣannaf*, iv, p. 444.
[228] *Origins*, pp. 144–145.
[229] Qur'ān, *Hashr*, 5.
[230] Ibn Hishām, *Sīrah*, vol. 3, p. 219.

Chapter Eight

The *Isnād* System: Its Validity and Authenticity

In any evaluation of the *isnād* system one must keep firmly in mind its central position in Islam. The belief that the *aḥādīth* handed down by the Prophet have the force of law is largely based on Qur'ānic injunctions. These *aḥādīth* came to us from the Prophet through chains of transmitters. They are, thus, the cornerstone of the Islamic faith and the code of ethics associated with it. Sufyān al-Thaurī (d. 161 A.H.) says: "The *isnād* is the believer's weapon; thus, when he has no weapon, with what will he fight?[1] Another scholar, Ibn Mūbarak (d. 181 A.H.), says: "*Isnād* is a part of religion *(dīn)*, and if there were no *isnād* everyone would be free to report what he wants."[2]

The *isnād* system is a unique system applied by Muslim scholars in the transmission of information relating to the Prophet. Although it was originally initiated for the transmission of *hadīth*, it has a great impact on the entire corpus of literature produced up to the fourth century. We find in the works of such well-known Arabic writers such as al-Jāḥiẓ (163–235 A.H.), Al-Mubarrad (210–286 A.H.), Ibn Qutaiba (213–276 A.H.], Abū Faraj al-Aṣfahānī (284–356 A.H.), and Abū 'Alī al-Qālī (288–356 A.H.), that they so often adopted the *isnād* system in recording their materials that they included *isnād*s even when writing jokes and light-hearted work.[3]

Beginning and Development of the *Isnād* System

The *isnād* system was born during the life of the Prophet and had developed into a proper science by the end of the first century A.H. It had

---

[1] Al-Ḥākim, [translated by Robson], Introduction (London, 1953), p. 10.
[2] Muslim, *Ṣaḥīḥ*, Introduction, p. 15.
[3] The *isnād* system was applied by these scholars and by others in different branches of knowledge, but the rules of strict criticism and the standards required by *Muḥaddithīn* were not maintained by those writers.

its beginnings in the Companions' practice of transmitting the *aḥādīth* of the Prophet when they saw each other. In the last chapter I alluded to the arrangements they made to attend the Prophet's circle in shifts and inform each other of what they had heard and seen. Naturally, in informing their colleagues they would have used sentences like "The Prophet did so and so" or "The Prophet said so and so." It is also natural that anyone gaining information at second hand, when reporting the incident to a third man, would disclose his sources of information and give a full account of the incident.

These methods, used in the early days for the diffusion of the *sunna* of the Prophet, were the rudimentary beginning of the *isnād* system. During the fourth and fifth decade of the Islamic calendar the system gained in importance because of the upheavals of the time. It is possible that the first fabrications of *aḥādīth* may have appeared in that period for political reasons.[4] Scholars became cautious and began to scrutinize the sources of the information supplied to them. Ibn Sīrīn (d. 110 A.H.) said: "They did not used to ask about the *isnād*, but when the civil war [*fitna*] arose, they said "Name to us your men." As for those who belonged to *Ahl Al-Sunnah*, their *aḥādīth* were accepted and as for those who were innovators, their *aḥādīth* were put aside.' "[5]

By the end of the first century, this practice had become a full-fledged science. The learning of at least a portion of the Qur'ān and the *aḥādīth* of the Prophet was already an obligatory duty of every Muslim. In response to this requirement, there was an outburst of educational activity throughout the Islamic world. For many centuries in the educational history of Islam the word "knowledge" (*'Ilm*) was applied only to the learning of *aḥādīth* and related subjects.[6] This zeal for the knowledge of *ḥadīth* gave birth to *al-Riḥla*, the journey to learn *ḥadīth*, which was counted one of the essential requirements for scholarship. Its importance is demonstrated by Ibn Ma'īn (d. 233 A.H.), who said that anyone who learns *aḥādīth* in his own city only and does not journey to acquire knowledge will not reach maturity.[7] These journeys increased the numbers of transmitters and resulted in the spread of *ḥadīth* throughout the many provinces of the Islamic world. Scholars undertook journeys to study with Companions and Successors and then returned home to spread the word.

Evidence for the transmission of *'Ilm* in this way is given by the thousands of *aḥādīth* with identical wording found in different parts of the Islamic world, which trace their origins back to a common source – the

---

[4] The recent research of Dr. 'Umar bin Hasan Fallātā shows that even up to 60 A.H., it is difficult to find a fabricated *ḥadīth* on the authority of the Prophet. See his doctoral thesis, *Al-Waḍ'ufī al-Ḥadīth*, Azhar University, Cairo, 1397/1977, p. 132.
[5] Muslim, *Ṣaḥīḥ*, Introduction, p. 15; see also *Studies*, p. 213.
[6] *Studies*, p. 183.
[7] Khaṭīb, *al-Riḥla*, (Damascus, 1395), p. 89.

Prophet or a Companion or a Successor. That identity of content and wording spread across so wide a distance at a time that lacked the immediacy of modern communication systems stands as a testimony to the validity of the *isnād* system.[8]

A few examples will illustrate this point:

EXAMPLE 1

حدثنا عبد العزيز المختار قال حدثنا سهيل بن أبي صالح عن أبيه عن أبي هريرة أن النبي صلى الله عليه وسلم قال : انما الإمام ليؤتم به فاذا كبّر فكبّروا ، وإذا ركع فاركعوا واذا قال سمع الله لمن حمده فقولوا : اللهم ربنا لك الحمد ، وإذا سجد فاسجدوا ولا تسجدوا حتى يسجد ، وإذا رفع فارفعوا ولا ترفعوا حتى يرفع ، وإذا صلى قاعداً فصلوا قعوداً أجمعون . [9]

Abū Huraira reported the Prophet saying: The *Imām* ought to be followed. So recite *takbīr* when he recites it, and bow down when he bows down. And when he says ("Allah hearkens to him who praises Him") سمع الله لمن حمده, [9] say ("O Allah, our Lord, praise be to thee") اللهم ربنا لك الحمد. And when he prostrates, you should prostrate. When he raises [his head] you should raise yours. You must not raise your [head] until he raises his. If he prays sitting, you should all pray sitting.

This *hadīth* has been recorded at least 124 times, with many dozens of scholars of different localities taking part in it. It is reported by 26 third-generation authorities, all of whom trace the origins of their knowledge to Companions of the Prophet. It is found almost in the same form or in the same meaning in all versions in ten different locations at this time (Medina, Mecca, Egypt, Baṣrah, Ḥims, Yemen, Kūfa, Syria, Wāsiṭ, and Ṭāif). Three of the 26 authorities heard it from more than one source.

Existing documentation shows that this *hadīth* was transmitted by at least ten Companions. We have details of the courses of transmission for seven of these ten, showing that they came originally from three different places – Medina, Syria, and Iraq.

The course of transmission from only one of the Companions – Abū Hurairah – shows clearly how the number of transmitters increased from generation to generation and how the *hadīth* became known in widely different locations. Abū Hurairah had at least seven students who transmitted this *hadīth* from him. Four of these belonged to Medina, two to Egypt, and one to Yemen. These students in turn transmitted to at least 12 others – five from Medina, two from Mecca, and one each from Syria, Kūfa, Ṭāif, Egypt, and Yemen. Similar patterns of transmission from the other Companions show the *hadīth* spread more widely – to Baṣrah, Ḥims, and Wāsiṭ – and reinforce the *hadīth* in Medina, Mecca, Kūfa, Egypt, and Syria.

---

[8] *Studies*, p. 15 (Arabic section) Not all the *aḥādīth* spread so widely. On the other hand, thousands of books have been lost which would presumably otherwise have provided evidence of the spreading of information on much larger scale.

[9] *Studies*, p. 15, 27–31 (Arabic section).

Chart 1 shows the *isnād* of this *ḥadīth* and traces it back to the Prophet, reading left to right.

EXAMPLE 2

حدثنا عبد العزيز بن المختار ، قال : حدثنا سهيل بن أبي صالح ، عن أبيه ، عن أبي هريرة عن النبي صلى الله عليه وسلم قال : اذا استيقظ أحدكم من منامه فليغسل يده ثلاث مرات فانه لا يدري أين باتت يده . [10]

Abū Huraira reported that the Prophet said: "When anyone among you wakes up from sleep, he must not put his hand in the utensil until he has washed it three times, for he does not know where his hand was during his sleep."

This *ḥadīth* was transmitted by five Companions – Abū Huraira, Ibn 'Umar, Jābir, 'Ā'isha, and 'Alī. In the second generation there are 16 transmitters, and 18 in the third. The *ḥadīth* is found in Medina, Kūfa, Baṣra, Yemen, and Syria in the second generation, and has spread to Mecca, Khurāsān, and Hims by the third generation. It has been recorded at least 65 times, with dozens of scholars taking part in its transmission.

Al-Zuhrī and al-A'mash narrate the *ḥadīth* on more than one authority. Ibn Hanbal endorsed it at least fifteen times, on the authority of Abū Huraira (see Chart 2).

EXAMPLE 3

حدثنا عبد العزيز بن المختار ، حدثنا سهيل بن أبي صالح ، عن أبيه ، عن أبي هريرة عن النبي صلى الله عليه وسلم قال : عمل ابن آدم كله له ، والحسنة بعشر أمثالها ، الا الصيام ، فانه لي وأنا أجزي به . يدع الطعام من أجلي ويدع الشراب من أجلي ويذر اللذة من أجلي . فاذا أصبح أحدكم صائما فلا يرفث ولا يفسق ، فان سب فليقل : اني صائم . وللصائم فرحتان ، فرحة عند افطاره ، وفرحة يوم يلقي ربه ولخلوفه أطيب عند الله من ريح المسك . [10]

Abū Huraira reported the Prophet saying: (that Almighty Allah has said) Every act of the son of Adam is for him; every good deed will receive tenfold except fasting. It is [exclusively] meant for me, and I [alone] will reward it. He abandons his food for My sake and abandons drinking for My sake and abandons his pleasure for My sake. When any one of you is fasting he should neither indulge in sex nor use obscene language. If anyone reviles him he should say, "I am fasting." The one who fasts has two [occasions] of joy: one when he breaks the fast and one on the day when he will meet his Lord. And the breath [of a fasting person] is sweeter to Allah than the fragrance of musk.

This lengthy *ḥadīth* has been transmitted by many scholars in parts. Ibn Hanbal has endorsed it at least 24 times. It is preserved in the collections of A'mash (d. 148 A.H.), Ibn Juraij (d. 150 A.H.), and Ibrāhīm b. Ṭahmān

---

[10] *Studies*, p. 16 (Arabic section).

Chart 1. Transmission of a *Ḥadīth* Concerning Prayer.

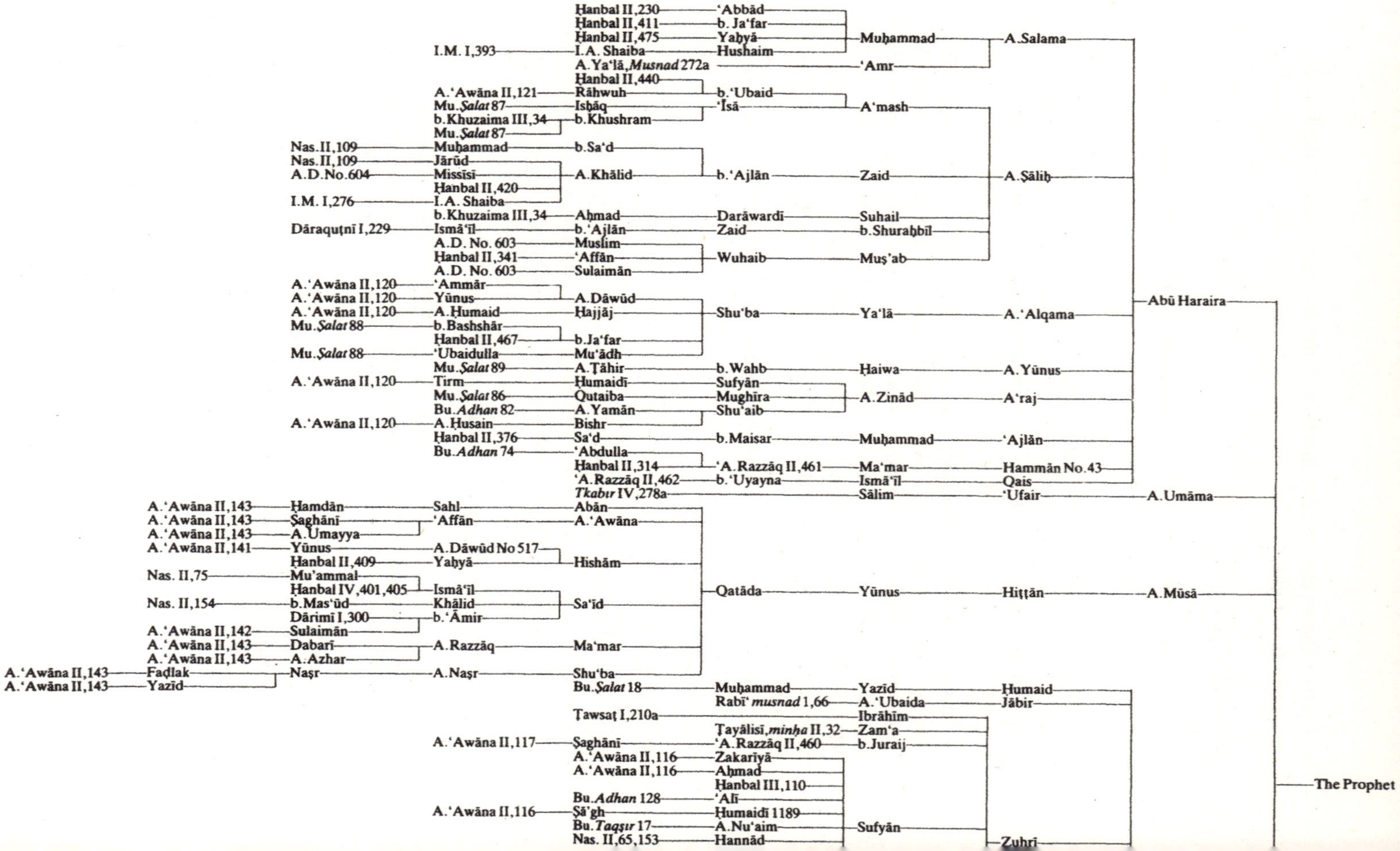

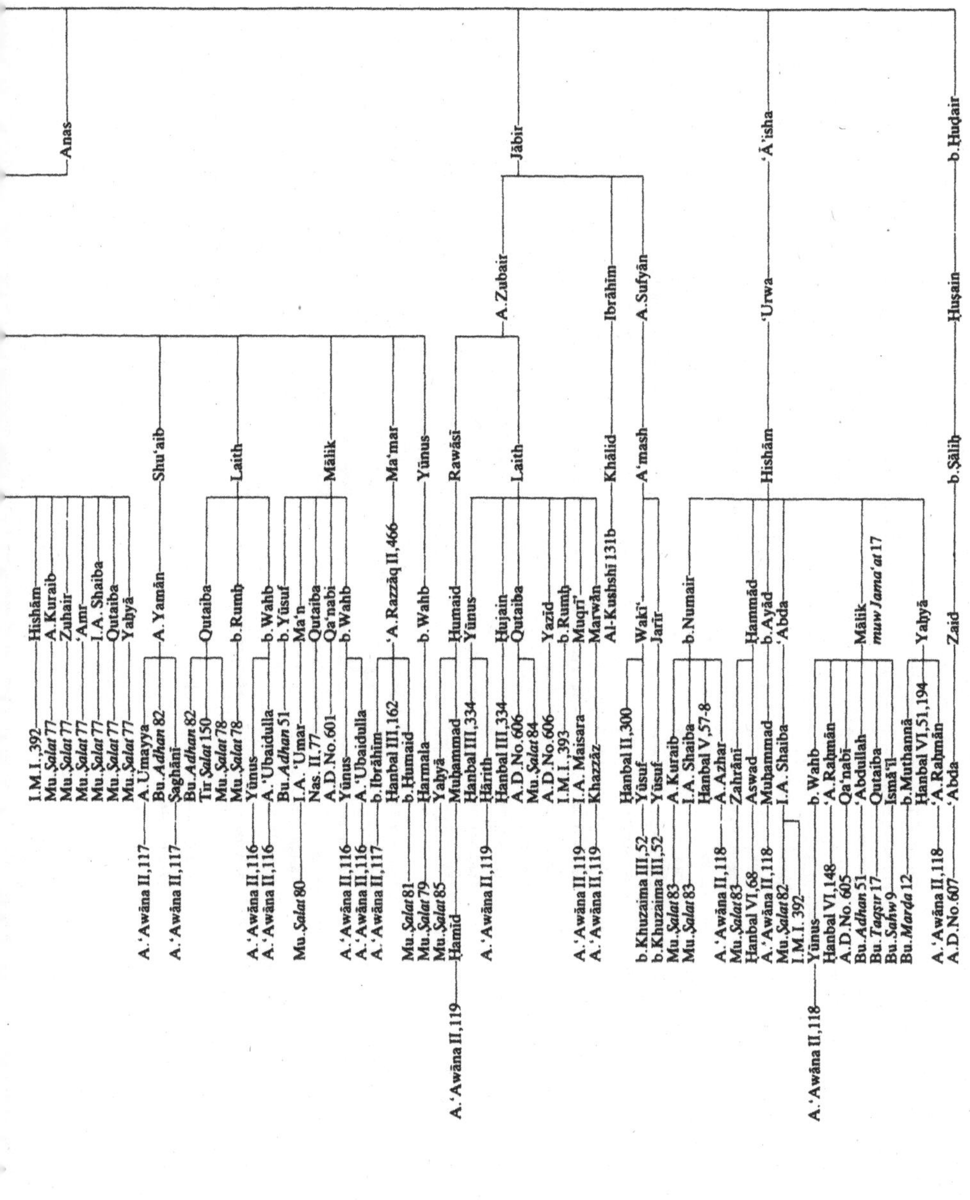
Anas
Jābir
'Ā'isha
b.Ḥuḍair
A.Zubair
Ibrāhīm
A.Sufyān
'Urwa
Ḥuṣain
Shu'aib
Laith
Mālik
Ma'mar
Yūnus
Rawāsī
Laith
Khālid
A'mash
Hishām
b.Ṣāliḥ
Hishām
A.Kuraib
Zuhair
'Amr
I.A. Shaiba
Qutaiba
Yaḥyā
A.Yamān
Qutaiba
b.Rumḥ
b.Wahb
b.Yūsuf
Ma'n
Qutaiba
Qa'nabi
b.Wahb
'A.Razzāq II,466
b.Wahb
Ḥumaid
Yūnus
Ḥujain
Qutaiba
Yazīd
b.Rumḥ
Muqrī'
Marwān
Al-Kushshī 131b
Wakī'
Jarīr
b.Numair
Ḥammād
b.Ayād
'Abda
Mālik
muw Jamā'at 17
Yaḥyā
Zaid
I.M.I. 392
Mu.Ṣalat 77
Mu.Ṣalat 77
Mu.Ṣalat 77
Mu.Ṣalat 77
Mu.Ṣalat 77
Mu.Ṣalat 77
A.'Umayya
Bu.Adhan 82
Ṣaghānī
Bu.Adhan 82
Tir.Ṣalat 150
Mu.Ṣalat 78
Mu.Ṣalat 78
Yūnus
A.'Ubaidulla
Bu.Adhan 51
I.A.'Umar
Nas. II,77
A.D.No.601
Yūnus
A.'Ubaidulla
b.Ibrāhīm
Ḥanbal III,162
b.Ḥumaid
Ḥarmala
Yaḥyā
Muḥammad
Ḥanbal III,334
Ḥārith
Ḥanbal III,334
A.D.No.606
Mu.Ṣalat 84
A.D.No.606
I.M.I.,393
I.A. Maisara
Khazzāz
Ḥanbal II,300
Yūsuf
Yūsuf
A.Kuraib
I.A. Shaiba
Ḥanbal V,57-8
A.Azhar
Zahrānī
Aswad
Muḥammad
I.A. Shaiba
b.Wahb
'A.Raḥmān
Qa'nabī
'Abdullah
Qutaiba
Ismā'īl
b.Muthannā
Ḥanbal VI,51,194
'A.Raḥmān
'Abda
A.'Awāna II,117
A.'Awāna II,117
A.'Awāna II,116
A.'Awāna II,116
Mu.Ṣalat 80
A.'Awāna II,116
A.'Awāna II,116
A.'Awāna II,117
Mu.Ṣalat 81
Mu.Ṣalat 79
Mu.Ṣalat 85
Ḥamid
A.'Awāna II,119
A.'Awāna II,119
A.'Awāna II,119
A.'Awāna II,119
b.Khuzaima III,52
b.Khuzaima III,52
Mu.Ṣalat 83
Mu.Ṣalat 83
A.'Awāna II,118
Mu.Ṣalat 83
Hanbal VI,68
A.'Awāna II,118
Mu.Ṣalat 82
I.M.I. 392
Yūnus
A.'Awāna II,118
Hanbal VI,148
A.D.No. 605
Bu.Adhan 51
Bu.Taqṣīr 17
Bu.Sahw 9
Bu.Marḍa 12
A.'Awāna II,118
A.D.No.607

Chart 2. Transmission of a *Hadīth* Concerning Waking from Sleep.

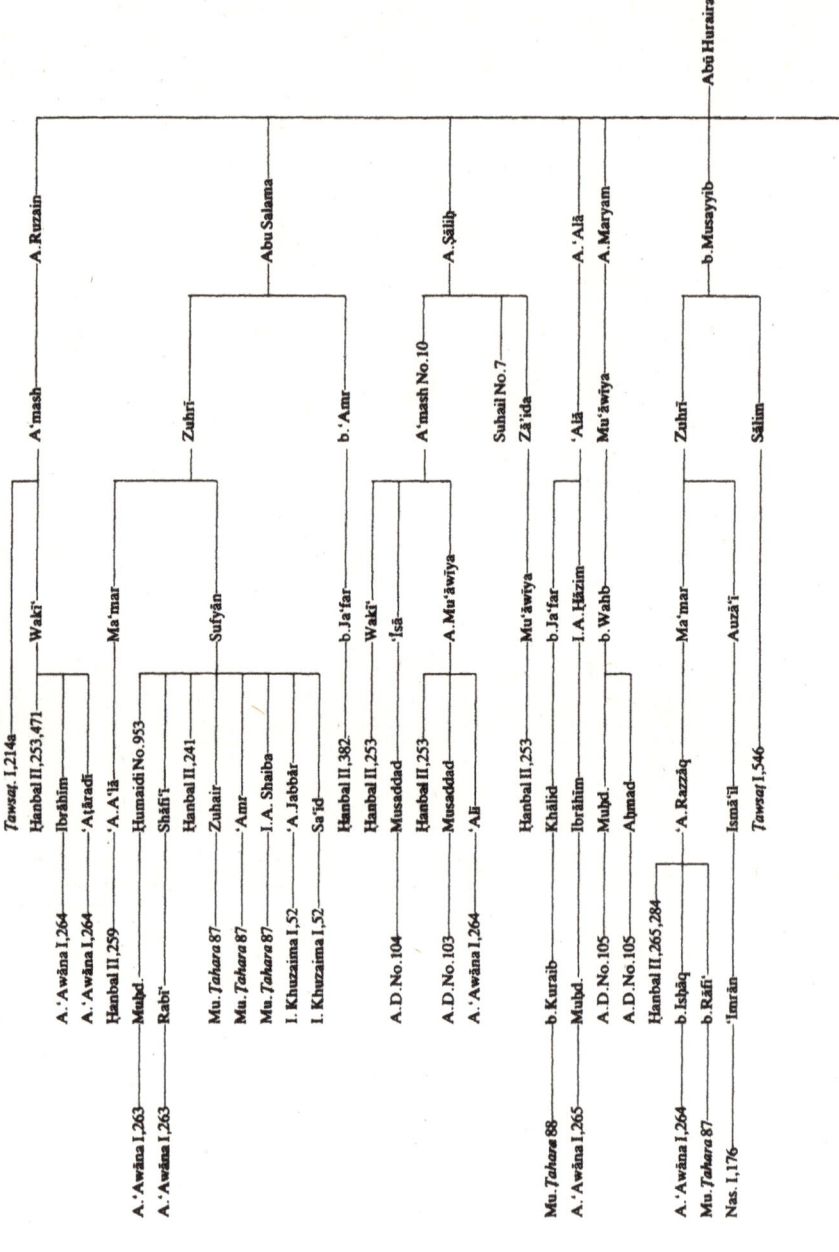

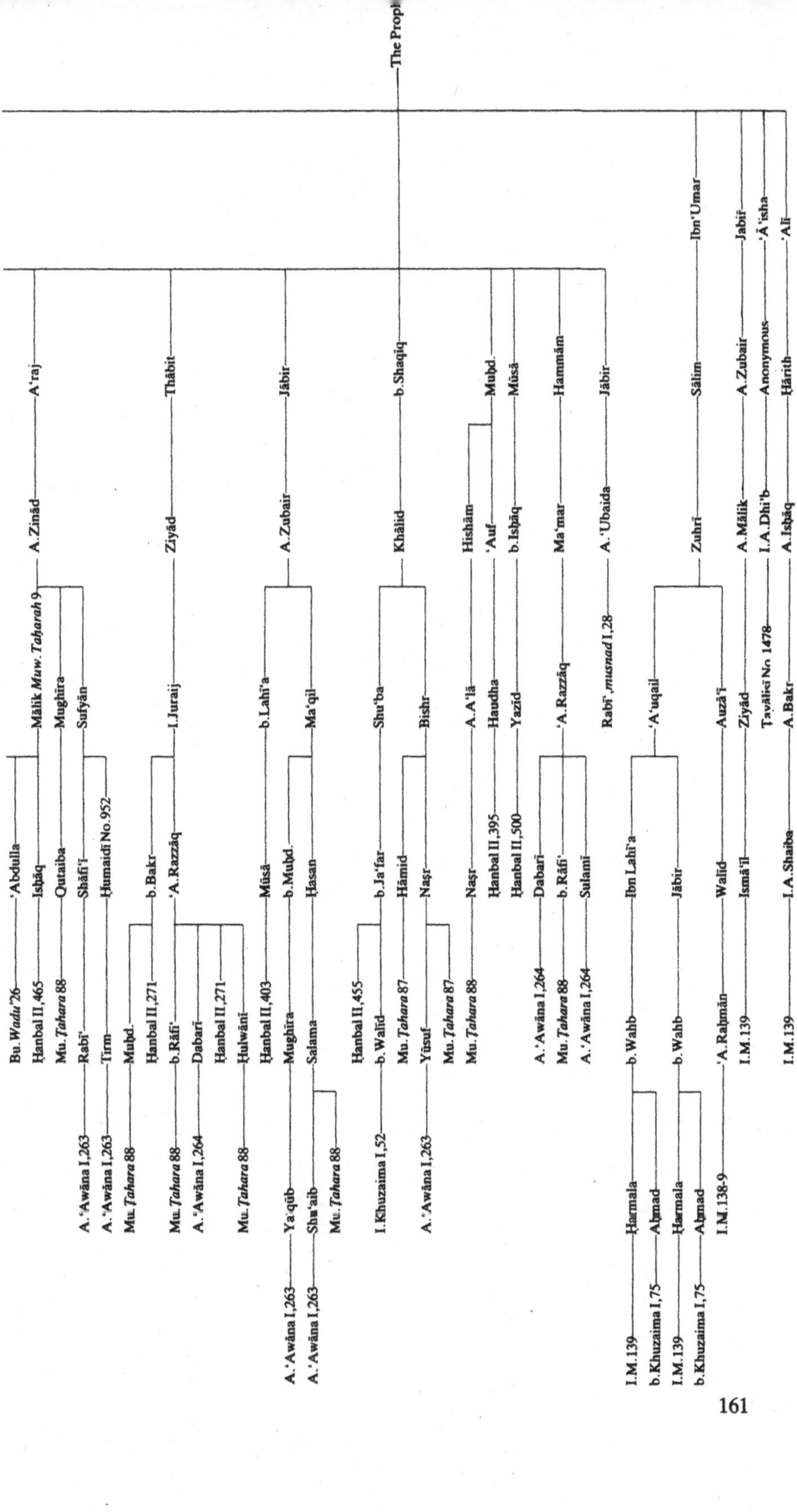

The Proph
A'raj
A. Zinād
Mālik Muw. Ṭahārah 9
Mughīra
Sufyān
'Abdulla
Isḥāq
Qutaiba
Shāfi'ī
Ḥumaidī No. 952
Bu. Wadu' 26
Ḥanbal II, 465
Mu. Ṭahara 88
Rabī'
Tirm
A. 'Awāna I, 263
A. 'Awāna I, 263
Thābit
Ziyād
I. Juraij
b. Bakr
'A. Razzāq
Muḥd.
Ḥanbal II, 271
b. Rāfi'
Dabarī
Ḥanbal II, 271
Ḥulwānī
Mu. Ṭahara 88
Mu. Ṭahara 88
A. 'Awāna I, 264
Mu. Ṭahara 88
Jābir
A. Zubair
b. Lahī'a
Ma'qil
Mūsā
b. Muḥd.
Ḥasan
Ḥanbal II, 403
Mughīra
Salama
Ya'qūb
Shu'aib
Mu. Ṭahara 88
A. 'Awāna I, 263
A. 'Awāna I, 263
b. Shaqīq
Khālid
Shu'ba
Bishr
b. Ja'far
Ḥāmid
Naṣr
Ḥanbal II, 455
b. Walīd
Mu. Ṭahara 87
Yūsuf
Mu. Ṭahara 87
I. Khuzaima I, 52
A. 'Awāna I, 263
Muḥd.
Hishām
A. A'lā
Naṣr
Mu. Ṭahara 88
'Auf
Haudha
Ḥanbal II, 395
Mūsā
b. Isḥāq
Yazīd
Ḥanbal II, 500
Hammām
Ma'mar
'A. Razzāq
Dabarī
b. Rāfi'
Sulamī
A. 'Awāna I, 264
Mu. Ṭahara 88
A. 'Awāna I, 264
Jābir
A. 'Ubaida
Rabī', musnad I, 28
Ibn 'Umar
Sālim
Zuhrī
'A'uqail
Ibn Lahī'a
Jābir
b. Wahb
b. Wahb
Ḥarmala
Aḥmad
Ḥarmala
Aḥmad
I.M. 139
b. Khuzaima I, 75
I.M. 139
b. Khuzaima I, 75
Auzā'ī
Walīd
'A. Raḥmān
I.M. 138-9
Jabir
A. Zubair
A. Mālik
Ziyād
Ismā'īl
I.M. 139
'Ā'isha
Anonymous
I. A. Dhi'b
Ṭayālisī No. 1478
'Alī
Ḥārith
A. Isḥāq
A. Bakr
I. A. Shaiba
I.M. 139

Chart 3: Transmission of a *Hadīth* Concerning Fasting.

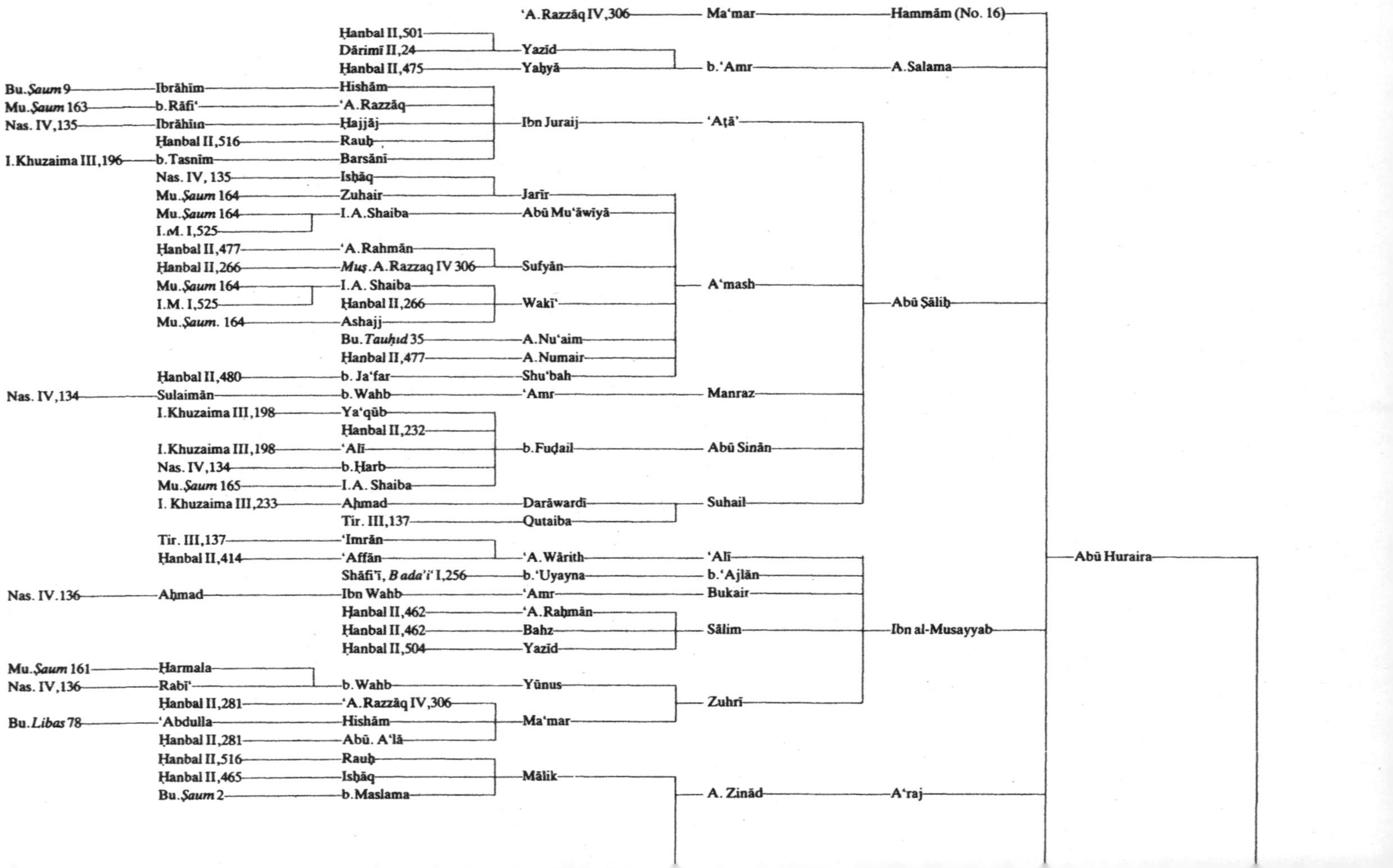

The Prophet
—Abū Huraira
—Abū Sa'īd Al-Khudarī
—b. Mas'ūd
—Bashīr
—'Ā'isha
—b. 'Umair
—'Uthmān
—b. A. Al-'Āṣ
—'Alī

—Sufyān — Shāfi'ī, Bada'i' I,256
         — Humaidī N.1010,1014
         — Ḥanbal II,458
         — Humaidī 1015

—Dāwūd
—Shu'ba — b. Ja'far — Bishr — I. Khuzaima III,197
—Maqburī
—b. 'Ajalān — Sufyān — 'Umar
—Ma'n
—I. A. Dhi'b — b. Ja'd 366
—'Ajalān — Ismā'īl — I. Rāhwaih 39a
—Qais — b. Tahmān 248a

—Muḥammad b. Ziyād — Shu'ba — Ṭayālisī I,121
                              — b. Ja'far — Ḥanbal II,457
                              — Yazīd — Ḥanbal II,504
                              — Ādam — Bu. Tauḥīd 504
—Ḥammād — 'A. Raḥmān — Ḥanbal II,466
—Sālim — Ṭabarānī Aws. I,54a
—Hishām — Mubd. b. Ja'far — Ḥanbal II,234,410
                           — Rauḥ — Ḥanbal II,516
                           — Yazīd — Ḥanbal II,234
—Ibn Sīrīn — Ḥaudha — Ḥanbal II,395
           — b. Tahmān 247b
           — I. Rāhwaih 65a

—Mūsā — 'Auf — 'Umar — Ismā'īl — I. Khuzaima III,198
—Ḥanẓala
—Jābir
—'Aṭīya — Dāwūd — Rabī' Musnad 84
        — Ma'n — Shaibān — Ḥarbal III,40
        — A. 'Ubaida — 'A. 'Azīz — Mu'āwīya — Mu Ṣaum 165
—Firās — Isḥāq — Ḥanbal III,5
—A. Ṣāliḥ — Ḍirār — b. Fuḍail — Ya'qūb — I. Khuzaima III,198
                              — 'Alī — I. Khuzaima III,198
                              — I. A. Shaiba — Mu Ṣaum 165

—A. Aḥwaṣ — Ibrāhīm — 'Amr — Ḥanbal I,446
          — A. Isḥāq — Shu'ba — Mubd — B. Bashshār — Nas. IV,134
—Ḥai — Qatāda — Ma'mar — 'A. Razzāq IV,308
—Umm Sālim — Ja'far — Yazīd — Tkabīr I,84b
—Yazīd — Khārija — Ḥanbal VI,240
—'Amr — Sufyān — Tawsaṭ I,252
—Ḥasan — 'Anbasa — Humaidī No.1011
—Muṭarrif — Sa'īd — Tkabīr V,9a
—b. Ḥārith — A. Isḥāq — 'Ubaidulla — Hilāl A'Alā — Ibn Ḥibbān N.931
—His Father — 'Alī — Zaid — Zaid, Musnad 202 — Nas. IV,132

163

(d. 168), transmitters from the students of Abū Huraira. It is also found in Shi'ite, Zaidi, and Ibadī sources.

Confining the discussion only to the third generation of narrators from Abū Huraira, who mostly belong to the first half of the second century of the Hijra, the following features appear: There are 22 third-generation transmitters – nine from Medina, five from Basra, four from Kūfa, and one each from Mecca, Wāsiṭ, Ḥijāz, and Khurāsān. These variously trace their source to 11 students of Abū Huraira, whose homes were in Medina, Baṣra, and Kūfa. A second interesting point is that not all the Medinese, Basrites, or Kūfans are the students of one man. Three of the Basrites trace the source of their knowledge to one Basrite, but the other two cite two different Medinese as their source.

Chart 3 shows the transmission of the *isnād* of this *ḥadīth* to classical collections.

Not all the *aḥādīth* were spread on this grand scale. Some were transmitted by a single scholar for two or three generations or even more. For example:

قال أبو هريرة ، قال النبي صلى الله عليه وسلم : « اذا صليت الجمعة فصل بعدها أربعا » .

Abu Hūraira reported the Prophet, saying: Whenever you pray *Jum'a*, pray four *rak'a* after it.[11]

This *ḥadīth* was transmitted by Abū Huraira only. From him, it was transmitted by Abū Ṣāliḥ, and from Abū Ṣāliḥ by his son Suhail. At least eight scholars transmitted it through Suhail. Chart 4 traces the transmission.

Chart 4: Example of Transmission Attributable to a Single Scholar.

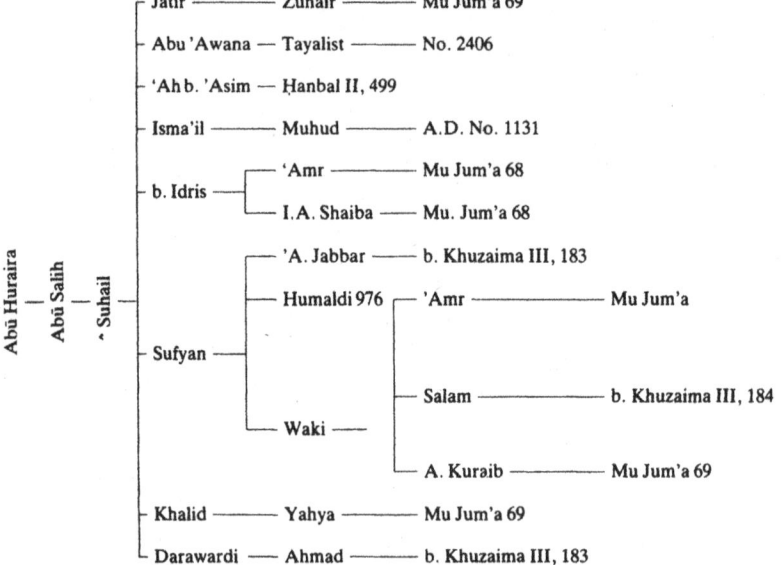

[11] *Studies*, p. 20 (Arabic section).

Without going into much detail, diagrams of these *aḥādīth* show how easy it was for *ḥadīth* knowledge to spread throughout the Islamic world and how the number of transmitters, in most cases, increased in each generation. Further down the chain, the number of narrators increases and the localities spread even farther into different provinces. This proves the early existence of the *isnād* system and shows how impossible it would have been to fabricate *isnāds* on this large a scale.

The above illustrations serve to show how well documented are the *isnāds* of the majority[12] of *aḥādīth*, how the system is used to examine the statements of the scholars, and how it was and can still be used for eliminating mistakes. The previous chapter described the efforts made by early scholars to distinguish between valid and invalid *aḥādīth*, and the rigorous methods they used to authenticate chains of transmission. Given centuries of this kind of activity, we are justified in accepting both the whole system of *isnād* and the methodology of *ḥadīth* scholars as valid scientifically.

Schacht seems to have believed that he had enough evidence to prove that the entire system is false. In this chapter, the examples he uses in support of his thesis will be examined, in order to demonstrate that his case rests on faulty logic and misunderstanding.

Schacht and the *Isnād* System

Schacht devoted an entire chapter of his *Origins of Muhammadan Jurisprudence* to the problem of *isnād*, and his findings were applauded by many scholars. Professor J. Robson considered it "a very valuable study which opens up new lines of research." He wrote:

> Dr. Schacht has studied the chains of authorities through whom legal traditions are transmitted and has put forward a most interesting theory. He has found *very often* that, while some legal traditions are transmitted through a variety of lines of authorities, they are liable to have a common transmitter at a certain stage in the chain. There may be a number of transmitters from him to succeeding generations, and the same may apply between him and the Prophet. Dr. Schacht has concluded that the tradition was made current either by this man, or by someone or some party who used his name. This is a very valuable contribution to the study of the development of Tradition, for it not merely suggests a date when certain traditions became attributed to the Prophet, but gives a certain value to the chain of authorities, suggesting that the later part of the chain is genuine, whereas the earlier part which goes back to the Prophet is fictitious . . .[13]

---

[12] I have demonstrated this position in three *aḥādīth* only. By going through *Studies*, Arabic section, 30 charts can be produced, and by going through Al-A'zamī, Ziyaur Rahmān's work on Abū Huraira, 1000 charts can be drawn on this grand scale for the *aḥādīth* transmitted by Abū Huraira alone.

[13] J. Robson, "*Muslim Tradition*," *Manchester Memoirs*, 90:7 (1951 – 52), 98–99 (italics mine).

Schacht's overall contention is that the *isnād* system may be valid for tracing traditions back to the second-century scholars, but that chains that stretch back to the Prophet and Companions are spurious. His argument can be summed up in six main points:

1. The *isnād* system began in the early second century or, at the earliest, the end of the first century.
2. *Isnāds* were put together carelessly and arbitrarily by those who wanted to "project back" their doctrines into the mouths of ancient authorities.
3. *Isnāds* were gradually "improved" by forgery and fabrication; early *isnāds* were incomplete, but all the gaps were filled in by the time of the classical collections.
4. Additional authorities were created in Shāfi'ī's time to meet the objections that were made to *aḥādīth* traced back to a single source.
5. "Family *isnāds*" are spurious, and so is the material presented in them.
6. The existence of a common narrator in a chain is an indication that the *ḥadīth* originated in the time of that narrator.

In addition to asking us to ignore the weight of evidence which points to the authenticity of the *isnād* system,[14] Schacht wants us to believe in a physical and psychological impossibility. First, he asks us to accept that *aḥādīth* with substantially the same wording or meaning could spring up in widely separated localities, a possibility now, with modern methods of communication, but hardly feasible several centuries ago. Then he asks us to accept either that these same narrators independently traced their sources back to a common source, or that they were conspirators in a vast confidence trick. Again, contemporary communications and the distances involved militate against such a possibility, let alone what we know of psychology. Surely such gross fabrication would not have gone unnoticed; someone would have come forward to point the finger of suspicion. And yet no one did. The burden of proof rests on Schacht; it is the aim of this chapter to show that he has not discharged that burden.

Origins of the System

Orientalists have differed in their views about the origins of the *isnād* system. According to Leone Caetani, 'Urwah (d. 94 A.H.), the oldest systematic collector of traditions, as quoted by Ṭabarī, used no *isnāds* and quoted no authority but the Qur'ān. Caetani therefore holds that, in the time of 'Abd al-Malik (d. 70 – 80 A.H.), more than 60 years after the Prophet's death, the practice of giving *isnād* did not exist. From this he concludes that the beginning of the *isnād* system may be placed in the

---

[14] See the text under the heading "Beginning and Development of the *Isnād* System" in this chapter.

period between 'Urwah and Ibn Isḥāq (d. 151 A.H.). In his opinion the greater majority of the *isnād* were created by *Muḥaddithīn* at the end of the second century, or perhaps the beginning of the third.[15]

Sprenger is another scholar who has argued that the writing of 'Urwah to 'Abd al-Malik does not contain *isnāds* and that it was not until later that he was credited with them.[16]

Horovitz has answered these arguments in his article "*Alter und Ursprung des Isnāds.*" He points out that those who have denied the use of *isnād* by 'Urwah cannot have consulted all his writings. Furthermore, he contends that there is a difference between what one writes when one is asked questions and what one does within learned circles. His conclusion is that the first entry of the *isnād* into the literature of *ḥadīth* was in the last third of the first century.[17]

Schacht ignores this argument and the evidence amassed by Horovitz, and simply reinstates Caetani's argument: "In any case, there is no reason to suppose that the regular practice of using *isnāds* is older than the beginning of the second century A.H."[18] He further says in the footnote: "Horovitz (in *Islam*, viii, 44 and in *Islamic Culture*, i, 550) has pointed out that the *isnād* was already established in the generation of Zuhrī (d. 123 A.H. or later), but to project its origin backwards into 'the last third of the first century A.H. at the latest' or 'well before the year A.H. 75', is unwarranted. Caetani (*Annali*, i, Introduction, 11), has shown that the *isnād* was not yet customary in the time of 'Abdalmalik (65–86 A.H.)."[19]

His denial of the early existence of *isnād* is a natural outcome of his theory regarding the *ḥadīth* of the Prophet. As there were no *aḥādīth* of the Prophet in the first century, according to Schacht, naturally there could be no *isnād*. The necessity for Schacht not to find first-century *isnāds* blinds him to any contrary evidence. In discussing the statement of Ibn Sīrīn (d. 110 A.H.) that the demand for the interest in *isnāds* started from the civil war *(Fitna)*, he says:

> We shall see later that the civil war which began with the killing of the Umaiyad Caliph Walīd b. Yazīd [A.H. 126], towards the end of the Umaiyad dynasty, was a conventional date for the end of the good old time during which the *sunna* of the Prophet was still prevailing; as the usual date for the death of Ibn Sīrīn is A.H. 110, we must conclude that the attribution of this statement to him is spurious. In any case, there is no reason to suppose that the regular practice of using *isnāds* is older than the beginning of the second century A.H.[20]

This whole argument, impugning a reliable source, is based on an

---

[15] For details, see *Studies*, pp. 213–214.
[16] *Ibid.* p. 214.
[17] See *Studies*, p. 214.
[18] *Origins*, p. 37.
[19] *Ibid.*, p. 37.
[20] *Origins*, pp. 36–37.

arbitrary interpretation of the word "*Fitna*." The assassination of Walīd b. Yazīd has never been a "conventional date" in Islamic history and was never reckoned as the end of the "good old time." This title is given only to the period of the Four Righteous Caliphs.

Further, there were many *Fitnas* before this date. There was the civil war between Ibn al-Zubair and 'Abd al-Malik b. Marwān about 70 A.H. But the biggest *Fitna* of all was the civil war between 'Alī and Mu'āwiyah, which produced a breach among Muslims that exists to the present day. Ṭāhā Ḥusain rightly described it as the fiercest quarrel of Islamic history.[21] The assassination of the Caliph Uthmān precipitated a *Fitna* even before this time.

In this context, it is difficult to see any justification for assuming that the *Fitna* referred to is the civil war that arose after the killing of Walīd b. Yazīd. Moreover, as was shown earlier in this chapter in the charts of the spread of *aḥādīth* in the Muslim world up to the first half of the third century, mass fabrication was impossible: thousands of scholars from Afghanistan to Egypt and from what is now the USSR to Yemen would have had to meet and agree on massive collusion. Another point that may be raised is that if the ancient schools of law – according to Schacht – were born in the second century, the traditionist movement would have had to come into existence at a later date. He saw no reason to suppose that the regular practice of using *isnāds* is older than the beginning of the second century, although he seems to have been prepared to admit that the irregular use of *isnād* may be dated even earlier, somewhere in the first century. The problem that needs resolution here is by whom were these *isnāds* used, since there were neither lawyers nor traditionists in existence.

Arbitrary and Careless Creation of *Isnāds*

In Schacht's view, "the *isnāds* were often put together very carelessly. Any typical representative of the group whose doctrine was to be projected back on to an ancient authority could be chosen at random and put into the *isnād*. We find therefore a number of alternative names in otherwise identical *isnāds*, where other considerations exclude the possibility of the transmission of a genuine old doctrine by several persons."[22] He goes on to quote six examples of alternative attribution in the generations preceding Mālik, and then gives four other examples of general uncertainty in the creation of *isnād*. I shall treat these two gro   f examples in turn.

Alternative Names

The six examples of alternation quoted by Schacht are:

1. Nāfi' and Sālim *(passim)*.

---

[21] Ṭāhā Ḥusain, [Cairo, 1951] *Al-Fitna al Kubrā 'Uthmān*, p. 5.
[22] *Origins*, p. 163.

2. Nāfi' and 'Abdallāh b. Dīnār (*Muw.* iv, 204 and *Ikh.* 149 f.).
3. Nāfi' and Zuhrī (*Muw.* iii, 71 and *Muw. Shaib.* 258).
4. Yayḥā b. Sa'īd and 'Abdallāh b. 'Umar 'Umarī (*Muw.* ii, 197 and *Muw. Shaib.* 207).
5. Yayḥā b. Sa'īd and Rabī'a (*Muw.* ii, 362 and *Tr.* 42).
6. Muḥammad b. 'Amr b. Ḥazm and Abū Bakr (b. 'Amr) b. Ḥazm (*Muw.* i. 259 and *Tr.* 101).[23]

Schacht gives no indication or evidence of the nature of the "other considerations" that would exclude the possibility of transmission of a genuine old doctrine by several persons. We therefore must assume what these might be. Did the people themselves not exist? Had they no opportunity to learn the doctrine from the same or different scholars? Was the content of the tradition not possible in the context of the times? In fact, these were all genuine historical people; all were of the same generation or lived in the same city for a period of 30 to 40 years, and there is no illogicality in the subject matter.

Let us now examine in detail each of the first six examples.

EXAMPLE 1: NĀFI' AND SALĪM

Schacht quotes no *ḥadīth* from these two sources. We can therefore only prove that the two scholars did exist and that they had the opportunity to learn from a common source. Their connection with Ibn 'Umar is well documented. According to Dhahabī, Nāfi' was a freed man of Ibn 'Umar who served his master for more than 30 years.[24] We are also told that he died in Medina in 117 A.H.[25] Sālim was the son of Ibn 'Umar. He died in 106 A.H,[26] 32 years after his father's death. At the end of the first century he was one of the most famous scholars in Medina, and one of the "seven lawyers" of that city. Living in the same city, and perhaps even in the same house, for 30 or 40 years, the two scholars had ample opportunity to learn from Ibn 'Umar.

EXAMPLE 2: NĀFI' AND 'ABDULLĀH B. DĪNAR

'Abdullah b. Dīnār was also a freed man of Ibn 'Umar with similar opportunity to learn *aḥādīth* from him. He is mentioned by the Shi'ite historian al-Ya'qūbī as one of the famous lawyers of Medina,[27] and is recorded by Bukhārī as a transmitter from Ibn 'Umar.[28] It is therefore more than likely that two men, Nāfi' and 'Abdullah b. Dīnār, could transmit the same *aḥādīth* from a single common source as they lived 60 or

---

[23] *Origins*, pp. 163–164.
[24] M. al-Dhahabī, *Tadhkirat al-Ḥuffāz*, (Hydrabad) vol. i, p. 88, reprint Beirut, N.D.
[25] *Tahd.*, vol. x, p. 414.
[26] *Taqrīb*, (Cairo, 1960), vol. I, p. 280. Cited hereafter as *Taqrīb*.
[27] A. A. Ya'qūbī, *Tārikh al-ya'qūbī* (Beirut, 1379-1960), vol. II, p. 309.
[28] M. al-Bukhārī, *at-Tārikh al-Kabīr* [Hydrabad, 1361], vol. iii, i, p. 81.

70 years together in the same city, and were freed men of the same person.

Is there any difficulty in the content matter of the *aḥādīth*? Here are the texts:

أخبرنا الشافعي ، قال أخبرنا مالك ، عن نافع عن ابن عمر ، أن رسول الله صلى الله عليه وسلم ، سئـل عن الضب فقال : « لست بـآكله ولا محرمـه » . (الأم ١٤٩/٧ اختلاف الحديث)

أخبرنا سفيان بن عيينة عن عبد الله بن دينار عن ابن عمر عن النبي نحوه . (اختلاف ، ١٤٩/٧)

مالك عن عبد الله بن دينار ، عن عبد الله بن عمر ان رجلاً نادى رسول الله ، فقال : يـارسول الله مـا ترى في الضب ؟ فقـال رسـول الله صلى الله عليـه وسلم : « لست بـآكله ولا محرمه » . (طـاستئذان ١١ (٤ : ٣٦٩) ط ، الشيباني ٢٢٠)

1. Shāfiʿī – Mālik – Nāfiʿ – Ibn ʿUmar: the Prophet was asked about the lizard *(al-ḍabb)*; he replied, "Neither do I eat it nor do I forbid it."[29]
2. Sufyān – ʿA. Dīnār – Ibn ʿUmar – the Prophet, as mentioned above.
3. Mālik – ʿA. Dīnār – Ibn ʿUmar – A man called to the Prophet, saying, "Messenger of Allah, what do you say about lizard?" Upon which the Prophet replied, "Neither do I eat it nor do I forbid it."[30]

Thus, Ibn ʿUmar says that the Prophet was asked about the eating of lizard, to which he replied: "I neither eat it nor forbid it." Lizards clearly did exist in those days, and there is no reason to suppose that everyone either liked or disliked eating them.

We have shown that both scholars were in a position to transmit this statement from Ibn ʿUmar. What other problem can there be? Transmission of this *ḥadīth* through Nāfiʿ is well documented by his students – notably, ʿUbaidullāh b. ʿUmar and Juwairiya b. Asmāʾ,[31] both of whom were colleagues of Mālik. Two students of Mālik, namely, Yaḥyā and Shaibānī, give its *isnād* as Mālik – ʿAbdullāh b. Dīnār – Ibn ʿUmar. Shāfiʿī, however, gives it the *isnāds* Mālik – Nāfiʿ – Ibn ʿUmar and Sufyān – ʿAbdallah b. Dīnār – Ibn ʿUmar.

Here we do find a contradiction, but it is as easy to believe it an omission of one of the authorities as to consider it an error of commission or carelessness. Mālik heard the *ḥadīth* from both sources. He transmitted many other *aḥādīth* from Nāfiʿ and could quite easily have transmitted this one from Nāfiʿ to Shāfiʿī without feeling the need to record it, in his *Muwaṭṭaʾ*, any more than that he heard it from ʿAbdullāh b. Dīnār.

We know that not all of his *aḥādīth* or legal opinions are contained in the *Muwaṭṭaʾ*, and many of his students (more than a thousand)[32] varied in the amount they transmitted from him. Thus, if a *ḥadīth* is transmitted

---

[29] *Umm.* vol. vii, p. 149. 5-Ibid.
[30] *Muw.* vol. iv. p. 369. *Muw. Shaib.* p. 220.
[31] *Ḥadīth* Nāfiʿ 115 and *Ḥadīth* Juwairīya 24 in *Studies*, Arabic section, pp. 131, 136.
[32] ʿAyād, *Tartīb al Madārik* (Beirut, 1387), vol. I, p. 279.

from him by a reliable scholar and is not found in *Muwaṭṭa'*, we cannot necessarily blame the scholar for carelessness on this ground alone.

Elsewhere, Schacht has impugned the Golden Chain of Mālik – Nāfi' – Ibn 'Umar, basing his objections to its authenticity on the age of Mālik and on the "client" relationship of Nāfi' to Ibn 'Umar. In his own words: "But as Nāfi' died in A.H. 117 or thereabouts, and Mālik in A.H. 179, their association can have taken place, even at the most generous estimate, only when Mālik was little more than a boy. It may even be questioned whether Mālik, whom Shāfi'ī charged elsewhere with concealing imperfections in his *isnāds*, did not take over in written form traditions alleged to come from Nāfi'."[33] He says in the footnote that "nothing authentic is known of Mālik's date of birth."[34]

If we consult the bibliographical works, however, we find that most of the scholars, even those who were born a little earlier than Mālik, state that he was born in 93 A.H.; a few put it in the early months of 94 A.H., a few in 90 A.H., and a few in 97 A.H.. But there is no one who maintains any date later than this. So Mālik was at least 20 years old, if not 24 or 27, when Nāfi' died. He transmitted in the *Muwaṭṭa'* from Nāfi' only 80 traditions of the Prophet, which cover in the printed text of Ibn 'Abd al-Barr about 15 pages.[35] Other *āthār* transmitted by Mālik on the authority of Nāfi' are not taken into account; if we take an equal number to those from the Prophet, then it would be some 30 pages. The teacher, Nāfi', and the student, Mālik, both lived in the same city until Mālik was about 24 years old, which makes it difficult to say that he might not have learned these 50 pages from his teacher.

The other point raised by Schacht is that Nāfi' was a client of Ibn 'Umar. But why should we believe that a man is dishonest because of this relationship, when he was clearly accepted among his contemporaries and the later authorities as most trustworthy?

EXAMPLE 3: NĀFI' AND ZUHRĪ

Zuhrī was born in Medina in about 51 A.H., and studied there until his thirties. He went to Syria and came back to Medina for some time, subsequently joining the Caliph's circle in Syria where he died in 124 A.H. Thus he lived in Medina at the same time as Nāfi', for 30 or 40 years. Historians tell us that they were colleagues, and that Zuhrī also learned from Nāfi'. Is there any evidence to prove that they could not transmit genuine doctrines from earlier authorities? Here are the original texts with the translation.

---

[33] *Origins*, pp. 176–177.
[34] *Origins*, p. 176, 4.
[35] *Tajrīd al-Tamhīd*, (Cairo, 1350) pp. 170–184.

١ - أخبرنا مالك ، أخبرنا الزهري عن سعيد بن المسيب قال : إذا آلى الرجل من امرأته ثم فاء قبل أن تمضي أربعة أشهر فهي امرأته لم يذهب من طلاقها شيء ، فان مضت لأربعة أشهر قبل أن يفيء فهي تطليقة وهو أملك بالرجعة مالم تنقض عدتها . (ط ٣ : ١٧٤ ، ط الشيباني ٢٥٨) . [36]

٢ - أخبرنا مالك أخبرنا نافع عن ابن عمر قال : ايما رجل آلى من امرأته فاذا مضت الأربعة أشهر وقف حتى يطلق أو يفيء ولا يقع عليها طلاق أو ان مضت لأربعة أشهر حتى يوقف . (ط ٣ : ١٧٣ ، الشيباني ٢٥٨) . [37]

٣ - عبد الرزاق عن أبي جريج ، قال أخبرني ابن شهاب ان ابن المسيب وأبا بكر بن عبد الرحمن قالا : اذا مضت الأشهر فهي واحدة وهو أحق بها . (المصنف ٦ : ٤٥٦) . [38]

٤ - عبد الرزاق عن معمر ، عن أيوب ، عن نافع عن ابن عمر قال : يوقف المولى عند انقضاء الأربعة فإما ان يفيء وإما أن يطلق . [39]

٥ - حدثنا سعيد قال ناهشيم قال عبد الحميد عن نافع عن ابن عمر انه قال في المولى عن امرأته : يوقف عند الأربعة أشهر فإما أن يفيء وإما أن يطلق . (سعيد بن منصور سنن ٣/٢/٣٢) . [40]

1. Mālik – Zuhrī – Ibn al-Musayyab: If a man pronounced *īlā'* [swore] to abstain from sexual intercourse with his wife for four months and later on changed his mind before the four-month period was passed, then she would remain his wife. If four months passed before he changed his mind, this would [automatically] be counted as a divorce but the husband would have the right to take her back as his wife if the waiting period had not passed.
2. Mālik – Nāfi' – Ibn 'Umar: If a man pronounced *īlā'* on his wife and the four-month period passed, he would have to make a choice. Either he would divorce her or he would take her back [there would not be any divorce automatically].
3. 'A. Razzāq – Ibn Juraij – Ibn Shihāb – Ibn al-Musayyab and Abū Bakr b. 'Abdul Raḥmān were both of the opinion that after an oath of *īlā'*, if four months passed it would be counted a divorce, and the husband would have the right to take her back.
4. 'A. Razzāq – Ma'mar – Ayub – Nāfi' – Ibn 'Umar: The one who pronounces *īlā* still has the right to keep his wife or divorce her even after the four-month period.
5. Sa'īd – Hushaim – 'Abdul Ḥamıd – Nāfi' – Ibn 'Umar said the man

---

[36] *Muw. Shaib*, p. 258, *Muw.* vol. 3. p. 174.
[37] *Muw. Shaib*, p. 258; *Muw.* vol. 3. p. 173.
[38] *Muṣannaf*, vol. 6, p. 456.
[39] *Muṣannaf*, vol. 6, p. 458.
[40] Sa'īd b. Manṣūr, *Sunan*, vol. 3, Part 2, p. 32.

who pronounces *īlā'* on his wife would have to make up his mind at the end of the four-month period: he could take his wife back or divorce her.

Here Zuhrī is transmitting the *fatwā* of Ibn al-Musayyab on *īlā'* (to swear to abstain from sexual intercourse with one's wife for four months). He was associated with Ibn al-Musayyab for more than seven years. Nāfi' is transmitting the *fatwā* of Ibn 'Umar on the same subject. We have seen that Nāfi' served Ibn 'Umar for more than 30 years. Thus both scholars had ample opportunity to learn the *fatwā* from the authorities they cite. Furthermore, there is a fundamental difference between the doctrine of Ibn al-Musayyab and that of Ibn 'Umar. Schacht does not recognize this and thinks it a single doctrine ascribed to two early authorities.

The disagreement between Ibn 'Umar and Ibn al-Musayyab can be traced back to different interpretations of the Qur'ānic verse, *sūra* ii, 226, so there is no reason to reject either statement on the grounds of content. Moreover, we have proof in other works that students of both scholars trace their knowledge of the *fatwā* back to them. Ibn Juraij, a colleague of Mālik, learned it from Zuhrī [41] and Ayyūb and 'Abdul Ḥamīd trace its origin to Nāfi'.[42] We must therefore conclude that both men transmitted the doctrine and that they learned it from the authorities they mentioned.

EXAMPLE 4: YAḤYĀ B. SA'ĪD AL-ANṢĀRĪ AND 'ABDALLAH B. 'UMAR AL-'UMARĪ

Yaḥyā b. Sa'īd al-Anṣārī of Medīnā was born in the second half of the first century A.H. He transmitted *ḥadīth* from Anas b. Mālik (d. 93 A.H.) etc. and died in 144 A.H.[43] 'Abdallah b. 'Umar (b. Ḥafṣ) al-'Umarī of Medina was born at the end of the first century A.H. and transmitted *ḥadīth* from Nāfi' etc. He died in 171 A.H.[44] Both transmit the following *āthār* from Muhammad b. Ibrāhīm al-Taimī (d. 120 A.H.) Is there any improbability in their both having met him? All three scholars lived in Medina and their dates are close enough together to permit their meeting, even if we accept that 'Abdallah b. 'Umar was only a young man at the time. Here is the original text with the translation:

١ - حدثني يحيى عن مالك عن يحيى بن سعيد عن محمد بن ابراهيم بن الحارث التيمي عن ربيعة بن أبي عبد الله بن الهدير أنه رأى عمر بن الخطاب يقرد بعيرا له في طين بالسقيا وهو محرم . (الموطأ ٣ : ٢٨٩) .[45]

٢ - أخبرنا مالك ، حدثنا عبد الله بن عمر بن حفص بن عاصم بن عمر بن الخطاب عن

---

[41] *Muṣannaf*, vol. iv, p. 450.
[42] *Ibid.*, p. 458.
[43] *Tahd.*, vol. xi, p. 223.
[44] *Tahd.*, vol. x, p. 327.
[45] *Muw.* vol. 3. p. 289.

محمد بن ابراهيم التيمي عن ربيعة بن عبد الله بن الهدير ، قال : رأيت عمر بن الخطاب رضي الله عنه يقرد بعيره بـالسقيا وهـو محرم فيجعله في طـين . (الموطأ الشيباني ٢٠٧) . [46]

٣ - عبد الرزاق عن ابن عيينة عن يحيى بن سعيد عن محمد بن ابراهيم عن ربيعة مثله ، الا أنه لم يقل في طين . (المصنف ٤ : ٤٥٠) . [47]

٤ - عبد الرزاق عن عبد الله بن عمر ، قال حدثنا محمد بن ابراهيم التيمي قال حدثنا ربيعة بن عبد الله بن الهدير قال : رأيت عمر بن الخطاب يقرد بعيره بالسقيا وهو محرم في طين . . (المصنف ٤ : ٤٤٩) . [48]

1. Mālik – Yaḥyā – Muḥammad – Rabī'a: He saw the Caliph 'Umar cleaning bugs from a camel near the place of Suqyā, (putting them) into mud, while the Caliph was *muḥrim* (proceeding for pilgrimage, and in such a state that he should not kill any living beings).
2. Mālik – 'Abdullāh – Muḥammad – Rabī'a said: "I saw 'Umar cleaning bugs from his camel near the place of Suqyā, putting them into mud, while he was in *iḥbrām* (proceeding for *Ḥajj*)."
3. 'Abdul Razzāq – Ibn 'Uyayana – Yaḥyā – Muḥammad – Rabī'a: The same except he did not mention the mud.
4. 'A. Razzāq – 'Abdullāh – Muḥammad – Rabī'a: "I saw 'Umar b. Khaṭṭāb cleaning bugs from his camel near the place of Suqyā (putting them into the mud while he was *muḥrim*)."

The *āthār* refers to Caliph 'Umar removing bugs from his camel while on pilgrimage. Given the existence of camels in Arabia and the well-established practice of undertaking pilgrimages, there can be little difficulty here. There seems to be only one objection: Schacht might be saying that two students of Mālik, Yaḥyā b. Yaḥyā and Muḥammad al-Shaibānī, both transmitted from Mālik the same *āthār* but were very careless in recording the *isnād*. The following are the *isnāds* of Yaḥyā and Shaibānī, respectively.

Yaḥyā's version: Mālik – Yaḥyā b. Sa'īd – Muḥammad b. Ibrāhīm – Rabī'a – 'Umar.

Shaibānī's version: Mālik – Abdallāh b. 'Umar – Muḥammad b. Ibrāhīm – Rabī'a – 'Umar.

One of Mālik's students names Yaḥyā as Mālik's authority, while another names 'Abdallāh b. 'Umar. Schacht calls this careless putting together of the *isnād*. We may just as easily assume that Mālik heard this

---

[46] *Muw. Shaib.* p. 207.
[47] *Muṣannaf*, vol. 4. p. 450.
[48] *Ibid.* p. 449.

athar from two of his teachers. The evidence of two of Mālik's contemporaries, Ibn 'Uyaynah (107 – 198 A.H.) and 'Abdar Razzāq al-Ṣanʿānī (126 – 211 A.H.), tends to support this point.

Ibn 'Uyayna transmitted this same *āthār* from Yaḥyā b. Sa'īd – Muḥammad b. Ibrāhīm – Rabī'a – 'Umar,[49] while 'Abdar Razzāq transmitted from 'Abdallah b. 'Umar – Muḥammad b. Ibrāhīm – Rabī'a – 'Umar.[50] This makes it quite clear that neither Shaibānī, nor Yaḥyā can be blamed for changing the names of the authority of Mālik. There were, in fact, two. One belonged to Iraqi school of law and lived in Kūfa, while the other was from *Ahl al-Ḥadīth* and belonged to Yemen. Clearly, Mālik learned these *āthār* from both authorities, sometimes naming one and sometimes another. This may be remiss of him in the eyes of future scholars, but he can hardly be blamed for carelessness – at least he has let us know two of his sources. But if Schacht continues to insist on carelessness, then he has to solve the riddle of probability of how a Yemenite, 'Abdur Razzāq, carelessly put together an *isnād* that coincides with the authority quoted by an early careless scholar of Iraq.

EXAMPLE 5: YAḤYĀ B. SA'ĪD AND RABĪ'A

Rabī'a b. Abū 'Abdar Raḥmān, was one of the most famous scholars in Medina known as Rabī'a al-Rāi'. He died in 136 A.H.,[51] thus he and Yaḥyā could easily have been part of the same learning circle for 50 years. They could both have heard this *fatwā* from Muḥammad b. Ibrāhīm, or one could have transmitted it to the other. Let us examine the text for any problems of content.

١ - قال الشافعي : « أخبرنا مالك عن يحيى بن سعيد عن محمد بن ابراهيم بن التيمي ، قال : تستحب العقيقة ولو بعصفور » (الأم ٧/٢٠٢)

٢ - « وحدثني عن مالك عن ربيعة بن أبي عبد الرحمن عن محمد بن ابراهيم بن الحارث التيمي أنه قال : سمعت أبي ، يستحب العقيقة ولو بعصفور » . (الموطأ ٣ : ٩٨)

٣ - « قال مالك : الأمر عندنا في العقيقة أن من عق فانما يعق عن ولده بشاة ، شاة ، الذكور والاناث . وليست العقيقة بواجبة ، ولكنها يستحب العمل بها . . . فانما هى بمنزلة النسك والضحايا لا يجوز فيها عوراء . . » (الموطأ ٣ : ٩٨-٩٩)

لم يذكر الشيباني هذا الأثر . . . انظر موطأ الشيباني ٢٢٥ - ٢٢٦ .

Here is the translation.

1. Mālik – Yaḥyā – Muḥammad said that *'aqīqa* [sacrificing an animal

---

[49] *Muṣannaf*, vol. iv, p. 450.
[50] *Ibid.*, p. 449.
[51] Ibn Ḥajar, *Taqrīb*, vol. 1, p. 247.

upon the birth of a baby] is desirable, even if one may sacrifice a sparrow.[52]
2. Mālik – Rabī'a – Muḥammad: He heard his father saying, "*Aqīqa* is desirable, even if one may sacrifice a sparrow."[53]
3. Mālik speaking about '*aqīqa* said: "Our opinion in the case of '*aqīqa* is that anyone who offers '*aqīqa* should sacrifice a sheep on behalf of his baby, one sheep for the boy or the girl. The '*aqīqa* is not compulsory, but to act accordingly is preferable [*mustaḥabb*]. . . . This is like the sacrifice of *Ḥajj* and *Uḍhīya*; therefore, any animal which has a defect is not acceptable.[54] However, Shaibānī did not record this statement.[55]

There can be no confusion here. Muḥammad b. Ibrāhīm gives his own or his father's opinion regarding '*aqīqa*. The one objection that might be raised is that Shāfi'ī traces the *fatwā* back from Mālik through Yaḥyā and Muḥammad b. Ibrāhīm, while Yaḥyā's version of the *Muwaṭṭa'* shows it coming through Rabī'a, and Shaibānī omits it totally. This is the same kind of problem as in the second example above, and can be met with the same argument: that there is every likelihood that Mālik heard the *fatwā* from two sources. Supposition is not a sufficient basis to prove otherwise. In any event, we should ask ourselves why later scholars would have wanted to invent an *isnād* for this *fatwā*. Being the wording of Successors, it has no weight in Shāfi'ī's eyes, and, moreover, it embodies an idea that both Mālik and Shāfi'ī rejected.

EXAMPLE 6: MUḤAMMAD B. 'AMR B. ḤAZM AND ABŪ BAKR (B. 'AMR) B. ḤAZM

The problem under discussion concerns praying in a single cloth. Mālik brought forward the following evidence:

1. The practice of the Prophet narrated by two Companions.
2. A saying of the Prophet to this effect.
3. The practice of two Companions, Abū Huraira and Jābair.
4. The practice of Muḥammad b. 'Amr b. Ḥazm.

However, Shāfi'ī reported the same practice but on the authority of Abū Bakr b. Ḥazm:

أخبرنا مالك عن ربيعة عن أبي بكر بن حزم أنه كان يصلي في قميص . فقلت أنا نكره هذا ،
فقال : كيف كرهتم ما استحب أبو بكر . (الأم ٧ : ٢٢٧ – ٢٢٨) .

Rabī'a reported about Abū Bakr b. Ḥazm that he used to pray in a shirt

---

[52] *Umm.*, vol. 7. p. 202.
[53] *Muw.*, vol. 3. p. 98.
[54] *Ibid.* p. 98–99.
[55] *Muw. Shaib.* p. 225–226.

[*qamīṣ*]. [The Medinese protagonist says]: "I say that we dislike it."
He inquired: "Why do you dislike that which was liked by Abū Bakr?"

The version of Shāfiʿī is most probably correct. Abū Bakr b. Ḥazm died in 117 or 110 A.H. or thereabouts[56] and Muḥammad b. ʿAmr b. Ḥazm died in 63 A.H.[57] The nickname [*kunya*] of Abū Bakr was Abū Muḥammad;[58] there may have been an Abū Muḥammad b. ʿAmr b. Ḥazm, and some scribe may have made a mistake in copying. As Shāfiʿī's version is correct, the mistake might well have been committed by the student of Mālik.

Schacht might say that his point is valid after all. But no scholar believes that he or any other scholar is infallible. Indeed, Schacht makes the same sort of mistake in this case. The full name of Abū Bakr b. Ḥazm is Abū Bakr b. Muḥammad b. ʿAmr b. Ḥazm[59] and not Abū Bakr b. ʿAmr b. Ḥazm as given by Schacht.

These six examples do *not* prove that *isnāds* were put together carelessly and in an arbitrary manner. In fact, if we adopt Schacht's view that *isnāds* were fabricated in the second century, we may find ourselves surprised that scholars widely scattered throughout the Islamic world were able to reach so much agreement on the *isnāds* they created. Without modern methods of communication this would seem improbable, if not impossible. Moreover, since we have shown that the alternative narrators were historically capable of having learned from the same source, the existence of alternatives would be evidence of great care, rather than carelessness, among the second-century scholars who "created" *isnāds*. Considerable research would have been required to establish that the alternatives in question were feasible. That is, the existence of alternatives serves to vindicate the traditional view, rather than to threaten it. Schacht's only justifiable complaint might be the omission of some of the authorities and the mentioning of only some of them.

General Uncertainty

Schacht quotes four more examples of what he calls "the general uncertainty and arbitrary character of *isnāds*."[60] Let us examine each of these examples in turn to determine what constitutes this uncertainty and arbitrary character.

Example 1

Schacht cites two stories about a *mudabbar*[61] slave, each with a different *isnād*:

---

[56] *Tahd.*, xii, 39.
[58] *Taqrīb*, ii, 195.
[58] *Tahd.*, xii, 24.
[59] See *Tahd.*, xii, 38.
[60] *Origins*, p. 164.
[61] A slave to whom freedom has been promised on the master's death.

1. Ḥafṣa killed a *mudabbar* slave who had bewitched her. Mālik – Muḥammad b. 'Abdalraḥmān b. Sa'd b. 'Zurāra – Ḥafṣa.[62]
2. 'Ā'isha sold a *mudabbar* slave who had bewitched her. Mālik – Abul Rijāl Muḥammad b. 'Abdalraḥmān [b. Ḥāritha] – his mother 'Amra – 'Ā'isha.[63]

Schacht maintains that these are two versions of the same tale: One of these versions is modeled on the other, and neither can be regarded as historical. It is obvious that the story was put into circulation in the generation preceding Mālik on the fictitious authority of one Muḥammad b. 'Abdalraḥmān, and this name was completed in such a way as to refer to two different persons in the two versions, it is at least doubtful whether Mālik met either of them.[64]

It is difficult to see on what grounds Schacht makes this assertion. The two stories are fundamentally different, in the people concerned (Ḥafṣa and 'Ā'isha) and in the fate of the slaves: one was killed and the other was sold. His contention that neither version is historical needs support to be accepted. We know that our forebears believed in witchcraft – many people still do – so actions of this type might well have been commonplace. The infectiousness of witchcraft hysteria is well documented (see, for example, the articles on Salem, Massachusetts and witchcraft in the *Encyclopaedia Britannica*) so it is more than likely that there would have been more than one instance of persecution.

As for the *isnād* itself, it is Schacht's stance always to be suspicious if he finds two people bearing the same name. A quick reference to the telephone directory of any Western city is enough to show the illogicality of this stance. Are people with identical names or only slight variations in name fictitious? In sum, the example gives no basis for a charge of uncertainty.

Moreover, there are scores of scholars of the early second century who transmitted traditions from these two authorities and differentiated between them.[65] One of them, Muḥammad b. 'Abdur Raḥmān b. 'Abdullah, was appointed governor of Yamāma by 'Umar b. 'Abdul 'azīz[66] and died in 124 A.H. The second one is Muḥammad Abū Rijāl, the date of whose death is not mentioned. As Mālik explicitly confirms that he learned from him personally,[67] there is no reason to suspect Mālik's statement. Since all these three belonged to Medina, there was every possibility that they met each other.

---

[62] *Muw.* iv., 49.
[63] *Muw. Shaib.*, 359; *Tr. III*, 93.
[64] *Origins*, p. 164. Schacht erroneously writes Jāriya instead of Ḥāritha, which I have corrected.
[65] See *Tahd.*, vol. ix, pp. 289, 295.
[66] *Ibid.*, p. 298.
[67] *Muw. Shaib.* pp. 299–300.

EXAMPLE 2

As a further example of uncertainty, Schacht cites:

> A tradition in *Muw.* 1, 371 reads: Mālik – Hishām – his father 'Urwa – 'Umar prostrated himself [on a certain occasion which is described], and the people prostrated themselves together with him. As 'Urwa was born in the caliphate of 'Uthmān, this *isnād* is 'interrupted' [*munqaṭi'*]. Bukhārī has a different, uninterrupted *isnād*. But old copies of the *Muwaṭṭa'* have 'and we did it together with him,' which is impossible in the mouth of 'Urwa. This of course is the original text of the *Muwaṭṭa'*. The same words occur in the text of a different tradition from the Prophet on the authority of Abū Huraira. This shows that the formulation of the text of the tradition came first, the *isnād* was added arbitrarily and improved and extended backwards later.[68]

It shows nothing of the sort. Ma'mar (95 – 153 A.H.), who died some 26 years before Mālik, quoted the same *athar* as follows:

« عبد الرزاق عن معمر عن هشام بن عروة عن أبيه أن عمر قرأ على المنبر سورة فيها سجدة ثم نزل فسجد وسجد الناس معه ، فقرأ في الجمعة التي تليها تلك السورة فلما بلغ قريبا من السجدة تهيأ الناس للسجود ، فقال : انها ليست علينا الا أن نشاء فقرأها ولم يسجد » .[69]

'A-Razzāq – Ma'mar – Hishām – his father 'Urwa: 'Umar recited a verse on the pulpit which contained *sajda* [prostration], then he came down and prostrated, and the people prostrated together with him. When he recited the same *sūra* on the next Friday [prayer] and was about to reach the point of *sajda*, the people prepared themselves to prostrate. 'Umar said, "It is not obligatory upon us to prostrate except if we wish": then he recited it and did not prostrate.

If one compares this with the printed text of the *Muwaṭṭa'* of Imām Mālik, one finds almost the same thing:

« وحدثني عن مالك ، عن هشام بن عروة ، عن أبيه ، أن عمر بن الخطاب قرأ سجدة وهو على المنبر يوم الجمعة ، فنزل ، فسجد ، وسجد الناس معه ، ثم قرأها يوم الجمعة الأخرى ، فتهيأ الناس للسجود ، فقال : على رسلكم ، ان الله لم يكتبها علينا ، الا أن نشأ فلم يسجد ، ومنعهم أن يسجدوا » . (الموطأ القرآن ١٦) .[70]

Mālik – Hishām – his father 'Urwa: 'Umar recited a verse containing *sajda* while he was on the pulpit on Friday, then he came down and prostrated. The people prostrated together with him. He recited the same verse on the occasion of the next Friday [prayer]. People prepared themselves to prostrate, then he said: "Take it easy. Allah did not make it obligatory upon us except if we wish to we can do it. Then he did not prostrate and forbade them from prostration."

That the *ḥadīth* was transmitted by Mālik's colleague Ma'mar is almost

---

[68] *Origins*, p. 164.
[69] *Muṣannaf*, vol. 3. p. 346.
[70] *Muw.*, *Qur'ān*, p. 16.

identical with the printed text of Mālik is enough proof that what was found in some copies of the latter is a late discrepancy. Schacht may not accept this, claiming that Ma'mar was older than Mālik, yet his recording did not invalidate Mālik's recording. We also find that two of Mālik's students, Shaibānī (d. 189 A.H.) and Qa'nabī (d. 221 A.H.), recorded almost the same text. Shaibānī's version is given first:

« قال محمد بن الحسن : بلغنا ان عمر بن الخطاب رضي الله عنه قرأ السجدة على المنبر يوم الجمعة فنزل ، فسجدوا ، ثم قرأها في الجمعة الأخرى فتهيأوا للسجدة ، فقال عمر : على رسلكم ان الله لم يكتبها عليكم الا أن نشأ ، فقرأها فلم يسجد ومنعهم ان يسجدوا . ذكر ذلك مالك بن أنس عن هشام بن عروة عن أبيه » . [71]

Muḥammad b. Ḥasan said: We learned that 'Umar b. Khaṭṭāb recited a prostrated verse containing *sajda* on the pulpit on Friday. He came down and prostrated and they prostrated together. He recited it on the next Friday. The people prepared themselves to prostrate. Then 'Umar said, "Take it easy. Allah has not made it obligatory upon you, except if we wish." Then he recited it and did not prostrate and forbade them from prostration. This was reported by Mālik on the authority of Hishām from his father 'Urwa.

Qa'nabī's version:

« أخبرنا أبو بكر قال حدثني اسحاق ، قال حدثنا القعنبي ، عن مالك عن هشام بن عروة عن أبيه أن عمر بن الخطاب رحمه الله قرأ السجدة وهو على المنبر يوم الجمعة ، فنزل فسجد وسجدوا معه ، ثم قرأها الجمعة الأخرى ، فذهبوا ليسجدوا ، فقال : على رسلكم ، أن الله عز وجل لم يكتبها علينا ، الا أن نشاء ، فقرأها فلم يسجد ومنعهم أن يسجدوا . » . [72]

Abū Bakr – Isḥāq – Qa'nabī – Mālik – Hishām – his father 'Urwa: 'Umar b. Khaṭṭāb recited verse containing *sajda* while he was on the pulpit on Friday, then he came down, and prostrated, and the people prostrated with him together. Then he recited the same on the next Friday. They were about to prostrate. He said, 'Take it easy. Allah did not make it obligatory upon us except if we wish.' Then he recited it and did not prostrate, and forbade them from prostration.

Thus the recording of the authorities older than Mālik and the recordings of Mālik's students tally with the printed text, which is more than enough proof of a later discrepancy. However, Schacht had no basis for believing that this "of course" is the original text of the *Muwaṭṭa'*, for I believe he did not see a copy written by Mālik himself. Moreover, the most famous commentator on the *Muwaṭṭa'*, Ibn 'Abd al-Barr (d. 463 A.H.), makes no mention of it in the versions of the *Muwaṭṭa'* he used. Nor is there any reference to "old copies" in the text and commentary of Zurqānī, from which Schacht took his quotation.

Here is the text:

---

[71] *Al-Ḥujja*, i, 287.
[72] Qa'nabī, *Muwaṭṭa'*, p. 146.

$$\text{أن عمر بن الخطاب قرأ سجدة وهو على المنبر فنزل فسجد وسجد الناس معه ... هكذا}$$
$$\text{الرواية الصحيحة وهي التي عند أبي عمرو ويقع في نسخ وسجدنا معه .. ثم قرأ يوم الجمعة}$$
$$\text{الأخرى فتهيأ الناس للسجود ، فقـال عـلى رسلكم .. فلم يسجـدوا ومنعهم أن}$$
$$\text{يسجدوا ...}^{73}$$

'Umar b. Khaṭṭāb recited *sajda* while he was on the pulpit. He came down and prostrated, and the people prostrated with him together ... This is the correct version which has been transmitted by Abū 'Amr, although in some copies it appears as "We prostrated with him ... Then he recited it on the next Friday. The people became prepared for prostration, upon which he said, "Take it easy." ... Then he did not prostrate and forbade them from prostration.

Zurqānī says that this is the correct version, although in *some* copies it appears as '*wa sajadna ma'ahu* (وسجدنا معه)

Every Arabist would reach the conclusion that it is a scribe's mistake; dropping a single letter *sin* س from سجد الناس was sufficient to make all these versions. Had it been the original text, as assumed by Schacht, then 'Urwa would have used the first-person personal pronoun plural number and the structure of the whole of the next sentence would have been

$$\text{فتهيأنا للسجود ... فلم نسجد ومنعنا أن نسجد .}$$

This is another proof that it is a later discrepancy. It is clearly unacceptable to cast doubt on the *isnād* of Bukhārī on the basis of a discrepancy that occurred in a later text.

EXAMPLE 3

Schacht tries to give the impression that various *isnāds* were concocted for two *aḥādīth* on this subject:

> The Iraqian doctrine which extends the right of pre-emption to a neighbour is expressed in two legal maxims: "the neighbour is entitled to the benefit of his promimity" (*al-jār aḥaqq bi-saqbih*), and 'the neighbour of the house is entitled to the house of the neighbour' (*jār al-dār aḥaqq bi-dār al-jār*). The first has the *isnād* 'Amr b. Sharīd – Abū Rāfi' – the Prophet (*Tr. I*, 49; *Ikh.* 260), the second the *isnād* Qatāda – Ḥasan Baṣrī – Samura – the Prophet (Ibn Ḥanbal, v. 8 and often; Ibn Qutaiba, 287). But the second was also provided with an alternative form of the *isnād* of the first: 'Amr b. Shu'aib – Sharīd – the Prophet (Ibn Ḥanbal, iv. 388).[74]

This hypothesis can be refuted by reference to contemporary sources. The version 'Amr b. Shu'aib – 'Amr b. Sharīd – Sharīd – the Prophet is recorded by Abū Yūsuf in his work the *Ikhtilāf Abī Ḥanīfa wa Ibn Abī*

---

[73] *Muw.* vol. 1, p. 371.
[74] *Origins*, pp. 164–165.

Lailā.[75] This work probably belongs to the first half of the second century, some one hundred years before Ibn Ḥanbal, and by Shaibānī[76] proving clearly that the *ḥadīth* was *not* "provided with an alternative form of the *isnād*" in the time of Ibn Ḥanbal or Shāfiʿī. However, it ought to be noted that the last quotation of Schacht (from Ibn Ḥanbal iv, 388) is misprinted. ʿAmr b. Shuʿaib did not transmit directly from Sharīd but from ʿAmr b. Sharīd, and this name was dropped either in printing or in transcribing. The same *ḥadīth* is printed on the next page of the same book (p. 389) where the correct version is given.

We may assume, then, that the second *ḥadīth* was transmitted by both Sharīd and Samura. Is it inconceivable that ʿAmr b. Shuʿaib should have heard it from ʿAmr b. Sharīd? Or that Qatāda should have heard it from both Ḥasan Baṣrī and ʿAmr b. Shuʿaib? In assuming that if the name of a scholar occurs several times in different *aḥādīth* on a subject, the *isnāds* were forged, Schacht demonstrates a surprising lack of understanding of the techniques of early Islamic scholars in using *isnād*. Typically, in teaching and learning, the early scholars preferred to refer to *isnāds* rather than books.[77] If a scholar were collecting material on a given subject, he would quote the *isnāds* of the *aḥādīth* available to him; thus for later authorities using his material he would become part of the *isnād*. His appearance in several different chains would mean only that he had gathered extensive material on the subject.

To demonstrate the fallacy inherent in Schacht's assumption, let us imagine that Mālik's *Muwaṭṭaʾ* was one of the many earlier source books that were lost. We would then find the *Muwaṭṭaʾ* material scattered throughout the classical collections, with *isnāds* passing through Mālik. Schacht's argument would lead us to the view that all these *isnāds* are forgeries. Moreover, the fact that mistakes are made does not invalidate the material in question. We know, for example, that there are some 200,000 differences and variations in existing Greek Bibles[78] and the same is true of many famous literary masterpieces. So even if mistakes in *isnāds* and *aḥādīth* exist, Schacht has produced no evidence that would cause us to impugn the good faith of the majority of transmitters or abandon the *ḥadīth* literature.

Gradual Improvement of *Isnāds*

One of Schacht's central contentions is that *isnāds* were gradually "improved" by forgery and fabrication, early incomplete *isnāds* being completed by the time of the classical collections. In his own words:

---

[75] Edited by Abul Wafā al-Afghānī (Cairo, 1357), p. 39.
[76] *Muw. Shaib.*, 305.
[77] See *Studies*, pp. 293–300.
[78] See P. Auvray and A. Barueq, *Introduction à la Bible*, p. 111.

The gradual improvement of *isnāds* goes parallel with, and is partly indistinguishable from, the material growth of traditions which we have discussed in the preceding chapters; the backward growth of *isnāds* in particular is identical with the projection of doctrines back to higher authorities. Generally speaking, we can say that the most perfect and complete *isnāds* are the latest. As is the case with the growth of traditions, the improvement of *isnāds* extends well into the literary period . . . The Muhammadan scholars chose to take notice of one particular kind of interference with *isnāds*, the *tadlīs*; we saw that Shāfi'ī disapproved of it, but minimized its occurrence.[79]

In support of this point, Schacht presents seven cases which will be discussed in detail below.

The general remarks of Schacht:

Āthār A. Y.: The editor has collected in the Commentary the parallels in the classical and other collections; a comparison shows the extent of the progressive completion, improvement, and backward growth of *isnāds*.[80]

Most of the Orientalists' misconceptions may be attributed to their choice of the wrong materials for the study of *isnād*. They use *sīrah* and *hadīth-Fiqh* literature instead of pure *hadīth* literature, ignoring the different nature of these books. This is rather like using science fiction works to learn about physics and chemistry – one may learn something of value, but the knowledge will inevitably be incomplete.

The early lawyers mention the importance of *isnāds* time after time, but they also state explicitly that, for the sake of brevity, they chose not to quote all the authorities and sources available to them. Their main concern was the legal point at issue and we can easily see that they would feel justified in not quoting *isnāds*, particularly if the *hadīth* in question was well known among the scholars. We find Abū Yūsuf, for example, saying that considerations of brevity prevented him from recording all the *ahādīth* and *isnāds* at his command.[81] Even Shāfi'ī remarks in places that he has heard unbroken *isnāds* for the *ahādīth* he quotes, but cannot remember them at the time.[82]

We must accept, first, that these scholars' knowledge was partial, and, second, that they omit in their works many details that were known to them. The following phenomena are common in *hadīth-Fiqh* literature as will be clear in the light of the Appendix I.

Omitting the *isnād* entirely where other sources prove they knew it.

Quoting only partial *isnāds* – citing either the immediate and highest authority, or various authorities at different points – where other sources prove they knew it in full.

---

[79] *Origins*, p. 165.
[80] *Origins*, p. 165.
[81] See Auzā'ī, p. 38.
[82] See *Umm*, vii, 311; *ar-Risālah*, 405; and Majid Khadduri', *Islamic Jurisprudence* (Baltimore, 1961), p. 254.

Mentioning only one channel of *isnād* from several available to them.

Using the expression "from a man" (عن رجل) or "from a reliable man" (عن الثقة) when the authority in question is elsewhere cited by name.

Appendix 1 gives examples of these patterns of *isnād* usage from the works of Ibn Isḥāq, Mālik, Abū Yūsuf, Shaibānī, and Shāfiʻī, quoting references to the sources that prove they *did* know the details they omitted. In the following paragraphs I shall confine myself to specific comments on the invalidity of the examples Schacht himself has chosen to "prove" this highly dubious point. I commented in the previous chapter on the fallacy inherent in the *e silentio* argument. This should be borne in mind throughout the discussion that follows.

EXAMPLE 1

Muw. iii 172 and *Muw. Shaib.* 364: Mālik – Zuhrī – Ibn Musaiyib and Abū Salama – Prophet; this tradition is *mursal*. Shāfiʻī [*Ikh.* 258 f.] has the same, but knows it also with the full *isnāds* Zuhrī – Abū Salama – Jābir – Prophet, and Ibn Juraij – Abul-Zubair – Jābir – Prophet. According to *Comm. Muw. Shaib.*, Ibn Mājashūn, Abū ʻĀṣim Nabīl and Ibn Wahb give it with a full *isnād* through Abū Huraira instead of Jābir, and so it occurs in Ṭaḥāwī, ii. 265: Abū ʻĀṣim Nabīl – Mālik – Zuhrī – Ibn Musaiyib and Abū Salama – Abū Huraira – Prophet. But Ṭaḥāwī remarks that the most reliable of Mālik's companions, including Qaʻnabī and Ibn Wahb, relate it with an imperfect *isnād*, that is, *mursal*.[83]

Schacht's comment on the *isnād* is based on his misunderstanding of the text of Ṭaḥāwī. He speaks here only of the *ḥadīth* transmitted by the students of Mālik, and not of *aḥādīth* coming through other channels. Some of Mālik's students transmitted it with full *isnāds*, but the more famous among them transmitted it as *munqatiʻ*.[84] This does not mean that no other *ḥadīth* with different *isnāds* existed. After recording the *ḥadīth* through Mālik, Shaibānī specifically says:

قد جاءت في هذا أحاديث مختلفة ، فالشريك أحق بالشفعة من الجار والجار أحق من غيره ، بلغنا ذلك عن النبي صلى الله عليه وسلم .

There are many different *aḥādīth* related on the subject . . . on the authority of the Prophet.[85]

In the light of this statement, it is clear that he is quoting only from a portion of the *ḥadīth* available. As Schacht points out, Shāfiʻī (*Ikh.* 258 f.) has the same *ḥadīth* with two separate full *isnāds*. That these were not

---

[83] *Origins*, pp. 165–166.
[84] Ṭaḥāwī, *Maʻāni al-Āthār*, ii, 265. *Munqatiʻ* means that the *isnād* is broken as one of the transmitters has been dropped and not mentioned.
[85] *Muw. Shaib.*, p. 364.

recorded by Mālik is not sufficient proof that they did not exist at the time. We have positive proof that the custom was to record some of the *isnāds*, while leaving others.[86]

EXAMPLE 2

Muw. iv. 35 and *Muw. Shaib.* 239: Mālik – Zuhrī – Ibn Musaiyib – Prophet; this tradition is *mursal*. Shāfi'ī (*Tr. VIII*, 14) has it with a complete *isnād* through 'a reliable man' [identified by Rabī' as Yaḥyā b. Ḥassān] – Laith b. Sa'd – Zuhrī – Ibn Musaiyib – Abū Huraira – Prophet. The name of Abū Huraira was inserted in the period between Mālik and Shāfi'ī and taken from the *isnād* of a parallel version with a sensibly different text (*Muw.* and *Muw. Shaib., loc. cit.*). In the same context, Shāfi'ī records the doubts of some Medinese regarding *isnāds* in general.[87]

First, there is a mistake in the reference at the beginning, which should read *Muw. Shaib.* 293.

Second, Schacht's statement is misleading. There are two *aḥādīth* on the subject recorded by Mālik and Shaibānī, one with *mursal isnād* and the other with complete *isnād*, both concerning the decree of the Prophet to pay *wergeld* in certain cases. One is Mālik – Ibn Shihāb – Ibn al-Musayyab – the Prophet; the other is Mālik – Ibn Shihāb [al-Zuhrī] – Abū Salama – Abū Huraira – the Prophet. Both Mālik and Shaibānī therefore, knew the *ḥadīth* with full as well as incomplete *isnād*.[88]

The third point which needs to be raised is that the subject matter of the *ḥadīth* recorded by Shāfi'ī with full *isnād* is not the same as that of the *ḥadīth* recorded by Mālik with incomplete *isnād*. The first *ḥadīth* says (قضى في الجنين في بطن أمه) ". . . he handed down a ruling regarding the fetus in its mother's womb. . ." while the second one says (قضى بالجنين على العاقلة) ". . . he handed down a ruling in which he required the tribal unit [of the defendant] to pay the *wergeld* for the fetus. . ." The first *ḥadīth* concerns *wergeld* while the second speaks about the parties or people who have to pay it – two quite different *ḥadīth* on two quite different matters. Scholars are unanimous on the first, but differ about the second. Schacht prefers to consider them parallel versions with sensibly different texts, which must cast doubts on his understanding of the Arabic text. Moreover, his comment that some Medinese expressed doubt regarding *isnāds* in general is based on a misunderstanding of Shāfi'ī's statement and style. As the second *ḥadīth* recorded by Shāfi'ī was not accepted by the Medinese, Shāfi'ī was refuting – as a lawyer – all the reasons that might

---

[86] See examples of careless naming cited in examples 21-24 in Chapter Seven and under the heading "Beginning and Development of the *Isnād* System" in this chapter.
[87] *Origins*, p. 166.
[88] *Muw.* iv, 35 (p. 855 in Fu'ād's edition); *Muw. Shaib.* 293.

cause the rejection of the *ḥadīth*; but no real doubt was being expressed by any party.

EXAMPLE 3

Muw. iv. 44: Yaḥyā b. Sa'īd – 'Amr. b. Shu'aib – 'Umar gives a decision, referring to an inconclusive statement of the Prophet. Ibn Māja [*Abwāb al-farā'iḍ*, *Bāb mīrāth al-qātil*], however, has a tradition with the *isnād* Muḥammad b. Sa'īd or 'Umar b. Sa'īd – 'Amr b. Shu'aib – his father [Shu'aib b. Muḥammad] – his grandfather 'Abdallah b. 'Amr – Prophet: a wordy, explicit statement, part of a composite speech.[89]

Schacht should have been aware that early scholars themselves rejected the *ḥadīth* recorded by Ibn Majah as spurious because the narrator, Muḥammad b. Sa'īd al-Shāmī, was notorious for fabricating *ḥadīth*.[90] This example proves how careful scholars were in eliminating false traditions, and, therefore, works against Schacht's case rather than for it.

EXAMPLE 4

Ris. 45: Shāfi'ī does not remember whether having heard a certain tradition with a reliable *isnād* and doubts whether it is well authenticated. But it exists in Bukhārī and Muslim with a first class *isnād* [see *ed. Shākir*, p. 315].[91]

But Shāfi'ī explicitly says:

All the traditions that I have cited [above] in an interrupted fashion were [originally] heard by me as uninterrupted, or are well-known traditions related by many people transmitting them from scholars who were acquainted with them through common knowledge; but I did not want to cite traditions that I had not fully memorized, nor did I have access to some of my books which I had lost [to verify them]; but I have verified the accuracy of what I memorized by checking it with the knowledge of scholars, and I have *summarized* it fearing that this book might become too long. I have, however, cited what might be *sufficient* without going into every aspect of it in an *exhaustive* fashion.[92]

In another place he says: "We know of no one who possesses knowledge of *all* the *sunnas* without failing to have a portion of it. So if the knowledge of all scholars is gathered, the entire *sunna* would be known. [However], if the knowledge of each scholar is taken separately, each might be found lacking in some portion of it."[93]

When Shāfi'ī himself admits that no one has knowledge of all *ḥadīth*, how can one cast doubt on a *ḥadīth* because Shāfi'ī is ignorant of it?

---

[89] *Origins*, p. 166.
[90] See any biographical work of *Muḥaddithīn*, for example, *Taqrīb*, ii, 164.
[91] *Origins*, p. 166.
[92] Khadduhrī, *Risāla*, p. 265 (italics mine).
[93] *Ibid.*, p. 89 (italics mine.)

Moreover, the *ḥadīth* was recorded with full *isnād* by two scholars who were earlier than Shāfiʿī: the Ibādī scholar Rabīʿ with the genuine *isnād* Abū ʿUbaidah – Jābair b. Zaid – Abū Saʿīd Khudrī – the Prophet[94] and the Ḥanafī scholar Shaibānī with the *isnād* Abū-Ḥanīfa – Ḥammād – Ibrāhīm – Abū Saʿīd al-Khudrī and Abū Hurairah – the Prophet.[95] Thus it may be concluded that the *ḥadīth* under discussion was well known with perfect *isnāds* even during the childhood of Shāfiʿī.

EXAMPLE 5

Ris. 59: Mālik – Rabīʿa – several scholars – ʿUmar; Shāfiʿī states that this *isnād* is 'interrupted'. But it has become complete in Ibn Ḥanbal, Bukhārī, and Muslim (see Zurqānī, iv. 200 and *ed. Shakir*, p. 435).[96]

The text of Shāfiʿī is: «فإن قال هذا منقطع . .». If someone says that this is a *munqaṭiʿ* [meaning a *ḥadīth* with imperfect *isnād*], Schacht did not read the text carefully enough. Shāfiʿī raised the issue but did not answer it; perhaps he forgot it or perhaps he was unsure and unwilling to commit himself. The real point is that this *ḥadīth* is recorded by Maʿmar (96–153 A.H.), a contemporary of Mālik who died a quarter of a century earlier than Mālik. He gives it with the following complete *isnād* in his book *Jāmiʿ Maʿmar*, which was published with the *Muṣannaf* of ʿAbdur Razzāq al-Ṣanʿānī: Maʿmar – Saʿīd al-Jurarī – Abū Nadhrah – Abū Saʿīd al-Khudrī – Abū Mūsā – the Prophet.[97] Thus, the above-mentioned *ḥadīth* was recorded with full *isnād* before the birth of Shāfiʿī.

EXAMPLE 6

Ris. 64: Shāfiʿī states that a tradition is *mursal* and generally not acted upon, implying that it is not confirmed by any version with a complete *isnād*. But it appears with a different, full *isnād* in Ibn Hanbal (see *ed. Shākir*, p. 467) and Ibn Māja [see Graf, *Wortelan*, 63, n. 1].[98]

It has been shown earlier in my work *Studies in Early Ḥadīth Literature* that "*Muḥaddithīn* used to judge every *ḥadīth* on its own merits." They would first consider the *isnād*, and would reject the *ḥadīth* if the *isnād* were defective, without scrutinizing the subject matter; because according to their criteria a *ḥadīth* cannot be authentic unless both its parts are perfect.

This point is clearly made in Appendix III of *Studies*. This is a collection of *aḥādīth* transmitted by Bishr b. al-Ḥusain on the authority of Zakarīyā b. ʿAdī from Anas b. Mālik from the Prophet, which are called spurious, though about one quarter of the *aḥādīth* of this collection are found in

---

[94] Ar-Rabīʿ, *Musnad* (Damascus, 1388/1968), p. 151.
[95] M. Shaibani, al-Āthār (Karachi, n.d.), 734.
[96] *Origins*, p. 166.
[97] *Muṣannaf*, X. p. 381.
[98] *Origins*, p. 166.

Bukhārī's and Muslim's Ṣaḥīḥ collections, and are called authentic. The only reason for discarding them is that it is maintained that Zakariyā did not hear all these *aḥādīth* from Anas, and they are falsely attributed to him.[99]

The same is true in this example. The *ḥadīth* to which Shāfi'ī refers is weak and unacceptable. But the same statement of the Prophet was transmitted by other channels unknown to Shāfi'ī. Later scholars, while they rejected the *ḥadīth* mentioned by Shāfi'ī, accepted the others, which were transmitted with a sound *isnād*.

Of the six examples which Schacht adduces in support of the gradual improvement of *isnāds*, we find four cases of full *isnāds* being recorded before the partial or incomplete version he quotes, one example that proves how diligent early scholars were in eliminating suspect *aḥādīth*, and another that shows the reluctance of scholars to cite an *isnād* unless they were certain of it.

Creation of Additional Authorities

Another of Schacht's central theories is that new *isnāds* and additional authorities were created with the intention of confirming a doctrine by apparently independent evidence: "Parallel with the improvement and backward growth of *isnāds* goes their spread, that is, the creation of additional authorities or transmitters for the same doctrine or tradition. The spread of *isnāds* was intended to meet the objection which used to be made to 'isolated' traditions'."[100]

Much of his argument rests on the *e silentio* thesis and his lack of understanding of the early scholars' methods of using *isnād* – points which have already been commented on at length. His view is merely supposition and the evidence he produces is inconclusive, as can be seen from looking at the examples he uses.

EXAMPLE 1

Mālik (*Muw*. ii, 54) refers, without *isnād*, to the instructions on the *zakāt* tax which 'Umar gave in writing. The same instructions are projected back to the Prophet, with *isnāds* through 'Umar and through other Companions, in Ibn Ḥanbal and the classical collections (see Zurqānī, *ad loc.*). The two oldest examples are two traditions in *Tr. II*, 9 (b): the one Medinese, through Ibn 'Umar from the Prophet, with the added remark that 'Umar instructed his agents to the same effect; the other Iraqian, quoted above . . . An earlier form of traditional authority for the identical Iraqian doctrine is represented by a tradition through Ibrāhīm Nakha'ī from Ibn Mas'ūd (*Āthār A.Y.* 423; *Āthār Shaib.* 49); the tradition from 'Alī in *Tr. II*, 9 (b) represents an unsuccessful primitive effort to systematize.[101]

---

[99] *Studies*, p. 305.
[100] *Origins*, p. 166.
[101] *Origins*, p. 167.

In a footnote he adds: "This does not mean, of course, that the tariff of the *zakāt* tax was not in fact fixed by 'Umar, but this cannot be concluded from the traditions."[102]

Earlier, he writes:

> *Tr. II*, 9 (b): Shāfi'ī – Abū Kāmil and others – Ḥammād b. Salama Baṣrī – Thumāma – [of Baṣra] – his grandfather Anas b. Mālik – his father Mālik gave him the copy of a decree of Abū Bakr on the *zakāt* tax and said: "This is the ordinance of Allah and the *sunna* of the Prophet." A parallel version in 9 (c) has: 'Abū Bakr gave him the *sunna* in writing. This tradition can be dated to the time of Ḥammād b. Salama; the connexion between Ḥammād and Thumāma is very weak.[103]

To summarize his arguments: (1) Mālik refers to the instruction given by 'Umar regarding *zakāt* without *isnād*; (2) In Ibn Ḥanbal and the classical collections it was improved upon in two ways: (a) projected back to the Prophet and (b) the *isnād* was completed.

To refute these arguments it is sufficient to refer to Abū Yūsuf, who recorded this *ḥadīth* through:

> Zuhrī – Sālim – Ibn 'Umar – the Prophet. The Prophet dictated a decree on *zakāt*, which was followed by Abū Bakr and then 'Umar.[104]

As far as the *ḥadīth* of Thumāma is concerned, he says that Anas handed him the document which was written by Abū Bakr for him. This *ḥadīth* has complete and sound *isnād*, but it is not accepted by Schacht who thinks that it can be dated to the time of Ḥammad b. Salamah (d. 167 A.H.). But suppose that it can be so dated: then surely Schacht should have mentioned that in the first half of the second century this tariff was attributed to the Prophet instead of "projecting forward" one hundred years to the time of Ibn Ḥanbal and later.

Moreover, his translation and statement contains mistakes. For example, the *isnād* is: Ḥammād – Thumāma – Anas – Abū Bakr, while Schacht has it: Thumāma – his grandfather Anas b. Mālik – his father Mālik, which is totally wrong. He further states that the connection between Ḥammād and Thumāma is very weak – against the statements of early biographers.[105]

It is generous of Schacht to grant that 'Umar fixed the *zakāt* tariff. The Qur'ān, however, demands it hundreds of times, and it is therefore more rational to suppose – without even looking to traditions which claim that it was fixed by the Prophet – that it must have been carried out in the time of the Prophet and must have been fixed by him. This is, however, mentioned in *ḥadīth* literature and other works.

---

[102] *Idem*, n.1.
[103] *Origins*, p. 73.
[104] *Kharāj*, p. 76.
[105] See *Tahd.*, II, 28–29.

EXAMPLE 2

Schacht cites this as an example of the creation of additional authorities to meet objections to isolated traditions:

> Mālik's tradition on the *khiyār al-majlis*, with the *isnād* Nāfi' – Ibn 'Umar – Prophet, must be later than the doctrine to the contrary which is common to the Medinese and the Iraqians (*Muw*. iii. 136; *Muw. Shaib.* 338). The classical collections (quoted in Zurqānī, iii. 136) have additional *isnāds*, some of which eliminate Nāfi' and branch off directly from Ibn 'Umar, or even eliminate Ibn 'Umar and go back to the Prophet through another Companion. These are certainly later developments.[106]

This statement should be considered together with an earlier reference by Schacht to the same *ḥadīth*:

> The *khiyār al-majlis* is enjoined in a tradition expressing a legal maxim: Mālik – Nāfi' – Ibn 'Umar – the Prophet said: 'The two parties to a sale have the right of option as long as they have not separated' (*Muw.* and *Muw. Shaib.*, loc. cit; *Tr. III*, 47). This is certainly later than 'Aṭā' and must have been put into circulation by Nāfi' or someone who used his name. Mālik states that there is no such practice...[107]

Let us first clear up the mistakes of fact. The opposing doctrine was *not* common in Medina and Iraq. The following authorities all held the same view:

Medina: Ibn 'Umar, Ibn al-Musayyab, al-Zuhrī, Ibn Abū Zinād.[108]
Mecca: 'Aṭā' and Ibn Abū Mulaika.[109]
Iraq: Shuraiḥ and Sha'bī.[110]
Baṣra: Ibn Sīrīn.[111]
Syria: Al-Auzā'ī.[112]
Egypt: Al-Laith b. Sa'd.[113]
Yemen: Ṭā'ūs.[114]

The only views that are at all contrary are those of Rabī'a [Medina] in one of the opinions ascribed to him, and Ibrāhīm al-Nakha'ī [Kūfa], who accepts the *ḥadīth* but differs in his interpretation of it. Abū Ḥanīfa (*Muw. Shaib.* 338) makes the same point.

Mālik did *not* say there was no such maxim. There has been much discussion in explaining the wording of Mālik. But it is quite clear that he

---

[106] *Origins*, p. 167.
[107] *Ibid.*, p. 160.
[108] Ibn Ḥajar, Fatḥ ul Bārī, IV, p. 330; also Ibn Abī Rabī' in one of his statements (Zurqānī, iii, 321).
[109] Bu., *Buyū'*, 44.
[110] Bu., *Buyū'*, 44; *Muṣannaf*, viii, p. 52; Wakī', *al-Quḍāt*, ii, p. 260.
[111] *Muṣannaf*, viii, 54.
[112] *Zurqānī*, ii, 322.
[113] *Zurqānī*, ii, 322.
[114] *Muṣannaf*, viii, 54.

does not deny *khiyār majlis*, because in the chapter on *khiyār majlis* he quotes the *ḥadīth*, and says:

ليس لهذا عندنا حد معروف ولا أمر معمول به فيه

"There is no limit known to us for the period of *khiyār*." Had he denied *khiyār* he would have said: ليس عليه العمل "There is no such practice."[115]

The *ḥadīth* was not necessarily put into circulation after the time of 'Aṭā'. Ibn Juraij records 'Aṭā''s statement that after completing the contract of sale, one should give the buyer the choice of either taking or leaving it. Ibn Juraij asked him whether it would be necessary to annul the contract if the buyer, having been given the option, took it and then regretted his choice before they separated. 'Aṭā' replied: "I do not think so if he has given him the choice after completing the transaction."[116] This does not prove that 'Aṭā' did not know the doctrine of *khiyār majlis*, merely that he interprets "separation" as closing of business on that particular topic – a quite valid difference in interpretation, which does not challenge the authority of the document. Even if he did not know the doctrine, this is not conclusive proof that it did not exist.

Now let us look at the evidence for the contention that Nāfi', or someone using his name, put this *ḥadīth* into circulation. Let us begin with the second assumption, that the originator might be someone using Nāfi''s name. The point has already been made that many books from the first and second centuries have been lost, but some early works do remain. This particular *ḥadīth*, or parts of it, is recorded through Nāfi' by several scholars: 'Ubaidullah b. 'Umar (d. 145 A.H.);[117] Ibrāhīm b. Ṭahmān of Khurāsān (d. 163 A.H.) through Mūsā b. 'Uqba of Madīna (d. 141 A.H.);[118] Ayyūb al-Sakhtiyānī of Baṣra (d. 131 A.H.);[119] and Juwairiyi b. Asmā' of Baṣra (d. 177 A.H.)[120] Some of these explicitly said that they read the *ḥadīth* to Nāfi' or heard it from him. We can, I think, assume that these students knew their teacher. Therefore, Nāfi' must have transmitted it himself. Moreover, the same *ḥadīth* was transmitted through other students of Ibn 'Umar.[121]

What evidence is there for the alleged creation of additional authorities? Let us review our findings. First prior to Mālik we have seen five *isnāds* from Nāfi' in books older than Mālik's. There are three other sources prior to Mālik through different Companions: (a) Samura,

---

[115] For detail see Aḥmad Noor Saif, "*Amal Ahl al-Madina*, Master's Thesis, Sharih College, Mecca, pp. 229–241.
[116] Shāfi'ī, *Umm*, iii, 3.
[117] See *Studies*, Arabic section, p. 131.
[118] Ibrāhīm b. Ṭahmān, *Juz'*, 253b.
[119] See Ibrāhīm b. Ṭahmān, *Juz'*, 253b.
[120] See Al-Sard (Shahīd 'Alī Ms. 539 Istanbul) 136b.
[121] Al-Ḥumaidī, *Musnad*, No. 655.

(b) through 'Alī, as recorded in a Zaidite book,[122] and (c) through Ibn 'Abbās, as recorded in an Ibadite book.[123]

Before Shāfi'ī, Ibn 'Uyayna recorded two other versions through Nāfi' and 'Abdullāh b. Dīnār from Ibn 'Umar.[124] Shāfi'ī, who died a hundred years before the last authors of classical collections, recorded this *ḥadīth* from Ibn 'Umar, Ḥakīm b. Ḥizām, Abū Barzah, and Samura. All these *aḥādīth* were transmitted on the authority of the Prophet. If we add to these early recorded *isnāds*, those of 'Alī and vi-Ibn 'Abbās, it would make altogether six Companions.

Classical collections contain the *ḥadīth* through Ibn 'Umar, Ḥakīm b. Ḥizām, 'Abdallah b. 'Amr, Abū Barzah, and Samura.[125] Thus the classical collections cite only one additional authority, 'Abdullah b. 'Amr, and do not record two authorities known prior to Mālik, 'Alī and Ibn 'Abbās. In view of these facts, one may say that the *ḥadīth* was so widely diffused, even prior to Mālik, that there was hardly a need to create new authorities for it.

EXAMPLE 3

Schacht's third lengthy example deserves careful consideration. Rather than quote, I shall summarize his argument. He is discussing the doctrine that the evidence of one witness confirmed by the oath of the plaintiff constitutes legal proof. The essence of his argument is that the doctrine grew out of the current practice and that only later was it attributed to authorities. I shall discuss each of his points in turn.[126]

(a) Tauba b. Nimr, the judge of Egypt, gave judgment [115 – 120 A.H.] according to this rule with no reference to a *ḥadīth*. Schacht assumes that this means no *ḥadīth* existed. In fact, Muslim judges and *muftīs* seldom mentioned the basis of their judgment. The most one can say is that Tauba did not mention the *ḥadīth*. Since in this case he deviated from the normal practice of requiring two witnesses, it would be equally logical to maintain that he knew it. Moreover, we see that this *ḥadīth* does *not* embody normal practice in Egypt. Laith b. Sa'd of Egypt (94 – 175 A.H.) rejects it,[127] which indicates that this practice was not commonly followed.

(b) Schacht claims that Medinese and Meccans held this doctrine in the middle of the second century, projecting it back to the old authorities Abū Salama, Sulaimān b. Yasār, Umayyad Caliph 'Umar b. 'Abdul 'Azīz, 'Abdul Malik, and Mu'āwīya. In fact, according to *opponents* of the doctrine, the view was held in Medina in the middle of the *first*

---

[122] Zaid b. 'Alī, *Musnad* Zaid, (Beirut, 1966) p. 263.
[123] Rabī', *Musnad* p. 152.
[124] Ḥumaidī, *Musnad*, 654–655.
[125] See *Jāmi' al-Uṣūl*, (Damascus, 1389), i, 574–580.
[126] See *Origins*, p. 167.
[127] See Ibn Ma'īn, *Tārīkh*, 164b. Zahiriya Ms 113 Damascus.

century.¹²⁸ Al-laith b. Sa'd says that when 'Umar b. 'Abdal 'Azīz was the governor of Medina he used to judge according to this doctrine, but when he became Caliph in Syria he abandoned this doctrine. Ruzaiq b. Ḥukaim wrote to him on this occasion, and 'Umar b. 'Abdal 'Azīz replied that he judged according to the doctrine while in Medina, but found people in Syria following the other doctrine, so he now also required two witnesses.¹²⁹ It is not the Medinese and Meccans who project the doctrine back to earlier authorities, in this case it is an opponent of the doctrine, who would hardly fabricate a *fatwā* to reinforce the opposite opinion. Similarly, it was Shaibānī, another opponent of the doctrine, who traced it to Mu'āwīya and 'Abdal Malik b. Marwān.¹³⁰

(c) Schacht believes that the Iraqians claimed "correctly" that the doctrine was unknown to Zuhrī, 'Aṭā', the old Medinese authorities, and the first Caliphs. First, let us repeat that ignorance by one scholar is *not* proof of nonexistence. We have already shown that it was an opponent of the doctrine who ascribed knowledge of it to the early Medinese. Shaibānī cites Zuhrī and 'Aṭā' in support of his opposition to the doctrine. The evidence simply shows that they did not follow the doctrine – this could mean either that they did not know it or that they were not convinced of its provenance. This is not conclusive proof; we have to accept that research into *isnāds* continued throughout the period and that doubt could properly exist until validity was finally proved.

(d) According to Schacht, later Medinese scholars falsely projected their doctrines back to the Iraqian authorities, Shuraiḥ, Sha'bī, 'Abdallah b. 'Utba b. Mas'ūd, and Zurāra b. 'Auf. The writings of Shaibānī and Laith show that this doctrine was held by Mu'āwīya in Syria and by 'Abdal Mālik b. Marwān and 'Umar b. 'Abdal 'Azīz in Medina. When they were Caliph and governor (20 – 100 A.H.) they must have decided many cases on the basis of this doctrine, so that it might well have been known to contemporary Iraqi scholars as well. Even 'Umar b. 'Abdal 'Azīz wrote to 'Abdul Ḥamīd b. 'Abdurraḥmān at Kūfa telling him to judge according to this doctrine.¹³¹ There is therefore no difficulty in believing that some Iraqi scholars, such as Shuraiḥ and Sha'bī, who were judges appointed by the Umayyads, might have held the same doctrine: there seems to be no necessity to project it back.¹³²

(e) Schacht maintains that several references to these old authorities describe the Medinese doctrine as *sunna*. In fact, only in the statement of

---

[128] Ibn Ma'īn, *Tarīkh*, 164b; Shaibānī, *Muw.* 361.
[129] Ibn Ma'īn. *Tarīkh*, 164b.
[130] *Muw. Shaib.* p. 361.
[131] *Umm*, VI, 274.
[132] For Shuraiḥ, see also Wakī, *Akhbār, Quḍāt*, II, 310; for Sulaimān al-Muḥaribī, Wakī', ibid. Vol. iii, p. 201; for Yaḥyā b. Yā'mur in Khurāsān, *Ibid.*, III, 305; Ayās b. Mu'āwiya, *Ibid.*, I, 340. For opposition to this doctrine, see Ibn Shubrama, *Ibid.*, III, 87; and Sawār, judge of Baṣra, *Ibid.*,

'Umar b. 'Abdal 'Azīz has the word *sunna* been used in this context.[133] Moreover, Schacht believes that *sunna* always means the living tradition. Our views on this have been stated in the discussions on *sunna* in Chapter 3.

(f) Mālik knew only one *mursal ḥadīth* in support of Medinese doctrine. We know Mālik's practice in quoting *isnād*.[134] Since he justified doctrines with elaborate arguments, Schacht believes that he would have quoted any relevant *ḥadīth* he had. This may well be so, but all we can say is that Mālik did not disclose the extent of his knowledge. The elaborate argument is undertaken because the *ḥadīth* is apparently in conflict with the Qur'ān, which demands two witnesses. Mālik was arguing this last point, so that he might have considered it unnecessary to produce further evidence from the traditions in favor of his viewpoint. However, it must be reiterated that, even if he did not know it with full *isnād*, this is not conclusive proof that it did not exist.

(g) Shāfi'ī refers to other *isnāds* and additional authorities in various places. Schacht considers this proof that the *isnāds* were fabricated and improved over time. Is this true? Some of the new evidence recorded by Shāfi'ī is found in the work of 'Abdur Razzāq al-Ṣan'ānī as quotations from the work of Ibn Juraij (80 – 150 A.H.), a scholar who was even older than Mālik. The *isnāds* are:

Ibn Juraij – Ibn Abū Mulaikah – 'Alqamah – Mu'āwīyah.[135]
Ibn Juraij – Ibn Abū Mulaikah – Ṣuhaib – Marwān.[136]
Ibn Juraij – 'Amr b. Shu'aib – Abū Zinād – the Prophet.[137]
Wakī' – 'Imrān – Abū Mijlaz – Zurārah b. Abū Awfā.[138]

Many *isnāds* therefore existed before or at least during the time of Mālik. Thus there could have been no need in the classical period to fabricate additional authorities.

Furthermore, the sequence and timing of Shāfi'ī's work contradict Schacht's contention. Schacht says: "In Mecca, the tradition was provided with an uninterrupted *isnād* of Meccan authorities (*Ikh.* 345): this was the only additional version which Shāfi'ī knew when he wrote *Tr. III*, 15. When he wrote *Ikh.* 346, he knew a further version with a Medinese *isnād*, relating it from the Prophet on the authority of two Companions. In *Umm*, VI, 273 ff, he quotes the following additional versions."[139]

Are we to assume that Shāfi'ī wrote sequential pages of *Ikh.* several

---

[133] *Umm*, vi, 274 – 275.
[134] See Appendix 1.
[135] *Muṣannaf*, viii, 336 – 337.
[136] *Ibid.*, viii, 337.
[137] *Ibid.*, viii, 338.
[138] *Muṣannaf*, viii, 337.
[139] *Origins*, p. 168.

months apart? Moreover, there is no evidence that the version quoted in *Ikh*. 345 is the only version Shāfi'ī knew when he wrote *Tr. III*, 15. In fact, all the evidence points in the other direction. Shāfi'ī's work *al-Umm* is in seven volumes, *Tr. III*, 15 forming part of the seventh volume. The seventh volume has only one *ḥadīth* reference, while Volume VI gives nine references. This would be considered normal scholarly practice, particularly since early scholars frequently state that for reasons of brevity they do not give all *aḥādīth* in a particular subject.

(h) In the classical collections, according to Schacht, the *isnād* in favor of the Medinese doctrine is complete and widespread. In fact, the classical collections give three *aḥādīth* that were mentioned by Shāfi'ī,[140] the *ḥadīth* of Ibn 'Abbas,[141] Abū Hurairah,[142] and Muḥammad b. 'Alī.[143] Two other *aḥādīth*, from Jābir[144] and Zabīb al-Anbārī,[145] are considered weak by many scholars. Shāfi'ī may or may not have known them and they may not be valid, but this is not conclusive proof of a wholesale creation of additional authorities, as Schacht would have us believe. Because there is no additional version and there were many *aḥādīth*, there could not be an objection that this was an isolated one. Since the earlier steps in his argument have been disproved, this minor anomaly is insufficient to bear the entire weight of his theory.

EXAMPLE 4

Introducing this example, Schacht says:

> We sometimes find that *isnāds* which consist of a rigid and formal chain of representatives of a school of law and project its doctrine back to some ancient authority, are duplicated by others which go back to the same authority by another way. This was intended as a confirmation of the doctrine of the school by seemingly independent evidence.
>
> A Medinese example is: Ibn 'Uyaina – 'Abdalraḥmān b. Qāsim – his father Qāsim b. Muḥammad – the opinions of 'Uthmān, Zaid b. Thābit and Marwān b. Ḥakam [*Tr. III*, 89 (a)]. The interruption in the *isnād* above Qāsim was remedied, and 'Abdalraḥmān b. Qāsim eliminated, in: Mālik – Yaḥyā b. Sa'id – Qāsim b. Muḥammad – Furāfiṣa b. 'Umair – 'Uthmān (*Muw. ii*, 151). Finally there appeared: Mālik – 'Abdallāh b. Abī Bakr – 'Abdallāh b. 'Āmir b. Rabī'a – 'Uthmān with a composite anecdote (*Muw. ii*, 192).[146]

This implies that the first version was that of Ibn 'Uyaina, and that this is the one which is defective in its *isnād*. This, however, is found in

---

[140] *Umm*, vi, 273–275.
[141] *Mu.*, 1712, A.D., 3607.
[142] *Tir.*, 1343.
[143] *Muw.* iii, 182.
[144] *Tir.*, 1344.
[145] A.D., 3612.
[146] *Origins*, p. 169.

Shāfi'ī's *al-Umm*, while the second and third versions are from Mālik's *Muwaṭṭa'*, which was compiled some 40 or 50 years earlier than Shāfi'ī. Are we to assume that Mālik "remedied" a fault that had not yet been committed?

Moreover, Mālik has two versions with complete *isnād*, and he goes against them.[147] He would be unlikely to fabricate *isnāds* in favor of a doctrine he did not support. Ibn 'Uyaina was a supporter of neither the Medinite school nor the Shāfi'ī school. In Schacht's term he was a "traditionist."[148] Would he then be likely to fabricate a *ḥadīth* to support either of them?

EXAMPLE 5

An Iraqi example (Duplication of *isnād* to confirm the doctrine of school).

As a further example of the same point, Schacht says:

An Iraqian example is: Abū Ḥanīfa – Ḥammād – Ibrāhīm Nakha'ī – 'Alqama b. Qais and Aswad b. Yazīd – Ibn Mas'ūd (*Āthār Shaib*. 22). This became: Muḥammad b. 'Ubaid – Muḥammad b. Isḥāq – 'Abdalraḥmān b. Aswad – his father Aswad b. Yazīd – Ibn Mas'ūd with Aswad and 'Alqama [*Tr. II*, 19 (g)].[149]

Schacht's statement is untenable on two counts. The first version is recorded by the Iraqi scholar Shaibānī, while the second version is recorded by the anti-Iraqi scholar Shāfi'ī. One may ask why one would invent a *ḥadīth* in favor of an opponent. Second, it was accepted neither by the Iraqians, as is explicitly stated by Shaibānī, nor by Shāfi'ī, as he declares in the same place. To confirm whose doctrine was it duplicated?

Family *Isnād*

One of the lesser theories, but one which nevertheless leads Schacht to reject many well-authenticated *aḥādīth* and *isnāds*, is his belief that all family *isnāds* are spurious:

> There are numerous traditions which claim an additional guarantee of soundness by representing themselves as transmitted amongst members of one family, for instance, from father to son [and grandson], from aunt to nephew, or from master to freedman. Whenever we come to analyse them, we find these family traditions spurious, and we are justified in considering the existence of a family *isnād* not an indication of authenticity but only a device for securing its appearance.[150]

Robson has said in this context:

---

[147] Zurqānī, II, 232.
[148] *Origins*, General Index p. 345.
[149] *Origins*, p. 169.
[150] *Origins*, p. 170.

Was the family *isnād* invented to supply apparent evidence for spurious traditions, or did genuine family *isnāds* exist which later served as models? It seems better to recognize that they are a genuine feature of the documentation, but to realize that people often copied this type of *isnād* to support spurious traditions. Therefore, while holding that family *isnāds* do genuinely exist, one will not take them all at face value.[151]

Of course, Robson is right. Scholars accept that not all family *isnāds* should be taken as genuine, as is quite obvious from their biographical works. Some of the examples of *isnāds* that were denounced on this basis are:

Ma'mar b. Muḥammad and his transmission from his father.
'Īsā b. 'Abdallāh from his father.
Kathīr b. 'Abd Allāh from his father.
Mūsā b. Maṭīr from his father.
Yaḥyā b. 'Abd Allāh from his father.[152]

But we should not go too far in our dismissal. If a statement of a father about his son or vice versa, or a wife about her husband, or a friend about a friend, or a colleague about a colleague is always unacceptable, then on what basis could a biography possibly be written? Early scholars researched this category thoroughly and dismissed suspect *isnād* and *aḥādīth*. It is therefore unnecessary to refer further to the examples Schacht advances in this part of his case.

The Common Link in a Chain

Another of Schacht's central theories is that the existence of a common link in a chain of transmission indicates that the *ḥadīth* in question originated at the time of that common member. This allows us to date the time of forgery. He writes:

> These results regarding the growth of *isnāds* enable us to envisage the case in which a tradition was put into circulation by a traditionist whom we may call N.N., or by a person who used his name, at a certain time. The tradition would normally be taken over by one or several transmitters, and the lower, real part of the *isnād* would branch out into several strands. The original promoter N.N. would have provided his tradition with an *isnād* reaching back to an authority such as a Companion or the Prophet, and this higher, fictitious part of the *isnād* would often acquire additional branches by the creation of improvements which would take their place beside the original chain of transmitters, or by the process which we have described as spread of *isnāds*. But N.N. would remain the [lowest] common link in the several strands of *isnād* [or at least in most of them, allowing for his being passed by and eliminated in additional strands of *isnād* which might have been intro-

---

[151] J. Robson, "The Isnād in Muslim Tradition," Glasgow University, Oriental Society Transactions, xv [1955], 23.
[152] See *Studies*, p. 246.

duced later]. Whether this happened to the lower or to the higher part of the *isnād* or to both, the existence of a significant common link [N.N.] in all or most *isnāds* of a given tradition would be a strong indication in favor of its having originated in the time of N.N. The same conclusion would have to be drawn when the *isnāds* of different, but closely connected traditions showed a common link.

The case discussed in the proceding paragraph is not hypothetical but of *common occurrence*. It was observed, though of course not recognized in its implications, by the Muhammadan scholars themselves, for instance by Tirmidhī in the concluding chapter of his collection of traditions. He calls traditions with N.N. as a common link in their *isnāds* 'the traditions of N.N.', and they form a great part of the traditions which he calls *gharīb*, that is, transmitted by a single transmitter at any one stage of the *isnād*.

A typical example of the phenomenon of the common transmitter occurs in *Ikh.* 294, where a tradition has the following *isnāds*:

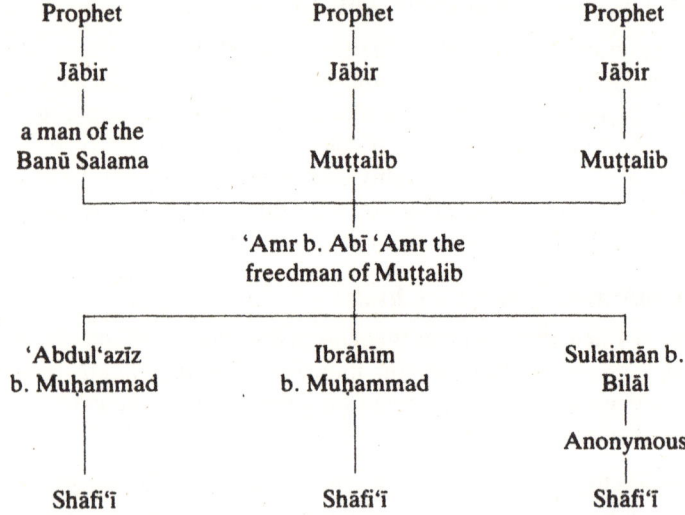

'Amr b. Abī' Amr is the common link in these *isnāds*. He would hardly have hesitated between his own patron and an anonymous transmitter for his immediate authority.[153]

In support of his argument, Schacht produces only one example. The diagram gives the false impression that there were three authorities from whom 'Amr had transmitted this *ḥadīth*. In fact, the name of his teacher, Muṭṭalib, occurs twice in the diagram. Hence it should be drawn as follows:

---

[153] *Origins*, pp. 171-172.

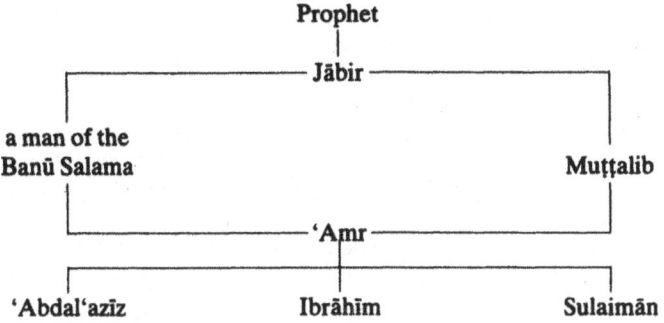

In addition, it seems that Schacht either overlooked the text of *Ikh.* 294 or did not understand it. Shāfi'ī, comparing three students of 'Amr, makes it clear that 'Abdal'azīz was wrong in naming the authority of 'Amr as a man of Banū Salama. Ibrāhīm Ibn Abū Yaḥyā was a stronger transmitter than 'Abdal'azīz and his statement is attested by Sulaimān as well. Hence, it appears that there is only one channel through which 'Amr has received his information. Accordingly the diagram would appear as follows:

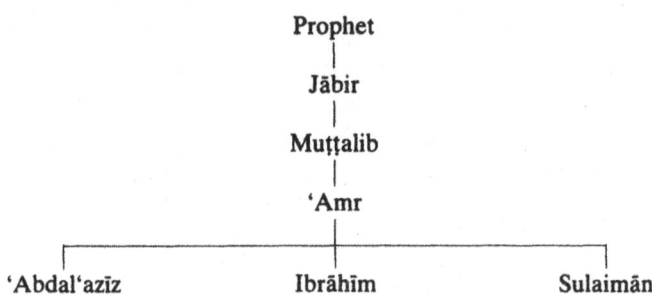

Even if we accept Schacht's explanation that 'Amr claimed that he received the information through different lines, it remains that this is a single case. On such meagre evidence a theory of "common occurrence" is unacceptable.

Scholars were, however, aware of the problems inherent in such situations and tried to judge each case on its merits. Here is an example. Dhababī says:

فانظر أول شيء إلى أصحاب رسول الله صلى الله عليه وسلم الكبار والصغار ، مافيهم أحد إلا وقد انفرد بسنة ، فيقال له : هذا الحديث لا يتابع عليه ، وكذلك التابعون ، كل واحد عنده ماليس عند الآخر في العلم . وما اتعرض لهذا فان هذا مقرر على ما ينبغي في علم الحديث . وأن تفرد الثقة المتقن يعد صحيحاً غريباً وأن تفرد الصدوق ومن دونه يعد منكراً وإن اكثار الراوي من الأحاديث التي لا يوافق عليها لفظاً أو اسناداً يصيره متروك الحديث . «
ميزان الاعتدال ٣ : ١٤٠ - ١٤١

Consider first of all, all the Companions of the Prophet, the older and younger ones. Each one of them had some knowledge of a certain *sunna* alone, not known to others. In this case it is said that this *ḥadīth* has not been attested by any other narrators. So is the case with Successors. Every one of them had some knowledge alone. I do not want to go into detail, because the subject has been discussed in the Science of *Ḥadīth*. If a scholar, trustworthy and accurate, narrated a *ḥadīth* alone, it would be counted as authentic but "strange."

If a scholar who was of a grade B such as *Ṣadūq* [truthful] or lower than him and narrated a *ḥadīth* and no one attested his statement, then it would be counted as *munkar*.

If a narrator relates *aḥādīth*, a good quantity of which are not testified by any other scholars' narrations, this would result in calling him *matrūk al-Ḥadīth* which means neither his narrations nor the *aḥādīth* transmitted by him could be taken to verify other scholars' *aḥādīth*.[154]

There are additional reasons which sometimes cause a man to appear as a "common transmitter" when he is in fact not. These stem from the methodology of tradition in quoting the information. The point has been discussed above in some detail.[155]

To take a modern example of where Schacht's approach would lead if followed through rigorously: a news reporter who gathers information from many sources and then publishes his findings in a newspaper would be considered to have fabricated the news items because thousands of readers would be able to refer only to him as their source.

In the final section of this chapter, I shall discuss in detail one of the examples Schacht uses to illustrate his point about the common transmitter. I shall not restrict myself to commentary on the "common transmitter" theory, but will comment in full on the implications of each of his theories as it arises.

Ḥadīth Barīra

It is worth examining the *Ḥadīth Barīra* example in detail. Schacht refers to it to show how "the argument drawn from a common transmitter can be used, together with other considerations, in investigating the history of legal doctrines."[156] Rather than quote I shall summarize his argument.

In tracing the legal history of this doctrine, Schacht appears to use five principles: customary practice at the time, the idea that a common link implies forgery, creation of new *aḥādīth* to support one with a suspect *isnād*, suppression of undesirable material, and insertion of authorities.

Customary Practice

Schacht claims that: " In the first half of the second century A.H. the sale

---

[154] Dhahabī, *Mīzān al-Iʿtidāl*, iii, 140–141.
[155] See the discussion under the heading "Arbitrary and Careless Creation of *Isnāds*" in this chapter.
[156] *Origins*, p. 172.

of *walā'* of a manumitted slave was customary and considered valid."[157] This implies – in Schacht's view – that any *ḥadīth* transmitted from the Prophet to object to this customary practice must be spurious.

His whole argument is based on a single piece of evidence recorded by Ibn Sa'd, V, 309, about the selling of *walā'* of Abū Ma'shar. Ibn Sa'd does not give his source of information, yet Schacht accepts it as genuine evidence and elevates this single instance into customary practice. But when the same Ibn Sa'd records eight documents giving his sources of information in detail relating to the Barīra incident,[158] he declares them spurious.[159] It is difficult to see then on what criteria one has to accept the statement of Ibn Sa'd concerning Abū Ma'shar.

Let us suppose, however, that the incident recorded by Ibn Sa'd is correct. Is a single incident proof of customary practice? Does this one incident prove that there were no *ḥadīth* prohibiting it? The number of jails in existence stand testimony to the human failing of breaking the law. Even if the case of Abū Ma'shar can be proved to be historical, there is no evidence in support of Schacht's contention that *aḥādīth* prohibiting the sale of *walā'* are of late origin.

Common Link

'Abdullāh b. Dīnār is the common link in the *isnād* of several versions prohibiting the practice of selling the *mukātab* slave. Schacht believes that the doctrine must therefore have originated in the generation before Mālik. I have already commented on the absurdity of assuming a man to be the originator of a false *ḥadīth* simply because he went to the trouble of researching a specific field. This is particularly foolish when all contemporary and later authorities believe him to be an authentic and reliable scholar.

The Medinese – according to Schacht – allowed the selling of the *mukātab* slave,[160] and 'Hishām is the common link in the several versions of this family *isnād*...[161] According to Schacht, family *isnāds* are spurious.[162] Therefore, what is attributed by Hishām to his father 'Urwa and his father's aunt 'Ā'isha is spurious. Hishām being the common link in several versions, careful application of Schacht's theories regarding the common link[163] lead to the supposition that the *ḥadīth* was fabricated in his time, either by him or someone who used his name.

Let us examine the implications of this. Did the transmitters from Hishām, who may well have traveled thousands of kilometers to learn

---

[157] *Origins*, p. 173.
[158] *Ibn Sa'd*, viii, 187, 188.
[159] *Origins*, p. 174.
[160] *Origins*, p. 173.
[161] *Idem*.
[162] *Origins*, p. 170.
[163] See *Origins*, pp. 171–173 and the discussion in this chapter under the heading "Gradual Improvement of *Isnāds*."

Chart 5. 'Hishām and the Ḥadīth of the Mukātab Slave.

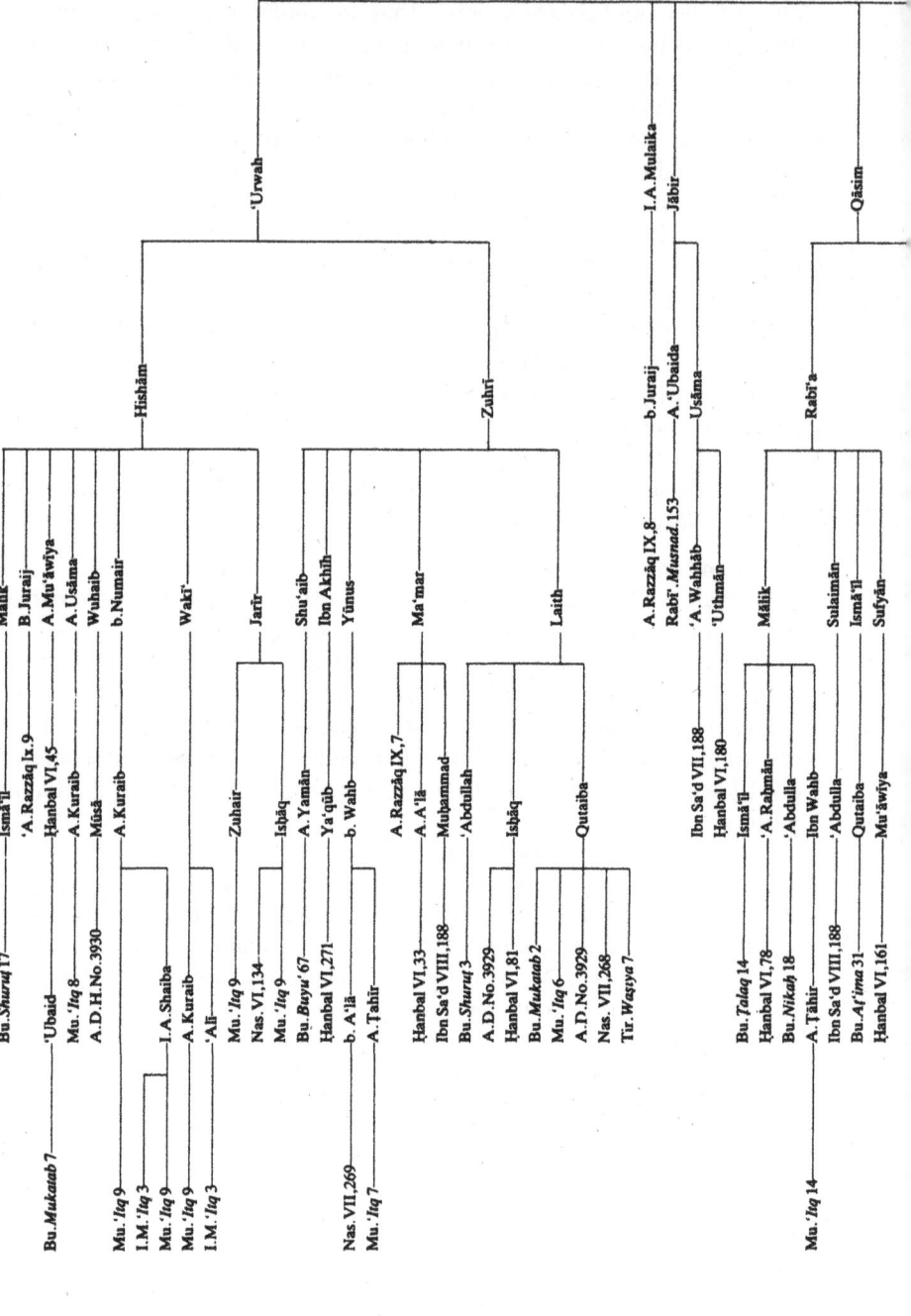

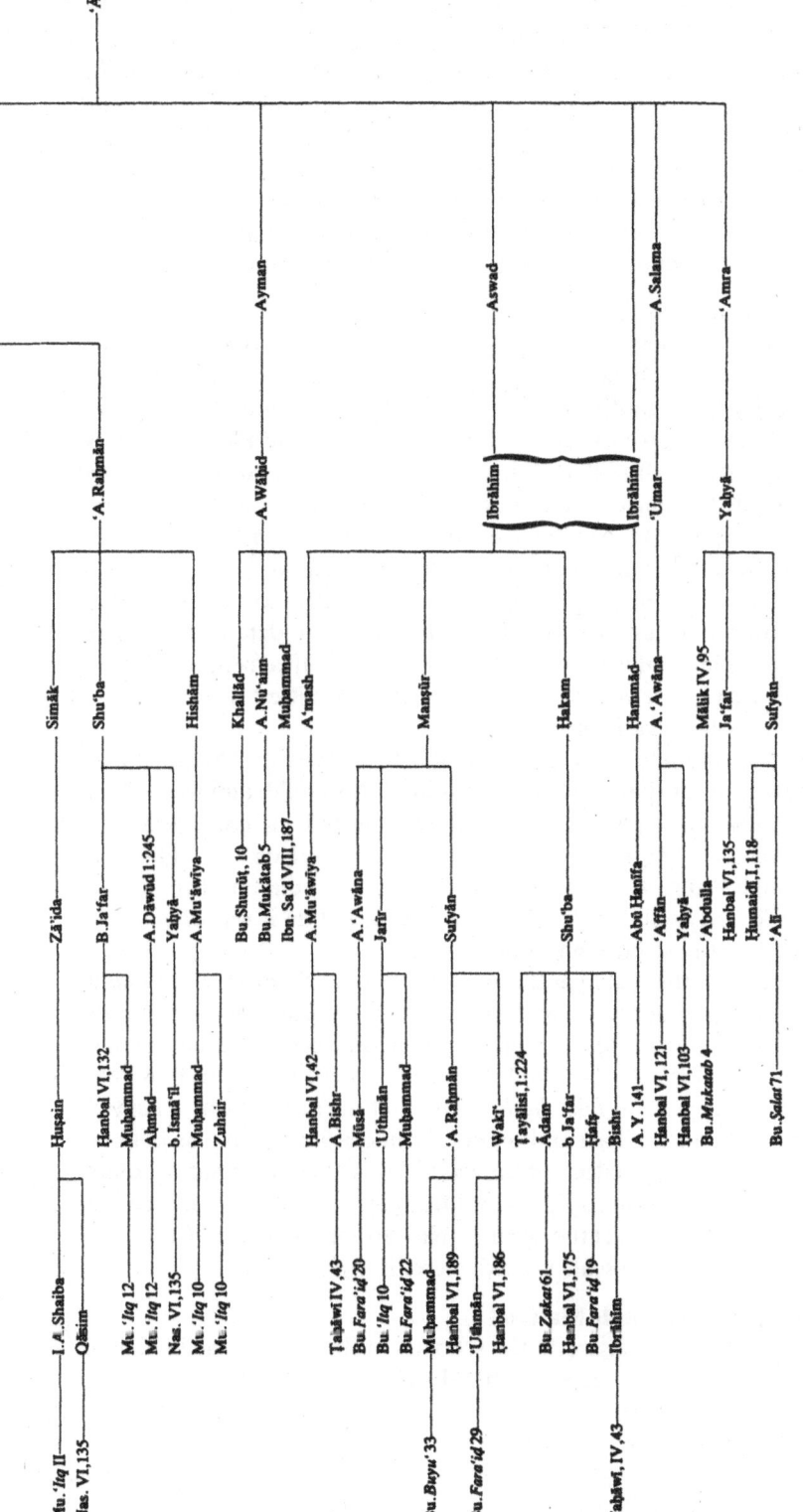

from him, not know the name of their teacher? Did some anonymous scholar convince several different students that they should fictitiously ascribe the *ḥadīth* to Hishām? We may assume that not all the students came to study at one time; must we then believe that some anonymous scholar waited for several years – maybe 30 or 40 – to waylay the students and relay to them a fabricated tradition in Hishām's name? Or did the students conspire among themselves to use Hishām's name?

Creation of Supporting Traditions
Let us consider the possibility that a new *isnād* was created bypassing this transmitter. Schacht believes that a new *isnād* was created bypassing Hishām, going through Zuhrī – 'Urwa – 'Ā'isha, and eliminating Hishām from the chain.[164] If we examine the *isnād* of Zuhrī and Hishām on this particular *ḥadīth*, we find that Zuhrī was also one of the lowest common links.[165] He died a quarter of a century before Hishām, which may be why Schacht prefers not to cite him as the original authority or, rather, fabricator, since this might date the birth of the *ḥadīth* before his "evidence" of the customary practice. There is really no reason, using Schacht's own theories, why we should not push the date even further back, to Ibrāhīm Nakha'ī who died (96 A.H.) half a century before Hishām and had at least four students who transmitted from him[166] – some of whom died even before Hishām.

Even the incomplete *isnād* chart available to us (see Chart 5) shows that many sources other than Hishām transmitted this *ḥadīth* and were older than he; those through whom it was transmitted included Nakha'ī, Qāsim, and Nāfi'. There was therefore no need to "create" an additional chain through Zuhrī. Or were all other *isnāds* created after Hishām and attributed to early scholars falsely? We have seen that it was impossible for anyone else to use Hishām's name.

Let us return to the first hypothesis – that it was Hishām who fabricated this *ḥadīth* and perhaps made arrangements for the duplication of *isnāds* bypassing him, entrusting his students with the secret and instructing them to ask scholars of a hundred years later or even more to fabricate new *isnāds* to support his false *ḥadīth*, and that the request was accepted by Ibn Ḥanbal and Bukhārī and others. Would Schacht have us believe that Hishām, the "originator" of the *ḥadīth*, was able to contact scholars scattered from Khurāsān to Egypt and from Syria to Yemen, informing them of the need to project the doctrine back to early scholars? Collusion and forgery on so wide a scale is hard to credit.

Suppression of Undesirable Material
In a further attempt to discredit the scholars of the time, Schacht claims that since the *ḥadīth* as narrated by Hishām (d. 146 A.H.) shows the

---
[164] *Origins*, p. 172.
[165] See Chart 5.
[166] See Chart 5.

Prophet and 'Ā'isha in a disconcerting light, the crucial point was formally mitigated in a version with the new *isnād* Mālik – Yaḥyā b. Sa'īd – 'Amra – 'Ā'isha, and a shortened one with the *isnād* Mālik – Nāfi' – Ibn 'Umar – 'Ā'isha...[167] Oddly enough, Bukhārī,[168] Muslim,[169] 'Abdur Razzāq,[170] and Ibn Ḥanbal[171] all record Hishām's version without noting or suppressing this "disconcerting" aspect of the Prophet's behavior. Moreover, Nāfi' died 30 years earlier than Hishām, and according to Schacht, Hishām's version most probably did not exist in the life of Nāfi'. Schacht thus asks us to believe that Nāfi' had the foresight to see that after 30 years Hishām would present the Prophet and 'Ā'isha in a disconcerting light, and thus mitigated the crucial point before its existence.

Insertion of Authorities

Schacht maintains that the name of the Iraqian authority, Ibrāhīm Nakha'ī, was introduced into two *isnāds* as a late counter move by the Iraqians against the prevailing Medinese doctrine. He quotes his source as Ṭaḥāwī (d. 321 A.H.) But 150 years before Ṭaḥāwī we find Ibrāhīm cited as an authority for this *ḥadīth* in Iraqi literature.[172] Schacht accuses the traditionists of projecting their doctrines back to early authorities. Here we might well accuse him of projecting his doctrines forward.

On the point of creating additional authorities, we may also note that the *ḥadīth* was accepted in the early days when only 'Abdullah b. Dinār was quoted as its authority. When the same *ḥadīth* was narrated by Ibn Mājashūn, through Mālik – Nāfi' – Ibn 'Umar, it was rejected because no other student reported this *ḥadīth* from Mālik.[173]

Can we really believe that scholars capable of such fine discrimination in a situation where a *ḥadīth* had only one accredited supporter would stoop to creating additional authorities?

---

[167] *Origins*, p. 173.
[168] *Bu. Shurūṭ*, 17; *Mukātab*, 7, etc.
[169] *Mu. 'Itq*, 7, 8, 9, etc.
[170] *Muṣannaf*, ix, 9.
[171] Ḥanbal, vi, 45.
[172] *A.Y.* 141.
[173] Zurqānī, iv, 99.

APPENDIX 1
THE USE OF ISNĀD IN *SĪRAH* AND *ḤADITH-FIQH* LITERATURE

THIS Appendix shows that early lawyers and biographers of the Prophet did not always feel it necessary to cite all the *asānīd* known to them or to quote full *isnāds*, since they were concerned with the subject matter rather different to *Muhaddithīn* (traditionists).

IBN ISḤĀQ
Omits authorities that were known to him:

    1a. Zuhrī—Ibn al Musayyab—the Prophet sent someone to 'Uyaynah . . .[1]

    1b. Ibn Isḥāq—'Āsim b. 'Umar—Zuhrī, the Prophet sent someone to 'Uyaynah.[2]

Zuhrī gives his authority as Ibn al-Musayyab, while Ibn Isḥāq, transmitting from him, leaves out this link in the chain. Wāqidī, however, mentions Zuhrī's authority.

Omits *isnād* known to him:

    2a. Ibn Isḥāq—'Abdur Raḥmān b. al-Ḥārith and others—Sulaimān b. Musā—Mākḥūl—Abū Umāmah—'Ubādah b. al-Ṣāmit concerning *anfāl* (booty).[3]

    2b. Ibn Isḥāq—'Ubādah b. al-Ṣāmit—the same incident.[4]

In quotation 2a we find Ibn Isḥāq using a complete uninterrupted *isnād*, while in quotation 2b in the same book, we find him omitting the *isnād* totally and quoting directly from the highest authority. It is interesting to note that the full *isnād* for the incident was recorded earlier than the interrupted one.

ABŪ ḤANĪFA
Frequently omits *isnāds*, but Abū Yūsuf and Shaibānī (often independently) record the same *aḥādīth* and *āthār* through Abū Ḥanīfa, giving either complete or partial *isnād*.

    3a. Abū Ḥanīfa—The Prophet, concerning oath.[5]

    3b. Abū Ḥanīfa—'Amr b. Shu'aib—his father—his grandfather—the Prophet.[6]

---

[1] Zuhrī, *Sīrah*; see 'Abdur Razzāq, *Muṣannaf*, v, 367; also Wāqidī, *Maghāzī*, 77.
[2] Ibn Hishām, *Sīrah*, iii, 223.
[3] Ibn Hishām, *Sīrah*, i, 642.
[4] Ibn Hishām, *Sīrah*, i, 666–667.
[5] Ibn Abī Lailā, 78.
[6] On the margin of Ibn Abī Lailā, 78–79, quoting Ṭalḥa b. Muḥammad.

4a. Abū Ḥanīfa narrated from the Prophet that he imprecated against enemies for one month only.[7]
4b. Abū Ḥanīfa—Ḥammād—Ibrāhīm—The Prophet.[8]
4c. Abū Ḥanīfa—Ḥammād—Ibrāhīm—'Alqamah—'Abdallah—the Prophet.[9]
5a. Abū Bakr did not imprecate until he died.[10]
5b. Abū Ḥanīfa—Ḥammād—Ibrāhīm—Abū Bakr.[11]
6a. Ibn Mas'ūd did not imprecate.[12]
6b. Abū Ḥanīfa—Ḥammād—Ibrāhīm—Ibn Mas'ūd, the same.[13]
7a. 'Umar did not imprecate.[14]
7b. Abū Ḥanīfa—'Abdul Malik—Zaid—'Umar imprecated in the war only.[15]
7c. Abū Ḥanīfa—Ḥammād—Ibrāhīm—Aswad lived with 'Umar for two years, and did not see him imprecating.[16]
8a. Ibn 'Umar asked Iraqians about their practice concerning imprecation.[17]
8b. Abū Ḥanīfa—Aṣṣalt-Ḥauṭ—Abū Ashsha'thā'—Ibn 'Umar.[18]
9a. 'Alī imprecated when he was fighting Mu'āwiya, and hence Kūfans learned from him. Mu'āwiya did it when he was fighting against 'Alī and hence Syrians learned from him.[19]
9b. Abū Ḥanīfa—Ḥammād—Ibrāhīm—'Alī and Mu'āwiyah.[20]
10a. Abū Ḥanīfa differed with Ibn Abī Lailā on *zakāt* on loan and reported in favor of his doctrine, a decision of 'Alī (without *isnād*).[21]
10b. Abū Ḥanīfa—al-Haitham—Ibn Sīrīn—'Alī, the same.[22]
11a. Abū Ḥanīfa transmitted a *ḥadīth* from the Prophet in support of his doctrine concerning liability (without *isnād*).[23]
11b. Abū Ḥanīfa—Ḥammād—Ibrāhīm—the Prophet.[24]

---

[7] Ibn Abī Lailā, 112.
[8] A.Y., 349; Shaibānī, *Āthār*, 212.
[9] A.Y., 350.
[10] Ibn Abī Lailā, 112–113.
[11] A.Y., 351; see also Shaibānī, *Āthār*, 212.
[12] Ibn Abī Lailā, 113.
[13] Shaibānī, *Āthār*, 210.
[14] Ibn Abī Lailā, 113.
[15] A.Y., 353.
[16] A.Y 354; Shaibānī, *Āthār*, 213.
[17] Ibn Abī Lailā, 113.
[18] A.Y., 355; Shaibānī, *Āthār*, 211.
[19] Ibn Abī Lailā, 113–114.
[20] A.Y., 352.
[21] Ibn Abī Lailā, 123.
[22] Shaibānī, *Āthār*, 290.
[23] Ibn Abī Lailā, 150.
[24] Shaibānī, *Āthār*, 561.

12a. Abū Yūsuf said in the case of capital punishment of Mā'iz it was reported by Abū Ḥanīfa from the Prophet (without giving *isnād*).[25]
12b. Abū Yūsuf—Abū Ḥanīfa—'Alqama—Ibn Barīdah—his father—the Prophet, the same.[26]
13a. Abū Ḥanīfa—'Alī, concerning liability of washerman.[27]
13b. Shaibānī—Abū Ḥanīfa—Bishr or Bashīr (Shaibānī doubted) Moḥammad b. 'Alī—'Alī, the same.[28]

MĀLIK

He often omits *isnāds* totally, while the complete *isnād* is known to him and recorded in the same book.

14a. Mālik—the Prophet concerning *I'tikaf*.[29]
14b. Mālik—Ibn Shihāb—'Amra—'Ā'isha—the Prophet.[30]
15a. Mālik—the Prophet, about prohibition of golden ring for men.[31]
15b. Mālik—Nāfi'—Ibrāhīm—his father—'Alī—the Prophet, the same.[32]
16a. Mālik—the Prophet prohibited certain transactions.[33]
16b. Mālik—'Abdallah b. Dinār—Ibn 'Umar—the Prophet, the same.[34]
16c. Mālik—Nāfi'—Ibn 'Umar—the Prophet, the same.[35]
17a. Mālik—the Prophet.[36]
17b. Mālik—Yaḥyā—'Umar b. Kathīr—Abū Muḥammad—Abū Qatādah—the Prophet.[37]
18a. Mālik—the Prophet.[38]
18b. Mālik—Ibn Shihāb—'Uthmān b. Isḥāq—Qabīṣa—Abū Bakr—Mughīra—the Prophet.[39]

Mālik omits some authorities from *isnād* known to him:

19a. Mālik—Ibn Shihāb—the Prophet concerning *Mu'takif's* entrance into the house.[40]

---

[25] Ibn Abī Lailā, 157.
[26] *A.Y.*, 719.
[27] Ibn Abī Lailā, 10.
[28] Shaibānī, *Āthār*, 764.
[29] *Muw.*, 317.
[30] *Muw.*, 316.
[31] *Muw.*, 912.
[32] *Muw.*, 80.
[33] *Muw.*, 644, 648, 649.
[34] *Muw.*, 640.
[35] *Muw.*, 640.
[36] *Muw.*, 455.
[37] *Muw.*, *Jihād* 18, p. 454.
[38] *Muw.*, 514.
[39] *Muw.*, 513.
[40] *Muw.*, 317.

19b. Mālik—Ibn Shihāb—'Urwah—'Amrah—'Ā'isha—the Prophet.[41]

Mālik omits some authorities from the *isnād*; colleagues of Mālik, such as 'Ubaidullah, who died 35 years earlier, record the same *ahādīth* through Nāfi' with complete *isnād*.

20a. Mālik—Nāfi'—'Umar wrote to his governors.[42]

20b. 'Ubaidullah—Nāfi'—Ṣafīya—'Umar wrote to his governors.[43]

21a. Mālik—Ibn 'Umar about slaves running to enemy territory.[44]

21b. 'Abdallah—Nāfi'—Ibn 'Umar, the same.[45]

22a. Mālik—Nāfi—Abū Lubāba—the Prophet.[46]

22b. 'Ubaidullah—Nāfi'—Ibn 'Umar—Abū Lubāba—the Prophet.[47]

23a. Mālik—Nāfi'—Sā'ibah—the Prophet.[48]

23b. 'Ubaidullah—Nāfi'—Sa'ibah—'Ā'isha—the Prophet.[49]

ABŪ YŪSUF

Believes firmly in *isnād*.

24a. Abū Yūsuf, arguing with Auzā'ī, says that this cannot be accepted unless it was reported through trustworthy transmitters.[50]

24b. Once again he says: Has Auzā'ī any authentic report with *isnād* from the Prophet on the subject through trustworthy narrators . . .[51]

But explicitly prefers brevity over comprehensiveness. He says:

24c. Had he not been afraid of making the book too long, he would have quoted *hadīth* with *isnād*.[52]

He further says:

27d. There are many *ahādīth* on the subject but if all were included the book would be too long.[53]

Omits *isnād totally,* although other writings show that he knew it.

25a. Abū Yūsuf says: The Prophet prohibited the killing of women and children . . .[54]

25b. Abū Yūsuf—'Ubaidullah—Nāfi'—Ibn 'Umar—the Prophet, same prohibitions with detail.[55]

---

[41] *Muw.*, 312.
[42] *Muw., Waqūt*, 6.
[43] *Studies*, 117, Arabic section.
[44] *Muw.*, 452.
[45] *Kharāj*, 200.
[46] *Muw.*, 975.
[47] *Studies*, 129, Arabic section.
[48] *Muw., Isti'zān*, 32, p. 976.
[49] *Studies*, 129, Arabic section.
[50] Auzā'ī, 5.
[51] Auzā'ī, 22.
[52] Auzā'ī, 30–31.
[53] Auzā'ī, 38.
[54] Auzā'ī, 66.
[55] *Kharāj*, 195.

29a. Abū Yūsuf says: We were reported on the authority of the Prophet, and from some of his Companions that the Prophet [and the Companions] gave three shares in the war for horsemen and one share for soldiers (راجل).[56]

29b. Abū Yūsuf—Qais—Muḥammad b. 'Alī—Isḥāq—Abū Ḥāzim—Abū Dharr—the Prophet.[57]

30a. Abū Yūsuf says: from 'Umar, Ibn Mas'ūd and 'Uthmān, they handed money [or goods] for partnership.[58]

30b. Abū Yūsuf—Abū Ḥanīfa—Ḥumaid b. 'Abdallah b. 'Ubaid—his father—his grandfather—'Umar gave him money of the orphan on partnership.[59]

30c. Abū Yūsuf—Abū Ḥanīfa—'Abdalla b. 'Alī—Al-'Alā b. 'Abdur Raḥmān b. Ya'qūb—his father—'Uthmān gave money on partnership.[60]

30d. Abū Yūsuf—Abū Ḥanīfa—Ḥammād—Ibrāhīm—Ibn Mas'ūd gave money to Zaid b. Khulaidah on partnership.[61]

31a. Abū Yūsuf—the Prophet, concerning sale of date tree.[62]

31b. Abū Yūsuf—Abū Ḥanīfa—Abu Zubair—Jābir—the Prophet, the same.[63]

32a. Abū Yūsuf—Abu Bakr donated 'Ā'isha. . . .[64]

32b. The same is transmitted by Zuhrī, who is sixty-two years older than Abū Yūsuf, with the following *isnād*: Zuhrī—'Urwah—'Āisha.[65] Gives only his immediate authority, when this authority supplies an *isnād*.

33a. Abū Yūsuf—Ibn Isḥāq and al-Kalbī—the Prophet dismounted in a valley . . .[66]

33b. Ibn Isḥāq describes the same, with full *isnād*: Ibn Isḥāq—Ṣadaqah b. Yasār—'Aqīl—Jābir—the Prophet.[67]

34a. Abū Yūsuf—Ibn Isḥāq—Zuhrī—the Prophet in the battle of Khandaq . . . .[68]

34b. The same from Ibn Isḥāq with the *isnād* Ibn Isḥāq—'Āsim—Zuhrī—the Prophet.[69]

---

[56] Auzā'ī, 21.
[57] *Kharāj*, 18–19.
[58] Ibn Abī Lailā, 30–31.
[59] Ibn Abī Lailā, 31–32.
[60] Ibn Abī Lailā, 31–32.
[61] Ibn Abī Lailā, 32–33.
[62] Ibn Abī Lailā, 14.
[63] Abū Yūsuf, *Āthār*, 829; Shaibānī, *Āthār*, 717.
[64] Ibn Abī Lailā, 47.
[65] *Studies*, 143, Arabic section.
[66] Auzā'ī, 90.
[67] Ibn Hishām, *Sīrah*, iii, 208.
[68] *Kharāj*, 207.
[69] Ibn Hishām, *Sīrah*, iii, 223.

34c. Zuhrī recorded the same incident in his own book through Ibn al-Musayyab.[70]

Omits some authorities, while knowing the *isnād* in perfect form.

35a. Abū Yūsuf—Ibn Isḥāq—Zuhrī—Yazīd b. Hurmuz, the scribe of Ibn ʿAbbās, reported that Najdah wrote to Ibn ʿAbbās.[71]

35b. Abū Yūsuf—Ibn Isḥāq—Zuhrī reported, saying Najdah wrote to Ibn ʿAbbās.[72]

35c. Abū Yūsuf—Ibn Isḥāq and Ismāʿīl—Ibn Hurmuz reported that Najdah wrote to Ibn ʿAbbās.[73]

Mentions only one of several authorities.

36a. Abū Yūsuf—Mujālid—Shaʿbī—ʿUmar wrote to Saʿd.[74]

36b. Mujālid—Shaʿbī and Ziyād—ʿUmar wrote to Saʿd.[75]

37a. Abū Yūsuf—Saʿīd—Qatādah—Sālim—Miʿdān b. Ṭalḥah—ʿUmar delivered a sermon on Friday....[76]

37b. Ibn Isḥāq—Anonymous—Miʿdān b. Ṭalḥah—ʿUmar.[77]

Uses the anonymous word for a man who is known, while dropping some of the authorities.

38a. Abū Yūsuf—Ibn Isḥāq and Ismāʿīl—Ibn Hurmuz—Najdah wrote to Ibn ʿAbbās.[78]

38b. Abū Yūsuf—Ibn Isḥāq and Ismāʿīl—anonymous—Ibn ʿAbbās wrote to Najda, replying to his letter.[79]

39a. Abū Yūsuf—Abū Ḥanīfa—Haitham—anonymous—ʿUmar concerning doubling the *Ṣadqah* on Banū Taghlab.[80]

39b. Abū Yūsuf—Abū Ḥanīfa—anonymous—ʿUmar, the same.[81]

SHĀFIʿĪ

He says:

40. We do not accept any *ḥadīth* unless it is transmitted by a trustworthy narrator and we know the trustworthiness of those who transmitted it from beginning to the end.[82]

41. There is an unbroken *isnād* for this *ḥadīth*, but I do not remember it at the moment.[83]

---

[70] See *Muṣannaf*, v, 367; Wāqidī, *al-Maghāzī*, 477.
[71] *Kharāj*, 198.
[72] *Kharāj*, 20.
[73] Auzāʿī, 38.
[74] Auzāʿī, 5–6.
[75] Auzāʿī, 35.
[76] *Kharāj*, 14.
[77] *Kharāj*, 118; there is a misprint in the name of Miʿdān.
[78] Auzāʿī, 38.
[79] Auzāʿī, 43.
[80] Abū Yūsuf, *Āthār*, 445.
[81] *Kharāj*, 120.
[82] *Risāla*, 398.
[83] *Umm*, vii, 311.

42. I have heard someone who gave the names of all the transmitters of this *ḥadīth*, but I do not remember the names.[84]

Omits *isnād*, although it was known to him.

43a. Shāfiʿī—the Prophet concerning the sale of slave.[85]

43b. Shāfiʿī—Ibn ʿUyaynah—Zuhrī—Sālim—Ibn ʿUmar—the Prophet, the same.[86]

44a. Shāfiʿī—Ibn ʿUmar—the Prophet, about the prayer in the battlefield.[87]

44b. Shāfiʿī—anonymous—Ibn Abū Dhiʾb—Zuhrī—Sālim—Ibn ʿUmar—the Prophet, the same.[88]

45a. He says: the *ḥadīth* of Anas is abrogated by that of ʿĀʾisha and does not give *isnād* (a man leading prayer while sitting).[89]

45b. Refers to *ḥadīth* but mentions neither narrators nor text.[90]

45c. The same *ḥadīth* with *isnād*; Ibrāhīm—Aswad—ʿĀʾisha—the Prophet.[91]

Omits intermediate authorities.

46a. In discussing the problem of unobligatory prayer after *Fajr* and *ʿAṣr* prayer, he says, "Some of our colleagues say that ʿUmar performed *Ṭawāf* (circumambulation) after *Fajr* prayer . . .[92]

The same is found in his authority with the following *isnād*.

46b. Mālik—Zuhrī—Ḥumaid—ʿAbdur Raḥmān—ʿUmar.[93]

Reporting on the Prayer in danger, he gives the following *isnād*:

47a. Shāfiʿī—Ibn ʿUmar—the Prophet.[94]

47b. And elsewhere, Shāfiʿī—Ibn ʿUmar—the Prophet.[95]

47c. The same, with complete *isnād*; Shāfiʿī—Muḥammad b. Ismāʿīl or ʿAbdallah b. Nāfiʿ—Ibn Abū Dhiʾb—Zuhrī—Sālim—Ibn ʿUmar—the Prophet.[96]

Uses the word anonymous when the narrator is known to him.

47d. Shāfiʿī—anonymous—Ibn Abū Dhiʾb—Zuhrī—Sālim—Ibn ʿUmar—the Prophet.[97]

---

[84] *Risāla*, 405; Khaddurī, 254.
[85] *Risāla*, 174–175.
[86] *Risāla*, 170.
[87] *Risāla*, 260.
[88] *Risāla*, 185.
[89] *Umm*, i, 151.
[90] *Umm*, i, 157.
[91] *Ikh*, vii, 100.
[92] *Risāla*, 327.
[93] *Muw.*, *Ḥajj*, 117.
[94] *Risāla*, 126.
[95] *Risāla*, 260.
[96] *Umm*, i, 197.
[97] *Risāla*, 185.

APPENDIX 2
MATERIALS OF
APPENDIX 1 IN ARABIC

Note: Appendix 2 contains Arabic text which reads right to left and, when compared to an English text, back to front. The Arabic reader will find that Appendix 2 begins on page 226. As an aid, the sequence of pages with the appendix (keyed "Appendix 2" joined with a Persian numeral) appears at the bottom of each page in Arabic.

صلى الله عليه وسلم صلى بهم في مرضه الذي مات فيها جالسا وصلوا خلفه قياما . »(١١١)

(١١٣) ٥٠ - بلُأشار الشافعي إلى مفهوم هذه الرواية في الأم . (١١٢)

(١١٤) ٥٠ - قال الشافعي : « وذكر ابراهيم عن الأسود عن عائشة عن النبي مثل معناه » الصلاة قائما خلف الإمام القاعد . (١١٣)

(١١٥) ٥١ - قال الشافعي : « وقد ذهب بعض أصحابنا إلى أن عمر بن الخطاب طاف بعد الصبح ، ثم نظر فلم ير الشمس طلعت ، حتى أتى ذا طوى وطلعت الشمس فأناخ فصلى . . . »(١١٤)

(١١٦)٥١- ب « حدثني يحيى عن مـالـك ، عن ابن شهـاب ، عن حميـد بن عبد الرحمن بن عوف ، أن عبد الرحمن بن عبد القاري أخبره : أنه طاف بالبيت مع عمر بن الخطاب بعد صلاة الصبح ، فلما قضي عمر طوافه ، نظر فلم ير الشمس طلعت ، فركب حتى أناخ بذي طوى ، فصلى ركعتين . . »(١١٥)

---

(١١١) الأم ١ : ١٥١
(١١٢) الأم ١ : ١٥٦ بدون ذكر الرواي ولا المتن .
(١١٣) اختلاف الحديث ٧ : ١٠٠
(١١٤) الرسالة ٣٢٧
(١١٥) ط الحج ١١٧

الإمام الشافعي واستعماله للأسانيد

٤٦(١٠٣)- أ قال الشافعي : « وقد روى فيه حديثا موصولا لا يحضرني ذكره »(١٠٢)

٤٦(١٠٤)- ب قال الشافعي : « وعليه اعتمدنا مع غيره في أن لا نقبل حديثاً إلا من ثقة ، ونعرف صدق من حمل الحديث من حين ابتدى إلى أن يبلغ به منتهاه »(١٠٣)

٤٦(١٠٥)- جـ قال الشافعي : « وقد سمعت من يصل هذا الحديث ولا يحضرني ذكر من وصله . . »(١٠٤)

٤٧(١٠٦)- أ قال الشافعي : « ثم كانت لرسول الله في بيوع سوى هذا سننا . . . ومنها ان من باع عبدا وله مال فماله للبائع إلا أن يشترط المبتاع »(١٠٥)

٤٧(١٠٧)- ب قال الشافعي : « أخبرنا ابن عيينة ، عن ابن شهاب عن سالم عن أبيه ، ان رسول الله قال : « من باع عبدا وله مال فماله للبائع إلا أن يشترط المبتاع »(١٠٦)

٤٨(١٠٨)- أ قال الشافعي : « وروى ابن عمر عن النبي صلى الله عليه وسلم أنه صلى صلاة الخوف خلاف هذه الصلاة في بعض أمرها ، فقال : . . . »(١٠٧)

٤٨ (١٠٩) - ب« أخبرنا مالك ، عن نافع ، عن ابن عمر ، أراه عن النبي صلى الله عليه وسم ، فذكر صلاة الخوف . . . »(١٠٨)

٤٩ (١١٠) - أ قال الشافعي : « أخبرنا رجل ، عن ابن أبي ذئب ، عن الزهري ، عن سالم ، عن أبيه عن النبي ، مثل معناه »(١٠٩)

٤٩ - (١١١) ب قال الشافعي : « أخبرنا محمد بن اسماعيل أو عبد الله بن نافع ، عن ابن أبي ذئب ، عن الزهري ، عن سالم عن أبيه عن النبي صلى الله عليه وسلم »(١١٠)

٥٠ - (١١٢) أ قال الشافعي : حديث أنس منسوخ « بحديث عائشة أن رسول الله

---

(١٠٢) الأم ٧ : ٣١١
(١٠٣) الرسالة ٣٩٨
(١٠٤) الرسالة ٤٠٥
(١٠٥) الرسالة ١٧٤ - ١٧٥
(١٠٦) الرسالة ١٧٠
(١٠٧) الرسالة ٢٥٩ - ٢٦٠
(١٠٨) الرسالة ١٨٤ - ١٨٥
(١٠٩) الرسالة ١٨٥
(١١٠) الأم ١ : ١٩٧

(٩٥) ٤٢ - أ قال الشيباني : « ولكنه بلغنا عن النبي صلى الله عليه وسلم أنه قال : لا يؤمن الناس أحد بعدي جالسا ... »(٩٤)

(٩٦) ٤٢ - ب« قال محمد : حدثنا بشر ، حدثنا أحمد ، أخبرنا اسرائيل بن يونس بن أبي إسحاق السبيعي ، عن جابر بن يزيد الجعفي ، عن عامر الشعبي ، قال رسول الله صلى الله عليه وسلم : لا يؤمن الناس أحد بعدي جالسا »(٩٥)

(٩٧) ٤٣ - أ قال الشيباني : « وبلغنا عن عمر بن الخطاب رضي الله عنه بينما هو يخطب ، اذ جاء رجل من أصحاب النبي صلى الله عليه وسلم يتخطى رقاب الناس حتى جلس .. »(٩٦)

(٩٨) ٤٣ - بقال الشيباني : « أخبرنا مالك ، أخبرني الزهري ، عن سالم بن عبد الله ، عن أبيه ، ان رجلا من أصحاب رسول الله صلى الله عليه وسلم دخل المسجد يوم الجمعة وعمر بن الخطاب يخطب الناس ... »(٩٧)

(٩٩) ٤٤ - أ قال الشيباني : « وقال مالك بن أنس في حديث عمر أنه كان يصلي الجمعة ثم يرجع بعد الجمعة فيقيل قائلة الضحى ... »(٩٨)

(١٠٠) ٤٤ - ب قال الشيباني : « أخبرنا مالك ، أخبرني عمي أبو سهيل بن مالك ، عن أبيه ، قال : كنت أرى طنفسة ... ثم نرجع فنقيل قائلة الضحى »(٩٩)

(١٠١) ٤٥ - أ قال الشيباني : « وكان علي رضي الله عنه يكبر من صلاة الفجر يوم عرفة إلى صلاة العصر في آخر أيام التشريق »(١٠٠)

(١٠٢) ٤٥ - ب محمد : « قال أخبرنا أبو حنيفة ، عن حماد ، عن ابراهيم ، عن علي بن أبي طالب أنه كان يكبر من صلاة الفجر من يوم عرفة إلى صلاة العصر من آخر أيام التشريف »(١٠١)

---

(٩٤) الحجة ١ : ٢٧٢
(٩٥) الموطأ للشيباني ١١٣
(٩٦) الحجة ١ : ٢٨١
(٩٧) الموطأ للشيباني ٧٢
(٩٨) الحجة : ٢٨٦ - ٢٨٧
(٩٩) الموطأ للشيباني ١٣٤
(١٠٠) الشيباني ، الجامع الكبير ١٣
(١٠١) الآثار للشيباني رقم ٢٠٥

أبي سعيد الخدري ، قال ، قال رسول الله صلى الله عليه وسلم : لا يحل لامرأة ، تؤمن بالله واليوم الآخر ان تسافر سفرا يكون ثلاثة أيام فصاعدا . . »(٨٥)

(٨٧) ٣٨ - أ قال محمد بن الحسن : « قال أبو حنيفة رضي الله عنه الصلاة على النبي صلى الله عليه وسلم أن يقول . . . بلغنا نحو ذلك عن النبي صلى الله عليه وسلم ، أخبرنا مالك بن أنس بنحو ذلك »(٨٦)

(٨٨) ٣٨ - ب قال الشيباني : « أخبرنا مالك ، حدثنا عبد الله بن أبي بكر ، عن أبيه ، عن عمرو بن سليم الزرقي ، أخبرني أبو حميد الساعدي ، قال ، قالوا : يا رسول الله كيف نصلي عليك ؟ . . »(٨٧)

(٨٩) ٣٩ - أ قال الشيباني : « . . . وكان صلى الله عليه وسلم فيما بلغنا يسلم عليه في الصلاة فيرد ، فلما كان بعد ذلك ، سلم عليه فلم يرد . . . »(٨٨)

(٩٠) ٣٩ - ب « عن أبيه ، عن أبي حنيفة ، عن حماد ، عن إبراهيم ، عن ابن مسعود رضي الله عنه لما قدم من أرض الحبشة سلم على رسول الله صلى الله عليه وسلم وهو يصلي فلم يرد عليه . . . »(٨٩)

(٩١) ٤٠ - أ قال الشيباني : « وقد بلغنا نحو هذا حديث من رسول الله صلى الله عليه وسلم رواه مالك بن أنس أن النبي صلى الله عليه وسلم قال : إذا أتيتم الصلاة فلا تأتوها وأنتم تسعون . . . »(٩٠)

(٩٢) ٤٠ - ب « وحدثني عن مالك ، عن العلاء بن عبد الرحمن بن يعقوب ، عن أبيه ، وإسحاق بن عبد الله أنهما أخبره ، أنهما سمعا أبا هريرة يقول ، قال رسول الله صلى الله عليه وسلم : إذا ثوب بالصلاة ، فلا تأتوها وانتم تسعون . . »(٩١)

(٩٣) ٤١ - أ قال الشيباني : « . . . لأن رسول الله صلى الله عليه وسلم ثبت عنه أنه قال : صلاة الليل مثنى مثنى »(٩٢)

(٩٤) ٤١ - ب قال الشيباني : « أخبرنا مالك ، أخبرنا نافع ، عن أبي عمر أن رجلا سأل رسول الله صلى الله عليه وسلم كيف الصلاة بالليل ، فقال : مثنى مثنى . . »(٩٣)

---

(٨٥) الحجة ١ : ١٦٧
(٨٦) الحجة ١ : ١٣٨
(٨٧) الموطأ للشيباني ١٥٦ - ٥٧
(٨٨) الحجة ١ : ٢٤٥
(٨٩) الآثار لأبي يوسف رقم ١٢٢
(٩٠) الحجة ١ : ٢١٧
(٩١) الموطأ ٦٨
(٩٢) الحجة ١ : ٢٧٣
(٩٣) الموطأ للشيباني ١١٧

Appendix 2 (١١)

(۷۸) ۳۳ - ب قال : « وحدثني محمد بن إسحاق ، قال حدثني من سمع طلحة بن معدان العمري ، قال خطبنا عمر بن الخطاب . . »(۷۷)

(۷۹) ۳٤ - أ قال أبو يوسف : « حدثنا محمد بن إسحاق وإسماعيل بن أمية ، عن ابن هرمز قال : كتب نجدة إلى ابن عباس رضي الله عنهما كان النساء يحضرن الحرب مع رسول الله صلى الله عليه وسلم . . . »(۷۸)

(۸۰) ۳٤ - ب قال أبو يوسف : « حدثنا محمد بن إسحاق وإسماعيل بن أمية ، عن رجل ، ان ابن عباس رضي الله عنهما كتب إلى نجدة في جواب كتابه ، كتبت تسألني عن الصبي متى يخرج من اليتم . . »(۷۹)

(۸۱) ۳٥ - أ « ثنا يوسف ، عن أبيه ، عن أبي حنيفة ، عن الهيثم ، عمل حدثه ، عن عمر بن الخطاب رضي الله عنه ، أنه أضعف الصدقة على نصارى بني تغلب عوضا من الخراج »(۸۰)

(۸۲) ۳٥ - ب قال أبو يوسف : « حدثنا أبو حنيفة ، عمن حدثه ، عن عمر بن الخطاب ، أنه أضعف الصدقة على نصارى بني تغلب عوضاً من الخراج »(۸۱)

الإمام الشيباني واستعماله للأسانيد

(۸۳) ۳٦ - أ قال محمد بن الحسن : « لا بأس بالاعتكاف في مساجد القبائل . . . كما لابد له من الخروج لحاجة الانسان وبلغنا ذلك عن رسول الله صلى الله عليه وسلم »(۸۲)

(۸٤) ۳٦ - ب قال محمد : « أخبرنا مالك ، أخبرنا ابن شهاب ، عن عروة بن الزبير ، عن عمرة بنت عبد الرحمن ، عن عائشة انها قالت : كان رسول الله صلى الله عليه وسلم إذا اعتكف يدني إلى رأسه فأرجله ، وكان لا يدخل البيت إلا لحاجة الانسان »(۸۳)

(۸٥) ۳۷ - أ قال محمد : « ألا ترون أن رسول الله صلى الله عليه وسلم قال : لا تسافر المرأة ثلاثة أيام الا ومعها ذو رحم . . . »(۸٤)

(۸٦) ۳۷ - ب أخبرنا أبو معاوية المكفوف ، عن الأعمش ، عن أبي صالح ، عن

---

(۷۷) الخراج ۱۱۷ - ۱۱۸
(۷۸) الأوزاعي ۳۸
(۷۹) الأوزاعي ٤۳
(۸۰) أبو يوسف ، الآثار ٤٤٥
(۸۱) الخراج ۱۲۰
(۸۲) الحجة على أهل المدينة ۱ : ٤۱٦ - ٤۱۷
(۸۳) الموطأ للشيباني ۱۸۸
(۸٤) الحجة ۱ : ۱٦۷

صلى الله عليه وسلم ، كما حدثني عاصم بن عمر بن قتادة ومن لا أتهم عن محمد بن مسلم بن عبد الله بن شهاب الزهري إلى عيينة بن حصن بن حذيفة بن بدر ، وإلى الحارث بن عوف بن أبي حارثة المري ، وهما قائدا غطفان ، فأعطاهما ثلث ثمار المدينة . . »(٦٩)

(٧١) ٣١ - ج وروى الزهري عن ابن المسيب « فبيناهم على ذلك إذ أرسل النبي صلى الله عليه وسلم إلى عيينة بن حصن بن بدر الفزاري وهو يومئذ رأس المشركين من غطفان ، وهو مع أبي سفيان : أرأيت أن جعلت لك ثلث ثمر الانصار أترجع بمن معك من غطفان ؟ »(٧٠)

(٧٢) ٣٢ - أ قال أبو يوسف : « حدثنا محمد بن إسحاق عن الزهري ، عن يزيد ، عن هرمز كاتب ابن عباس ، قال : كتب نجدة إلى عبد الله بن عباس يسأله عن النساء . . »(٧١)

(٧٣) ٣٢ - ب قال : « وحدثني محمد بن إسحاق ، عن الزهري ، أن نجدة كتب إلى ابن عباس رضي الله تعالى عنهما يسأله عن سهم ذوي القربى . . »(٧٢)

(٧٤) ٣٢ - ج قال أبو يوسف : « حدثنا محمد بن إسحاق وإسماعيل بن أمية عن ابن هرمز ، قال : كتب نجدة إلى ابن عباس رضي الله عنهما كان النساء يحضرن الحرب مع رسول الله صلى الله عليه وسلم . . »(٧٣)

(٧٥) ٣٣ - أ قال أبو يوسف : « حدثنا مجالد بن سعيد ، عن الشعبي ، عن عمر رضي الله عنه أنه كتب إلى سعد بن أبي وقاص ، إني قد أمددتك بقوم ، فمن أتاك منهم قبل أن تتفقأ القتل فاشركه في الغنيمة »(٧٤)

(٧٦) ٣٣ - ب « وحدثنا مجالد ، عن عامر الشعبي وزياد بن علاقة الثعلبي ، ان عمر رضي الله عنه كتب إلى سعد بن أبي وقاص رضي الله عنها : قد أمددتك بقوم ، فمن أتاك منهم قبل أن تتفقأ القتل فاشركه في الغنيمة »(٧٥)

(٧٧) ٣٤ - أ قال أبو يوسف : « وحدثنا سعيد بن أبي عروبة ، عن قتادة ، عن سالم بن أبي الجعد ، عن معدان بن أبي طلحة اليعمري ، أن عمر بن الخطاب قام في يوم الجمعة خطيبا . . . »(٧٦)

---

(٦٩) سيرة ابن هشام ٣ : ٢٢٣
(٧٠) سيرة الزهري ، المصنف ٥ : ٣٦٧ ، الواقدي ٤٧٧
(٧١) الصحيح يزيد بن هرمز ، الخراج ١٩٨
(٧٢) الخراج ٢٠
(٧٣) الاوزاعي ٣٨
(٧٤) الاوزاعي ٥ - ٦
(٧٥) الاوزاعي ٣٥
(٧٦) الخراج ١٤

(٦٢) ٢٧ - د قال أبو يوسف : « حدثنا أبو حنيفة ، عن حماد ، عن إبراهيم ، أن عبد الله بن مسعود رضي الله عنه أعطى زيد بن خليدة مالا مقارضة »(٦١)

(٦٣) ٢٨ - أ قال أبو يوسف : « وكذلك بلغنا عن رسول الله صلى الله عليه وسلم أنه كان يقول : من اشترى نخلا له ثمرة مؤبرة فثمره للبائع إلا أن يشترط ذلك المشتري »(٦٢)

(٦٤) ٢٨ - ب « قال حدثنا يوسف ، عن أبيه ، عن أبي حنيفة ، عن أبي الزبير ، عن جابر بن عبد الله رضي الله عنهما عن النبي صلى الله عليه وسلم أنه قال : من باع نخلا مؤبرا أو عبدا فثمر النخل ومال العبد للبائع إلا أن يشترط المبتاع »(٦٣)

(٦٥) ٢٩ - أ قال أبو يوسف : « بلغنا عن أبي بكر رضي الله عنه أنه نحل عائشة أم المؤمنين رضي الله عنها جذاذ عشرين وسقا من نخل له بالعالية »(٦٤)

(٦٦) ٢٩ - ب « حدثنا أبو اليمان ، أخبرني شعيب ، عن الزهري ، أخبرني عروة بن الزبير ، أن عائشة قالت : كان أبو بكر نحلني جاد عشرين وسقا »(٦٥)

(٦٧) ٣٠ - أ « أخبرنا محمد بن إسحاق والكلبي ، أن رسول الله صلى الله عليه وسلم نزل واديا ، فقال : من يحرسنا في هذا الوادي الليلة ؟ فقال رجلان : نحن . فأتيا رأس الوادي »(٦٦)

(٦٨) ٣٠ - ب « قال ابن إسحاق : وحدثني عمي صدقة بن يسار ، عن عقيل بن جابر عن جابر بن عبد الله الأنصاري ، قال : خرجنا مع رسول الله صلى الله عليه وسلم في غزوة ذات الرقاع من نخل .. فنزل رسول الله صلى الله عليه وسلم منزلا ، فقال : من رجل يكلؤنا ليلتنا هذه ، قال فانتدب رجل من المهاجرين ورجل آخر من الأنصار »(٦٧)

(٦٩) ٣١ - أ قال أبو يوسف « حدثني محمد بن إسحاق عن الزهري أن رسول الله صلى الله عليه وسلم أراد يوم الخندق أن يفتدى بثلث ثمار المدينة »(٦٨)

(٧٠) ٣١ - ب قال ابن إسحاق : « فلما اشتد على الناس البلاء بعث رسول الله

---

(٦١) ابن أبي ليل ٣٢ - ٣٣
(٦٢) ابن أبي ليل ١٤
(٦٣) آثار أبي يوسف رقم ٨٢٩ ، انظر أيضاً آثار محمد ٧١٧
(٦٤) ابن أبي ليل ٤٧
(٦٥) حديث الزهري ، دراسات ١٤٣ ، الحديث/٦
(٦٦) الاوزاعي ٩٠
(٦٧) سيرة ابن هشام ٣ : ٢٠٨
(٦٨) الخراج ٢٠٧

الحديث عن رسول الله صلى الله عليه وسلم إلا بشاهدين . ولولا طول الكتاب لأسندت لك الحديث »^(٥٢)

(٥٣) ٢٤ - ج قال أبو يوسف : « وما جاء في هذا من الأحاديث كثير ، لولا طول ذلك لكتبت لك من ذلك شيئاً كثيراً »^(٥٣)

(٥٤) ٢٥ - أ قال أبو يوسف : « فقد نهى رسول الله صلى الله عليه وسلم عن قتل النساء والأطفال والصبيان .. »^(٥٤)

(٥٥) ٢٥ - ب قال أبو يوسف : « وحدثني عبيد الله ، عن نافع ، عن ابن عمر ، قال وجدت امرأة مقتولة في بعض مغازي النبي صلى الله عليه وسلم فنهى عن قتل النساء والولدان »^(٥٥)

(٥٧) ٢٦ - أ قال أبو يوسف : « بلغنا عن رسول الله صلى الله عليه وسلم وعن غيره من أصحابه أنه أسهم للفارس بثلاثة أسهم ، وللراجل بسهم ، وبهذا نأخذ »^(٥٦)

(٥٨) ٢٦ - ب قال : « وحدثنا قيس بن الربيع ، عن محمد بن علي ، عن إسحاق بن عبد الله ، عن أبي حازم ، قال : حدثنا أبو ذر الغفاري رضي الله تعالى عنه ، قال : شهدت أنا وأخي مع رسول الله صلى الله عليه وسلم حنيناً ومعنا فرسان لنا ، فضرب لنا رسول الله صلى الله عليه وسلم ستة أسهم أربعة لفرسينا وسهمين لنا ، فبعنا الستة الأسهم بحنين ببكرين »^(٥٧)

(٥٩) ٢٧ - أ قال أبو يوسف : « وقد بلغنا عن عمر بن الخطاب رضي الله عنه وعن عبد الله ابن مسعود وعن عثمان بن عفان رضي الله عنها ، أنهم أعطوا مالاً مضاربة »^(٥٨)

(٦٠) ٢٧ - ب قال أبو يوسف : « حدثنا أبو حنيفة عن حميد بن عبد الله بن عبيد الأنصاري ، عن أبيه ، عن جده أن عمر بن الخطاب رضي الله عنه أعطى مال يتيم مضاربة فكان يعمل به في العراق ، ولا يدري كيف قاطعه على الربح »^(٥٩)

(٦١) ٢٧ - ج قال أبو يوسف : « وحدثنا أبو حنيفة ، عن عبد الله بن علي عن العلاء بن عبد الرحمن بن يعقوب ، عن أبيه ، أن عثمان بن عفان رضي الله عنه أعطى مالاً مقارضة يعني مضاربة »^(٦٠)

---

(٥٢) الأوزاعي ٣٠ - ٣١
(٥٣) الأوزاعي ٣٨
(٥٤) الأوزاعي ٦٦
(٥٥) الخراج ١٩٥
(٥٦) الأوزاعي ٢١
(٥٧) الخراج ١٨ - ١٩
(٥٨) ابن أبي ليلى ٤٢
(٥٩) ابن أبي ليلى ٣٠ - ٣١
(٦٠) ابن أبي ليلى ٣١ - ٣٢

(٤٣) ٢٠ - ب« وحدثني عمرو ، نا سليمان ، نا شعيب ، نا عبيد الله ، عن نافع ، عن صفية بنت أبي عبيد أن عمر بن الخطاب رضي الله عنه كتب إلى أمراء الاجناد . »(٤٣)

(٤٤) ٢١ - أ « حدثني يحيى عن مالك أنه بلغه أن عبدا لعبد الله بن عمر أبق . . »(٤٤)

(٤٥) ٢١ - ب« حدثنا عبد الله بن عمر ، عن نافع ، عن ابن عمر أن عبدا له أبق . . »(٤٥)

(٤٦) ٢٢ - أ مالك « عن نافع عن أبي لبابة أن رسول الله صلى الله عليه وسلم نهى عن قتل الحيات التي في البيوت »(٤٦)

(٤٧) ٢٢ - ب« . . عبيد الله ، عن نافع ، أن عبد الله أخبره ، أن أبا لبابة أخبره أن رسول الله صلى الله عليه وسلم نهى عن قتل الجنان إلا أن يكون الابتر التي في البيوت »(٤٧)

(٤٨) ٢٣ - أ « وحدثني مالك عن نافع عن سائبة ـ مولاة لعائشة ـ أن رسول الله صلى الله عليه وسلم نهى عن قتل الجنان التي في البيوت إلا ذا الطفيتين فانهما يخطفان البصر . . »(٤٨)

(٤٩) ٢٣ - ب« . . . عبيد الله ، عن نافع ، أن سائبة أخبرته أن عائشة رضي الله عنها زوج النبي صلى الله عليه وسلم قالت : ان رسول الله صلى الله عليه وسلم نهى عن (قتل) الجنان . . . »(٤٩)

الإمام أبو يوسف واستعماله للأسانيد

(٥٠) ٢٤ - أ قال أبو يوسف : « فان هذا ليس يقبل الا عن الرجال الثقات ، فمن هذا الحديث ؟ . . »(٥٠)

(٥١) ٢٤ - أ قال أبو يوسف : « فهل عنده (يعني الأوزاعي) أثر مسند عن الثقات أن رسول الله صلى الله عليه وسلم أسهم فارس غزا مع راجلا . . »(٥١)

(٥٢) ٢٤ - بقال أبو يوسف : « كان عمر رضي الله عنه فيما بلغنا ، لا يقبل

---

(٤٣) دراسات في الحديث النبوي ص ١١٧ (الجزء العربي)
(٤٤) الموطأ ٤٥٢
(٤٥) الخراج ٢٠٠
(٤٦) الموطأ ٩٧٥
(٤٧) دراسات في الحديث النبوي ١٢٩ (الجزء العربي)
(٤٨) الموطأ ٩٧٦
(٤٩) دراسات في الحديث النبوي ١٢٩ (الجزء العربي)
(٥٠) الأوزاعي ٥
(٥١) الاوزاعي ٢٢

(٣٤) ١٦ - ب« مالك ، عن عبد الله بن دينار ، عن عبد الله بن عمر أن رسول الله صلى الله عليه وسلم قال : من ابتاع طعاما فلا يبعه حتى يقبضه »(٣٤)

(٣٥) ١٦ - ج « عن مالك ، عن نافع ، عن عبد الله بن عمر أن رسول الله صلى الله عليه وسلم قال : من ابتاع طعاما فلا يبعه حتى يستوفيه »(٣٥)

(٣٦) ١٧ - أ قال مالك : « ولم يبلغني أن رسول الله صلى الله عليه وسلم قال : من قتل قتيلا فله سلبه إلا يوم حنين »(٣٦)

(٣٧) ١٧ - ب« مالك عن يحيى بن سعيد ، عن عمر بن كثير بن أفلح ، عن أبي محمد مولى أبي قتادة ، عن أبي قتادة بن ربعى انه قال : خرجنا مع رسول الله صلى الله عليه وسلم ... من قتل قتيلا له عليه بينة فله سلبة »(٣٧)

(٣٨) ١٨ - أ قال مالك « ولا ميراث لأحد من الجدات إلا الجدتين لأنه بلغني أن رسول الله صلى الله عليه وسلم ورث الجدة ، ثم سأل أبا بكر عن ذلك حتى أتاه الثبت عن رسول الله صلى الله عليه وسلم أنه ورث الجدة فأنفذه لها . »(٣٨)

(٣٩) ١٨ - ب مالك « عن ابن شهاب ، عن عثمان بن إسحاق بن خرشة ، عن قبيصة بن ذويب ، قال : جاءت الجدة إلى أبي بكر الصديق تسأل ميراثها ، فقال لها أبو بكر : مالك في كتاب الله شيء ، وما علمت لك في سنة رسولة الله صلى الله عليه وسلم شيئاً ، فارجعي حتى أسأل الناس ، فسأل الناس ، فقال المغيرة بن شعبة حضرت رسول الله صلى الله عليه وسلم أعطاها السدس .. »(٣٩)

(٤٠) ١٩ - أ مالك « عن ابن شهاب أن رسول الله صلى الله عليه وسلم كان يذهب لحاجة الانسان في البيوت »(٤٠)

(٤١) ١٩ - ب« مالك عن ابن شهاب عن عروة بن الزبير عن عمرة بنت عبد الرحمن عن عائشة زوج النبي صلى الله عليه وسلم نحوه »(٤١)

(٤٢) ٢٠ - أ « مالك عن نافع مولى عبد الله بن عمر أن عمر بن الخطاب كتب إلى عماله »(٤٢)

---

(٣٤) الموطأ ٦٤٠ ؛ أنظر أيضاً الموطأ ٦٢٩
(٣٥) الموطأ ٦٤٠
(٣٦) الموطأ ٤٥٥
(٣٧) الموطأ ٤٥٤ - ٤٥٥
(٣٨) الموطأ ٥١٤
(٣٩) الموطأ ٥١٣
(٤٠) الموطأ ٣١٧
(٤١) الموطأ ٣١٢
(٤٢) الموطأ ٦

حين اعترف عنده ماعز بن مالك رضي الله عنه وأمر به أن يرجم ، هرب حين أصابته الحجارة فقال رسول الله صلى الله عليه وسلم : فهلا خليتم سبيله ، حدثنا بذلك أبو حنيفة يرفعه إلى النبي صلى الله عليه وسلم . »(٢٥)

(٢٦) ١٢ - ب« قال : ثنا يوسف ، عن أبيه ، عن أبي حنيفة ، عن علقمة بن مرثد ، عن ابن بريدة عن أبيه ، عن النبي صلى الله عليه وسلم . . . »(٢٦)

(٢٧) ١٣ - أ قال أبو حنيفة : « وبلغنا عن علي بن أبي طالب رضي الله عنه أنه قال : لا ضمان عليهم ، (يعني على القصار والصباغ . . .)»(٢٧)

(٢٨) ١٣ - ب« محمد ، قال : أخبرنا أبو حنيفة ، عن بشر أو بشير ـ شكى محمد ـ عن أبي جعفر محمد بن علي أن علي بن أبي طالب كان لا يضمن القصار ولا الصائغ ولا الحائك »(٢٨)

الإمام مالك واستعماله للأسانيد

(٢٩) ١٤ - أ قال مالك : « وقد بلغني أن رسول الله صلى الله عليه وسلم أراد العكوف في رمضان ثم رجع فلم يعتكف حتى إذا ذهب رمضان اعتكف عشرا من شوال »(٢٩)

(٣٠) ١٤ - ب مالك عن ابن شهاب ، عن عمرة بنت عبد الرحمن ، عن عائشة أن رسول الله صلى الله عليه وسلم أراد أن يعتكف . . . »(٣٠)

(٣١) ١٥ - أ قال مالك : « وأنا أكره ان يلبس الغلمان شيئا من الذهب لأنه بلغني أن رسول الله صلى الله عليه وسلم نهى عن تختم الذهب »(٣١)

(٣٢) ١٥ - ب« عن نافع ، عن ابراهيم بن عبد الله بن حنين ، عن أبيه ، عن علي بن أبي طالب ، ان رسول الله صلى الله عليه وسلم نهى عن لبس القسى وتختم الذهب »(٣٢)

(٣٣) ١٦ - أ « قال مالك : « وقد نهى رسول الله صلى الله عليه وسلم عن بيع الطعام قبل أن يستوفى »(٣٣)

---

(٢٥) ابن أبي ليلى ١٥٧
(٢٦) الآثار لأبي يوسف ٧١٩ نحوه مفصلا
(٢٧) ابن أبي ليلى ١٠
(٢٨) الشيباني ، الآثار رقم ٧٦٤
(٢٩) الموطأ ص ٣١٧
(٣٠) الموطأ ٣١٦
(٣١) الموطأ ٩١٢
(٣٢) الموطأ ٨٠
(٣٣) الموطأ ٦٤٠ ، وانظر أيضاً ٦٤٤ ، ٦٤٨

(١٧) ٨ - أ ‏« قال أبو حنيفة : « وان عبد الله بن عمر رضي الله عنهما لم يقنت ، وقال يا أهل العراق أنبئت ان أمامكم يقوم لا قاري قرآن ولا راكع ، يعني بذلك القنوت »(١٧)

(١٨) ٨ - ب ‏« قال ثنا يوسف ، عن أبيه ، عن أبي حنيفة ، قال ثنا الصلت بن بهرام ، عن حوط ، عن أبي الشعثاء ، عن ابن عمر ، أنه قال لأبي الشعثاء : أنبئت ان أمامكم بالعراق يقوم في آخر ركعة من الفجر لا تالي قرآن ولا راكع »(١٨)

(١٩) ٩ - أ ‏« قال أبو حنيفة : « وأن عليا رضي الله عنه قنت في حرب يدعو على معاوية ، فأخذ أهل الكوفة عنه ذلك ، وقنت معاوية رضي الله عنه بالشام يدعو على علي رضي الله عنه فأخذ أهل الشام عنه ذلك »(١٩)

(٢٠) ٩ - ب ‏« حدثنا يوسف بن أبي يوسف ، عن أبيه ، عن أبي حنيفة ، عن حماد عن ابراهيم أن عليا رضي الله عنه قنت يدعو على معاوية رضي الله عنه حين حاربه ، فأخذ أهل الكوفة عنه ، وقنت معاوية يدعو على علي فأخذ أهل الشام عنه »(٢٠)

(٢١) ١٠ - أ ‏« قال أبو يوسف : « وكان ابن أبي ليلى يقول : زكاة الدين على الذي هو عليه . فقال أبو حنيفة رضي الله عنه : بل هي على صاحبه الذي هو له إذا خرج . كذلك بلغنا عن علي بن أبي طالب رضي الله عنه . »(٢١)

(٢٢) ١٠ - ب «محمد ، قال : أخبرنا أبو حنيفة ، قال حدثنا الهيثم ، عن ابن سيرين ، عن علي بن أبي طالب ، قال : إذا كان لك دين على الناس فقبضته فزكه لما مضى »(٢٢)

(٢٣) ١١ - أ ‏« قال أبو يوسف : « وإذا نفحت الدابة برجلها وهي تسير ، فان أبا حنيفة رضي الله عنه كان يقول : لا ضمان على صاحبها لأنه بلغنا عن رسول الله صلى الله عليه وسلم انه قال : الرجل جبار . . »(٢٣)

(٢٤) ١١ - ب «محمد ، قال : أخبرنا أبو حنيفة ، حدثنا حماد ، عن ابراهيم عن النبي صلى الله عليه وسلم قال : العجماء جبار ، والقليب جبار ، والرجل جبار ، والمعدن جبار ، وفي الركاز الخمس »(٢٤)

(٢٥) ١٢ - أ ‏« قال أبو يوسف : « وقد بلغنا ـ عن رسول الله صلى الله عليه وسلم

---

(١٧) ابن أبي ليلى ١١٣
(١٨) أبو يوسف ، الآثار ٣٥٥ ، أيضا الشيباني ، الآثار ٢١١
(١٩) ابن أبي ليلى ١١٣ - ١١٤
(٢٠) أبو يوسف : الآثار رقم ٣٥٢
(٢١) ابن أبي ليلى ١٢٣
(٢٢) الآثار الشيباني رقم ٢٩٠
(٢٣) ابن أبي ليلى ١٥٠
(٢٤) الشيباني ، الآثار رقم ٥٦١ وانظر آثار أبي يوسف رقم ٤٣٥ رواه مثله لكنه لم يذكر : الرجل جبار .

(٧) ٤ - أ قال أبو يوسف : « كان أبو حنيفة ينهى عن القنوت في الفجر ، وبه نأخذ ، ويحدث به عن رسول الله صلى الله عليه وسلم انه لم يقنت إلا شهراً واحداً حارب حياً من المشركين فقنت يدعو عليهم »(٧)

(٨) ٤ - ب « حدثنا يوسف بن أبي يوسف عن أبيه ، عن أبي حنيفة ، عن إبراهيم عن النبي صلى الله عليه وسلم انه لم يقنت في الفجر إلا شهراً واحداً حارب حياً من المشركين قنت يدعو عليهم ، لم ير قانتا قبلها ولا بعدها »(٨)

(٩) ٤ - ج « حدثنا يوسف ، عن أبيه ، عن أبي حنيفة ، عن حماد ، عن ابراهيم ، عن علقمة ، عن عبد الله رضي الله عنه ، عن النبي صلى الله عليه وسلم مثله »(٩)

(١٠) ٥ - أ (أبو حنيفة) « وان أبا بكر رضي الله عنه لم يقنت حتى لقي بالله عز وجل »(١٠)

(١١) ٥ - ب « قال حدثنا يوسف بن أبي يوسف ، عن أبيه ، عن أبي حنيفة ، عن حماد ، عن ابراهيم ، أن أبا بكر رضي الله عنه لم يقنت حتى لحق بالله تعالى »(١١)

(١٢) ٦ - أ (أبو حنيفة) « وان ابن مسعود رضي الله عنه لم يقنت في سفر ولا حضر »(١٢)

(١٣) ٦ - ب « محمد ، قال : أخبرنا أبو حنيفة عن حماد عن ابراهيم أن ابن مسعود لم يقنت هو ولا أحد من أصحابه حتى فارق الدنيا - يعني في صلاة الفجر »(١٣)

(١٤) ٧ - أ (أبو حنيفة) « وأن عمر بن الخطاب رضي الله عنه لم يقنت »(١٤)

(١٥) ٧ - ب « قال : ثنا يوسف بن أبي يوسف ، عن أبيه ، عن أبي حنيفة ، عن عبد الملك بن ميسرة ، عن زيد بن وهب أن عمر رضي الله عنه كان يقنت إذا حارب ويدع القنوت إذا لم يحارب »(١٥)

(١٦) ٧ - ج « قال : ثنا يوسف بن أبي يوسف ، عن أبيه عن أبي حنيفة ، عن حماد ، عن ابراهيم ، عن الأسود ، قال : صحبت عمر رضي الله عنه سنتين لم أره قانتا في سفر ولا حضر »(١٦)

---

(٧) ابن أبي ليلى ١١١ - ١١٢
(٨) أبو يوسف ، الآثار ٣٤٩ ، أيضاً الشيباني الآثار رقم ٢١٢
(٩) أبو يوسف ، الآثار ٣٥٠
(١٠) ابن أبي ليلى ١١٢ - ١١٣
(١١) أبو يوسف الآثار ٣٥١ ، انظر أيضاً آثار محمد الشيباني رقم ٢١٢
(١٢) ابن أبي ليلى ١١٣
(١٣) آثار محمد الشيباني رقم ٢١٠
(١٤) ابن أبي ليلى ١١٣
(١٥) أبو يوسف ، الآثار رقم ٣٥٣
(١٦) أبو يوسف ، الآثار رقم ٣٥٤ ، أيضاً الآثار للشيباني ٢١٣

ابن إسحاق واستعماله للأسانيد

(١) ١ - أ   وروى الزهري عن ابن المسيب : « فبيناهم على ذلك إذ أرسل النبي صلى الله عليه وسلم إلى عيينة بن حصن بن بدر الفزاري وهو يومئذ رأس المشركين من غطفان ، وهو مع أبي سفيان : أرأيت ان جعلت لك ثلث ثمر الانصار أترجع بمن معك من غطفان ؟ . . . »(١)

(٢) ١ - ب   قال ابن إسحاق : « فلما اشتد على الناس البلاء ، بعث رسول الله صلى الله عليه وسلم ، كما حدثني عاصم بن عمر بن قتادة ومن لا اتهم ، عن محمد بن مسلم بن عبيد الله بن شهاب الزهري ، إلى عيينة بن حصن بن حذيفة بن بدر ، وإلى الحارث بن عوف بن أبي حارثة المري ، وهما قائدا غطفان ، فأعطاهما ثلث ثمار المدينة . . . »(٢)

(٣) ٢ - أ   قال ابن إسحاق : « وحدثني عبد الرحمن بن الحارث وغيره من أصحابنا عن سليمان بن موسى ، عن مكحول ، عن أبي أمامة الباهلي . . . قال سألت عبادة بن الصامت عن الأنفال ، فقال : فينا أصحاب بدر نزلت حين اختلفنا في النفل ، وساءت فيه أخلاقنا ، فنزعه الله من أيدينا ، فجعله إلى رسوله ، فقسمه رسول الله صلى الله عليه وسلم بين المسلمين عن بواء »(٣)

(٤) ٢ - ب   قال ابن إسحاق : « فكان عبادة بن الصامت ـ فيما بلغني ـ إذا سئل عن الأنفال قال فينا معشر أهل بدر نزلت حين اختلفنا في النفل يوم بدر . فانتزعه الله من أيدينا حين ساءت فيه أخلاقنا فرده على رسول الله صلى الله عليه وسلم فقسمه بيننا عن بواء »(٤)

أبو حنيفة واستعماله للأسانيد

(٥) ٣ - أ   قال أبو حنيفة : « بلغنا عن رسول الله صلى الله عليه وسلم أنه قال : « اليمين على المدعى عليه والبينة على المدعي »(٥)

(٦) ٣ - ب   أخرجه طلحة بن محمد من طريق أبي يوسف عن الإمام عن عمرو بن شعيب عن أبيه عن جده مرفوعا : البينة على المدعي واليمين على المدعى عليه إذا أنكر . »(٦)

---

(١)   سيرة الزهري ، انظر المصنف ٥ : ٣٦٧ ، الواقدي ٤٧٧
(٢)   سيرة ابن هشام ٣ : ٢٢٣
(٣)   سيرة ابن هشام ١ : ٦٤٢
(٤)   سيرة ابن هشام ١ : ٦٦٦ - ٦٦٧
(٥)   ابن أبي ليل ٧٨
(٦)   هامش ابن أبي ليلى ٧٨ - ٧٩

Bibliography

Abbot, Nabia, *Studies in Arabic Literary Papyri,* vol 2, Chicago, 1967.
Abdul Rahim, *Muhammadan Jurisprudence,* Lahore, 1968.
'Abdur Razzāq al-Ṣan'ānī, *Muṣannaf,* 11 vols, edited by Ḥabībur Raḥmān Al-A'zāmī, Beirut, 1390–1392.
Abū Dāwūd, *Sunan,* edited by M. M. 'Abdul Ḥamīd, 2nd imp, Cairo, 1369.
Abū al-Husain, Muḥammad b. 'Alī, *Al-Mu'tamad,* 2 vols, edited by Ḥamidulla, Damascus, 1964.
Abū Khaithama, Zuhair b. Ḥarb, *al-'Ilm.* Damascus. (ND)
Abū 'Ubaid, al-Qāsim b. Sallām, *al-Amwāl,* edited by Ḥāmid al-Fiqī, Cairo, 1953.
Abū Yūsuf, Ya'qūb b. Ibrāhīm, *al-Āthār,* edited by Abul Wafā al-Afgānī, Cairo, 1355/1937.
────── *Ikhtilāf Abī Hanīfa wa Ibn Abī Lailā,* edited by Abul Wafā Al-Afgānī, Cairo, 1957.
────── *al-Kharāj,* 2nd ed., Cairo, 1352.
────── *al-Radd 'alā Sīyar al-Auzā'ī,* edited by Al-Afgānī, Cairo, 1357.
Abū Zur'a, 'Abdur Raḥmān al-Dimashqi, *Tārīkh,* Fatih Ms. 4210, Istanbul.
Aḥmad Nūr Saif, *'Amal Ahl al-Madīna,* Master's thesis, Sharī'a College, Mecca, 1392 (Printed Cairo, 1397).
Anderson, J. N. D., "Recent Developments in Sharī'a Law," *Muslim World* 40, 1950.
Ansārī, Zafar Isḥāq, "The Early Development of Islamic Fiqh in Kufa," Doctoral thesis, McGill University, 1966.
────── "Islamic Juristic Terminology Before Shafi'ī," *Arabica,* 19, 1972.
Arberry, A. J., *The Koran Interpreted,* Oxford, 1964.
Auvray, P. and Barucq, *An Introduction a la Bible,* Paris, 1936.
'Ayāḍ, al-Qāḍī 'Ayāḍ b. Mūsā, *Tartīb al-Madārik,* edited by Aḥmad Bukair Maḥmūd, Beirut, 1387/1967.
────── Al-Ilmā', edited by Ṣaqr, Cairo, 1970.
Al-A'zamī, M. M. *Kuttāb an-Nabī, al-Maktab al-Islamī,* Beirut, 1394/1974.
────── *Ḥadīth Methodology and Literature,* Indianapolis, 1977.
────── *Studies in Early Ḥadīth Literature,* Beirut, 1388/1968.
Al-A'zamī, Z. Raḥmān, *Abū-Huraira fī dau'i Mariyātihī,* Master's thesis, Sharī'ā College, Mecca, 1392.
Azdī, Yazīd b. Muḥammad, *Tārīkh al-Mauṣil,* edited by Abū Ḥabība, Cairo, 1387/1967.
Al-Baihaqī, Aḥmed b. al-Husain, *al-Sunan al-Kubrā,* 10 vols., Hyderabad, 1344.
Al-Balādhurī, *Liber Expungnationis Regionum,* edited by M. J. de Goeje, Leiden, 1866.

―――― *Futuḥul Buldān,* edited by Ṭabbā', Beirut, 1957.
Al-Bāqillānī, Muḥammad b. Ṭayyib, *Al-Intiṣār,* Ms Bayazit, 18671, Istanbul.
Bevan, A. A. (editor), *Al-Naqā'id* (reprint), Beirut.
Al-Bihārī, Muḥibbulla, *Musallam al-Thubūt* (reprint), Beirut.
Bravmann, M. M., *The Spiritual Background of Early Islam,* Leiden, 1972.
Al-Bukhārī, Muḥammad b. Ismā'īl, *al-Jāmi' al-Ṣaḥīḥ,* printed with *Fatḥ al-Bārī,* (see Ibn Ḥajar).
―――― *Raf' al-Yadain,* Delhi, 1299.
―――― *al-Tārīkh al-Kabīr,* 8 vols., Hyderabad, 1361.
―――― *at-Tārīkh aṣ-Ṣaghīr,* Allahabad, 1325.
Caetani, Leone, *Annale dell' Islam,* 10 vols., 1905–1926.
Coulson, N. J., *Conflict and Tension in Islamic Jurisprudence,* Chicago, 1969.
―――― *A History of Islamic Law,* Edinburgh, 1964.
Cowan, J. Milton, *A Dictionary of Modern Written Arabic,* Wiesbaden, 1961.
Dāraquṭnī, 'Alī b. 'Umar, *Sunan,* edited by 'Abdulla Ḥāshim al-Yamānī, 4 vols., Cairo, 1386.
Dārimī, 'Abdullah b. 'Abdur Raḥmān, *Sunan,* edited by M. A. Dahmān, 2 vols., Damascus, 1349.
Al-Dhahabī, Muḥammad b. Aḥmad, *Tadkirat al-Ḥuffāẓ,* 4 vols., 4th imp., Hyderabad.
―――― *Mīzān-al-I'tidāl,* 4 vols., Cairo, 1382/1963.
―――― *The Encyclopaedia Britannica,* Encyclopaedia Britannica Inc., Chicago, Illinois.
Ennamī, 'Amr, *Studies in Ibadism,* Beirut, 1392.
Fallata, 'Umar b. Ḥasan, *Al-Waḍ'u fī al-Ḥadīth,* Doctoral thesis, Al-Azhar University, Cairo, 1397.
Fasawī, Ya'qūb b. Sufyān, *Al-Ma'rifa Wa attārīkh,* Ms. Esad Effendi, 2391 Istanbul (edited by al-Umary), 3 vols., Baghdad, 1394.
Fazzārī, Ibrāhīm b. Muḥammad, *Al-Siyar,* Qarwiyin Library, Ms. no. 139, Fez.
Fitzgerald, S. V., "The Alleged Debt of Islamic to Roman Law," *Law Quarterly Review,* vol. 67, Jan. 1951.
Fyzee, A. A. A. *Outlines of Muhammadan Law,* 3rd ed., Oxford, 1964.
Gibb, H. A. R., *Muhammadanism,* London, 1964.
―――― "Review on *Origins of Muhammadan Jurisprudence,*" *"Journal of Comparative Legislation and International Law,* 1951, 114.
Goitein, S. D., *Studies in Islamic History and Institutions,* Leiden, 1965.
Goldziher, I., *Muhammadanische Studien,* translated by S. M. Stern, London, 1967.
Guillaume, A., *The Life of Muhammad,* the translation of the *Sīra* of Ibn Isḥāq, Oxford, 1955.
al-Ḥākim an-Nisāburī, Muḥammad b. 'Abdullah, *al-Mustadrak,* 4 vols.,

Hyderabad (reprinted in Beirut).
Ḥamīdullah, Muḥammad, *al-Wathā'iq as-Sīyasīyah*, 3rd ed. Beirut, 1968.
Hammām b. Munabbih, *Ṣaḥīfa*, 5th rev. ed. edited by Ḥamidulla, Hyderabad, 1380.
Hasan, Aḥmad, *The Early Development of Islamic Jurisprudence*, Karachi, 1970.
Al-Hudhalien, *Dīwān*, 2 vols., Cairo, 1385.
al-Ḥumaidī, 'Abdullah b. az-Zubair, *Musnad al-Ḥumaidī*, 2 vols., edited by Ḥabibur Raḥmān al-A'zamī, Karachi, 1963.
Husain, Ṭahā, *Al-Fatna al-Kubrā*, Cairo, 1951.
Ibn 'Abdul Barr, *Tajrīd al-Tamhīd*, Cairo, 1350.
Ibn Abī Ḥātim al-Rāzī, 'Abdur Raḥmān, *al-Jarḥ wat-Ta'dīl*, 9 vols., with introduction, Hyderabad, 1360–1373.
Ibn al-Athīr al-Jazarī, Al-Mubārak b. Muḥammad, *Jāmi' al-Uṣūl*, 11 vols., edited by A. Arnāwūṭ, Damascus, 1389.
Ibn Ḥajar, Aḥmad b. 'Alī, *Fatḥ ul-Bārī*, 13 vols., edited by F. 'Abdul Bāqī, Cairo, 1380.
——— *Tadhīb at-Tahdhīb*, 12 vols., Hyderabad, 1325–1327.
——— *Taqrīb at-Thadhīb*, 2 vols., edited by A. A. Laṭīf, Cairo, 1960.
Ibn Ḥanbal, Aḥmad b. Muḥammad, *al-'Ilal wa Ma'rifat ar-Rijāl*, edited by Talat Kocyigit, Ankara, 1963.
——— *Musnad*. 6 vols., Cairo, 1313 (reprinted in Beirut).
Ibn Ḥazm, 'Alī b. Aḥmad, *Muḥallā*, 11 vols., edited by Aḥmad Shākir, Cairo, 1352.
Ibn Ḥibbān, Muḥammad, *Al-Majrūḥīn min al-Muḥaddithīn*, Ms. Ayasofi No. 496, Istanbul.
Ibn Hishām, *Sīra*, edited by Musṭafa as-Saqqā and others, 4 vols., 2nd imp., Cairo, 1375/1955.
Ibn Kathīr, Ismā'īl b. 'Umar, *Tafsīr Ibn Kathīr*, 7 vols., Beirut, 1385/1968.
Ibn Khair, Muḥammad al-Ashbīlī, *Fihrist*, reprinted in Baghdad, 1963.
Ibn Khuzaima, Muḥammad b. Isḥāq, *Ṣaḥīḥ Ibn Khuzaima*, 4 vols., edited by M. M. A'zamī, Beirut, 1391–1397.
Ibn Ma'īn, Yaḥya, *Tārīkh*, Zahiriya Ms. No. 113, Damascus.
Ibn Mājah, Muḥammad b. Yazīd, *Sunan*, 2 vols., edited by F. 'Abdul Bāqī, Cairo, 1373–1954.
Ibn Manẓūr, Muḥammad, *Lisān al-'Arab*, Beirut.
Ibn al-Muqaffa', *Āthār Ibn al-Muqaffa'*, Beirut, 1966.
Ibn al-Murtaḍā, Aḥmad b. Yaḥyā, *Ṭabaqāt al-Mu'tazila*, edited by Susanna Diwals-Wilzer, Wiesbaden, 1961.
Ibn Sa'd, Muḥammad b. Sa'd, *at-Ṭabaqāt al-Kabīr*, 9 vols., edited by E. Sachau, Leiden, 1904–1940.
Ibn Ṭallā', *Aqḍīyat Rasulillah*, edited by Z. Al-A'zamī, Beirut, 1978.
Ibn Wahb, 'Abdullah, *Le Djami d'Ibn Wahb*, edited by S. David Weill, Cairo, 1939.
Ibrāhīm b. Ṭahmān, *Juz'*. Zahiriya, Ms. No. Majmū'lo, Damascus.

Introduction, translated by J. Robson, London, 1953.
Juwairīya b. Asmā', *Ṣaḥīfa,* Sehid Ali Ms. 539, Istanbul.
Al-Kattānī, 'Abdul Ḥaie, *Al-Trātīb al-Idārīya,* 2 vols., reprinted in Beirut.
Khadduri, Majid, *Islamic Jurisprudence, A Translation of Shāfi'ī's Risālah,* Baltimore, 1961.
Khalīfa b. Khayyāṭ, *Tārīkh,* edited by S. Zakkar, 2 vols., Damascus, 1968.
—— *Tabaqāt,* 2 vols., edited by S. Zakkar, Damascus, 1967.
Khallāf, 'Abdul Wahhāb, *'Ilm Uṣūl al-Fiqh,* Kuwait.
Khatīb al-Baghdādī, Aḥmad b. 'Alī, *Tārīkh Baghdad,* 14 vols., Cairo, 1931.
—— *Al-Faqīh wa al-Mutafaqqih,* 2 vols., Riyādh.
—— *Sharaf Aṣḥāb al-Ḥadīth,* Ms.
—— *Al-Kifāya,* Hyderabad, 1357.
—— *Al-Rihla fī Ṭalab al-Ḥadīth,* edited by N. 'itr, Damascus, 1395/1975.
—— *Al-Jāmi'li Akhlāq ar-Rāwī,* Ms. Alexandria Municipal Library.
Al-Khayyāṭ, 'Abdur Raḥmān b. Muḥammad, *al-Intiṣār,* edited by A. N. Nader, Beirut, 1957.
El-Kindī, Muḥammad b. Yūsuf, *The Governors and Judges of Egypt,* edited by Rhuvon Guest, Leiden, 1912.
Lane, E. W., *Arabic English Lexicon,* Edinburgh, 1867.
Mālik b. Anas *Muwaṭṭa',* 2 vols., edited by F. 'Abdul Bāqī, Cairo, 1370/1951. (If reference is to volume and page, then refer to Zurqani's *Commentary on Muwaṭṭa',* as used by Schacht.)
Margoliouth, D. S., *The Early Development of Muhammedanism,* London, 1914.
Muir, Sir William, *The Life of Mahomet,* 3rd ed., London, 1894.
Muslim b. Al-Ḥajjāj al-Qushairī, *Ṣaḥīḥ Muslim,* 5 vols., edited by F. 'Abdul Bāqī, 1374/1955.
—— *at-Tamyīz,* edited by M. M. al-A'ẓamī, Riyadh, 1395/1975.
Nasā'ī, Ahmad b. Shu'aib, *Sunan,* 8 vols., Cairo, 1383/1964.
Al-Nawāwī, Muḥyuddīn b. Sharaf., *Tahdhīb al-Asmā',* 2 vols., reprinted in Beirut.
Penrice, John, *Dictionary and Glossary of the Koran,* London, 1875.
Al-Qa'anabī, *Muwaṭṭa',* edited by 'Abdul Hafiẓ Manṣūr, Tunis N.D.
al-Rabī' b. Ḥabīb, al-Frāhīdī, *Musnad,* Damascus, 1388/1968.
Raḥman, Fazlur, *Islamic Methodology in History,* Karachi, 1965.
Robson, J., "Ibn Isḥāq's Use of Isnād," *Bulletin of the John Rylands Library,* 38:2 (March 1965) 449–465.
—— "The Isnād in Muslim Tradition," *Glasgow University Oriental Society Transactions XV* (1965) pp. 15–26.
—— "Muslim Traditions—the Question of Authenticity," Memoirs and proceedings, Manchester Lit. Philosophical Society, vol. XCIII (1951), No. 7.

Rusainī, 'Abdullāh Ṣāliḥ, *Fiqh al-Fuqahā' as-Sab'a*, Master's thesis, Sharī'a College, Mecca, 1392.

Saḥnūn, *Al-Mudawwana al-Kubrā*, 16 vols., Cairo, 1323–1324.

Sa'īd b. Manṣūr, *Sunan*, 2 vols., edited by H. Raḥmān al-A'zamī, Malegeon, 1967.

Schacht, Joseph, *An Introduction to Islamic Law*, Oxford, 1964.

—— *The Origins of Muhammadan Jurisprudence*, 2nd ed., Oxford, 1959.

Shāfi'ī, Muḥammad b. Idrīs, "On the Margins of Kitāb l-Umm," *Ikhtilāf al-Ḥadīth*, vol. VII.

—— *Ar-Risāla*, edited by Aḥmad Shākir, Cairo, 1358/1940.

—— *Al-Umm*, 7 vols., 1st ed., Cairo, 1321–1325.

—— *Sunan, Badā'i' al-Minan*, arranged by Sā'ātī, 1st ed., Cairo.

Shaibānī, Muḥammad b. al-Ḥasan, *Al-Āthār* 1385/1965 (with Urdu commentary), Karachi.

—— *al-Ḥujja 'alā ahl al-Madīna*, edited by S. M. Ḥasan, Hyderabad, 1385/1965.

—— *Muwaṭṭa'*, edited by 'Abdul Ḥa'ī al-Lakhnawi, Lucknow, 1306.

Sibā'ī, Muṣṭafā, *As-Sunna wa Makanatuhā*, Cairo, 1380/1961.

Snouck, Hurgronje C., *Mohammedanism*, 1916.

Subkī, 'Abdul Wahhāb b. 'Alī, *Ṭabaqāt Al-Shāfa'īya al-Kubrā*, 10 vols., edited by A. Ḥilw, Cairo, 1964.

Suyūṭī, 'Abdur Raḥmān b. Abū Bakr, *Hama'ul Hawāmi' sharh Jama'ul Jawāmi'* reprinted in Beirut.

—— *Tadrīb ar-Rāwī*, 2 vols., edited by A. A. Latīf, Cairo, 1379.

—— *Al-Itqān fi 'ulūm al-Qur'ān*, 4 vols., edited by M. A. Ibrāhīm, Cairo, 1967.

Ṭabarānī, Sulaimān b. Aḥmad, *Al-Mu'jam al-Kabir* Ms. Fatih, 1198 vols. 3–4, No. 465, Istanbul, edited by H. A. Salafī, Baghdad, 1978.

at-Ṭabarī, Muḥammad b. Jarīr. *Annales (Tārikh at-Ṭabarī)* edited by A. Abul Faḍl Ibrāhīm (paging according to De Goeje's edition, Leiden, 1879–1901).

at-Taḥāwī, Abū Ja'far, Aḥmad b. Muḥammad, *Sharḥ Ma'ānī al-Āthār*, 4 vols., Cairo.

Ṭayālisī, Abū Dāwūd, *Minḥat al-Ma'būd Fī Tartīb Musnad at-Tayālisī Abū Dawūd*, compiled by Sā'ātī, 1st ed., Cairo, 1372.

Tha'ālibī, Muḥammad b. Al-Ḥasan, *Al-Fikr al-Sāmī*, 2 vols., edited by A. A. Al-Qari, Medina, 1977.

at-Thānawī, Muḥammad b. 'Alī, *A Dictionary of Technical Terms*, Calcutta, 1862.

at-Tirmidhī, Muḥammad b. 'Īsā, *al-Jāmi'*, 5 vols., edited by Aḥmad Shākir and others, Cairo, 1356.

Tyan, E. *Histoire l'Organisation judiciare en pays d'Islam*, 2nd ed., Leiden, 1960.

Wakī', Muḥammad b. Khalaf, *Akhbār al-Quḍāt*, 3 vols., Cairo, 1366/1947.

Wāqidī, Muḥammad b. 'Umar, *Kitāb al-Maghāzī*, edited by Marsden Jones, London, 1966.
Al-Yamānī, Mu'allimī, *Al-Anwār al-Kāshifa*, Cairo, 1378.
al-Ya'qūbī, Aḥmad b. Abū Ya'qūb, *Tārikh al-Ya'qūbī*, Beirut, 1379/1960.
Zaid bin 'Alī, *Musnad*, Beirut, 1966.
Ziriklī, Khairuddīn, *Al-A'lām*, 10 vols., Cairo, 1373.
Zurqānī, Muḥammad, *Commentary on Mālik's Muwaṭṭa'*, 4 vols., Cairo, 1310.

Index

A

'Abdah 128
'Abdal 'azīz 198
'Abdal Karīm 126
'Abdallāh b. 'Āmir b. Rabī'a 195
'Abdallāh b. 'Amr. b. Al-'Āṣ, 120, 192
'Abdallāh b. Dīnār, 169, 170, 192, 200, 205
'Abdallāh b. 'Umar 'Umarī 169, 173–175, 186
'Abdallāh b. 'Utba b. Mas'ūd 193
'Abdallāh ibn Ibāḍ 29
'Abd al-Malik 29, 166, 167
'Abd al-Malik b. Marwān See also 'Abdul Malik 168, 193
'Abd al-Raḥmān b. Aswad 196
'Abd al Raḥmān b. Qāsim 195
'Abdul Ḥamīd 172, 173
'Abdul Jabbār, Qāḍī 74
'Abdul Karīm 127
'Abdullāh 131
'Abdullāh b. 'Amr. 113
'Abdullāh b. Fuḍāla 22
'Abdullāh b. Idrīs 113
'Abdullāh b. Mas'ūd 21
'Abdullāh b. Muḥarrir 137
'Abdullāh b. 'Umar 49
'Abdul Majid 148
'Abdul Malik 23, 32, 108, 116, 126
'Abdul Malik b. Maisara 138, 139
'Abdul Malik b. Marwān 42
'Abdul Malik b. Ya'lā 22
'Abdul Qais 109
'Abdur Raḥmān 24
'Abdur Raḥmān b. 'Auf 23
'Abdur Raḥmān b. Udhaina 21
'A. Razzāq 127, 128, 172, 174, 179, 204
'Abdur Razzāq 137, 147, 148
'Abdur Razzāq al-Ṣan'ānī 175, 187, 194
Abī Ḥanīfa See Abū Ḥanīfa
Abū Al-Dardā' 110, 151, 152
Abū 'Alī al-Qālī 154
Abū 'Amr. 181
Abū Bakr (b. 'Amr) B. Ḥazm, 169, 176, 177, 180, 187
Abū 'Āṣim Nabīl 184
Abū Bakr b. 'Abdur Raḥmān 172
Abū Bakr 23, 29, 30, 32, 36, 49, 65, 79, 91, 102, 106, 112, 117, 130, 131, 142, 153
Abū Barzah 192
Abū Faraj al-Aṣfhānī 154
Abū Ḥanīfa 33, 63, 66, 67, 70, 72, 78, 86–88, 94, 116, 121–124, 126–128–131, 133–135, 137–145, 147, 152, 153, 181, 187, 190, 196
Abū Ḥātim al-Rāzī 91, 92
Abū Huraira 47, 110, 133, 134, 146, 150, 156, 157, 162, 176, 179, 184, 185, 187, 195
Abū Jamara 128, 152
Abū Kāmil 189
Abul Aswad 49
Abul Husain 74
Abul Zubair 184
Abū Mālik 127
Abū Ma'shar 200
Abū Mijlaz 194
Abū Mūsā al-Ash'arī 21, 22, 24, 110, 121
Abū Mūsā 194
Abū Nadhrah 187
Abū Qilābah 25, 147 (of Basra)
Abū Rāfi' 181
Abū Sa'īd al-Khudrī 111, 127, 150
Abū Sa'id Khudrī 187
Abū Salama 192
Abū Salama b. 'A. 'Auf. 43–45, 47, 191–192
Abū Ṣāliḥ 162
Abū 'Ubaidah 187
Abū Zinād 150, 194
Abū Yūsuf 51, 55, 56, 63, 66, 67, 70–72, 78, 88, 90, 106–108, 120, 121, 126, 129, 131–140, 142–149, 153, 181, 183, 184, 189
Abū Zur'ah 113
'Adī b. Ḥātim 12
Aḥmad Noor Saif 60
'Ā'isha 32, 92, 93, 113, 114, 157, 178, 201, 204
'Alī b. Abī Ṭālib 21, 24, 35, 37, 38, 52–54, 65, 91, 111, 130, 131, 141, 157, 168, 192
'Alqama 131, 194 (Alqama b. Qais)
A'mash 143, 157
'Āmir 24
'Āmir b. Sa'īd 150
'Amr. 127, 128
'Amr. b. al-'Āṣ 21, 178, 204
'Amr b. Abī 'Amr 198, 199
'Amr b. Ḥazm 21
'Amr b. Sharīd 181, 182
'Amr b. Shu'aib 181, 182, 186, 194
Anas 110, 129, 173, 187–189

Anderson 16
A'raj 150
Ashtar 37
Ashyam al-Ḍibābī 23
'Āṣim 127
Aswad b. Yazīd 196
'Aṭā' 127, 132
'Attāb b. Asīd 21
'Auf b. Abū Jamīla 74
'Auzā'ī 51, 52, 55, 64–67, 70, 72, 90, 91, 94, 106, 107, 135–138, 140, 148, 153, 190
Ayād 127
Ayas b. Ṣubaiḥ Abī Maryam 21
Ayyūb 126, 127, 142 (Ayyub of Basra) 147, 172, 173
Ayyūb al-Sakhtiyānī 112, 191 (of Basra)

B

Baihaqī 138
Bakr 127
Barā' b. 'Āzib 110
Bishr b. al-Ḥusain 187
Bravmann, M. M. 44
al-Bukhārī 112, 114, 138, 142, 149, 150, 179, 181, 186–188, 204

C

Coulson, N. J. 23, 25
Caetani, Leone 173

D

Ḍahhāk b. Qais 22
Ḍahhāk b. Sufyān 23
Dāraquṭnī 138
Dārimī 89
Dhahabī 169, 199
Diḥya al-Kalbī 21

F

al-Faḍl b. 'Abbād 113
Farazdaq 29
Fazārī 51
Fāṭima b. Qais 114
Fazlul Raḥmān 16, 17
Fitzgerald, S. V. 23
Furāfiṣa b. 'Umair 195
Furai'a 23

G

Goldziher, I. 105

H

Ḥafṣa 178
Haitham 144
Ḥajjāj b. Arṭāt 133
Ḥakīm b. Ḥizām 146, 192
Ḥakam 139, 140
Ḥammād b. Salamah 112, 126–128, 131, 142, 147, 187, 189, 196
Ḥamza 178, 204
Ḥarmala 153
Hārūn al Rashīd 139
Ḥasan b. 'Alī 24
Ḥasan al-Baṣrī 22, 29, 74, 124–126
Ḥasan Baṣrī 116, 181, 182
Ḥasan b. 'Umaira 138–141
Hishām b. Hubaira 22, 24, 127, 129, 179, 180
Hishām 201, 204
Horovitz, J. 167
Ḥudhaifa b. al-Yamān 21
Ḥujr b. 'Adī 24
Ḥumaid 133–135
Ḥumaidī 127
Hurgronje, C. Snouck 22
Ḥusain 38, 128
Hushaim 172

I

Ibn 'Abbās 23, 49, 111–113, 126–128, 139, 140, 146–148, 152, 192, 195
Ibn 'Abd al Barr 171, 180
Ibn 'Abdul Ḥakam 89
Ibn Abī Ḥatim al-Rāzī 114
Ibn Abī Lailā 66, 88, 183 (Ibn Abu Laila); 134, 135, 142, 144, 181, 182
Ibn Abū Mulaika 190, 194
Ibn Abū Zinād 190
Ibn al-Mubārak 112
Ibn al-Muqaffa' 37, 40, 41–43, 96
Ibn al-Musayyab 44, 63, 133, 134, 172, 173, 184, 185, 190
Ibn al-Qayyim 114
Ibn al-Zubair 168
Ibn Buraidah 111
Ibn Dinār 146
Ibn Fulān 32, 33

Ibn Ḥajar 150
Ibn Ḥanbal 157, 181, 182, 187–189, 204
Ibn Isḥāq 133, 136, 153, 166, 167
Ibn Jubair 127, 128
Ibn Juraij 135, 142, 145, 147, 148, 152, 157, 172, 173, 184, 191, 194
Ibn Ma'īn 112, 155
Ibn Māja 151, 186, 187
Ibn Mājashūn 184, 205
Ibn Mas'ūd 22, 24, 96, 109, 111, 113, 120, 126, 128, 129, 131, 132, 143, 144, 147, 188, 196
Ibn Mubārak 154
Ibn Musaiyib 43
Ibn Qāsim 57–59
Ibn Qusaiṭ 49
Ibn Qutaiba 74, 92, 154, 181
Ibn Sa'd 128, 136, 207
Ibn Sa'īd 80
Ibn Shihāb See Zuhrī
Ibn Sīrīn 155, 167, 190
Ibn Ṭallā' 20
Ibn 'Umar 22, 23, 32, 50, 58, 61–63, 81, 91, 119, 120, 128, 131, 138–142, 146, 148, 149, 152, 153, 169–173, 189–192, 204
Ibn 'Uyaynah 126–128, 147, 150, 174, 192
Ibn Wahb 49, 127, 149, 153, 184
Ibrāhīm Ibn Abū Yaḥyā 198
Ibrāhīm b. Ṭahmān 157, 191
Ibrāhīm Nakha'ī 24, 66, 88, 126–132, 145, 147, 188, 190, 196, 201, 204
'Ikrimah 126, 127, 152
Imām Muslim 92, 149, 152
'Imrān 194
'Imrān b. Ḥuṣain 21
'Īsā b. 'Abdallāh 197
Isḥāq 129, 180
Ismā'īl 150
Iyās b. Mu'āwīya 22

J

Juwairīya b. Asmā' 170, 191
al-Jāḥiz 154
Jābir 157, 194, 195
Jābir b. Zaid 129, 187
Jābir b. Zaid Al-Azdī 24

K

Ka'b b. Sūr 22
Kathir 'Abdallāh 197
Khālid al-Hudhali 29
Khālid b. Walīd 140–142, 153

Khayyāṭ 74
al-Khirrīt 38
Kuraib 113
Khubaib 32

L

Laith 127
al-Laith b. Sa'd 190, 192, 193
Lane, E. W. 61

M

Maimūna 113
Majīd Khaddurī 104
Mālik
(Mālik b. Anas in ()) 30, 32, 33, 43–50 (55), 56–64, 69 (72), (77), 77–82, 84, 87, 94, 115, 116, 118, 119, 121, 122, 124, 130, 131, 133–138, 141, 142, 145–153, 168, 170–180, 182, 184, 185, 187–192, 194–196, 200, 204, 205
Mālik b. Abū 'Āmir 128
Mālik b. al-Ḥuwairith 105
Ma'mar 127, 128, 145, 147, 152, 172, 179, 180, 187, 197
Ma'qal b. Yasār al-Muzanī 15
Margoliouth, D. S. 36, 37, 40
Marwān 23, 146, 147, 194, 195
Maṭar b. Ṭahmān 74
Miqsam 139, 140
Mis'ar 127, 128, 139
Moses 11
Mu'ādh 23
Mu'ādh b. Jabal 21
al-Mua'llamī al-Yamānī 114
Mu'āwīya 108, 110, 111, 130, 131, 168, 192–194
al-Mubarrad 154
Mughīrah 23
Muhallab 38
Muḥammad 7, 8, 10, 11, 13, 15–17, 24, 39
Muḥammad b. 'Abdalraḥmān b. Sa'd b. Zurāra 178
Muḥammad b. 'Abdur Raḥmān b. 'Abdullāh 178
Muḥammad b. Abū Bakr 59
Muḥammad b. Abī Yaḥyā 153
Muḥammad Abū Rijāl b. 'Abdur Raḥmān (b. Hāritha) 178
Muḥammad b. 'Alī 195
Muḥammad b. 'Amr b. Ḥazm 169, 176, 177
Muḥammad b. Ḥasan 180

Muḥammad b. Ibrāhīm al-Taimī 173–176
Muḥammad b. Isḥāq 196
Muḥammad b. Muslim 113
Muḥammad b. Saʻīd 186
Muḥammad b. ʻUbaid 196
Muḥammad b. Yaḥyā b. Ḥayyān 150
Muir, W. 7
Mujāhid 127, 128, 135
Mūsā b. Anas 22
Mūsā b. Maṭīr 197
Mūsā b. ʻUqba (of Medina) 191
Muslim 186–188, 204
Muṭarrif 38
Muʻtazila 73, 74, 94
Muttalib 198

N

Nāfiʻ 49, 63, 131, 138–141, 142, 145, 146, 148, 149, 168–173, 190–192, 204, 205
Nasāʼī 149

Q

Qaʻnabī 180, 184
al-Qāsim 49, 50, 139 (only as Qasim)
Qāsim b. Muḥammad 60–61, 148, 149, 195
Qāsim 204
Qāsim b. ʻAbdur Raḥmān 143
Qatādah 74, 181, 182

R

Rabīʻ 57, 59, 60, 77, 80, 81, 151, 187
Rabīʻ bin Ḥabīb 133, 147
Rabīʻa 49, 149, 169, 174, 175, 176, 187, 190
Robson J. 203, 204
Ruzaiq b. Ḥukaim 193

S

Saʻd 22
Ṣafīya 131
Saḥnūn 49, 50
Sāʼib 124
Saʻīd 127, 172
Saʻīd al-Jurairi 187
Saʻīd b. al-Musayyab 44, 49
Saʻīd b. Jubair 122, 126
Saʻīd ibn Abī ʻArūba 74
Ṣāliḥ b. Kaisān 80, 84
Sālim 49, 121, 148, 149, 168, 169, 189
Sallām 127

Samūra 181, 182, 191, 192
Satān 11
Schacht, Joseph 15, 17–20, 25–29, 36, 37, 40, 41, 43–68, 70, 72–82, 84–96, 100, 103–108, 115, 116, 118–153, 166–169, 171, 177–190, 192–204
Shaʻbī 19, 25, 142, 190, 193
Shafiʻī 36, 37, 43, 45, 52, 53, 55, 60, 62, 64, 66, 67, 72–77, 79–82, 84–90, 92, 96–104, 118, 127, 130, 132–134, 137, 146–149, 152, 153, 166, 170, 171, 176, 177, 182–192, 194–196, 198
Shaibānī 33, 55, 63, 66, 67, 70–72, 78, 88–90, 107, 108, 119–123, 126–129, 131, 136, 137, 142–144 (Also as Muhammad Shaibani), 146, 147, 153, 174–176, 179, 182, 184, 185, 187, 193, 196 (as Muhammad al-Shaibani)
Sharīd 182, 183
Shuʻaib b. Muḥammad 186
Shuʻba 143
Shuraiḥ 190, 193
Shuraiḥ (of Kūfa) 22, 144
Sprenger, A. 167
Suddī 127
Sufyān 113, 170
Sufyan al-Thaurī 154
Ṣuhaib 194
Suhail 162
Sulaimān 43, 44, 45, 128, 192, 198
Suwaid 38

T

Ṭabarī 59, 166
Ṭaḥā Ḥusain 168
Ṭaḥāwī 88, 90, 151, 184, 204
Ṭalḥah 37
Tauba b. Nimr. 192
Tāʼūs 24, 139, 190
al-Thaurī 88, 127 (Thauri), 135
Thumāma b. ʻAbdullāh 22
Thumāma (of Baṣra) 189
Tirmidhī 198
Tyan, E. 22

U

Ubai b. Kaʻb 21
ʻUbaidullāh 128, 138, 139, 140, 141, 170, 191
ʻUmaira b. Yathrabī 22
ʻUmar b. Dharr Hamdānī 126
ʻUmar b. ʻAbdal Azīz 45, 49, 65, 91, 148, 178, 192–194

'Umar (b. Khaṭṭāb) 21–24, 29, 30, 32, 35, 36, 49, 63, 70, 71, 86, 87, 91, 102–104, 106, 110, 114, 120, 121, 127–131, 143, 144, 146, 152, 157, 174, 175, 179–181, 186–189
'Umar b. Sa'īd 186
Umm al-Dardā' 151
Umm Salama 92
Umm Salamah 119
'Uqail 150
'Uqbah b. 'Āmir al-Juhanī 21
'Urwa 24, 63, 113, 132, 166, 167, 179–181, 200
'Urwa b. Zubair 49
'Uthmān 23, 29, 37, 38, 40, 41, 49, 102, 128, 168, 195

W

Wakī' 194
Walīd b. Yazīd 167, 168
Wāqidī 133
Wāṣil b. 'Atā' 74

Y

Yaḥyā b. 'Abd Allāh 197
'Yaḥyā b. Ādam 113
Yaḥyā b. Ḥayyān 150
Yaḥyā b. Sa'īd 49, 59, 169, 170 (Yahya only) 173 (Yahya b. Said al-Ansari), 174–176, 195, 204
Yaḥyā b. Yaḥyā 174, 186
Ya'lā b. 'Umayyah 135
Ya'qūb 128
Yazīd 139

Z

Zabīb al-Anbārī 195
Zaid 127
Zaid b. 'Alī 39
Zaid b. Arqam 111
Zaid (b. Thābit) 21, 24, 146, 195
Zakarīyā b. 'Adī 187, 188
Zuhrī 32–34, 44, 46, 47, 63, 80, 84, 107, 108, 128, 133, 134, 141, 150, 157, 167, 171–173, 184, 185, 189, 190, 193, 201, 204
Zurqānī 149, 152, 180, 181, 187–189
Zurāra b. Abī Awafā 21, 194
Zunārah b. Abū Awfa 193